Mothers, Fathers, and Others

Mothers, Fathers, and Others

New Essays

SIRI HUSTVEDT

SCEPTRE

First published in Great Britain in 2021 by Sceptre
An imprint of Hodder & Stoughton
An Hachette UK company

1

Louise Bourgeois SELF PORTRAIT, 1990–1994
Dry point, etching and acquatint on paper
27 x 9 1/2"; 68.6 x 42.5 cm.
Photo: Christopher Burke
© The Easton Foundation / VAGA at Artists Rights
Society (ARS), NY and DACS, London 2021

A CIP catalogue record for this title is available from the British Library

Hardback ISBN 9781529376647
Trade Paperback ISBN 9781529376654
eBook ISBN 9781529376661

Interior design by Carly Loman

Printed and bound in Great Britain by Clays Ltd, Elcograf S.p.A.

Hodder & Stoughton policy is to use papers that are natural, renewable
and recyclable products and made from wood grown in sustainable
forests. The logging and manufacturing processes are expected to
conform to the environmental regulations of the country of origin.

Hodder & Stoughton Ltd
Carmelite House
50 Victoria Embankment
London EC4Y 0DZ

www.sceptrebooks.co.uk

CONTENTS

PREVIOUS PUBLICATIONS, LECTURES, AND SUNDRY ORIGINS

"Stones and Ashes" was first published in Heide Hatry, *Icons in Ash*, Barrytown, NY: Station Hill, 2017, 243–47.

A shorter version of "A Walk with My Mother" was written for Sommar i P1, annual summer programming on Swedish Radio, the national radio channel, August 2020.

"States of Mind" appeared as "State of Mind: A Mingling" in *Granta* 140, 2017, 55–57.

"Mentor Ghosts" was written for an essay collection edited by Nancy K. Miller, *Two Way Street: Feminists Reclaim Mentorship*, not yet published.

"Open Borders" is a revised version of a speech delivered at the Guadalajara International Book Fair, December 2, 2019.

"Notes from New York" was published as "I Think of the Sirens as New York's Heartbreaking Music," *Financial Times*, April 24, 2020.

"Reading During the Plague" appeared online at Literary Hub as "Fairy Tales and Facts: Siri Hustvedt on How We Read in a Pandemic," April 13, 2020.

"When I Met You I Saw Myself as Another" was written for the annual Tübinger Poetik-Dozentur, 2016, held at the University of Tübingen in Germany. The text appeared in a book: Siri Hustvedt and Vittorio Gallese, *Fühlen, Errinern, Schreiben zwichen Wissenschaft und Poesie, Tübinger Poetik Dozentur 2016*, edited by Dorothee Kimmich and Alexander Philipp Ostrowicz, Künselsau: Swiridoff, 2017.

A version of "The Future of Literature" was a lecture delivered at Litteraturhuset in Oslo, Norway, on September 5, 2017. It was published as a booklet: *Siri Hustvedt om Literaturens Fremtid*, Oslo:

Litteraturhuset, 2018. It was also published as a not-for-sale booklet, *El poder de la literatura*, Seix Barral, 2019.

"The Sinbad Variations: An Essay on Style" was published as a book with photographs by Reza Deghati in Spain, *Ocho viagos con Sinbad*, Madrid: La Fabrica, 2011, and in a French edition as *Au pay des mille et une nuits*, Arles: Actes Sud, 2011.

"He Dropped His Pen" was the introduction to Jane Austen, *Persuasion*, London: Folio Society, 2016.

"Visiting St. Francis" was titled "Learning to See What Is in Front of Me," written as a Meditative Story podcast, a partnership between WaitWhat and Thrive Global, released December 2, 2019.

"Both-And" is a revised, much longer version of a talk given at the Museum of Modern Art in New York City for an evening event: New Perspectives on Louise Bourgeois: A Conversation with Juliet Mitchell and Siri Hustvedt, November 7, 2017.

"What Does a Man Want?" began as a seven-page entry on *misogyny* as part of a dictionary on social passions, *Passions Sociales*, edited by Gloria Origgi, Paris: Presses Universitaire des France, 2018, 401–408.

TILLIE

My paternal grandmother was ornery, fat, and formidable. She cackled when she laughed, brooded for reasons known only to her, barked out her sometimes alarming opinions, and spoke a Norwegian dialect impenetrable to me. Although she was born in the United States, she never mastered the "th" sound in English and opted for a straight "t" instead, referring to "tings" and "tunderstorms" and "Tanksgiving." When I was a child her hair was thick and white, and when loose, it fell almost to her waist. Before I knew her, it had been auburn. It thinned over the years, but I remember my awe when I saw it down. That happened only at night after she had unpinned her bun in front of the hazy mirror in the tiny, musty, mildewed bedroom of the farmhouse where she lived with my grandfather, who had his own even smaller room under the eaves just up the narrow wooden steps on a floor we were rarely allowed to visit. Once her hair had fallen and her nightgown was on, my grandmother took out her teeth and put them in a glass by the bed, an act that fascinated me and my sister Liv because we had no body parts that could be removed at night and replaced in the morning.

The extractable teeth, however, were only one piece of an altogether marvelous, if sometimes intimidating, being. Our grandmother peeled potatoes with a paring knife at what seemed to me the speed of light, hauled logs from the woodpile near the house, and yanked open the heavy door to the root cellar with a single gesture as strong as any man's before she led us down to the cold, dank domain where canned goods stood in their glass jars on shelves lined up against earthen walls. It was a place that smelled of the grave, a thought that may or may not have occurred to me then, but the excursion was always accompanied by a whiff of threat—by the fantasy that I would be left below with the jars and the snakes and the ghosts in blackness.

She was the only grown-up we knew who enjoyed telling poop jokes. She rocked with laughter over our plop-plop funnies as if she were a child herself, and when she was in a good mood, she told us stories from the long lost days of her own childhood, how she had learned to turn handsprings and cartwheels and walk on a wire and how she and her brothers hoisted sails on their sleds and were blown hard and fast across the frozen lake near the farm where she grew up. Before we went "visiting"—a word that signaled we were about to hop in the old Ford and "call" on various neighbors—Grandma put on her straw hat with the flowers on it that hung on a hook inside the front door and grabbed her black handbag with the gold clasp that had her little coin purse inside it, and we were off.

My grandmother died when she was ninety-eight. She has been a ghost in my life for some time, but she has been returning lately in a mental image. I see Matilda Underdahl Hustvedt coming toward me carrying two heavy pails of water. Behind her is the rusted hand pump that still stands on the property and behind the pump are the stones, which were once the foundation of the old barn that had been torn down long before I was born. It is summer. I see my grandmother's cotton housedress buttoned up the front. I see her low breasts, wide body, and thick legs. I see the loose flesh under her arms jiggle as she walks straight-armed with the enameled metal buckets, and I see her fierce red-rimmed sunken eyes behind her glasses. I feel the heat of the sun and the hot wind that blows across the undulating flats of rural Minnesota. I see an immense sky and the broad blank horizon interrupted by copses of trees. The memory image is accompanied by a mixture of satisfaction and pain.

Tillie, her friends called her Tillie, was born in 1887, the daughter of an immigrant father, Søren Hansen Underdahl, and Søren's second wife, Øystina Monsdattar Stondal, who was probably an immigrant herself, but my father doesn't mention this in the family history he wrote for us, so I cannot report on it. In all events, Øystina's father was wealthy, and he left each of his three daughters a farm. Tillie grew up on her mother's property in Ottertail County, Minnesota, near the town of Dalton. When Tillie was eight, her mother died. A story my grandmother told us, and my father's sister, tante (Aunt) Erna, told us, and my mother told us, too, about the eight-year-old Tillie gained the status of a family legend. After Øystina's death, the local minister came to visit the family and do whatever Lutheran ministers did over the bodies of the departed. Sometime before the man left the premises, he piously intoned to all present that the woman's untimely death had been "God's will." And then my grandmother, long before she was my grandmother, stamped her foot in a rage and shouted, "It is not! It is not!" And she was glad she had done it, and we were glad, too.

Tillie never visited "the old country." She never saw her father's first home, Undredal in Sogn, with its tiny church fitted close to the steep cliff of the mountain that rises straight up from the fjord. She never indicated any desire to see it that I overheard. She was rarely sentimental. Her husband, my grandfather Lars Hustvedt, traveled to Norway for the first time when he was seventy. He inherited some money from a relative and used it for a plane ticket. He went to Voss, where his father had been born, and was embraced warmly by relatives he had never met. Family lore has it that he knew "every stone" on the family farm, Hustveit, by heart. My grandfather's father must have been homesick, and that homesickness and the stories that accompanied the feeling must have made his son homesick for a home that wasn't home but rather an idea of home. We acquire the feelings of others, especially beloved others, and imagine that what we have never seen or touched belongs to us, too, by imaginative connection.

My father made a life of that imaginative connection. After fighting in New Guinea and the Philippines during World War II and a stint in the occupation army in Japan, he returned home and went to college on the G.I. Bill and eventually earned a Ph.D. at the University of Wisconsin, Madison, in Scandinavian studies. He taught Norwegian language and literature at St. Olaf College in Northfield, Minnesota, and served as secretary of the Norwegian American Historical Association, organizing and annotating a vast archive of immigrant papers, a post for which he was never paid.

In the text he left for us called *The Hustvedt Family*, there is scant information about his mother's family, except what I have related about Øystina's inheritance. My father's conscious identity was formed by the paternal line, and he uncovered as much as he could about the men from Voss who came before him, his grandfather and great-grandfather and great-great-grandfather. I do not think it occurred to my father to look deeply into his maternal lineage. Tillie may not have saved any documents or letters from her parents. She was literate but did not attend school after the second grade. Her letters to her soldier son are fluent but sometimes ungrammatical.

It is only as an adult that I have been able to meditate on the problem of omission, on what is missing rather than what is there, and to begin to understand that the unsaid may speak as loudly as the said.

At the very least, my grandmother irritated my father. I recall him bristling when she made ignorant pronouncements about the state of the world or scowled in silence at the table. He rarely scolded, but his face was a map of unhappiness, and I felt the conflicts between mother and son as deep scrapes cut into the general vicinity of my chest, which sometimes became unbearable, and I would ask to be excused and flee the mostly unarticulated family turmoil for the garden, where I could study the still green Concord grapes slowly turning blue on the arbor or fling myself onto the lawn and concentrate on biting into the sweet white ends of blades of grass. Even then, I knew that behind my father's irritation were stories I could feel but would never hear.

Grandpa was a gentler soul than Grandma. Forty of the sixty acres of farmland were lost to the bank during the Depression, and this narrative explained their penury. They must have subsisted on social security. I don't really know. My father's salary was meager, and we lived from month to month for years, so whatever help he may have given them couldn't have been considerable. My grandfather's livelihood as a farmer ended long before I knew him.

I have no memory of my grandparents in conversation or of them touching each other. We have photographs of them, however, sitting side by side.

Grandpa was an inward, taciturn man who read the newspaper thoroughly, followed politics closely, sat for long stretches in a chair in the cramped living room, chewed tobacco and spat into a Folgers coffee can at his feet. He smiled benevolently at our drawings and gave us striped candy from a jar he kept in the kitchen. After Lars died, my father told me "more than half" of his love for "the place"—by which he meant the farm—had disappeared. I was eighteen, and I pondered over this cryptic pronouncement, which I took to mean that he had loved his father more than he loved his mother.

When Tillie was dying, my mother spent some time with her alone. She grabbed my mother's hand and moaned, "I should have been nicer to Lars. I should have been nicer to Lars."

After his mother died, my father made a speech at the funeral, during which he called her "the last pioneer." My father made excellent speeches. He wrote well and with wit. But there is a detached quality to the eulogy, as if he is surveying his childhood from a great distance, and his link to the woman who bore and suckled and cared for him is missing. Where did it go? Did it vanish into the bitterness of his parents' marriage? Is there another element, too, one far more obscure and hard to define? Did the debt to her disappear into the forgotten land of the mother and mothers, the speechless realm of the womb where every human being begins and from which every human being is born, a territory Western culture has studiously repressed, suppressed, or avoided to a degree I have come to regard as spectacular? The omission of Tillie's side of the family came "naturally" to my father because in the world of my childhood, we did not tell time by mothers, only by fathers. It is the father's name that marks one generation and then the next. I suspect now that *The Hustvedt Family* served in part to rehabilitate the patriarchs that had been squashed by history, a history that included what my father witnessed as a boy—his own father's humiliating losses, which the son through intense identification internalized as his own.

My grandmother suffered losses too. She inherited money from her father, put it in the bank, and saved it. I do not know how much it was, but it was *her* money. Years later, after my grandfather's brother, David, lost both his legs in a work accident on the West Coast, she gave up the money to pay for his prosthetic legs. The money was sent, but the brother disappeared. Many years later, David Hustvedt died in Minneapolis, where he had been selling pencils on the street. He managed to get around by inserting his knees into a pair of shoes. On the street he had been known as "Dave the Pencil Man." I used the story in a novel, *The Sorrows of an American.*

My parents are dead. As I write this, my mother has been dead for only three months. She died on October 12, 2019, at the age of ninety-six. My father died on February 2, 2004. I will be sixty-five on February 19, 2020, the same day my mother would have turned ninety-seven if she had lived. Neither of them died young, and even if I die soon, today or tomorrow, I will not die young either.

My parents met at the University of Oslo in 1950 or 1951. My mother was a student there, and my father had a Fulbright Fellowship. Born in Mandal, my mother moved to Askim, a town just outside Oslo, when she was ten years old. Rather stupidly, it took me a while to realize that both my parents spent the high bloom of their youth at war or under occupation. My father was nineteen when he received notice for duty. My mother was seventeen when the Nazis invaded Norway on April 9, 1940.

Within a few years of meeting the grandson of Norwegian immigrants, my mother became a Norwegian immigrant herself and found herself married and living in Minnesota.

My mother didn't know that the parents of the handsome American she had met at the American Club in Oslo lived on a farm without running water, that they had no electricity until my father put it in after the war, and that neither of them had finished grade school, much less high school. She didn't know that two woodstoves were all they had for heating during the frozen Minnesota winters. My father withheld all this from my mother. He let her discover it for herself. The reasons for his secrecy are buried with him.

As children, my sisters and I did not think of our grandparents as poor. It wasn't that we didn't know what the word meant, but rather that we didn't believe it was a word that applied to members of our own family. *Poor* summoned fairy tales, the man and woman with three daughters or three sons who lived in a cottage in the woods or distant urban "slums," visible to us only in sweeping gray tones on TV. It seems that my grandparents had managed reasonably well when my father, the oldest of four, and his sister, Erna, the second child, were still small, but when the Depression hit, the delicate equilibrium of the household was rocked and then it collapsed. The people lived on, but the farm I remember seemed to have been stopped in time, circa 1937. Paralysis defined the place.

We four sisters and our cousins had the run of that place when we visited in summer. It was our Wonderland. We climbed onto the seat of the tractor that sat in the high grass near the orchard of apple and pear trees. We perched happily on the carcass of an old car abandoned on the property. We loved the rain barrels lined up beside the house and the mysterious mounds of junk stored in the little white garage, including a discarded refrigerator, the sight of which terrified me because I had heard a story about a boy who closed himself inside of one and died. I loved the basin that served as a sink and the bar of gray Lava soap with grit in it made especially for farmers and mechanics. I loved the bowl and the long-handled dipper we used to drink water. I remember running with a side ache, grass stains on my knees and palms, cuts and bug bites, going inside for Band-Aids and drinks of lemonade and wild games of cops and robbers, shipwreck, tornado, kidnapping, and pirate.

When my mother confessed to Tillie that she was pregnant with me in July before my parents' wedding day in August, my grandmother blew air from between her lips, made a "puh" sound, and waved her hand to dismiss the subject. It was of no account. "Grandma didn't care at all," my mother said to me many years later as we sat up talking late one night.

There is a story my father could not bring himself to write, one he did not include in the family history or in the memoir he wrote about his life, but which at some point I heard, not from him but from his sister or one of his brothers, a story that was subsequently confirmed by my mother. At the height of the Depression, a government inspector visited the farm, declared that the dairy cows were infected with hoof-and-mouth disease, and ordered them killed. After the terrible thing had been done, it came out—I do not know how—that the cows had not been sick. The inspector had been wrong. There was no recompense.

I have carried the image of that carnage in my head for years, carnage I never saw.

I think my father hated the place as much as he loved it.

The landscape is unchanged. The farmland still rolls on for miles and miles, now under the auspices of vast farms or "agribusiness." The farmhouse on its remaining twenty acres stands as an empty monument to family memory, not far from Urland Church, where my father's ashes are buried in a box in a grave close to the wood that butts up against the cemetery. Beside him in another box are half of my mother's ashes. The four daughters will take the other half of what was once my mother to Norway this summer, to Mandal where she was born. Close to them lie my grandparents Lars and Matilda, my uncle Morris, my uncle Mac McGuire, an Irish policeman who married tante Erna, died when he was only fifty-two, and ended up among the Norwegians after death. The land looks the same, but the immigrants and their Norwegian-speaking children are dead. My father's generation, the third, the last one to still speak the language, are almost all dead now, too. The children of my generation who came after them disappeared into white America. For many, their connection to their immigrant past is tenuous at best, reduced to a couple of talismans—a tightly knit Norwegian sweater or a plate of lefse—the soft unleavened potato bread, my grandmother's specialty. It is best spread with butter, sprinkled with sugar, then rolled up, and eaten quickly or slowly, depending on one's inclination.

Brutally hot in summer and beset by blizzards and temperatures far below zero in winter, Minnesota's climate is extreme. Life on the prairie was a periodic struggle to survive weather. My father recalled drought, locusts, and roads closed for long periods by "the snows." When the roads were impassable by car, they traveled by sled with the horses, a memory that brought a smile of pleasure to my father's face. Tillie was terrified of icy roads and preferred to stay put when the ugly sleet fell and warnings arrived on the radio or television. I remember her cracking anxious voice coming from the telephone as she spoke to my father. She would not take the half-hour drive to Northfield under those conditions. Tillie must have remembered some frightening experience with slippery roads, but I do not know what it was.

We are all, to one degree or another, made of what we call "memory," not only the bits and pieces of time visible to us in pictures that have hardened with our repeated stories, but also the memories we embody and don't understand—the smell that carries with it something lost or the gesture or touch of a person who reminds us of another person, or a sound, distant or close, that brings with it unknown dread. And then there are the memories of others that we adopt and catalogue with our own, sometimes confusing theirs with ours. And again, there are memories that change because the perspective has been wrenched into another position—my grandmother has returned to me in a different guise. She has been rerembered and reconfigured.

By the time my great-grandfather Ivar Hustvedt arrived in Minnesota in 1868, the Dakota tribe had ceded 24 million acres of land to the U.S. government in the 1851 treaty of Traverse des Sioux, which pushed the Dakota, a nomadic people, onto a narrow reservation along the Minnesota River. In 1853, the land was opened to settlement, and the Norwegians began to arrive. In 1862, during the Civil War, betrayed by broken treaties and facing starvation, a small number of Dakota retaliated against a family of settlers and, after that, battles raged across Minnesota. Dakota, immigrants, and U.S. soldiers died. My grandparents must have heard stories, stories about what had come before their parents arrived, stories about the Indian Wars and the Civil War, in which a regiment of Norwegians, led by the staunch abolitionist Colonel Hans Christian Heg, fought for the Union. They were drafted the moment they set foot on the Minnesota territory. The men spoke no English. They conducted the business of war in Norwegian.

In answer to a letter from his brother Torkel, who had written to him of his plans to emigrate, Ivar told his brother not to come.

Those who emigrated from Norway, a quarter of the country's total population when all was said and done, those who came in great waves during the nineteenth century and into the twentieth, were not people of means. Many were farmers without a farm—the second and third and fourth sons who were not destined to inherit anything. They moved to the cities for work, but work was not always forthcoming, and there was land in *Amerika*. The men came alone or they brought their women with them. Some of these people managed life on the plains, the immigrant type gobbled up into the American myth of stout pioneers who "tamed" the "virgin" territory. But many others returned home. Some went mad. In 1932, Ørnulf Ødegård conducted a large psychiatric study that found that the number of Norwegian immigrants treated for psychotic disorders in Minnesota was significantly higher than those of both Norwegians who had stayed put and native-born Americans of Norwegian descent. Ødegård speculated that the difference was due to the arduous realities of being a stranger in a strange land.

Of course, this is the wide, long view of things, a view my grandmother never took, I'm sure, as she fought to keep her children fed and clothed after her husband had gone to work as a hired hand on neighboring farms and later crossed the country to work in a defense plant in Washington State during the war. Father and son met out there. My father had been assigned to an intelligence unit, training in Oregon as part of a provisional plan by the allies to invade Norway. His qualifications: He had tested high on an IQ test and spoke Norwegian. In his memoir, my father remembers that when he met his father, the man was wearing his wedding ring and that it made him happy. Nowhere else in the memoir is there any description of bitterness and alienation between his parents. There is no other mention of wedding rings on or off, or the pain of a naked finger as opposed to one wearing the sign of the marital pact.

My grandmother used to say she shouldn't have married Lars. We all heard her. We all thought it was a terrible thing to say.

I don't know when my grandfather lost heart and disappeared into himself. I know he had nightmares and would wake up yelling and that he once punched the ceiling of the little bedroom where he slept. How I know this I don't remember, but secrets traveled in the family, secrets heavy with emotion. I felt they were like stones stored in hidden pockets in a big man's overcoat, and wearing that coat meant being weighed down by shame. Did the grown-ups imagine we children didn't feel it? Is it possible that I felt it more than my sisters and cousins? I have used the image of a tuning fork before, but that is how I recall my child self, as a reverberating instrument, not of sounds, but of feelings in the various rooms where I found myself with the grown-ups and their tangled emotions of love and hate that must have mingled with my own and a fervent wish to be free of the oppressive lot of them. But that wish was as unspeakable for me as it was for my father. My great luck is that I can write it now.

Scandinavians in general and Norwegians in particular are often cast as stoic and repressed people who live their torments offstage rather than on it. Henrik Ibsen paraded secrets and ghosts and the anguish and guilt they created in the people possessed by them in full view of the theatergoing public. My father taught Ibsen's plays. It was his favorite course. When he was dying, he asked me what I thought of *Romersholm*, and I wished I remembered the play better. I reread it after he died. It is dense and deep and clotted with sexual-political fears and hopes, spoken and unspoken. At the center of the play is Rebecca West, a figure of striving ambition, immense psychological complexity, and moral ambiguity. She is guilty of driving Beata, the wife of Romers, the man she loves, to suicide. She is also a creature of soaring idealism, quiet rage, and strategic intelligence. Ibsen penetrated the impossible position of women in the world of the fathers with a ferocious clarity. "Assuredly, you were the strongest at Romersholm," Romers says to Rebecca. "Stronger than Beata and I together."

My grandfather didn't have my grandmother's strength. He didn't have her chutzpah—to steal a word from another immigrant culture I married into, the culture of Eastern European Jews who also arrived in large numbers in the nineteenth century. Tillie made and sold lefse to stave off desperation. There was another rumor that she had taken something from a store once—that she had *stolen*. My mother told me this in a low voice. The details are missing. Maybe Tillie *stole*. She didn't go to jail. I am not scandalized.

The story I want to tell now came to me from my mother, but it belonged to Grandma. One summer, my cousins who lived in Seattle came to visit their family in the Midwest. Uncle Stanley was the only Hustvedt offspring who had moved far away. He and his wife, Pat, were strict parents. Their many sanctions and threats of punishment were directed only at their own four children, but when I was in earshot of the authoritarian directives, I would feel my limbs turn rigid and my heart speed up in vicarious alarm. They lived in one world, and we in another, and it was strange when the worlds collided at the farm. I knew my laissez-faire parents disliked the foreign regime, but they tolerated the alien doings in silence. Of the grown-ups, only Grandma made her disapproval known. She winced, muttered, shook her head, and clucked when her son and daughter-in-law issued their commands. This I remember.

What I can't remember because I wasn't there is that Stanley and Pat left their children with Grandma and Grandpa for a couple of days to go off on a trip alone. Grandpa isn't part of the story, but wherever he was, it's hard to imagine that he was possessed by any desire to interfere with his wife's plans. Grandma told my mother that she and the children watched the car with the parents in it drive off, pass Urland Church, and disappear over the shallow hill. Then she turned to her temporary wards, nodded at them, and said, "Okay, now, *go wild*." They took the cue. They howled, hooted, rolled in the driveway dirt, threw whatever was handy, ran in and out of the house, slammed doors, kicked trees and fences, and spat at each other in an orgy of freedom as my grandmother watched them, seated calmly on the lawn, smiling with conspiratorial pleasure.

How weary I am of the well-worn narratives about grandmothers, the objects of so much cultural gibberish, and not only of the pink greeting card variety, although there is much of that. "A grandma is warm hugs and sweet memories," the inspirational writer Barbara Cage informs us. How convenient the platitudes and stories of Grandma's warmth, goodness, sacrifice, and poignant suffering have been, told and retold to comfort later generations and defuse all threat of their opposites.

Tillie was a difficult woman. She did not choke back her rebellion or thwart her caustic laughter or her open mirth. And she did not disguise her fury when it arrived.

In her book *Emotions in History—Lost and Found* (2011), Ute Frevert writes, "Since antiquity, rage has been seen as a feature of the powerful." I watched Brett Kavanaugh on television, now a justice on the U.S. Supreme Court, as he raged with tears in his eyes at the indignity of it all. How could he, *he*, the anointed boy of the law, be accused by that woman professor, Christine Blasey Ford, of sexual assault? Rage is a privilege of the powerful, of white men in America. It is not for the rest of us, who must guard it or eat it whole. The woman must sit humbly as she testifies in a soft, calm, ladylike voice, eager to "help" her interrogators.

"My anger has meant pain to me but it has also meant survival and before I give it up I am going to make sure there is something at least as powerful on the road to clarity," Audre Lorde said in her speech "The Uses of Anger: Women Responding to Racism." Lorde's anger charged her brilliance and electrified the prose of her essays. She knew onto whom it was directed and why, including white feminists who had closed their eyes to uncomfortable and ugly truths. My grandmother had no such exquisite clarity, no such intellectual acumen, no such philosophical penetration into her lot. She was a white woman subject to the bewildering realities of marriage and subsequent poverty and the shame that came with it. She had the anger. It helped her survive.

Her ghost has come back to me hauling buckets of water, a woman who delighted and frightened me at once, whose image had been, at least in part, filtered through my father's ambivalence, the mingled love and hate he could never really speak about. There is nothing simple, heroic, or pure about this ghost. I am well aware that there is much about her that remains hidden to me, much that I will never know. Time has altered Matilda Underdahl Hustvedt in her granddaughter's mind. I remember how she broke the silences over and over again.

2020

MY MOTHER'S OCEAN AND
HOW IT BECAME MINE

Before the ocean, there were stories of the ocean, my mother's stories from Mandal, a town located on the most southern tip of the coast of Norway, where she lived on a small mountain in a house overlooking the flat expanse of the North Sea with her parents and her three siblings in a state of nearly paradisiacal happiness, if she is to be believed (and I have mostly believed her, while acknowledging that memories of childhood are usually colored in the rosy hues of joy or the bleak shades of misery, and far less often in the varying grays of ambivalence), but it is certain that the salt wind blew the smell of fish and brine over the sand and rocks and cobblestone streets where my mother walked and ran and climbed as a girl and that the tales she told as a woman wafted into the minds of my three sisters and me, residents of Northfield, Minnesota, who gazed out the window at vistas of corn and alfalfa fields and low-strung barbed-wire fences, behind which cows grazed and left their pies to dry in the sun, but we knew no ocean except the one that came by way of our mother's accounts, and that is how we discovered the invigorations of maritime life without having lived it.

My great-grandfather was a captain who commandeered his ship, the Mars, *to the South Seas.* This sentence of indisputable fact sent me into high reverie as a child. The dim figure of the Norwegian patriarch mingled with Captain Smollett in *Treasure Island* and the ambiguous Captain Nemo in the film I had seen at least six times before I was twelve (thanks to the Grand Movie Theater's Saturday matinees for children): *20,000 Leagues Under the Sea.* And then there was Uncle Oskar, my grandfather's older brother, a first mate, who sailed to Coconut Island off the coast of Australia, married a Melanesian princess, and returned to

Norway with that highborn lady, but he sailed to India, too, and carried home a red tea set of fine, thin porcelain as a gift for my grandmother, which my mother keeps to this day in a glass cabinet in her room in the retirement home where she now lives in landlocked Minnesota.

But my favorite stories are my mother's intimate ones, of trips to the beach during the long days of summer when night is never truly night, but rather a deepening of blue above that soon gives way to increasing sunlight, and I see my mother's tante Andora in her sagging wool swimming costume as she throws herself into the water, takes a few brisk strokes, stands up, and wades toward land, but before she steps onto the beach, she performs a ritual that mystifies my mother: Andora leans over, scoops up a handful of water, and sprinkles its contents down the front of her oversized swimwear, anointing first her right breast and then her left. And I see my great-aunt on another day, too, striding toward the boat that will take the family to one of the small islands offshore, when all at once the elastic of her underpants gives way, and the garment slides down her legs to her ankles as my mortified young mother looks on, but the unruffled Andora steps out of the fallen bloomers, snags the silky heap with the toe of her shoe, gives it a neat kick, catches it, stuffs it into her purse, and keeps on walking. Such are the wonders of life by the sea.

2017

STONES AND ASHES

I keep one of my father's passports on a shelf above my writing desk. He died on February 2, 2004. He was cremated and then buried in the small cemetery of the rural church in Minnesota he attended as a boy. It is a short walk from there to my grandparents' small farmhouse, which now stands empty, its white paint scarred with gray. The immense maple tree, the grape arbor, the peony and lilac bushes, the pear and apple trees are still vigorous. They are no longer tended by anyone, but the bushes and trees bloom, and the fruit comes back every year.

We visit the grave. We plant flowers.

What are we visiting?

No human culture discards its dead without ceremony. To leave the dead without rites is ignominy. It seems that even the Neanderthals buried their dead.

Although it was long thought that mourning was an exclusively human trait, research suggests that other primates, elephants, and some birds grieve for their fellow creatures, that cultural practices handed down from one generation to the next are not ours alone.

The variety of human customs that attend death is stupefying.

The Vikings placed the corpse in a longboat, set it on fire, and pushed it out to sea.

The Zulus burn the dead person's property because they fear the presence of the spirit in those things.

Pierre Clastres, the French anthropologist who wrote an account of the two years he spent with an isolated people in Paraguay, *Chronicle of the Guayaki Indians*, reported that members of the community were vague and unforthcoming when he inquired about their death rituals. One person would say one thing, another something else. It made no sense to him. Not long before Clastres left the tribe, an old woman (who had not been told that the outsider was to remain ignorant) informed him that the Guayaki eat their dead. The consumption of corpses was intended to break the connection of spirit to body, and thereby free or banish the spirit so it could do no harm to the living.

Human beings grieve, fear, and worship the dead.

In a village in northern Thailand in 1975, I frightened the children, who thought I was a spirit. They had never seen a person so tall, white, and blond. They ran away from me shouting "pii, pii," the Thai word for *ghost*.

The people of many cultures mark out space for the dead: burial grounds, stones, totem poles, urns, mausoleums, tombs cut directly into the rock face of cliffs, tombs suspended from mountainsides, and coffins elevated on stilts yards above the earth.

Lewis Mumford wrote, "The city of the dead antedates the city of the living." He argued that people wanted to live close to the burial places of their ancestors, to whom they were drawn with mingled feelings of worship and dread, and that is how the city was born: necropolis before metropolis.

But there is also the literal preservation of the dead: embalming, mummification, various forms of holding on to the corpse. In the Museo Chileno de Arte Precolombino in Santiago, one of the curators explained to me that a long-vanished tribe in what is now Chile were a hunting-gathering people, but they engaged in elaborate rituals and embalming practices. This came as a great surprise to anthropologists because they did not expect such sophistication from hunter-gatherers. Their afterlife was given far more attention than their before-life.

The Aborginal people in northern Australia preserve and paint the bones of the dead.

A people in Africa wear the bones of the dead while they mourn. The English of the Victorian period were partial to jewelry made from the hair of a dear, dead person.

In part because burial space is limited and graves must be turned over in sixty years, increasing numbers of South Koreans are converting the ashes of their loved ones into colorful strings of beads that can be displayed at home.

My grandmother used to hear my grandfather moving around the farmhouse after he died. Once she saw him lift his hat from the hook on the back of the kitchen door. It is not uncommon for people to hallucinate the dead in their grief, but the phenomenon is poorly studied, perhaps because scientists resist the idea of ghosts. These specters mostly bring comfort to people in mourning. They are vivid reincarnations of a lost beloved, waking dreams of fervent wishes.

One woman I read about saw her deceased cat roaming contentedly in the rooms they once shared.

Few of us are free of the feeling that death, that most ordinary of all ordinary facts about human existence, is also unutterably strange. When the person is no longer there, we try to preserve what was in what is— with signs and tokens. People die around me, but when I care for the dead person, the loss is of me, not outside me. "It is the dead, not the living, who make the longest demands," Antigone says to her sister Ismene in the play by Sophocles. "We die forever." The tragic heroine refuses to let her brother go without tending to his body, without giving him the funeral rites he deserves. She defies the legal decree that has forbidden it, even though she knows it means her own death.

It is true that we are forever dying. It is also true that we cannot treat the bodies of our dead as if they were no different from the trash we routinely take out to the curb. We must symbolize the loss and care for the remains in one way or another. How we do that depends on our culture, but cultural practices evolve and change.

I will be burned and then buried in Green-Wood Cemetery in Brooklyn on top of or underneath my husband, depending on which one of us dies first. When we found the spot in that huge necropolis, I felt happy. How odd that feeling was. I do not want to die. I am always worrying that I will die before I have written what I still hope to write, and yet, I am pleased with the plot, pleased to think of it verdant in spring and summer, rouged in fall, and desolate or white in winter, despite the fact that I, snuffed of all consciousness, will not enjoy the shifting seasons anymore.

I love the Tom Waits song with its insistent refrain, "We're all gonna be just dirt in the ground." I sing along. I dance. I laugh. I am not sure why.

I am glad the ground where my father's ashes are buried is marked with his name.

As I write this, my mother is ninety-three. She has asked her four daughters to bury half of her ashes beside my father and to take the other half to her native Norway. She wants us to scatter them on the graves of her parents in the town of Mandal, where she was born and spent her childhood. On the small mountain that rises above those graves is the house my grandfather designed and where my mother lived as a girl. From there one can look straight out to the sea.

2017

A WALK WITH MY MOTHER

I have been remembering my mother's walk. It was a determined walk, but with a light step. I can still hear and feel its decisive, confident rhythm. She loved to walk—in the Minnesota woods, the Norwegian mountains, on beaches everywhere—and she walked hard and long every day until a spate of illnesses slowed her down at the age of ninety. She walked for pleasure. She walked to feel the wind, sun, snow, or rain in her face and to discover marvels along the way—wild flowers, tall grasses, sea glass made round by the surf, stones in surprising colors, fallen bark, and gnarled branches.

My mother, Ester Vegan Hustvedt, died on October 12, 2019. I am glad she died before the pandemic. It would have been impossible for me to sit beside her and hold her if she were dying now in the summer of 2020. The walking mother I remember is a particular woman, born in Mandal, Norway, in 1923, the youngest of four children, whose family left that town when she was ten and moved to Askim outside Oslo. She lived through the Nazi occupation and its deprivations and by 1954 she was in the United States, married to my father. My mother is not "The Mother," an archetype or cliché that inevitably shows up when mothers are invoked, a person squeezed into male/female hierarchies or the cult of the Great Mother or the Virgin Mary or Mother Nature or the mother of soft-focus advertisements in parenting magazines. And yet, mother ideas invade mothering with a stark morality of good and evil that rarely touches fathering.

At my fiftieth birthday party, which was also my mother's eighty-second birthday, my mother made a speech. She began, not with my birth, but with the moment she felt quickening, a tremor in her belly, the signal of her first pregnancy. She spoke of her intense joy, and I thought to myself: It is good to be a child wanted by her mother. The simple fact that every person begins inside another person haunts motherhood. The simple fact that most women push the infant out of their bodies haunts motherhood. The fact that many women feed their children from the milk in their breasts haunts motherhood. Without a female reproductive system there is no quickening, no labor, no birth or nursing.

My mother often said she thought infancy was too short. She had four daughters, and she relished our earliest stage of life. She told me that when she gave birth at forty to my youngest sister, Ingrid, she knew it was probably the last time, and she felt a pang of loss. My mother's labors were short and intense—all of them under three hours. Unlike other women of that era in the United States, she was never anesthetized, and her preferred birth position was squatting. In the last five years of her life, she lived in a room in an assisted living facility. As she lay in bed, she looked directly at four black-and-white photographs of her children as babies. When we spoke on the telephone almost every day, I would ask her what she was doing. Often she would answer, "I'm looking at the babies." Her oldest baby was then sixty-four.

She was a passionate mother, a mother who in many ways fulfilled a fantasy about mothers propagated in postwar, mid-century America. She worked at home until her children were all in school and never had what is called a "profession." For the first day of school, Christmas, and Easter, she sewed four matching dresses for her daughters. She sewed clothes for our dolls, too, and knit them sweaters. When we returned home on the bus every day after long hours of reading and arithmetic and sometimes tense, confusing dramas with other children, we each sat on a stool in the kitchen, ate the cookie or cake our mother had baked for us, and told her what was new. She laid out our clothes for school, put towels in the dryer so they would be warm when we emerged from the bath, shined our patent leather shoes with Vaseline for special occasions. She ironed beautifully. She loved a house in perfect order, copper that shone, dust-free surfaces, glass of sparkling clarity. She threw enviable dinner parties. She was proud of her housewifery skills. Cleanliness and elegant arrangements brought her sensual pleasure.

Although women have always borne children, ideas about mother-hood have changed over time. In ancient Greece, women were child-bearers confined to their homes with few rights, but Greek mythology features powerful and frightening female characters. Think of the Amazons, the women warriors; the snake-haired Medusa, who turns men to stone; and Medea, who murders her children. In myth, it seems, Greek women took their bloody revenge. Despite intense fears of female sexuality during the medieval period, Christ was often portrayed as a maternal figure. The ancient belief, which persisted for centuries, that mother's milk was transformed blood reinforced the image. As a mother nurtured her young, Christ nurtured the flock with his blood during the Eucharist.

But the self-sacrificing, patient queen of the domestic realm, who assumed the moral education of her children, was born in the eighteenth century. The French philosopher Jean-Jacques Rousseau deserves considerable credit for her creation. This ideal woman was more than merely a subject of her husband's rule. She had her own domain inside the house caring for her children. "The true mother, far from being a woman of the world," Rousseau wrote, "is as much a recluse in her home as the nun in her cloister . . ." The true mother was a middle-class creature. Poor and working-class women have never been in a position to stay home. Enslaved women had no control over their own bodies or their families. Only women of the middle classes were called upon to realize the ideal Virginia Woolf rebelled against. "Killing the angel in the house," she wrote, "was part of the occupation of a woman writer."

My mother's father was postmaster in Mandal and a landowner in a region of Norway known for its Pietism, a trait it has never thrown off. It remains part of Norway's "Bible belt," a bastion of conservative values including resistance to gender equality. My mother was never particularly religious, and she did not believe women should be either submissive or silent. Nevertheless, she lived in a world in which male and female labor was strictly divided, and the importance of the former over the latter went unquestioned. Years after my father died, my mother told me that his habit of interrupting her when she spoke had hurt and angered her. When she confronted him about it, he was hurt and angry.

My mother championed the good manners she had learned as a child. The repertoire included special rules for girls: keeping their knees tightly together, folding their hands in their laps, and curtseying to adults— behavior to be strictly observed in company. At the same time, Ester let her daughters run wild in the woods behind the house and roam for miles and get scraped by barbed wire and sucked by leeches and come home wet, filthy, and bug-bitten with dogs, frogs, salamanders, and grasshoppers in tow.

In Northfield, Minnesota, the small town my mother dropped into by marriage, women were mostly wives and mothers. When I was growing up, I don't ever recall meeting an older married woman without children. She must have existed, but I can't remember her. There was a gaggle of widows in town, several old maids who taught school or held down secretarial jobs until they died, and two aging unmarried sisters who lived together, one of whom had a Ph.D. and had been a history professor. They wore shawls and sturdy old lady shoes. I must have imagined being married one day and having children. I loved my dolls, but even as a child, I had dreams of becoming an artist. I would live somewhere far away and make art.

Where do I situate my own beloved mother in the ideal mother/real mother dichotomy? In *Of Woman Born: Motherhood as Experience and Institution* (1976), Adrienne Rich distinguished between two meanings of motherhood: "the *potential relationship* of any woman to her powers of reproduction and to children; and the *institution*, which aims at ensuring that potential—and all women—shall remain under male control." The distinction is important, but it is not at all clean. An institution is established law, practice, or custom. The institution of motherhood is not a building we walk into and out of. It is a social structure with rules that organizes collective behavior, a structure that is also internal and often unconscious, a learned way of being. My husband had an aunt who used to spur her daughters to action with the following threat: "Brush your teeth or you won't get married."

No person can be lifted out of the world in which she lives. No person can be stripped of context. Our desires are shaped by experience, by pleasures and pains, and dos and don'ts. The newborn person has pleasures and pains—sensations that soothe or hurt her—and learned patterns are established early, rhythms of feeling that take on meaning and become part of her. Every helpless infant needs constant care. In the world I grew up in, the primary caretaker was almost always the birth mother, but this is not universally true. Lone mothering is not a rule. There have always been others—fathers and wet nurses and nannies and grandmothers and uncles and cousins. In her work the evolutionary biologist Sarah Hrdy developed the idea of "cooperative breeding," a trait not unique to humans. Elephants, chimpanzees, lemurs, and many species of birds are also cooperative breeders. Human mothers were and are aided by what Hrdy calls "alloparents," others in the group that lend a hand. "Unless early hominin mothers had been able to count on significant alloparental as well as paternal contributions for the care and provisioning of extremely costly, slow-maturing young, the human species simply could not have evolved." A Swahili proverb articulates the idea perfectly: "A single hand cannot nurse a child."

I was thirty-two when my daughter, Sophie, was born, exactly the age my mother was when I was born. In the early months of Sophie's life I had a strong sensation of being awash in fluids, hers and mine. I felt as if I had expelled from my body a kind of mobile attachment. She could be passed around to my husband, my mother, sisters, to her nanny, and to others, but she would end up back on my body, although she was no longer inside it. For me, there was more pleasure than pain during those long, short first months of her life. Unlike my mother, I had help. It was exhausting nevertheless, and, at times, overwhelming, trying to calm her. Sophie was not a relaxed character. She wriggled and kicked and howled. She hardly slept. My husband and I bounced and rocked her in our arms and in her carriage. Even when I wasn't holding her, I found myself bouncing up and down as if I had become a brainless windup toy.

And yet, I loved stroking her bald head, looking into her enigmatic little face, watching her stare back at me and purse her mouth in small involuntary sucking motions. I loved her unmarred skin and its golden color, her tiny soft fingernails, and her flailing, undisciplined limbs. I loved her small body curled into mine when I nursed her, the foaming milk that leaked from the corners of her mouth as she grunted and sucked, a little animal of greed, comic in her complete lack of self-consciousness. I loved feeling the pressure of her tiny fist around my finger. I loved the smell of her. I fell in love with her. She is thirty-two now. I am still in love with her.

A few days after Sophie was born, my mother sat on the edge of the bed in the apartment in Brooklyn where we lived at the time, and she said to me in a voice of mild surprise, "You look as if you've always had a baby in your arms." Sophie was my post-dissertation baby. I became pregnant not long after my defense for a Ph.D. at Columbia in English literature. My experience with my daughter is my own—it is not intended to stand in for universal motherhood. That may be the crux of the matter. Motherhood has been and is drowned in so much sentimental nonsense with so many punitive rules for how to act and feel that it remains a cultural straitjacket, even today. The metaphor is highly conscious. The straitjacket used to restrain psychiatric patients is an apt image for what Rich meant by keeping women under male institutional control. When the maternal becomes a static concept, a fantasy about sacrificial nurturing without limit, it serves as a moral weapon to punish mothers who are perceived as wild. And because the institution is not a building or a rule book but a way of being that is part of collective life itself, it is also a weapon that strikes mothers from the inside as shame or guilt.

When Sophie was not yet two, we were traveling somewhere as a family. I cannot recall which airport we were negotiating or where we were headed. I know I was harried and tired, draped with bulging bags, and descending on an escalator with my child in her stroller. My husband was somewhere behind us. All of sudden, Sophie lurched forward, and I saw in a single horrified instant that she was not belted in. I grabbed her, pulled her back, and disaster was averted. A businessman gliding in front of me with a small square briefcase witnessed the close call. He gave me a look I have never forgotten. It was a look of disgust, and the shame I felt was so bruising I have never shared this story with anyone until now. In his eyes I saw myself: a monster of negligence, the bad mother.

It has taken me years to understand that the man on the escalator was an incarnation of the violent *moral* feelings in the culture directed at mothers. He made no move to block my child's potential fall. He showed no sympathy for my terror or subsequent relief. He was a figure of pure, brutal judgment. Had the person on the escalator been not me but my husband, I am certain his eyes would have carried another message: The poor man; where's his wife? Although feminists have long rebelled against the confining ideology of motherhood, the disgusted judge is not a figure of the past. After Rachel Cusk published *A Life's Work* (2001), in which she wrote about the shock, alienation, and loss of self she felt while caring for her baby daughter, she was excoriated by reviewers, many of them women, as a narcissistic "self-obsessed bore." Her longing to write and the barriers maternity created between her and her work induced not mild reproof but opprobrium.

I vividly remember listening to a woman rail against, not me, but Harriet Burden, one of my characters. A university professor had invited me to a book club to discuss my novel *The Blazing World*. As the book's author, I had wrongly expected polite treatment. Harriet, my aggressive, ambitious, and bitter artist so offended one of the women, she turned on me with open fury. Harriet was damned lucky, she said. She should have been content with her good life, plenty of money, and raising her children. Later, I wondered what desires she had squelched in the name of motherhood.

Until Sophie was six, my husband, Paul Auster, who is also a writer, wrote for many hours a day in a studio, while I was relegated to a desk in the living room of our small apartment. We moved to a house then, and I acquired a room of my own. Even with a study, my child's needs often smothered mine. I had periods of feeling drained, confused, and angry about how hard it was to work, but I was not desperate or depressed. Why? If I had thought my child's infancy and early childhood were permanent, I imagine I would have gone mad. I have often thought of the immense difficulties people must face who have children who for one reason or another cannot leave home and remain forever dependent.

My mother adored her own mother, Tobine, who died at eighty-nine.

My *mormor,* the Norwegian word for mother's mother, was a gentle, intelligent, deeply affectionate woman. Ester's ease and happiness while in Tobine's company was palpable. Seeing them together gave me pleasure. In the final two years of my mother's life when her memory steadily grew worse, she would sometimes say to me, "*Hvor er Mamma?*" "Where is Mamma?" I would tell her Mormor was dead, upon which she would look surprised, nod sadly, and reorient herself to this truth. Patterns often repeat across generations. Seven years after the cruel and stupid response to her book, Cusk published an article in *The Guardian* on March 21, 2008, "I have a bad relationship with my own mother," she wrote, "and was pitched by motherhood into the recollection of childhood unhappiness and confusion." This insight is not developed in the book. I suspect it arrived later.

If we carry in ourselves the joy and pain of our own early care, then the birth of a child may well unleash those feelings, but why we have those feelings is far more difficult to divine. "People can't help what they feel," my mother liked to say. Actions, on the other hand, are subject to inhibition. It is ridiculous to pretend that ambivalent feelings are not part of parent-child relations—that love and hate might not be directed at the same small person. Fathers are indulged for feeling jealous of infants or for mourning the days before paternity arrived. They have often been depicted as comic, hapless creatures, deserving of universal pity. Such indulgence is rarely afforded to mothers. Mothers are punished for what they feel or don't feel.

One of the great cultural ironies is the idea that maternal intimacy with a child is automatic, guaranteed by blood or by genes, and the mother simply follows her natural instincts. It is ironic because this notion is itself a distortion of human reality. We are intensely social animals and our societal arrangements vary enormously from place to place, time to time, but also from family to family and from person to person, and this social flexibility is part of our slow-developing species. My mother told me the story of her own aunt, a rather stiff, upright woman, whose children would run right past her and leap into the arms of the housekeeper whom they called Dudda. Dudda gave the cousins hugs and kisses and petted and played with them. It was Dudda who did the mothering in that house. The arrangement suited my great-aunt, it seems, who according to my mother didn't appear to resent the beloved Dudda.

Learned social habits become part of the established rhythms of our lives, which are sociological, psychological, and biological all at once. It is useless to divide nature from nurture. Even at the level of molecular biology, we know that gene suppression and expression may depend on what happens in the animal's life. Multiple shocks, for example, may prevent gene expression, but this effect can also be reversed or erased. Human beings are dynamic, not static creatures. Nothing illustrates this better than a long life.

My mother had a childhood, youth, and adulthood before she had children, and a life that went on for many years once her daughters had left home. My father died when my mother was eighty. She lived on for another sixteen years. She traveled widely, spent almost every summer in Norway, made intimate friends, followed American politics closely, had strong left-leaning opinions, read many books, and took her long, daily walks. At ninety, after several illnesses, she rather suddenly became old and frail. Recent memories began to vanish. When I visited her in spring during her last years, I would take her out into the garden of the assisted living facility in a wheelchair. We would talk about what we saw—buds breaking open, the subtle shades of green around us. We examined pine cones, admired butterflies and ladybugs. Inevitably, during a lull in our conversation, my mother would lift her face to the sun, close her eyes, and smile.

Human lives are in continual flux. My mother was the child who almost died of scarlet fever at the age of three. What she remembered from that near-death experience was lying in bed with a chocolate bear or dog—its animal identity remained unclear. She was the child who sat on a stool as her mother milked the family cow, Rosa, a cow her father had purchased before anyone in the family knew how to milk. The family's maid refused to take the job, but Mormor learned, and as she milked, she made up one story after another for Ester, who, whenever there was a pause, would say, "And then, Mamma, and then." My mother was the child with enormous eyes in a sailor suit in a photograph with her three siblings also dressed as seafarers—de rigueur for middle-class children of the era. My mother was the seventeen-year-old who was woken by her mother's voice on April 9, 1940: *Stå opp. Det er krig.* Get up. It's war.

She was the young woman, who, late the same year, was part of a spontaneous demonstration against the occupation, which began with her, her brother, and a few friends singing the national anthem and shouting their support for the king and their hatred for Hitler around the Christmas tree in the town square. It swelled to a crowd of about eight hundred people, who then took their protest to the houses of known Nazis and German sympathizers in town to continue shouting and singing. Later, my mother, her brother, and others considered ringleaders were interrogated. My mother said she was indignant that the Norwegian official who interviewed her softened her answers for the record. She was given a choice—pay a small fine of thirty crowns or spend nine days in jail. My mother chose jail.

I suspect that early in the occupation the administrators of the new justice were unsure about what to do with a rebellious gymnasium student, an Aryan girl, after all, not a Jew or a foreigner. They wanted to make an example of her but had not given up on the idea that the Nordic natives in a Nordic country might fall into line. My mother became the single inmate in a moldering unused prison in Mysen, which the Nazis apparently opened temporarily to house the only person in Askim who had refused to pay the fine. Although I have tried to track later use of that prison, I have found no records. In 1944, the Germans began building a concentration camp in Mysen, but the war ended before it was finished.

A member of Nasjonal Samling, the Norwegian fascist party, oversaw Ester Vegan's nine days of incarceration. She remembered her cell vividly. It had a high barred window, a table, chair, and cot. A bucket in the corner served as the toilet. Like a character in Dickens, she was fed green potatoes and gruel. She read. She read either *How Green Was My Valley* or *Kristin Lavransdatter*, or both. She left the prison with a bloated belly and her patriotism intact. Although her children were extremely proud of their mother's noble jail sentence, my mother stressed that she never doubted that after nine days she would be released. She also emphasized her naïveté. She took the hardship as an adventure, not unlike ones she had read about in novels. She also said that only a few months later, no one would have dared protest the occupation openly. All insurrection went underground.

What interests me, however, is my mother's resilience, a quality that she had throughout her life. She bounced back—not just from a short jail sentence, but from hardships of all kinds, and many illnesses. In psychiatry, *resilience* is a term with a clinical meaning used to describe a person's ability to cope with stress and trauma. This capacity involves multiple factors—the chorus of a person's bodily systems and how they respond to stress; psychological or cognitive factors, such as flexible thinking, not being stuck in a pessimistic rut; and finally, a person's "social support" network. Lonely, isolated people often lack resilience. Much remains unknown about how resilience actually works, but whatever it is, my mother had it.

When she couldn't find student housing in Oslo after the war, she slept on a gurney in a veterinary laboratory where a friend of hers worked. She sneaked in after everyone had gone home and left early in the morning. Her coat was her only bedding. There was no heat. She remembered the metal of the gurney was ice cold and the chemical smell in the room strong. It was used for animal surgery.

I will never forget watching my mother as she traipsed lightly and happily across a swinging footbridge high above Taroko Gorge in Taiwan. It was 1975, and the bridge was missing planks. Others were broken. With every step one took, the bridge bounced and swung. Far below I saw rocks, rushing water, and my death. I was nineteen years old and breathless with terror. When I finally arrived on solid ground, white and nauseated, my mother turned to me gaily and said, "You weren't afraid, were you?" I wish I could remember what I said to her. In some versions of the memory, I declare loudly that I was horrified and in others I shrink in shame. I have no idea which version is true.

When my mother called to tell me in 1979 that she had been diagnosed with breast cancer after finding a lump, which was, in her words, "the size of a walnut," she said her first thought was: "Well, why *not* me?"

I did not see my mother until after she had a radical mastectomy. Neither my parents nor I had money for a plane ticket. Although I was intensely worried about her, I remained in New York and continued my studies. I returned home for a visit in summer as planned. A few minutes after I had walked into the house, my mother looked at me and said, "I want you to see it." She removed her blouse and bra and showed me the long scar where her breast used to be. Her forthright display of the healed but ugly wound had a powerful effect on me. Bodily mutilation is no small thing. I can still see her standing opposite me with her erect posture and a resolute expression on her face. That enduring image has given me strength by example, a sense that I, too, could weather such a loss. I further remember my mother telling me husbands who shrank from their wives because they had lost a breast were "disgusting." Fortunately, my father was not one of them.

It is a banality to say that people both change and stay the same. Heraclitus, the philosopher of the late sixth century BCE whose work remains with us only as fragments, is probably most famous for the words "You cannot step in the same river twice." But this is not actually what the fragment says: "In the same river we both step and do not step, we are and are not." This is far more mysterious. The river continues to flow, to move, and the water in it is forever changing although it remains the same river. I will not attempt to interpret the "we are and are not." In biology, however, there is a concept called homeostasis, an old idea with a newish name. It identifies the dynamic adjustments the living body makes to internal and external realities that keep it going as itself. It changes so it can remain the same.

Difference and sameness are among the most difficult philosophical concepts to parse. The three-year-old Ester who had recovered from a near-fatal fever and looked with pleasure at a chocolate animal is not the ninety-six-year-old woman who sat beside me at the edge of her bed while she was dying, the woman who refused to lie down, who clenched her fists and said, "What is the matter with me? I have never felt like this before." And yet, the child and the old woman belong to the single trajectory of a life in time, early and late.

The woman I knew changed. She secured a job in the library at the college where my father was a professor. She studied French. She embraced her freedom as a mother of older and then adult children. She hired a cleaning lady who came twice a month. But when my father was ill, first from cancer and then from emphysema, and could no longer move without a cane and later without a wheelchair, she did the legwork. She took care of him. Times change.

I remember that my mother could be exhausted by her life, too. I remember all the money worries my parents had when I was a child. My mother had to budget with excruciating care. I remember her tired, drawn face. I remember her voice cracking when she scolded us. She could be furious. I have often wondered what I would have done with *four* children. I had *one*. She put us all to bed right after dinner—six thirty. I remember lying awake and making up stories because I couldn't sleep. As an adult, I once asked her why our bedtime was so early. She said she needed time for herself, time with my father, a little peace. I felt stupid for asking.

For years my mother suffered from chronic pain. She had operations to fuse damaged discs in her spine, but the pain did not go away. She had severe arthritic damage in her neck that flared up regularly. At some point she was also diagnosed with fibromyalgia. My mother was proud, vain, and competitive. Despite evidence to the contrary, she claimed she never had fevers, detected spots on her clothing no one else could see, and kicked higher and harder than anyone else in her exercise classes. She spent long hours writing deep papers for a book club to which she belonged. She wanted those papers to shine, to be the best. Although she had a B.A. degree, she said to me many times, "I thought I would at least have gotten a masters." A regret. We all have them.

Every human being is a complex amalgam of features we recognize only because they are repeated in time. I remember the mother of my early childhood, the bedtime rituals, her hugs and kisses, the feel of her skin, the wondrous smell of her in the dim light, the lamp that stood in the hallway so Liv and I would not lie in total darkness. My mother would adjust the crack in the door exactly to our liking—opening and closing it by an inch, two inches, half an inch—until we sang out, "Just right!" I remember Liv and me "cozying up" with her, one girl under each arm. I remember her kneeling before me to button up my sweater and the feel of her tying a scarf around my neck, the gentle tug at the end of the process as she arranged it, and I remember the feeling of a woolen hat being pulled securely over my ears. "I want my darlings to be warm." My mother's presence was comfort, safety, happiness. I was in love with my mother, and my passionate attachment to her never ended. It remains with me after her death. The physical intimacy between us changed, but that too never ended. My mother and I embraced and caressed each other until the end of her life. When she was really old, I would often lie beside her in her bed and gently rub her arm.

As her daughters grew older, my mother was wary of intruding on our privacy. She believed in knocking on doors, not barging through them. She never forced conversations. When we talked, she listened to me carefully, her eyes returning to mine throughout our dialogue. When I was a teenager, she was especially careful, aware no doubt that I boiled with thoughts and feelings and secrets. "Don't do anything you don't really want to do," she told me. The sentence passed through me like a bolt of electricity. I have written about that wise sentence once before. I now know she offered the same advice to at least one other daughter. It can only be given to a person who is not an unbridled hedonist or a psychopath, of course, but I have returned to her words again and again. I knew at the time it was mostly, although not entirely, sexual advice. If you don't really want it, sex will be bad. Don't accommodate pushy men. Her words helped me.

Accommodation in many forms was expected of the nice middle-class girl in my midwestern world. Smiles and nods and gold stars were the rewards for her role as sensitive reader of the desires of others. She resisted stepping forward to speak for the second time because she might be seen as a know-it-all. Rather than correct her teacher's blatant error of fact, she let it pass. She was chronically helpful and pathologically cheerful. And, if accommodation meant continually doing things she did not *really want* to do, the inevitable anger and aggression she felt were suppressed because other people came first. After a while, she couldn't even recognize those emotions for what they were anymore. The nice middle-class girl played a maternal part long before she took on the role of mother, *if* she took on the role of mother. This social pressure was part of the invisible institution intended to keep women under control.

Has anything changed? In the United States, the country of the quick fix, the Internet is dense with lists for improving one's motherhood. "17 Habits of Very Happy Moms" includes the directive "leave the house now." This is not an exhortation to abandon your children as Ibsen's Nora does when she walks out the door at the end of *A Doll's House*. "Fresh air, sunlight and nature are believed to be critical mood enhancers for women, and moms can get this little lift while pushing strollers or swings." Are we to infer from this that outdoor conditions do not lift men's moods? The writer of "Ten Simple Ways to Be a Great Mom" offers deeper if more abstract instructions: "Show unconditional love to your child," "Let your child be a child," and "Take care of yourself." The author of this blithe advice seems to believe that these vague notions should be immediately available to readers and further to be wholly un-aware that unconditional love, letting your child be a child, and taking care of yourself might at times be at odds.

During my survey of the countless Internet sites on good mothering, I noticed that the photos of pretty mothers with laughing children at-tached to these columns were mostly of white women (but white, Black, or brown, they were seen frolicking with their children in spotless interi-ors or groomed backyards). Just as women working brutally long hours in factories in the nineteenth century were probably not reading *The Glory of Woman: On Love, Marriage, and Maternity*, I suspect mothers working several jobs to keep themselves and their children alive are not indulging in the perusal of "ten simple ways to be a great mom."

The legacy of the Angel of the House in contemporary Western culture lingers in these bland lists aimed at middle- and upper-middle-class women, touted as "easy" and "simple," but which have a decidedly punitive undertow—*good* carries the dread of *bad* with it, after all. It is as if there is a critical juncture when one turns into the other, as if the good mother is a state that can be achieved and then retained in perpetuity. The good mother is frozen in time and thus will never go bad. She lives on in the newly slender glamorous mothers in their gleaming kitchens on Instagram, cuddling offspring who have unwittingly been entered into a global visual competition that turns on envy. Technology speeds things up, but it doesn't manufacture the maternal fantasy. The "very happy mom" is an imaginary static being, a maternal figment used as a gilded hammer to beat the real mother into shape.

Although nearly all of these advice blogs emphasize "taking time for yourself" and resisting "perfect motherhood," the underlying assumption of radical maternal accommodation to the child remains. "Taking time for yourself" means that you have already given yourself over to the children, that your time is not your own, so you must snatch moments here and there *for yourself*. Compare this to the suggestion I stumbled on in a parallel list for fathers: "How to Be a Great Dad—12 Awesome Tips." One of those awesome tidbits is the following: "Spend your spare time with them [the children]." *Spare* time is *extra* time. The father's time belongs to him, and rather than head for the pool hall, he can dole out minutes benevolently to his progeny if he so chooses.

"A good father," a man named Julian Marcus writes on a site with the suspiciously defensive name InnocentDads.org, is "a pillar of strength, support, and discipline." This phallic "pillar" closely resembles the ideal father touted in my own childhood—a remote but solid figure who walked into the house after work in time for a formal heart-to-heart talk with son or daughter before dinner, but who nevertheless retained enough authority to induce fear in his children. This hardly constitutes a new image of fatherhood. On a site called Fatherly, I discovered an article written by Rob Palkovitz, a professor of human development and family sciences at the University of Delaware: "Kids with Involved Dads Thrive. So Do the Dads." Palkovitz touts "involved" fatherhood as a boon not only to the child but to the father. This "dad" gains skills "that he can apply elsewhere, such as at work." He continues, "A close father-child relationship develops the dad's capacities for evaluating, planning, and decision making—all part of executive function." He winds up his piece by saying "Father-child relationships are not, in short, just about kids."

In other words, there are selfish reasons for men to be involved with their children. Our man of family science appears to be highly conscious of the fact that sacrifice is not a selling point for men. On the other hand, if you pitch them on the idea that being an active parent will improve "executive functions," they may buy the argument. There's nothing wrong with selfishness in men. In fact, it's an admirable quality. How will they get ahead if they don't look out for themselves? Palkovitz does not say that this involved "dad" might make more money "at work," but the promise of promotion and bettering one's chances in the race seem to lurk in the background. Mothers are not mentioned at all. Wouldn't "involvement" with her children also increase a woman's evaluating, planning, and decision-making skills, which she could then employ "at work"? Aren't agency, will, and judgment essential to mothering children? Imagine the following message: "Mother-child relationships are not, in short, just about kids."

What goes unsaid in these popular sites about how to be a good parent is far more important that what is actually articulated. "Don't do anything you don't really want to do" could not be proffered as advice by these purveyors of cultural platitudes who are busy pandering to an audience that is not seeking enlightenment so much as confirmation for what they already believe: "Mom, you have the right to a guilt-free bath." "Dad, you can feel good about yourself if you forgo your golf game to spend quality time with Freddy and Muffin." I confess to feeling nauseated by this world of American "moms" and "dads." The words once reserved for children's use within the family as expressions of intimacy, *Mom* and *Dad*, have become ubiquitous for *mother* and *father*, as if some mainstream mouthpiece is dead set on using infantile and familiar expressions for all people who become parents. The many parents who do not fit into these neat mom and dad categories, adoptive parents, gay and lesbian parents, and trans parents among others, must look elsewhere—at niche blogs and lists on the cultural margins.

And yet, what is the *really wanting* my mother spoke of and what does it mean for mothering? Accommodation is a necessary part of collective human life. It means making room for the other. It may mean letting go of pleasure now in the name of a future good. This should sound political because it is. Anyone who cares for a newborn becomes a being of accommodation to that helpless, speechless, spastic person for a time. Without that accommodation to a baby's needs, the baby cannot survive. On the other hand, the person who believes that an exhausted, miserable, depressed woman left alone with an infant deserves her fate simply because she's the "mom" participates in the cultural misogyny directed at mothers. Cusk quotes a reviewer in her *Guardian* article: "If you had a baby, you did so because you wanted one. If you are suffering sleep deprivation so severe you're hallucinating, that was your choice." Although irony cannot be discounted, I assume the reviewer meant what she wrote. There is no acknowledgment that children are a shared responsibility, not only in a family but in a society. There is no acknowledgment either that a woman who desperately needs sleep might not be in the best position to care for a child. Parents who care for children in societies that care about children, that offer paid parental leave, healthcare, childcare, and early education have it much easier than parents in the UK and the United States. Both countries consistently rank at the bottom in UNICEF's annual Child Well-Being in Rich Countries Report Card.

People cannot help what they feel, but they can help what they write. They can also make an effort to examine why they feel what they feel. Why so vindictive? Did you *really want* to write that cruel sentence and publish it for the whole world to see, and if you did, what was your motive? Isn't the underlying assumption of this reviewer that human beings are monads who make choices in a vacuum? You made your bed, now lie in it. But where do thoughts and choices come from? I do not think it is possible to talk about an isolated mind. Every person has an inner sense of her narrating consciousness, her inner speech, but the words we use are collective, not private. We are made in and through others. Our decisions are founded on a complex mingling of feelings and circumstance, both of which are influenced by the power or lack of it we have in society and the cultural ideas to which we have access—that include dos and don'ts and images of good and bad mothers, which may serve as justifications after the fact. We, all of us, often spin out *reasons* for why we did what we did on hindsight and then project them onto others: I managed to do it, bitch. Now so can you.

Don't do anything you don't really want to do is a way of saying: I have faith in your desire. I have faith that your desire is not purely impulsive, that you are a thoughtful, ethical person who can imagine how you might hurt others by what you do but also how you yourself might be hurt and made unhappy by giving into someone else. My mother was not at all worried about the fate of the boys in my life when I was fifteen. She was worried about me, and her ethics included my caring for me. She was worried young men who had the power advantage would manipulate her child. She was worried about my own weakness and desire to please. My mother did not think I would regret wholehearted love-lust for another person. She was not a prude or an advocate of virginity before marriage. When I became sexually active later, we discussed contraceptives.

My pondering of the sentence has gone on for years, and its meaning has expanded and evolved into continual reflection on possible regret. When asked to participate in an event, I think through how much I want it. Am I just being amenable? Am I merely flattered? Is it a duty I am proud to perform or do I feel pressured and uncomfortable? Will it help my work? How badly do I need the money? I refuse to allow sexist questions to go unremarked upon because I know I will feel bad later. "What is it like to be a wife, mother, *and* a writer?" a Polish television journalist asked me. I asked her if she would pose the same question to a male writer. She said no. What is it like to be a husband, father, *and* a writer?

My mother might have balked at asking a man writer that question. She had been steeped in a world in which women catered to the needs of men, not because they were perceived as strong but because their many weaknesses meant they should be indulged. Sometimes late in her life during our phone conversations, I would tell her what we were having for dinner. "But does Paul *like* fish?" she would say. When I asked her if my preferences shouldn't also be considered, she would say she couldn't help it. "I was raised that way, you know." My mother's sometimes excessive concern for "the husband" irritated me but never hurt me. Why? She was also the person who, after my father died, said to me, "Now you are head of the family." We were walking in the woods near my sister Ingrid's country house. I laughed and said, "What about you?" No, she didn't want the job. I was apparently next in line for the position, which required a vague authority associated with masculinity but which didn't require a man. Maybe by then she had had enough responsibility for others.

If my mother had died before my father or if she had not lived almost a decade after his death in her own apartment, our relationship would have been different. During those years, it entered a deeper register. A woman in her eighties and a woman in her fifties spent time together because they really wanted that time together. I have vibrant memories from my visits to her in Minnesota. We spent hours talking about books, politics, family. We lingered over shared beloved texts. Dickinson, Austen, James, and Wharton leap to mind. We laughed a lot. She spoke to me about her marriage to my father, about its pleasures and torments, how she wished he could have been more open, freer. We listened to each other with attention, urgency, and respect and spoke honestly but not rashly. I recall asking her a question to which she replied, "I do not want to talk about that." I did not press her.

On another occasion I asked her why she and my father had planned their children in two pairs. I was born first. Liv arrived only nineteen months later. Then there was a gap of four years before Asti was born. Fifteen months after that, she gave birth to Ingrid.

My mother looked at me. "What are you talking about?" she said. "You were all accidents."

The question was answered. I had nothing more to say.

She had a couple of suitors after my father died. One of them was an intelligent, handsome widower. She rejected him. "His face is too soft," she told me. I wasn't exactly sure what this meant, but I gathered that the deficit, one I couldn't see myself, meant there was no erotic spark. On another occasion, she met a man at a formal dinner. They had met earlier when my father was still alive, and for some reason I can't recall, the two of them had ended up in a car alone together, and they had talked as he drove. She remembered it as a lively, engaged conversation accompanied by the electric charge of strong mutual sexual attraction. Upon meeting her again, the man took her hand, "held it too long," and looked deeply into her eyes. She told me she went to pieces without showing it outwardly. She swooned internally at his touch, felt she could melt into the floor. She loved it. Nothing came of it. The man remained married to the woman he had been married to all those years before, but his touch persisted in her memory as a moment of radiant pleasure. This is not a story a thoughtful parent would share with a young child. It was a story that could be told only between intimate adults.

What does her motherhood to me have to do with the friendship that bloomed in that opening after my father's death during a time when my mother again became the hero of her own life? She mourned my father and went on. She made her own decisions without having to consult him or bow to his culinary desires. She made her own friends. She was resilient, yes, but I also think she welcomed her newfound freedom. She did not say this in so many words, but I felt and saw it. She also recognized that her freedom was to an important degree predicated on the fact that my hardworking father had both saved and been clever about money, which was left to her. She was by no means a rich woman, but she did not have financial worries. Before my father died, my mother had never written a check. The division of labor between them wasn't merely conventional; it was rigid. My mother was very much a creature of her time and the male/female stereotypes of the historical collective mind, but how do these affect love?

Familial intimacy is not chosen. No one chooses to be born. Class, color, sex, the shape of our noses and the length of our feet are not willed characteristics, although various desires and interventions can affect these qualities later in our lives. Nevertheless, we do not choose our families or their various arrangements. The German philosopher Heidegger referred to this as *Geworfenheit*, "thrownness" or "being thrown." We are not thrown into the world. We are *born* out of someone, and I have always been annoyed by this typical philosophical avoidance of the physicality of birth. Nevertheless the term refers to what human beings cannot control, such as kinship systems, languages, social conventions, and brutal hierarchies of oppression.

In the preface to the 1984 edition of *Notes of a Native Son*, James Baldwin wrote, "I am what time, circumstance, history have made me, certainly, but I am, also, much more than that. So are we all." This sentence is often quoted. What is not quoted is what comes immediately after: "The conundrum of color is the inheritance of every American, be he/she legally or actually Black or White. It is a fearful inheritance for which untold multitudes, long ago, sold their birthright." He goes on to say, "This horror has so welded past and present that it is virtually impossible and certainly meaningless to speak of it as occurring, as it were, in time." Sameness, difference, and repetition are deeply embedded in the latter sentence. Time moves like water, but it's the same damned river. The horror, Baldwin notes, is the same. And yet, the idea that human beings are simply the products of time, circumstance, and history does not allow for the significant fact that we are "more than that."

It is that "moreness" that is hard to comprehend and fit into theories. We are born into institutions, and they survive us. Slavery ended, but its legacy has warped every U.S. institution into the present. As for the long-standing fantasies of maternal love among the white middle classes and what it is supposed to look like, I can think of few texts better able to explode such myths as universal than Toni Morrison's novel *Beloved*, which explores the traumas of slavery, its effects on maternal love, the idea of the self in time, and that quality of "more" Baldwin addressed. Rather than see her children returned to slavery, Sethe decides to kill them. She succeeds in killing one of them. There is a term for this act: altruistic filicide. Let us not pretend that there are not women in the world who face such choices now.

Neither my mother nor I was ever confronted with the day-in and day-out miseries of racism or the shocking realities of enslavement and its effect on the generations that followed, including countless people who are examples of human resilience that seem supernatural under the circumstances. One has only to remember how many children were born to slave women raped by their masters. The imagination is powerful. Imagine those mothers. I think all experience must be part of our understanding of motherhood. It must be expansive and complex, not narrow and simple.

I was born a month early with what the physician said were "undeveloped lungs." He informed my mother I would probably die. Over and over, she told me that as she waited to discover my fate, she said to herself that she had never been so unhappy in her life. My mother referred to this horrible moment every time I visited her, as if my actual person remained something of a miracle for her.

Many women fall in love with their children, and they do so under highly various circumstances, including terrible hardship. Love takes different forms and families are organized in different ways. Every child is drawn into the vicissitudes of a life with others who must care for her if she is going to live and thrive, and every person attaches herself to important others for better and for worse. If I had not been born from my mother, our intimacy would not have been as profound. If she had not always been there in my life until just last year, it would have been different. Surely ideas about mothers and daughters and families that circulated in our culture—a mixture of Norwegian and American conventions and dos and don'ts—were part of our relationship too. And yet, our love was also forged over time and through our mutual idiosyncratic experience.

I knew she wanted for me what I really wanted for myself, even if her desires were not identical to my own. When her own mother died, she said to me, "It is strange to lose a person who only wanted the best for you." This only-wanting-the-best is empathy. Empathy is not being the other person. It is feeling into the other person. The philosopher Edith Stein called empathy "a foreign experience." Empathy recognizes difference. I feel the loss of my mother's empathy. My loss also includes a sense of bewilderment that I have never felt before after someone I love has died. It has been hard to understand how it is possible that my mother is *nowhere*. How can she be nowhere?

I remember walking on a beach with my mother in South Carolina. I was already married to Paul. We had no child yet, but the idea of a child was in the air. As we walked and talked, my mother said, "Of course one loves one's children, but it is just as important to *respect* them." When she said the word *respect*, her voice took on the stern, rough quality she saved for the truly important. My mother took love for granted. She was wrong about this, but it was difficult for her to imagine not loving her children—it seemed automatic. The other piece was not as automatic. You are not your child and because you are not she, you are duty bound to respect that person's separateness from you.

After attending the funeral of a friend, my mother complained to me that she had been unable to recognize the person she had known. The friend had drowned in a barrage of clichés and false praise. My mother despised what she perceived as distortions of the truth, particularly when they were also hypocritical. For our mother's funeral, my sisters and I decided that we would be brief and honest. We knew our mother's refined sense of the ridiculous had to be mentioned. She would roar with laughter when others would have been self-pitying or at least peevish—when she slipped and fell hard on the ice, when the car broke down, when the dog ran away with the dinner roast, when she put pepper instead of cardamom in the rolls. Her uncanny penetration of human character had to be mentioned, too, the way she could smell deceit and lies but also goodness in people she met when it was not apparent to others. Two of her granddaughters spoke of their grandmother as a being with almost magical powers of insight—a witch.

This is the story I chose because although my sisters and I share many stories about my mother, this one belongs to me alone, and I knew it wouldn't be repeated at the funeral. Three years after my father died, when my mother was eighty-three, she and I traveled to Portugal to visit my husband, who was directing a film there, and Sophie, who had a part in the movie. It was late May. The weather was mild and mostly sunny. Every day, I would get up and write in the hotel room. I worked into the early afternoon, but when I was finished for the day, Mamma and I went out to explore Sintra, a small city beloved by the Romantics for its moist microclimate, steep mountains, splendid gardens, and Moorish castle. We took long walks, hiked up and down a mountain, looked closely at plant life and architecture, and talked and talked and talked.

In the evenings we would join Paul, Sophie, and various members of the cast and crew in Azenhas do Mar, a village not far from Sintra close to the film set, where we had dinner in a simple restaurant that over-looked the sea. We ate fresh fish, vegetables, and salads, drank wine, and talked. One evening after we had ordered, we sat looking out at sky and beach and water. The air was cool and the swiftly setting sun illuminated the horizon and the low clouds above it. My mother was looking out intently when she said, "I'm going down to the beach." Irène Jacob, the movie's lead actress, forty-five years younger than my mother, was game. "I'll go with you!" she said. The rest of us remained at the table and watched the two women run down the steps and onto the beach. I saw the dark figure of my mother kick off her shoes and roll up her pants. I saw Irène follow her lead, and soon the two of them were in the ocean up to their knees, then their hips, their arms lifted over their heads. The light vanished, but we could hear their hoots of pleasure. Several minutes later, they returned to us laughing, drenched to the skin, and slid into their chairs just as the food arrived. Unless I am inventing it, there were blankets that helped remove the chill.

What I know for certain is that my mother turned an exultant face to me and said, "I could die here." It was not the comment I had expected, but I felt her emotion—her keen sense of freedom, happiness, complete-ness. Just as I was absorbing her words, *I could die here*, she went on. "But then you and Paul would have to fly my body back to the States, and that would be so involved and complicated. No," she said, "it's not a good idea."

I laughed. It was typical of my mother. She had a great gift for seizing the moment and sucking whatever joy was to be gotten out of it, but she also had a strong moral imagination. She thought beyond her own death to the responsible adults left behind to make arrangements for her corpse. Unless a human being turns against life itself, she cannot *choose* her death. Years later, my mother would often say to me, "I want to live. I want to live, you know." When it was hard for her to remember what I had just said to her on the phone and she would ask me again what she had asked me before, I always answered her, but sometimes during our conversations she would describe what was in the room in front of her. She loved the orchids that grew in her window, orchids that startled me with their powers to return. Because she forgot, she sometimes overwatered them and, at other times, she left them to parch, but those orchids sprouted new buds again and again, as if they were an extension of my mother's embodied being, which seemed to flourish against all odds.

The doctors told us she would die after she returned from a bout of sepsis at the hospital when she was ninety. She had already survived a long fall down our stairs in Brooklyn that resulted in a broken foot, congestive heart failure, and pseudo-gout that turned her thin legs into gigantic swollen logs. They told us her body was shutting down. It was just a matter of time. But my mother did not die. She lived on, and her daughters became accustomed to having a mother who cheated death.

The day before she died, my mother did not know me anymore. She had recognized me two days earlier, the day I arrived, and from time to time the following day, but on the last day I was with her, there was nothing in her eyes for me or anyone else. That was the day she sat, and as she sat, I could feel the strain of every tightened muscle in her body. From early that morning to well into the afternoon of October 11, 2019, she batted away every effort from the aides to get her to lie down. From time to time, her head would drop forward from weariness, but their kind suggestions that she would be more comfortable lying back in bed were useless.

There is a name for what happened to my mother—terminal delirium, or terminal restlessness. When people are dying, they sometimes become hallucinatory, belligerent, or simply agitated. The hospice nurse had seen it many times before. She asked me if it wouldn't help if I encouraged my mother to lie down. She said "the family's" interventions were often more effective than those of the "staff."

"I will *not* tell her," I said. I was adamant. "This is my mother's death, and I will not interfere."

She did not insist.

I had to leave my mother that day. I held her, cried on her, and told her I loved her, even though she did not hear me. We like to separate syndromes, conditions, and illnesses from persons, as if they belong to no one, but this is a false way to think about sickness. Sickness is part of us, and sickness that ends in death varies from person to person. In her fierce defiance of and resistance to death, I recognized the woman I knew, the woman who wanted to live.

Within hours of my departure, my sisters Asti and Ingrid arrived. My mother had lain back on her pillow, was in and out of consciousness, and then she was not conscious anymore. The morphine had had its effect. They heard the death rattle around seven in the evening of October 12. A moment after eight, I received a text from Asti. "It happened. Peaceful." I was sitting on the sofa in our library with my husband. We were expecting her imminent death. We had been holding vigil, but the words arrived as a sharp blow, and I let out a long bestial howl I didn't know I had in me and moaned, "Mamma is dead, dead, dead." My husband did not say stop. He was not embarrassed. He loved her too. I wailed like a small child.

I have never experienced a grief as pure as the grief I feel for my mother—a particular woman, Ester Vegan Hustvedt, whom I knew and loved passionately. Yes, she was my mother. She gave birth to me, but my love was honed by my intense admiration for her and my profound friendship with her over time.

What if she had been born in another historical period, earlier or later? How would her motherhood have been different? What if her own mother had resented her rather than doted on her? Did her near-death at three make her more precious to my grandmother? What if her father, who died during the war of heart failure, had lived? What if she had been a working-class girl and not a girl deeply imprinted with middle-class mores? What if she had married one of her beaus before my father? She had been in love with a painter. We had a portrait he had done of her in the house, although it never hung on the wall. She was mysterious about him. What if she hadn't lived in two languages, Norwegian and English? *What ifs* are fantasies, but they are not ludicrous. We have not solved the mystery of the becoming that is a human life.

Months passed before my mother came to me in a dream. I was waiting for her. My father and my mormor had both visited me in potent dreams not long after they died. My mother arrived near the end of a complicated dream about heartless Republicans that took place outdoors somewhere in my hometown. I had been explaining to one of them, an empty-faced white woman with an elaborate hairdo, that my mother was dead, and I was grieving. She ignored me. Irritated by her indifference, I walked away, turned a corner near a strange tower, and ran into my mother. She was taking a walk. I knew she was dead in the dream, but I didn't tell her because I didn't want to spoil our reunion. I looked down into her face and she smiled. I felt it was her real face, her old face, but not as old as at the end. She wanted to walk together, and so we did. She walked quickly, a little ahead of me as she always used to, striding confidently through the grass as I followed behind her.

2020

STATES OF MIND

State of mind is defined in Merriam-Webster as a person's emotion or mood; in other words, as a kind of internal human weather, turbulent or calm, sunny or gloomy, hot or cold. That climate is sometimes clearly visible on a person's face or in her posture, but not always. (Inner states can be hidden.) And like the shifting patterns of actual weather, states of mind are unstable. In a moment, one mood may become another. I cannot remember what I was thinking when my sister called to tell me our father had died, but the thought, whatever it was, fled my mind and was instantly replaced by the work of absorbing the truth of his death. The phone call changed my state of mind in seconds. I am often amazed at how dramatically sunshine lifts my mood and how quickly clouds depress it, how listening to Bach's cantata 147, *Jesus bleibet*, inevitably sends me into a rapture of tender, high feeling, no matter how glum I may have been before the first note sounds. Because I attended a Lutheran church as a girl, I grew up with Bach. The cantata is an amalgam of bracing music I love and diffuse religious memory. There are Dickinson poems I read to induce a state of mind: a radical, vivid, fierce clarity I find nowhere else: "He stuns you by degrees— / prepares your brittle substance / for the ethereal blow."

Often before I fall asleep, I enter a state of loose reverie. My eyes are closed, and my thoughts variously jolt or dance or lapse fluidly from one associative thought to another, and my mood seems to chase the words or pictures that rise unbidden to mind and either ease me into slumber or prick me awake. It is not simple to draw a hard line between states of mind and our perceptions of the world, our memories of it, or our imaginative fantasies that draw from both perceiving and remembering it. The world as we experience it is in us and of us. My father is no one now, not a person anymore, and yet he has haunted my dreams since he died, and dreams are most definitely states of mind, another form of consciousness and another form of perception, not of the outside world directly but of its residue reconfigured in the hallucinatory phantasms that visit us nightly.

When I was very young, I believed my mother could read my state of mind. When she doubted my honesty, she would say, "May I look into your eyes?" If I was innocent, I would gaze soberly into those maternal eyes. If I was guilty, I would squirm and resist the test. My mother obviously did not need to be a clairvoyant to gauge my truthfulness. All she had to do was look at me. But long after I had given up thinking of my mother as a supernatural being, I found it unbearable to look her directly in the eyes and tell an untruth. She was, I think, my conscience incarnate. My guilt was bound up with her gaze. Infants are not guilty. Like shame and pride, guilt is a social emotion born of our attachments to others, and that nasty form of self-punishment becomes active only when a person is able to see himself as others see him. It is born of reflective self-consciousness. My child self could not bear to be seen as a bad person by my mother because as she looked at me I saw my sorry self through her eyes. A guilty state of mind is by its very nature one made between and among people.

It is a cultural habit in the West to think of the mind as a locked room, a sealed adult domain that thinks, calculates, and makes decisions, wise or unwise, but which is fundamentally isolated from the minds of others. Many hundreds of thousands of words have been written about the problem of other minds. How do I know you are not a zombie, someone who walks and talks and acts a lot like me, but has no consciousness? And if you are human, your internal weather, your sunny days and gusting winds, your high or low temperatures are not mine, and unless your face is a map of your moods or you tell me about them, I will not know what is happening in your mind. And then, even if you do tell me, you might be lying and lying far better than the four-year-old Siri lied.

I expect every person has been deceived, lied to, and betrayed. We misread others and suffer for it. We also often read the minds of other people with a high degree of accuracy. And we don't just witness the moods of others; sometimes we catch them. Emotions are contagious. A toddler hurts himself, falls down, and the unhurt child watching him begins to howl. Feelings spread as yawns do. We do not plan to come down with another person's mood, but it steals inside us anyway. Empathy is a shared state of mind, one feeling shared by two or more minds. Your sadness becomes mine. My empathy may become a vehicle of insight for me and therefore help me to help you or it may debilitate me altogether, make me so sad I am no good to you whatsoever. Empathetic states are not necessarily beneficial to either person, but the fact that these states exist is further testimony to the truth that human beings are social animals that rely on other animals like ourselves to become ourselves.

But there is another form of shared mind that is not the subject of research studies or philosophical treatises as far as I know. I have been living with the same person for thirty-six years. I cannot read this man's mind. He has recesses in his personality I strongly suspect I have never seen. Mysteries abound. And yet, time has produced an uncanny mental mirroring between us. A friend tells a story, and it triggers an immediate, identical association in each of us. Before my husband opens his mouth, I know what he will say, or before I speak, he knows what I will say. The link between heard story and our spontaneous double response is rarely obvious and why our two heads appear to have summoned exactly the same material at exactly the same instant strikes us as inexplicable. It happens again and again and more and more.

It may be that two minds in two heads that have been in close proximity for many years, minds linked by dialogue and shared secrets, by conflict and reconciliation, by grief and joy and humor and all-around continual bumping into each other coalesce at various moments to become a single state of mind. The winds rise, and the clouds begin to move, and the sun comes out at just the same time in two heads rather than one.

2017

MENTOR GHOSTS

I am fascinated by the idea of mentorship, even though I have few of my own stories to tell as either protégé or wise counselor. The word itself, *mentor*, triggers a hunger from a time in my life that is now gone, the ache for an attachment to someone who recognized me as worthy of the life I had chosen for myself. Although I knew I wanted to write from a young age—thirteen—and I have read and studied and written ardently ever since, the overwhelming feeling I have to this day on the subject of mentors is that I never came home.

Home? Why *home*? I suspect that my mentor fantasy was one of longing for both recognition and repair. It taps primary desires because the two sides of the mentoring couple recapitulate the child/parent relation but at a later stage of life and in a more conscious form. No one chooses a parent, after all. A mentor must be sought out and cajoled or seduced into playing the role. And for the one who is sought, admiration is a potent elixir. Mutuality is key in the formation of the pair, but hierarchy is also a given.

"I applaud, I mean I value, I egg you on in, your study of the American life that surrounds you," Henry James wrote to Edith Wharton, who was almost twenty years younger than he was. She loved him. He loved her. She had money. He didn't. This evened things out between her and "the Master." There were some irritations between them—a low-grade rivalry—but more love than competition. No sex, but influence. Wharton grew weary of critics insisting on her likeness to James.

Sherwood Anderson wrote a letter of recommendation for the young Ernest Hemingway—I see the door open to Gertrude Stein's salon, an enchanted interior. There are paintings on the walls. I hear voices but the words are indecipherable. Alice B. Toklas is in the kitchen "with the wives." In *A Moveable Feast*, Hemingway is cruel to Stein. He punched back at his mentor, whose influence on him had been profound. She was called "The Mother of Modernism." He called his own mother, Grace Hall Hemingway, "my bitch mother" and "a dominating shrew." They say Grace Hall loved a woman. In Hemingway, love and hate, masculine and feminine, are strung together into an indistinguishable lump. He feared that lump.

In his ingratiating first letter to the great Lev Tolstoy, Ivan Bunin made a bid to be mentored: "I am one of the many who have followed your every word with great interest and respect." Bunin's groveling worked. After the two had known each other for years, Bunin wrote, "Right now I feel like crying and kissing your hand as if you were my own father!"

Samuel Beckett was a research assistant to his idol, James Joyce. "That's what it was," Beckett said about Joyce's work, "epic, heroic, what he achieved." Peggy Guggenheim noted that Beckett worked "like a slave" for Joyce. Lucia Joyce, a gifted choreographer and dancer, was infatuated with her father's handsome acolyte. Beckett took Lucia out. He appeared with her here and there, but he didn't return her feelings. He was interested in *her father*. He was humoring the *father*. This is the homo-social love story James Knowlson tells in his biography of Beckett. But Joyce accused Beckett of leading his beloved daughter on. The rift between the two men lasted for years.

Beckett had to cleanse himself of Joyce's influence. He had to become other to Joyce.

The lovely Lucia went mad. She survives among the wives and daughters in literature's kitchen.

Before I met and married him, a young Paul Auster met his literary hero, Samuel Beckett, in Paris. He was twenty-five years old. The painter Joan Mitchell made the introduction. Beckett was kind, interested. He looked at the young man and said, "So Mr. Auster, tell me all about yourself." "Mr. Auster" had no idea what to say.

Beckett's influence is visible in some plays Paul wrote when he was in his twenties. I read them later and told him so. After that, if it's there, the influence isn't easily seen. The complete digestion of another writer's work may mean it becomes invisible.

In 1980, when I was a twenty-five-year-old graduate student in English literature at Columbia University, I wrote a letter to Djuna Barnes. I had received her address by chance.

I was carrying Barnes's novel *Nightwood* with me on the subway. An elderly woman noticed, asked me about it, and I gushed love for the book. She said that her husband, who taught at Princeton, knew Barnes, and that if I wanted to write to my hero, she would send me the address. Two or three days later, a postcard arrived in my mailbox. *Nightwood* was still new to me. I had written a paper on it, and when I sat down at my typewriter, I wanted to convey to its author the dancing complexities I had found in her novel. My letter must have been passionate, but I was also highly conscious of the need for restraint, to keep the letter short but astute. It went through a number of revisions until I felt it was just right, and I sent it off.

Two years later, after I had moved to Brooklyn, a letter typed on what I guessed was an old Underwood arrived in the mail: It said, "Dear Miss Hustvedt, Your letter has given me great difficulty." Another line followed and that was all. The signature read: "Djuna Barnes." How I managed to lose that letter I cannot say. What was wrong with me? Why don't I recall the second line? I know I didn't take her response as an insult either. I read it as a tribute to me, the youthful letter writer who had disturbed the peace of the old recluse at 22 Patchen Place. She died a month later at the age of ninety. I remember reading the obituary in the *New York Times*.

I didn't expect the famously isolated, crotchety Djuna Barnes to mentor me. I was surprised that she wrote back. And yet, I am glad she received the letter and glad it gave her difficulty. Djuna Barnes is my phantom mentor.

The vagaries of my desire for someone to recognize me as worthy of the life I had chosen are painful on hindsight. What was the life I had chosen? I could have attended a writing program, given myself up to the instruction of older poets and novelists, but I didn't. I went to graduate school in English instead. I wanted to study, to read a lot, and learn to think well. I also wanted to pay the bills in that place known as the future.

"I'm not sure you want to become a professor," my father said to me after I had been in graduate school for several years. He was a professor. Did he mean he thought I wasn't cut out for it? Did he think I should write and not eat? Did he feel bad about his own career? Did he think I would be unhappy? I couldn't form the words to ask any of these questions.

After he had read my dissertation, my father said, "It doesn't read like a dissertation." That was it. Nothing more. I should have spoken up then, asked him to explain, but I didn't. I was hurt to the quick.

On hindsight my memories on the subject of mentors have acquired a certain bitterness, something I didn't feel when I was young and eager and floundered toward likely candidates who regularly resisted or slapped away my overtures.

Several times I approached the attractive young professor and Joyce scholar during my first year of college. She had a head of dark curls. I did not interest her the way the young men in class interested her. She chose one of them. Young professor L. didn't last long at St. Olaf College in Northfield, Minnesota. It was a Lutheran place with Lutheran mores, which didn't mean Eros wasn't rushing madly around the classrooms. It meant you couldn't let on that you were running after him, especially if you were a teacher and a woman.

I remember another college professor from whom I hoped to get some direction. He was a large, sweaty man with thick-rimmed glasses. I sat in his office as he savaged a paper I had written on Dreiser's *Sister Carrie*. His teeth on edge, he spat venom in my direction and never took his eyes off my breasts. Why so hostile? What I wrote about that second-rate writer has long vanished. The paper may well have been bad. What I remember is that I couldn't understand why the professor was so angry at me. The breast business should have been a clue, but I just felt stunned and puzzled.

And then there was the professor I visited during my first year at Columbia. I had a letter of introduction from one of his colleagues at another university. Although cold, curt, and stiff, Professor S. agreed to look at my work. When I returned for his comments, he led me, page by scrawled-over page, through an evisceration of the prose, the argument, and the sorry mind that had produced such drivel. I said nothing, although I no doubt thanked him before I left.

Again: his inexplicable rage. I think he smelled my ambition.

Even at the time, I knew the paper wasn't as bad as all that. With a few revisions that had nothing to do with Professor S.'s campaign of carnage, I delivered it in a seminar on nineteenth-century literature and philosophy. The prominent curmudgeon, Professor M., in charge of the Lit-Phil seminar thought the paper excellent. And yet, during office hours, M. was stiff, reluctant to talk, forbidding. I did not dare ask him to be my dissertation adviser, although he was the expert in my field. He ended up as head of my defense committee, however, and lauded my thesis in front of his five male colleagues. "There are sentences here I wish I had written myself."

I remember his sentence. Once uttered, some sentences stay for a lifetime. They are burned into memory by strong emotion. In an essay I called such phrases "brain tattoos."

A brain tattoo: "What are you doing in graduate school? You look like Grace Kelly." I did not look anything like Grace Kelly, but the comment ended all hope of my working with Professor H., who had spoken it, one of the few women in the English department and a feminist. I was and am a feminist. It was in her class that I gave the Djuna Barnes paper, and it was after I had given the paper, and we left the room together, that she spoke those words to me. What did my looks have to do with it? She seemed to think *Nightwood* was incomprehensible, so it might not have worked out between us anyway. Many years later, I came to know that she had felt mistreated and was unhappy in the department. The sentence may have carried other meanings I was in no position to read.

In my twenty-seven years of school, there was a single teacher who responded to my bid for instruction, help, dialogue, mutuality. I was a junior in college. The subject was Russian intellectual history. The professor's classes had a reputation for being difficult. The rumors had spread that he was hard to please, graded low, bristled at platitudes and lazy answers, all of which attracted me. He taught with a stringent vigor I found electrifying, and for two years I felt the soaring pleasure of being recognized by him as a student of unusual gifts. He pushed me to read closely and to argue carefully. Under his guidance, I wrote on the nihilist strains in Tolstoy's work. That was when I ran across the adoring apostle Bunin for the first time. I felt my intellectual powers bloom.

We met for coffee. We talked about ideas, literature, life. Our relations were warm, respectful, and correct. We became friends. He read the essays I wrote when I applied to graduate school. I loved him for encouraging my ambition, for taking me in, for praising my writing, but I never told him to his face. I never said, "Right now I feel like crying and kissing your hand as if you were my own father."

The ghosts of the familial haunt these ties between student and teacher. As a young woman, I longed for approval and affection from paternal quarters, from those who had authority. I now think it is a good thing that my yearning went mostly unanswered.

This memory from 2017: I am standing on a balcony looking out over Lake Como talking to a German colleague, a professor of American literature. We are at a conference where we are both giving papers on narrative medicine. It turns out he is a friend of Professor M. at Columbia, the one who admired the reviled paper and later my dissertation. My colleague says, "I saw him last week. He is so proud of you." I feel a thrill of happiness. The joy is immediately followed by irritation. Why didn't he let me know he had followed my work? It would have meant something to me if I had known. Then I am further annoyed. Why should I care? I am sixty years old with the feelings of a child.

Professor M. died last year. I intended to go to the memorial. I had it written on my calendar. I forgot. The better word for what happened, I suspect, is *repressed*.

"I applaud, I mean I value, I egg you on . . ." This came as a fulfillment for Wharton because she had sent her work to the Master, but the story to which he was referring in the letter he came across himself, and he wrote his admiration spontaneously.

Fathers and mothers, but also fathers who are more like mothers, and mothers who are more like fathers, at least if one takes the point of view of literary canons and our ideas about mothers and fathers and feminine and masculine. Henry James swam in what we have come to think of as the feminine, and Gertrude Stein in what we imagine is the masculine. It is supposed to be the boys and men who duke it out in an Oedipal battle for literary or scholarly or scientific prominence. I have seen iterations of all these—the slugging and the pissing. The girls and women stand outside the ring or stay in the kitchen. But really the feminine and the masculine are all mixed up, impure, a mélange, a mess. Aren't we all lumps of the two?

No wonder people long for living as a person truly in-between. We called it androgyny back in the day, but I didn't look or dress the part; it was/is psychic: the mutations of gender are all over my work from the beginning. One of my early poems, published in *The Paris Review* in 1983, is titled "Hermaphroditic Parallels."

An oddity of my personal story is that from a distance I was assigned a mentor who is not, was not, and has never been my mentor: my husband. I am the humble student in this fantasy that pops up regularly in articles, reviews, papers, other kinds of traveling literary news, and interviews.

More brain tattoos:

The most painful: "I think your husband wrote it." I was on tour in Germany for my first novel, *The Blindfold*, in 1993. The journalist was insistent, and I could feel his rage. He said my husband ran a "literary factory" in Brooklyn. At the time I thought he meant it. Now I am convinced it was a ruse to hurt me. He thought the book was very good.

"Your first two novels are just like your husband's," a journalist in Amsterdam said to me in 2004. "Please explain to me why you think so?" I asked him. The man reddened. "I was just trying to be provocative."

"Everyone knows you learned psychoanalysis from Paul Auster," a friendly woman confidently stated in an interview.

Words from a journalist in Chile in 2017: "Your knowledge of neuroscience comes from your husband? Mr. Auster reads neuroscience, doesn't he?" Mr. Auster has never read a neuroscience paper in his life.

I attend a lecture by my husband. The academic who introduces him tells the audience that Paul Auster is an expert on the work of the French psychoanalyst Jacques Lacan. Afterward, I explain to the man that Paul read one essay by Lacan in 1966. I read Lacan carefully. Some of his work informed my dissertation. The man was annoyed. I was supposed to remain silent.

A breathless Auster fan approached me at a party in Copenhagen. He wanted to talk to me about my husband's knowledge of the Russian theorist M. M. Bakhtin. "But," I say, "Paul never read Bakhtin. I read him. Paul borrowed the story from me." (In his introduction to *The Dialogic Imagination*, Michael Holquist explains that during the siege of Leningrad, Bakhtin used his manuscript on the German Bildungsroman as cigarette paper. In the screenplay for the film *Smoke*, into which Paul inserted the tale, he made the story memorable, a brain tattoo: "He smoked his book.") "I love Bakhtin," I said to the man, in hope of further conversation. But the man did not love that I loved Bakhtin. His face fell. He looked stricken and ran away.

I have hundreds of not-my-mentor-become-my-mentor stories. It can't be *you*. It couldn't have come from *you*. It must be the hero-mentor-man. It is comic, and it is tragic. To grant authority to the wife somehow undermines the husband's authority, even if the actual living, breathing husband does not feel that way at all and says so in print. In *A Life in Words*, a book-long conversation with I. B. Siegumfeldt, "Siri is the intellectual in the family, not me, and everything I know about Lacan and Bakhtin, for example, I know from her." They project onto the hero. If I, woman-writer-wife, am given authority, he, and by the magic of identification, they, are emasculated and shamed by the "dominating shrew."

We all have our phantoms.

Epic. Heroic. That's what it is. It's love. It's hate. It's a mix.

I have taught only rarely, so my opportunities to mentor have been few. I am lucky to live from my work. I am fond of the young residents I teach every month in a seminar on narrative psychiatry in a hospital in New York City. No doubt, the doctors in my class have physician mentors. It happens that young writers and scholars approach me for a favor. I read their manuscripts and the bound galleys of their books. I write blurbs and endorsements. Sometimes I detect the light of admiration in their eyes. In my case, anyway, such admiration is an elixir that must be drunk slowly, carefully, and rarely.

I remember the pleasure of that brief time when I was mentored. I also remember the sting of rejection and the paternal ghost who haunted my mentor fantasy and those who foisted their own your-husband-is-your-mentor fantasies onto me. I will stick with the phantom I never knew and from whom I received only two lines. She is a mentor of the purely literary kind, the kind that never leaves the pages of a book or a letter.

2019

OPEN BORDERS: TALES FROM THE LIFE OF AN INTELLECTUAL VAGABOND

When I was still a kid, my parents, three sisters, and I took several car trips across the United States in the summers. We piled into our old station wagon, to which my father had attached an open wooden trailer he had built himself. He was extremely proud of his frugal handiwork that had saved the family untold numbers of dollars. Once car and trailer had been fully loaded with family and gear respectively, we headed east or west or south from Minnesota. We spent the nights in campgrounds under our green canvas tent, side-by-side in sleeping bags or lying awake and listening to my mother snore. We became expert fire builders, did a lot of singing, and ingested a great many 99-cent breakfast specials.

I do not want to give you the wrong impression. We were not a happy-go-lucky bohemian family traveling willy-nilly in search of adventure. These trips were planned by my father with military precision. They were tightly budgeted with numerous contingency plans at the ready. My father was a professor, but he had been a farm boy who witnessed the devastation of the Great Depression at home and a soldier who survived the Battle of Luzon in the Philippines during World War II. He was not about to expose his wife and daughters to the wild winds of chance and the chaos that might follow.

On the occasions when unanticipated shocks disrupted my father's master strategy, he did not welcome them. At such moments, we children were lucky to have our mother, an immigrant who had spent the first thirty years of her life in Norway, including five long years under Nazi occupation. Despite her own experience of hardship, she had a different, less stringent view of things. When the aging station wagon we had driven thousands of miles to the West Coast and back broke down a mere five miles from home and my father began to mutter dark oaths of rage and despair under his breath, my mother burst into uncontrollable laughter. I will never forget it. In an instant, tragedy became comedy.

On one of those extended family outings when I was fourteen, we paid a visit to the Four Corners Monument, a place where the borders of four states—Arizona, Colorado, New Mexico, and Utah—meet. We sisters had great fun situating ourselves so we occupied four states at once—hands in two states, feet in the other two. It was also possible to simply lie down on the quadrapoint and be in four distinct regions at the same time. I loved this experience of promiscuous habitation, however silly. It was, at the very least, a lesson on borders—artificial and natural. The borders of most early states in the U.S. were drawn according to geographical realities: rivers, lakes, oceans, and then later, according to technological innovation, along railroad lines that severed the land, or just politics. What is certain is that the natural borders of land and sea rarely take geometrical form. They are bumpy and wavy, not square.

Present-day borders of countries, cities, and towns are often a mix of nature, history, human whim, and artifice, but few territorial borders can be understood as separate from the ideas that shaped them. Colonialism carved up the world in ways that continue to create political, economic, and ecological convulsions. Think of the brutal ideologies summed up in expressions such as the White Man's Burden, Manifest Destiny, and *Lebensraum*. The U.S. annexation of Texas in 1836, which had been Mexico and was not recognized as not Mexico by Mexico, led to a blurry and disputed boundary between the two countries, a war, and no final border until 1853. Where does one place begin and another end? How can we tell? Who gets to draw the lines?

Even as a teenager, I understood there was something ridiculous about the Four Corners, that the straight lines etched into the stone floor of the monument and marked with the names of the four states to immortalize the intersection were a purely human way of marking space. The soil lying underneath the stone must have looked pretty much the same. Soil has names, too, silt or clay or loam, but it isn't identified by the words *Utah*, *Colorado*, *Arizona*, and *New Mexico*. Human-made borders are delineated by signs, fences, walls, checkpoints, passport queues. But actual lines in the earth are more rare. There was something else that struck me about the monument, a *pompous promise of permanence*. Hadn't we seen the ruins of the Anasazi people on the same trip?

This essay is based on a speech I gave at the Guadalajara International Book Festival. I chose the title of the talk before I wrote it, and when I looked at the words, "Open Borders: Tales from the Life of an Intellectual Vagabond," the Four Corners, a place I hadn't thought of for many years, sprang into my mind. The words triggered the mental image, which in turn sparked memories of family trips and my parents, who are now both dead, and the differences in their personalities that gave them different perspectives on the same misfortune, and how tragedy for one was comedy for the other.

My guess is that the memory served as a spatial metaphor for what has now been my long writing life, one that has taken me across many disciplinary borders from the humanities to the sciences. I have refused to live comfortably in a single state—to draw out the metaphor—and instead use insights from several fields in both my fiction and nonfiction. My passion for novels and poems, which began very early, led to my becoming a writer, but also to a degree in literature.

Reading is a form of traveling and the literate are granted an unusual gift. We are allowed to move into rooms and walk down streets and listen to the stories and thoughts of people who died long ago. And reading is the path into the structure of ideas that inform various fields. Neurobiology, anthropology, physics, and psychoanalysis do not view the world from the same perspective, nor do they have the same vocabularies. Penetrating their perspectives also means learning their languages and their systems of classification.

These disciplines are like separate states or countries, each one existing within its own carefully drawn borders. Extreme specialization can make dialogues across borders difficult, even impossible. Different fields of knowledge run on different assumptions that in turn create different ways of perceiving and understanding the world. Those deep assumptions are not always apparent. Sometimes they are invisible, a kind of tacit agreement among the people working inside the discipline, whether it's physics or history. This doesn't mean there aren't arguments inside a given field. There are lots of arguments in every field, but they are rarely about first, second, or third questions. In other words, the boundaries of thought have been established, usually over long periods of time. And then, every once in a while, workers in the field begin to see that the lines they have drawn between one thing and another and the ground they assumed to be holding everything up begins to fragment or crumble. This is especially easy to see in experimental sciences. Repeated experiments suggest something unexpected, something that should not be, and the workers have to shake up their assumptions, redraw the lines, and think again. Thomas Kuhn made this idea famous in his book *The Structure of Scientific Revolutions*. He referred to the fundamental assumptions scientists accept to be true as *paradigms*. The overturning of Newtonian physics by quantum physics is a good example of a paradigm change.

These are not esoteric concerns. They affect every one of us and are founded on something simple if mysterious. We all encounter the world first as newborns and then as children and adults, and we interact with other people and objects, and as we age we remember some things but not others. We learn to represent the world to ourselves in words and pictures, and in order to do this we have to know where one thing ends and another begins. The boundaries may seem obvious. When I see a squirrel running across my garden, I identify the furry rodent as distinct from the tree and the brick wall in my backyard. We know, however, that the blind person who has his sight restored as an adult does not see what I see, but rather a blur of motion and images that lack the coherence of the world he lived in when he was blind—a world that was ordered by his other senses.

We take for granted that our own human boundaries end with the organ that is our skin, for example. But every person was once a cluster of dividing cells inside the body of another person, and her dreams and worries and the food she ate cannot be separated from the embryonic being who became a fetus and, after birth, a newborn person, who spent the next year clinging to her or to someone else before walking around on her own. Nor is the adult a perfectly independent being. Every person has orifices that are open to the outside. She or he sees, hears, touches, smells, breathes, eats, urinates, defecates, mingles with other bodies in erotic encounters, loves, hates, suffers, thinks, and imagines. When we remember or imagine, we miraculously lift ourselves out of our bodies and move in spaces that are not right in front of our eyes but somewhere else. I remembered the Four Corners, however imperfectly, and traveled in time. When I read *Wuthering Heights* by Emily Brontë for the first time at age thirteen, I shuddered in terror. I crossed the borders of my immediate experience into another world, and that world became part of my experience, lodged bodily in the workings of my brain in memory.

The human animal has long been in the business of representing the world in one form or another and through it creating order. Saying the word *squirrel* or drawing a squirrel evokes that creature but is not the creature itself.

A big philosophical question turns on the problem of how we do this. No one really knows. What are those words and pictures inside our heads and how do we draw the lines or borders between things? Are they inside the person doing the perceiving or outside in the real world or, more subtly, what is the relation between inner and outer borders? There is a world, but how do we perceive it? Drawings, sculptures, and maps go back to prehistoric times. Writing seems to be much more recent, although some scholars have questioned the moment of its beginnings. I think that discussion is wide open.

I am deeply interested in prehistoric art because it can shed light on human perception, on what we may share as a species and also how cultures make us different from one another. In 2017, a painting in a cave on the island of Sulawesi in Indonesia was discovered and has now been dated. The lively hunting scene was painted 44,000 years ago. Small part-human, part-animal figures are running after wild pigs and buffalo-like creatures with ropes and spears. The chase is vividly depicted. Like cave paintings in other parts of the world, the animals and human figures stand out in relief against the rock. Details of the landscape are not part of the image. Creatures that move willfully take precedence over sky and grass and other background information. The representations of living beings move in emptiness.

Therianthropes, the part-animal, part-human figures of the Sulawesi image, also pop up in prehistoric art far away from Indonesia. The Lion Man or Löwen Mensch (the consensus seems to be this ivory carving is male, not female, although its genitals are ambiguous), which is about 40,000 years old, was discovered in many tiny pieces inside the Stadel cave in southern Germany in 1939, and then was painstakingly reassembled. The hybrid creatures in Indonesia and Germany blend species' features, the way I sometimes do in my dreams when I discover that I have branches growing from my arms or am dragging around a heavy tail. The beings in these paintings and sculptures are not evolutionary realities but imaginative overlaps between or among humans and other animals. The significance of these blurrings is murky, although there are a number of theories about them, usually related to supernatural belief and the spirit world.

Monsters or mixes of various creatures are part of countless mythologies around the world, as is the art of shape-shifting. A god turns into a beast for a short period and then returns to herself. Some psychotic patients have reported vivid experiences of being transformed into animals as well, a phenomenon documented in the psychiatric literature. Turning into the other sex is another common metamorphosis. I didn't know until recently that there is a contemporary therianthrope community. They call themselves therians or otherkins, and, from what I understand, they have a deep personal sense of being somehow not human but animal, or being something other than fully human. Human beings are, of course, placental mammals, but the conviction of those who belong to this community seems to be distinct from this simple fact of our animal nature.

Despite the many thousands of years that separate me from the artists on Sulawesi or in Swabia, their representations of animals and therianthropes aren't wholly incomprehensible to me. Did those people perceive and represent animals more or less the same way I do? When I draw a squirrel, I perceive its outlines first and go from there. The contents of Ice Age dreams and visions must have been taken from the daily experiences and beliefs of those Ice Age people, just as my dreams usually originate in events of the preceding day. What do they and I have in common and how are we radically different? If I could leap back in time and jump into one of their bodies and then remember the experience I had had, would I feel they were seeing and representing in ways wholly incomprehensible to me, or would I feel some kinship between us?

In his book *Kant and the Platypus*, Umberto Eco offers another animal story. When Marco Polo made his journey to Asia between 1271 and 1295, he came across an animal that mystified him. Because the beast had a horn on its forehead, he identified it as a unicorn, despite the fact that the animal didn't correspond to any conventional picture of a unicorn he had seen, and he admitted it had the feet of an elephant, the hair of a buffalo, was black, and looked nothing like the unicorn of fantasy. It was, in fact, a rhinoceros. "Often," Eco writes, "when faced with an unknown phenomenon, we seek that scrap of content, already present in our encyclopedia, which for better or worse seems to account for the new fact." Eco was deeply influenced by the American philosopher Charles Sanders Peirce's theory of signs, and he takes his reader through the philosophical complexities involved in how we perceive, recognize, and name the various creatures and objects that inhabit our world, forms of classification. Eco uses the term *cognitive type*, or CT, to refer to what Marco Polo had in his head—his personal and cultural encyclopedia. *Unicorn* had an entry there. *Rhinoceros* did not. Expectation shapes perception. When what you perceive fits with the past, you move on because you are seeing what you expected to see. But when something altogether new comes along, that surprising information changes brain function. A reorientation of the inner encyclopedia is needed.

Perception depends dramatically on one's particular situation and particular encyclopedia of knowledge. Marco Polo integrated the animal into a known group or species, the unicorn, rather than classify it as an altogether new creature or hybrid. You could say his mental economy was conservative. Why invent a whole new species when there was a serviceable one in existence already? Albrecht Dürer made his 1557 woodcut of a rhinoceros without ever having seen the animal. The descriptions of the animal's fearsome strength resulted in Dürer supplying the animal with human-looking armor, an extra horn on its backside, and reptilian scales on its legs. However imaginatively embellished, it still looks very much like a rhinoceros.

Images of the past also reveal perceptual biases we no longer share with our ancestors. Until the eighteenth century, anatomists interpreted female genitalia as a version of male genitalia but inverted. In his book *Making Sex: Body and Gender from the Greeks to Freud*, Thomas Laqueur quotes the Renaissance anatomist Berengario, "the neck of the uterus is like the penis, and its receptacle with testicles and vessels is like the scrotum." Laqueur twists the phrase "seeing is believing" into "believing is seeing." This makes the point exactly. The drawings that accompany the texts written by anatomists who had dissected human bodies and had intimate knowledge of them illustrate the female vagina not as vaguely like a penis but with the precise form of a hollow penis. The female parts are all there, but they are seen through a particular lens. And, as Laqueur points out, this cannot be written down as error or folly. "A whole world view makes the vagina look like a penis to Renaissance viewers." They, too, had a classification system. In the Renaissance, indeed, going back to the Greeks, the cognitive type or schema for human bodies was male, and women were "defective" or lesser versions of a universal masculine standard of anatomical perfection. Like Marco Polo's unlikely unicorn, female difference was integrated into a broader category or type—the male body.

The popular view of such phenomena goes something like this: "Oh, weren't they silly back in the old days. Couldn't they see what was right in front of their eyes?" I call this reaction: the hubris of the present. If you think that such biases have vanished from intellectual pursuits, I am here to tell you that you are wrong. Perception is founded on past experience, and that past includes our various cultures and languages and metaphors and categories for this or that, our particular knowledge about many subjects, our early childhoods with our families, and the hurtful and happy feelings that accompany those childhoods that are written into our bodies with brains in them and are crucial to determining our perception of and responses to various people, objects, and events that come our way. We divide. We make borders. We classify. And those divisions, borders, and classifications are often unconscious.

Sex difference remains crucial to contemporary understanding of how the world turns. In fact, I am astounded by how many things that have no sex get one. In the United States and much of the West, physics is masculine; poetry is feminine. But this is not true everywhere. In Iran, poetry is not girlish. It has a strong masculine image. In the United States, steak is masculine; salad is feminine. Pink is for girls. Blue is for boys. Early in the twentieth century, the reverse was true. The sciences have invested heavily in masculine and feminine imagery as well. Take the still popular picture of the heroic spermatozoa swimming bravely up the vaginal canal in a life-and-death competition with millions of rivals on his way to pierce the fat, lazy egg eagerly awaiting his penetration. An online version of *Anatomy and Physiology Textbook* (2013) for medical students describes this as a "race," during which the ejaculated sperm must "overcome" countless "obstacles" to reach the prize.

The problem with this high-speed hurdling metaphor is that it seems to be wrong. There are indeed obstacles to successful fertilization, but the current scientific story is that sperm are most likely *passively* transported upward by the muscular contractions of the uterus and oviducts. (See Robert Bramigan and Larry Lipschultz, "Sperm Transport and Capacitation," in Global Library of Women's Medicine, 2008.) In a 2018 essay for *Aeon*, "The Macho Sperm Myth," the biological anthropologist Robert D. Martin argues that such fantasies have interfered with research in embryology and blinded scientists to actual biological processes. In her now classic 1991 essay, "The Egg and the Sperm: How Science Has Constructed a Romance Based on Stereotypical Male and Female Roles," Emily Martin notes that "recent research suggests the almost heretical view that sperm and egg are mutually active partners." This is indeed what was emerging then and has emerged since. It takes two to tango.

My research in contemporary embryology reveals that much of the vocabulary remains the same. Battle imagery is common: "aggressive" sperm, "invasions" of the uterine lining, and the ongoing "war" for resources between mother and fetus. Scientists are excessively fond of absolute borders and sealed hermetic spaces through which no impurities travel. This mode of thought is rooted in the seventeenth century and the idea of mechanism; our bodies are machines and each little part has a special job to do. Mingling processes have not been popular since. For example, until very recently, the pregnant mother's uterus and her placenta were thought to be sterile, untouched by any bacteria. The controversy over the sterile uterus and placenta continues, but recent research on the microbiome—all the microbes human beings live with and need to survive—has challenged the conventional thought. Microbiota have foreign DNA we not only tolerate but depend on. The microbiome has created a revolution in thinking about us, about what's foreign and what's not, and how we define our own borders.

Scientists have not spent much time speculating on why they had assumed these female reproductive organs were sterile in the first place. It seems that in 1900, Henri Tissier proposed that the healthy uterus was sterile and kept that way during pregnancy by the cervical plug that a woman develops during her pregnancy, an anatomical border. Tissier compared this bodily barrier to one of the Seven Wonders of the Ancient World, the Colossus of Rhodes, a 33-meter-tall statue of the male sun god, Helios, erected on the island of Rhodes as a gatekeeper to guard the entrance to the city and protect it from invasion.

One may well wonder how apt the image of the looming Helios is for the mucus that forms over a pregnant woman's cervix from cervical secretions. Tissier's anatomical colossus isn't even hard; it's gelatinous, gooey. The woman expels the plug when she is in labor, but she often doesn't recognize it as a distinct thing—it often appears as "bloody show." Although "germs" have gained their reputation as evil for a reason, our repulsion has not been fully warranted. A nice title for a highly technical science paper from 2018 describes the current dilemma about the new impure uterus perfectly: "Uterine Microbiota: Residents, Tourists, or Invaders?" (James Baker, Dana M. Chase, and Melissa Herbst-Kralovetz, *Frontiers in Immunology* 9, 2018.)

Let me be blunt. The sterile womb and related ideas in biology—the belief, for example, that the nervous, endocrine, and immune systems had no interaction, an idea that has also turned out to be wrong—are founded on a high alarm in Western culture about mixing that long predates mechanistic thinking. The desire to pinpoint everything on an anatomical map, to draw precise boundaries between one thing and another, has resulted in a reluctance to tolerate ill-defined borders. Utah is not New Mexico and New Mexico is not Colorado or Arizona.

Fantasies can't be separated from knowledge. Sterile uteruses and placentas were desirable because they meant that the fetus was kept isolated in an antiseptic container away from the mother, where it grew in a clearly defined space with inviolate borders rather than mingling with the larger female body in which it was lodged. After all, the fetus could be male, and the idea that male and female mix creates queasiness about contaminated categories. Western culture has a long tradition of fleeing feminine pollution. It is vital to understand the protective urge to ward off the mixing that is embedded in clean separation. The profound irony here is that embryology itself is about mixing. Sperm and ovum together create a zygote with the DNA of both parents and the gestation inside a woman's body that follows is a dance of cellular exchange, entanglements, and still poorly understood traffic patterns that involve the mother, her placenta, and her embryo.

One of the books I return to again and again is by the anthropologist Mary Douglas, *Purity and Danger: An Analysis of the Concepts of Pollution and Taboo* (1966). I read it first as a graduate student. I have reread it several times since and have quoted from it in my essays. The book, as great books often do, has grown inside me over the years. "All margins are dangerous," Douglas writes. "If they are pulled this way or that, the shape of fundamental experience is changed. Any structure of ideas is vulnerable at its margins. We should expect the orifices of the body to symbolize its particularly vulnerable points. Matter issuing from them is marginal stuff of the most obvious kind . . . The mistake is to treat bodily margins in isolation from all other margins." In other words, the body and the body politic cannot be separated, and border crossing is fraught with peril. It is important to stress that ideas about pollution change from culture to culture. Douglas cites menstrual blood as filthy in some cultures but not at all in others; excrement is vile and dangerous in some societies, in others, it's just a joke.

Disgust has become a vast area of study in recent years. There are jokes about the birth of a whole new field: "disgustology." Evolutionary psychologists and some social neuroscientists argue that disgust evolved in human beings to protect them from contamination, that we are naturally built to be revolted by human waste, people who look sick, rotting plums, and maggoty meat. Tiny babies wrinkle up their noses when they taste something bitter, but do they have ready-made sensory disgust networks? Evolution does not explain why the human objects of disgust are so variable from place to place or why small children are not averse to eating their snot or playing with their excrement, nor does it explain why some people develop such a high degree of disgust sensitivity that they may wash with a pathological intensity that injures their skin. Compulsive cleaning, checking, or making sure that the pencils on your desk are always perfectly lined up, the striving for immaculate order in all aspects of life, may result ironically in the total derangement of that person's life. Obsessive-compulsive disorder can be a terrible affliction.

My mother had a zeal for cleaning and fastidiousness. When she set the table for guests, she used a measuring tape to make sure the plates were perfectly equidistant. Fortunately, her passion, common in Scandinavia, didn't fall into the unmanageable range. I have been known to clean violently while in the grip of anxiety. My father was organized, too, as I have already noted. I once found a bunch of keys in a small drawer in his study with the label: "Unknown Keys." Planning, measuring, fixing, and cleaning are methods of control, getting the world in habitable shape, but it's good to have a clear idea of what we are doing and why we may attach moral qualities to these acts.

"Dirt," Douglas writes, "is the by-product of a systematic ordering and classification of matter, in so far as ordering involves a rejection of inappropriate elements." Inappropriate elements, dust, dirt, slime, and oozing liquids mess up the order of things. These elements might be saliva, tears, feces, or nail clippings, but they can also be the stranger, the witch, the immigrant, or the Jew. Bodily categories and social categories and their metaphors are related. Ambiguous characters are blends of cognitive types, hybrids. They are people who don't fit expected societal patterns and must be contained and kept in their place. If they refuse to go willingly into their proper box, they are punished. Their punishment serves as a form of collective cleansing and a restoration of order.

Openings along the border of the body or the border of a country represent the danger of leakage and intrusion. In English we have a number of phrases that go directly to the point: "toeing the line" and "staying in line" mean accepting authority, following the rules, just as being "out of line" means the opposite. "The hard-liner" is a person who adheres without compromise to the given boundaries of conduct. He—it is often a he, although by no means always—has taken a position to defend hard borders and plug all the leaks. From this perspective, sterility represents the perfect, pure, and inviolable state, which may be political, religious, or intellectual.

When I was a graduate student in English in the late seventies, I read a lot of philosophy as well as literature. I asked permission to attend a seminar on Immanuel Kant in the philosophy department. The philosophy department was on the seventh floor of Philosophy Hall, one floor above us. Despite its proximity to the world of letters on six, I had never set foot in that hallowed space, but once I secured permission through the proper channels, I was granted the right to press the elevator button and move up. I was confident that I had read enough and was more than smart enough to make my way into the difficult terrain of pure reason. I felt excited, buoyant, and eager to learn. I pressed seven, stepped out on a floor that looked very much like the one below, made my way to the assigned room, and walked through the door. What I remember is this: At the end of the table sat an older white man with a beard, smoking a pipe, and around him at the table were nine young white men, all with beards and all smoking pipes. So this was what philosophy looked like!

On the floor below, cigarettes were the tobacco source of choice. Everybody smoked then, but no literature student I knew smoked a pipe.

I pause to add that this memory cannot be accurate. There had to be at least a couple of beardless fellows at the table and, no doubt, a couple who didn't smoke pipes. Nevertheless, that is the image that remains in my head, and there must have been enough bearded pipe-smokers to give me a universal impression. As I walked through the door, I felt their eyes fall upon me. And then I saw them visibly stiffen as if they were not several beings but one. I felt as if I had ushered a noxious smell into the room. No one acknowledged me either by word or gesture. The professor did not introduce me. I took a seat at the table near the door. At one point, I summoned the nerve to comment. Whatever I said, it was received coldly, and then ignored. No one responded. It was as if I had not spoken. I endured the hour in a state of frozen misery. I felt bewildered, ashamed, and humiliated. When the class was over, I rushed out, took the elevator one floor down, and never returned. I knew I was not a resident of the philosophy department, but I had naïvely expected to be welcomed as a tourist. After all, I had secured the proper paperwork from legitimate authorities to cross that particular border.

What interests me now about the story is how puzzled I was at the time. I mentioned it to no one. Despite my feminism, I wasn't prepared for that reception. In 1979, I can remember only three women out of sixty-five professors in the English department at Columbia. I do not believe there was a single woman in philosophy at the time. My mistake was to believe that my questions, my insights, my curiosity would win the day. Being treated as a polluting invader made me feel bad and dirty, even though I had done nothing to feel bad and dirty about.

I had run into a wall of philosopher gatekeepers, a version of the Colossus of Rhodes, duty bound to protect the seventh floor from interlopers. Territorial impulses pervade the academy. Get off my turf and don't touch my expertise are common sentiments, but this story has an extra element: my sex. The higher regions of the mind, of objectivity, proof, and cold reasoning, were not for me. The working cognitive type or schema they all must have shared had blocked my entrance to the rarefied sanctum of the seventh floor.

Comedy or tragedy? There is something ridiculous, even hilarious about those philosophy boys with their facial hair and smoking accessories policing the borders of their discipline from feminine stink. I was not mortally injured, and I have continued to be an avid reader of philosophy. It was, however, a prime example of what the sociologist Pierre Bourdieu calls "symbolic violence." The boys did not have to rise up as one and push me physically from the room. They did not lay a hand on me. According to Bourdieu, symbolic violence is a show of force that legitimizes the social order and its hierarchies. Deeply held beliefs about social structure, class, sex, and race may be so deeply embedded in the way people perceive, think, move, feel, and act that they come to feel these perceptions, thoughts, gestures, feelings, and acts are "natural," ordained by nature.

The anatomist who saw penises in vaginas had a good knowledge of anatomy, after all, but the physical details he uncovered in the cadavers he dissected and the ideas that shaped his perception could not be disentangled. Rather, the borders and their configurations seemed to be present in nature itself. Bourdieu further argues that the victim of symbolic violence must be complicit in it—must also believe that the punishment meted out is somehow right and natural. My shame at the time was an indication of both my powerlessness and my complicity. My running from the room confirms it, and this strikes me as a bit tragic on hindsight.

Countless experiences of this sort, some far worse, have trained me to speak up and calmly question the motives of the gatekeepers, motives of which they are often not fully conscious. What they are conscious of are strong feelings, feelings of moral purity and righteousness. How could I or another woman or outsider—immigrant, gay, trans, brown, Black, lower class, disabled, or otherkin person—have the gall to claim *authority*? Authority, after all, is legitimate power. Social psychologists have done numerous studies on the backlash visited upon ambitious women who don't toe the line.

I like the story of the philosophy boys because the politics are not the ones we in the United States like to summon regularly these days—of ignorant, uneducated white people who cheer when the malignant narcissist-in-chief howls, "Send her back!" The philosophy boys knew their philosophy. The philosophers on their syllabi were men. They knew their Plato and his immortal soul that escapes the passions of the body that try to drag it down, and they knew that bodies and emotions are feminine, and the intellect masculine. They knew their Aristotle. All living things have souls, but only human beings have rational souls, and this helped Aristotle explain why the body and the body politic are connected. Every soul has both rational and irrational elements in it, but women, alas, have too much of the latter. The most rational rule, the less rational serve. "The male is by nature superior and the female inferior," he wrote, "the male ruler and female subject" (*Politics* 1, 1254b). Slaves, too, were inferior, as were children, whose rational faculties were not yet developed. The influence of Plato and Aristotle on Western thought has been immeasurable.

Not a single one of us is free of the cognitive schemas that help us organize the world and bias us accordingly, which does not mean that the human species doesn't share attributes that link us as a species with certain traits and abilities that distinguish us from microbes, squirrels, and the unicorns of imagination. Squirrels don't have libraries or seven thousand extant squirrel languages, at least as far as we know. Anyone who speaks more than one language knows there are words in one language that capture a feeling or thought the other languages don't have. I was granted two languages from early childhood, Norwegian and English. Speaking two languages means crossing borders. It means that the languages are inside and outside you at once. Sometimes they merge into one. When my mother was still alive, we would speak Norwegian and English to each other and what we referred to as "blandet," mixed—a hybrid blend of the two, which could be called Nordish. I have stolen this invented word from one commonly used in American English—Spanglish.

Learning the hermetic languages of several disciplines is not so different from studying foreign languages. The intellectual vagabond cannot easily stick to the straight and narrow or toe the line because she is working with several classification systems at once. Residing in four or more states can be uncomfortable, but it allows the traveler a plural perspective, and it makes purity and its radical ally, sterility, seem ridiculous. There's always going to be some mess, and the truth is we need the mess to help us ask questions about why things are the way they are and how they might be different. No single classification system with strict borders, no encyclopedia in any particular field can contain the shifting borders of dynamic human experience.

"Purity," Douglas writes near the end of her book, "is the enemy of change, ambiguity, and compromise." The purists and hard-liners share a mania for rigid classification and declare war on cracks, leaks, openings, mixing, and hybrids. Borders of all kinds are volatile. It is a mistake to treat bodily borders as separate from all other borders.

"Why should *Pennsylvania*, founded by the *English*, become a colony of *Aliens*, who will shortly be so numerous as to Germanize us instead of our Anglifying them, and will never adopt our language or customs, anymore than they can acquire our complexion?" (italics in the original). (Benjamin Franklin, *Observations Concerning the Increase of Mankind, Peopling of Countries, &c.*, 1751.)

"Examine the history of the Roman Catholic Church throughout all time . . . It is her office to destroy every healthy organization which exists within the sphere of her pestiferous influences. She is the serpent that gives no alarm—a moral plague spot in a political miasma." (Anonymous, *To Those Born on American Soil Who Know Nothing*, 1854.)

"The flood gates will be down and a turgid sea of aliens will inundate our seaports." (Madison Grant, *Current Opinion*, 1923.)

"The Jew represents an infectious illness." (Joseph Goebbels, "Total War Speech," 1943.)

"Islam is a creeping mold infestation. Islam is a virus. It is a deadly virus spreading throughout Europe and the West." (Neal Boortz, U.S. syndicated radio host, 2006.)

"Muslims are like the African carp. They breed quickly and are very violent and they eat their own kind." (Ashin Wirathu, Buddhist monk in Myanmar, 2013.)

"Likewise, tremendous infectious disease is pouring across the border. The U.S. has become the dumping ground for Mexico and, in fact, for many parts of the world." (Donald Trump, 2015.)

"Parasitic class of anti-white vermin." (Unite the Right speaker in Charlottesville, Virginia, 2017.)

"Africa wants to kick down the door . . . and Europe is under invasion already." (Viktor Orbán, 2018.)

"Freedom is only possible when the virus is eradicated." (Leaked Chinese party document on the Uighurs, 2019.)

"Send her back!" (Donald Trump, 2019.)

The man who occupies the White House in 2019 is terrified of germs. He insists that all visitors wash their hands before they enter the Oval Office. The word *disgust* punctuates his speeches. Women are disgusting animals, pigs. Breast-feeding is disgusting. He has a horror of menstruation—"bleeding from her wherever." Immigrants "have violated our borders" as an indistinguishable *liquid* force. They "pour" over the boundary in waves, floods, and tides. They invade like vermin. They infest and swarm and must be kept out by a great wall that is big, beautiful, impenetrable, and perfect.

U.S. anti-miscegenation laws that criminalize interracial marriage, 1661–1967.

The U.S. Chinese Exclusion Act, 1882.

Japanese U.S. citizens in concentration camps in California, Arizona, Wyoming, Colorado, and Arkansas, February 19, 1942–March 20, 1946.

Dutch citizens in Japanese internment camps in the East Indies during World War II, 1942–1945.

Nazi euthanasia program, Operation T4: psychiatric patients, the mentally and physically disabled, those deemed incurable. Nazi death camps: Jews, Roma, Sinti, Jehovah's Witnesses, lesbians, and gays. "The final solution."

Border patrol. Detention centers at the border. Children without their parents in cages, sobbing. Parents without their children. Humiliation, fear, and shame. The stink of bodies in crowded cells. People can't wash. Lice and flu outbreaks. Corpses.

Symbolic violence and real violence. One becomes the other. Where is the border between them? Words and deeds. No one, no body is closed. We are open beings living among and dependent on others. We are all born from the body of someone. No discourse or discipline of purity, no wall, no barrier, no gatekeeper or colossus will alter the truths of mixing and change.

In 228 or 226 BCE, an earthquake destroyed the Colossus of Rhodes, but pieces of it were said to have remained where they had fallen for centuries. When an Arab force captured the city in 653, the statue was melted down and sold to a Jewish merchant who, according to the story told by Theophanes, loaded the bronze onto nine hundred camels and carried it away.

2019

NOTES FROM NEW YORK

APRIL 23, 2020

From the house I share with my husband in Brooklyn, there is little to see these days except the empty street and the occasional masked forlorn pedestrian. But as I sit at my desk and write, I hear the sirens all day. Every alarm signals a person in crisis, and that person's fate is inevitably bound to the fates of others—family and friends. It is a noise that deserves moral attention. I have come to think of the sirens as the city's heartbreaking music, a high-pitched dirge that accompanies the number in the newspaper every day: 731, 779, 799. Grim as the daily count of corpses in New York State may be, it is surely too low. Until recently, the city has not recorded the cause of death as COVID-19 unless the person was tested. Those who died at home were not tested, and there are many of them. On April 12, the number fell. There is talk of a "plateau" and a "flattened curve"—human suffering charted on a graph.

I have lived in this dense, jostling city for more than forty years, and it is surely a testament to our new reality that I find myself longing to push through the door of the Q or F or number 2 train with a hundred other people and stand tightly pressed against shoulders, heads, elbows, knees, oversized packages, and bulbous backpacks as I breathe in the smell of sweat mingled with pungent and vague culinary odors that waft through the car.

On March 11, five days after I taught my seminar in narrative psychiatry to psychiatric residents at Weill Cornell Medical College in Manhattan, visited a department store, walked twenty blocks with hordes of fellow New Yorkers, and took three taxis (I avoided the subway because the virus had arrived), I fell ill with something. My husband came down with the ailment a few days later. The symptoms lingered for a while, but they were never serious. We recovered. On March 22, a friend forwarded a tweet from a physician alerting his colleagues about a fellow doctor who had tested positive for the virus. The man had chest constriction, cough, severe headache, body aches but *no fever*: an exact description of my symptoms. Our family physician suspects we had it. He suspects he had it. None of us had access to a test.

"Everyone that wants a test can get a test," Donald Trump told reporters on March 6, the same day I was out and about in Manhattan.

Rampaging illness and economic paralysis are global, but the pandemic is different in different countries; and within a single country, it is different in different cities; and within a city, the degree of suffering varies from neighborhood to neighborhood. In New York City, it depends on class, color, immigration status, and job description. Just as they did during the yellow fever epidemic of 1795, the cholera epidemic of 1832, and the flu pandemic of 1918, moneyed New Yorkers have fled town for their country houses to wait out the scourge, leaving behind the crowded and vulnerable poor who cannot afford "social distancing." According to Merriam-Webster, the term *social distancing* was born in 2003.

When words and images "go viral," they spread with the speed of a highly contagious virus across media to infect millions. The metaphor is apt. For a brief time, anyway, a viral message is alive in its readers and viewers and becomes a form of mass cognition. The metaphor *viral* for this form of speedy, voluminous communication might be said to once have had its own viral character, which began about ten years ago. It is now part of the English language.

A literal virus is a biological zombie. It occupies a borderland between the dead and the living. Virologists argue steadily about whether to categorize it as one or the other. Although viruses are composed of the same nucleic acids found in our own cells, they cannot reproduce without a host organism. They require the complex cellular machinery of a host to synthesize their proteins and replicate their DNA or RNA. They insert their own genes into the host cells to create a hybrid genome. Viruses are a ubiquitous part of the biosphere. They are inside and outside us. The human virome consists of all the viruses in our bodies and plays an essential role in our immune responses. Some viruses benefit their hosts. Others kill them.

The language we use to talk about a real infectious disease matters. The governor of New York, Andrew Cuomo, who holds a daily briefing for the state's citizens, has been forthright about the present dangers and clear about safety measures. He has also shared with the public what remains unknown and has demonstrated compassion for people who are ill or working on what has come to be called "the front lines"—people in hospitals and grocery stories, people delivering mail and packages and retrieving our garbage. In March, Donald Trump suggested that SARS-CoV-2 could be banished by magical thinking. It would "disappear" "like a miracle," perhaps in April. He referred to it as "their new hoax," a deception presumably cooked up by Democrats to discredit him. He personified it as the "Chinese" virus, a figment with possible Mexican relatives. "We need the wall now more than ever!" he retweeted on March 10. The message originated with the far-right group Turning Point USA.

Trump has repeatedly suggested that closing national borders and stopping air travel is an efficient method for halting the spread of the virus. On January 31, he barred most foreigners who had visited China from entering the United States. He then claimed the virus had been "pretty much" "shut down." At a rally on February 28, he said, "Border security is also health security." For years, he has employed metaphors of immigrants as biological contaminants that infect the white body politic with their impurities. In a 2015 speech, he turned "Mexican immigrants" into a mysterious liquid force: "tremendous infectious disease pouring across the border." The president's immigrant-as-pathogen rhetoric has a long and ugly history in the United States. An article in *The Saturday Evening Post* from 1923 by W. T. Ellis may stand as exemplary. Immigrants constitute a "stream of impurity" and "a tide of pollution."

In 2018, the *American Journal of Public Health* published "The 1918 Influenza Pandemic: Lessons Learned and Not," a series of articles on *how to prepare for the coming pandemic*. That same year, the Trump administration fired the members of the pandemic response team and did not replace them. In their introduction to the papers devoted to the topic, Wendy Parmet and Mark Rothstein identify the three "leading threats to global public health" as "hubris, isolationism, and distrust." The hubris is scientific and technological—a faith in fancy new tools. We do have high-tech tools, but as the authors point out, they are "woefully ineffective" in halting the spread of influenza, and, I will add, coronaviruses. Isolationism is the naïve belief that closing a nation's borders will keep a virus at bay. "Xenophobia, rather than science," they write, "helps to explain the call for travel bans." Distrust is a loss of faith in government, journalism, and science. The United States, which has the highest number of deaths from COVID-19 in the world, is a country riddled with distrust.

Viral figures of speech have collided and mingled with an actual virus. "We, all of us, grave or light, get our thoughts entangled in metaphors and act fatally on the strength of them," George Eliot's narrator famously commented in *Middlemarch*.

The body politic is a metaphor for a collective entity—the nation. Human beings are not viruses, even though viruses are, in fact, part of all of us. The human virome is in intimate interaction with the bacteria in our bodies, the microbiome. We need these fellow travelers to live. Every person is a multiplicity, a community of symbiotic relations that includes a diversity of DNA. In light of this, philosophers of biology have begun to question how to draw the lines between "us" and "them" and whether such divisions make any sense at all. The human body is an ecosystem that depends on the ecosystems around it. And we are social animals, heavily dependent on others like us for our survival. The pandemic has surely brought home how dependent every one of us is on the elaborate societal arrangements that sustain us, from running water in the tap to food on the grocery store shelves.

And this is where the irony becomes most acute. The political rhetoric of closed borders and impenetrable walls, of "lock her up" and "send her back," of shutting down and shutting out, of purity and impurity, of us versus them, this language of hubris, isolation, and distrust in the midst of a public health emergency, is killing people. It is a rhetoric that articulates a pernicious fantasy of the isolated, autonomous person who gave birth to himself and needs no one. The lone cowboy, the self-made man, the rugged individual are American iterations of this fictional being, inevitably a male, white being. The nightly installments of *The Donald Trump Show*, disguised as briefings on the coronavirus, during which the commander in chief boasts, swaggers, and punches, but never betrays the slightest sign of empathy for another person or guilt for his own actions, serve as the perfect theatrical embodiment of a ruinous ideology.

The failure of the Trump administration to prepare for an inevitable pandemic, to listen to virologists, epidemiologists, and public health experts and act decisively and quickly when the threat arose; the incompetence, chaos, and lies that have accompanied every decision; the lack of tests, ventilators, and protective gear that would have saved lives are the direct result of an ideology, which along with its xenophobia, racism, and misogyny, is profoundly anti-intellectual. The income inequality that has been growing in this country since the early seventies and the brutal racial disparities of our private health care system have become only more visible during the pandemic. I think this deserves moral attention.

There will be an end to the pandemic, although we don't know what that will look like now. They say 20,000 to 30,000 New Yorkers died when influenza swept through the city in 1918. The estimate for the global death toll that year is 50 million. In the United States, most people forgot all about it. I suggest we not forget this pandemic, if only because our ecosystems, inside and outside of us, are vulnerable. I suggest the blind virus that leapt from an animal to a human being sometime last year has made it clear that we are inextricably entangled with and dependent on one another and must also coexist with other mammals and birds and insects and plants and bacteria and viruses on this small and fragile earth.

2020

READING DURING THE PLAGUE

APRIL 13, 2020

Reading is an intimate encounter that every person can have during a pandemic. No social distance is required. In our current world of restricted movement, the book is a geography where complete freedom remains possible. But *what* a person reads during a pandemic, it seems to me, has no moral quality. The moral decision has already been made. Protect yourself to protect others. Stay put if you can. But no one is obliged to steep herself in the science of virology or the earth's complex ecosystems or novels about the plague or poems about death and dying. They are all possible choices—as is a turn to comedy, a form distinguished by its ending: It all works out. The fairy tale is another buoyant genre. The hero or heroine is tested sorely, but in the end, he or she is rewarded with happiness. And fairy tales have magic. The laws of nature are overturned and replaced by human desires. Human beings often believe their wishes will come true, and they often do so without reason. Reading offers a safe road to a variety of vicarious gratifications.

The question is: If you are well and at home and have enough to eat and can concentrate on a book, do you read toward or away from your fear? Reading for comfort and escape is readily explicable. But why read about what you fear? Since Aristotle used the word *catharsis* in his *Poetics* without explaining exactly what he meant, philosophers have puzzled over the undeniable fact that people take a weird pleasure from art that describes terrible events. Why do we enjoy weeping over the sorrows of characters in books? Why do gruesome stories of war, murder, and even uncontrollable contagions seem to relieve some of the pressure and anxiety of this real moment when the authorities scramble to find room for the growing number of corpses in New York City?

Why bother with art, after all? Why not consume every factual tidbit available about the virus and its spread, the best mask to wear, or how to clean your groceries to avoid contamination? Isn't this the age of facts versus fakery? What could fiction with its imaginary ramblings possibly give anyone at such a time, except an escape into the unreal? "Just the facts, ma'am" has become a mantra in an age of lies, the lifebuoy to which the noble opposition clings to keep from going under. When a statement from on high, "We have it totally under control," actually means "We have no control over it whatsoever," public outrage is entirely reasonable, but facts, important as they are, remain limited and puny things that must be interpreted. For example, what does a brand-new fact (or possible fact)—more men are dying of coronavirus than women—actually mean? It could mean the data is unreliable and incomplete. It might be related to modulating genes on the X chromosome that affect the immune system. Maybe the female double X is somehow protective. It could be related to the fact that men have more untreated health conditions than women because they see doctors less often—a sociological reality that makes them more vulnerable. Macho stoicism becomes risk factor.

One can easily imagine a novelist taking this possible fact and pushing it across a limit—only men are vulnerable to a new plague that has taken over the globe, a scourge that leaves the XY demented, frail, or dead. The very survival of the species is threatened. The startling numbers of sick and dying men have turned the age-old hierarchy upside down. All authority now lies with the clear heads and strong hands of those who had long been dubbed "the weaker sex."[*] From a scientific point of view, the narrative is highly dubious. Despite much advertising to the contrary, male and female physiologies are more the same than different. And yet, as far as I can tell, almost every novel or story that somehow relates to disease epidemics has been popping up on "what

---

[*] A reader of this book, Chelsea Cohen, pointed out to me that this is in fact the plot of the successful graphic novel series Y. I had no idea of its existence when I invented a possible story.

to read during the virus" lists. Does the fact that these exist testify to something more than filling up culture pages or screens with the timely and relevant?

In a country that denigrates the humanities and champions STEM fields, a country that cuts budgets for all the arts, a country in which poetry, the novel, and the arts in general are regarded as mostly fluffy, imaginary stuff for women (who are the principal consumers of all art), I have wondered why at this moment articles about imaginative fiction have been appearing all over the place. A number of these writers are not literary people, but they have taken to promoting the wisdom of the imaginary. Camus's *The Plague* is selling well. In France, it is topping bestseller charts. Katherine Anne Porter's *Pale Horse/Pale Rider*, which takes place during the 1918 flu pandemic, has been receiving renewed attention. I read it again. Its delirium passages are extraordinary. Although I haven't read anyone who has been explicit about why some people turn to literature during a crisis, I suspect that implicit in these literary resurrections is an understanding that "the news" and "facts" are impersonal, and even when they are advertised as *personal*, they fill a slot, the "heartwarming story," for example—half a minute on an adorable toddler waving through the glass at Grandpa, or a noble nurse on "the front lines," or the sweet young woman who carries groceries for the old lady next door. They are intended as a momentary lift for the reader or viewer "at home." The emotional manipulation is calculated. When it is good, literature moves the personal into other territory altogether and in the process becomes collective.

There are countless novelists who manipulate readers as mercilessly as television producers. They fulfill the expectations of their readers and their books sell like hotcakes. They serve an important purpose in the culture, just as comfort food does. In my own life, I have found that certain detective novels slide through me like water, and if I stumble across one I have already read, I do not remember it until late in the game, sometimes not at all. This kind of reading is like eating chocolate in bed. I am all for it. And yet, it may be that during moments when death is close and perhaps imminent, at least some readers crave an experience that is beyond what they expect, beyond the endlessly repeated platitudes on radio and TV and the Internet. My own tolerance for breathless reports on the virus has plummeted. I turn them off now.

At the last dinner party I attended, on March 7, Boccaccio's *Decameron* (1350–1353) came up. I found myself thinking about the book again. Memorable fragments returned to my mind—the randy nuns who take turns with the supposedly deaf and dumb gardener until they exhaust him completely, the knight who tells such a bad story to a lady that her heart thumps and she begins to sweat, and the doctor who while trying to diagnose the illness of a young man notices that every time a young woman enters the room, his patient's pulse quickens. The mystery is solved. Lovesickness.

Although I remembered that the prologue was about the Black Death, I had forgotten the details. Boccaccio gives a vivid description of "the deadly pestilence" wending its way through Florence. The narrator describes the apple- and egg-sized tumors that grow in the groins and armpits of the afflicted, the contagion's spread from person-to-person contact but also from touching infected garments. I was particularly fascinated by the various responses to the plague, all of which can be seen in New York City during the present pandemic. There are those who withdraw to live "a separate and secluded life" of imagined safety, others who throw themselves into mad revelry and flout all authority, and a third, more moderate group that tries to be sensible, neither terrified nor negligent. Everyone is vulnerable. The corpses pile up, and the city becomes a "sepulcher." My reading felt cathartic.

The seven women and three men who flee the plague for the countryside in *The Decameron* tell one another stories to pass the time while the death germ rages through the city. They tell one another stories of wit and agency and passion. They are tragic and comic. They are stories about our vulnerable erotic and mortal bodies, about being alive but also knowing we will die. They are about the flights our imaginations take—for better and for worse. They are stories for now.

2020

WHEN I MET YOU I SAW MYSELF AS ANOTHER

When I met you I saw myself as another. It's a strange sentence, but what does it mean? Its meaning is ambiguous, but not completely open. There is an "I character," a narrator, and a "you character," the person to whom the narrator speaks. We know that the "I" and the "you" have met sometime in the past, and we know that the meeting between them somehow caused the narrator to see herself or himself as another person. The meeting caused an estrangement inside the narrator, by which she or he became foreign to herself or himself. How this happens the sentence doesn't tell. We don't know who the two people are, what kind of meeting they had, how long it lasted, or where it took place.

The sentence is abstract, but it can be filled with details: *When I met you last year for the first time, and you looked me in the eyes and called me Zoe, which is not my name, I saw myself through your eyes as another person altogether, and even though I knew you must have mistaken me for someone else, I felt a sudden desire to be Zoe.* The story could go in many directions from here. There might be a real Zoe in the story, a third character, who looks very much like our narrator. On the other hand, the you character might be playing a game with the narrator. Perhaps Zoe is the heroine of a play the you character is writing and when the playwright meets the narrator, she has an uncanny feeling that her character has come to life. The possibilities proliferate.

The truth is every story is addressed to another person, even if that other person is the self. Stories are dialogical by nature. When I tell myself a story about myself, when I use the word *I* in a sentence, when I represent myself to myself, my "I" implies a "you." Further, by telling myself a story about my close call with a bus yesterday, for example, I have to recollect myself in the past as I was then, and my remembering is an imaginative act by which I become another to myself. If I run into a friend on the sidewalk in Brooklyn, stop him, and say, "You'll never believe what happened to me yesterday," and go on to tell him that I was almost run over by a bus, but was saved by an old woman who looked frail but turned out to be remarkably strong because she grabbed me at the last minute and pulled me out of danger, my friend will imagine me and the bus and the old woman in his mind. He won't see in his mind what I see in my mind, but he will generate some pictures of the accident that almost happened anyway. If he is a good friend, he will nod and pat me on the back and let me know how happy he is that I wasn't crushed by the bus but survived to tell him the story.

What if I turn the bus story into a fiction, into words on a page? Who is telling the story then? It isn't "I" but my narrator, another "I" with another past. I may be the *author* of the story but I am not the *narrator* of the story. In this case, there is no real person telling the story. I, the author, am now doubly alienated from myself. I am not only representing myself to myself in language as a narrating "I," I have taken on another "I," another storyteller of a fictional tale talking to a "you," but also to the reader. *On April 6, 1986, I was walking down Seventh Avenue, dreaming as usual, paying no attention to what was going on around me. The light turned green. I took several steps into the street, heard the blast of a horn, saw a huge orange bus careening toward me, smelled its exhaust, and froze in terror. Then a hand grabbed my arm, and I felt myself yanked violently backward onto the sidewalk where I fell hard on the cement, just before the bus screeched to a stop exactly where I had been standing seconds before, and there you were looking down on me—half my size, twice my age, with a frightened expression on your small face, breathing heavily. We didn't know then that our friendship would last for years. I didn't know then that meeting you by chance the afternoon you saved me from being flattened by a bus in Park Slope in Brooklyn would change my view of myself forever.*

The strange, abstract little sentence was intended to launch a story. But it was also meant to interrogate the back and forth that is part of every meeting between two people. Although I cannot imagine perfectly how you see me, your face and your gestures and your words are felt by me during our exchange. I mean *felt*. Even if I am actively analyzing our encounter as it takes place, I am sensing what goes on between us before I can articulate it. Do your eyes meet mine now and again or are they constantly averted? Do you smile at me a couple of times or do you keep your lips tight and pursed, even when you are speaking? Maybe while you are talking to me, I notice that every few seconds you glance at something or someone across the room. Your restlessness agitates me, affects my breathing. I feel my face tighten. Perhaps I turn my head to see what has captured your interest, and I notice that a famous actress has just arrived at the party. I guess that you would rather speak to her. Suddenly, I see myself through your eyes: I am boring. It's terrible to be boring. I've been talking about my interests, and you find them dull. Flustered and embarrassed, I politely excuse myself and release you to the actress. On the other hand, maybe after a couple of seconds of reflection, I decide I am not boring. Maybe I am offended by your inattention. I think to myself that you are a social climber attracted to celebrity, a shallow person I am happy to abandon. My interpretation of you depends not only on your subtle but meaningful expressions, gestures, and words, but on my view of myself, my confidence, humility, my past experiences with others, and how I understand my place in the world.

Maybe the actress's name is Zoe Banks, and maybe Zoe Banks is a character in the story I am writing. Maybe the narrator of the story who is at the party decides to take revenge on her bored interlocutor and sow confusion in the room. Maybe the imp of the perverse seizes her and she gives in to its prodding. She walks across the room, sidles up close to Mr. Bored, and extends her hand to the actress. "Hi," she says, "My name is Zoe Banks. What's your name?"

2016

THE FUTURE OF LITERATURE

The future is the land of our expectations, hopes, fantasies, and projections, which is to say the future is a fiction. If this imaginary place appears too bleak and miserable to inhabit comfortably, some people lose the desire to go on. Human beings need the idea of a good future in order to live in the present, and yet, the future belongs to imaginary, not real time, because it has not yet been lived, and what we imagine it will be is largely shaped by our past experiences and how we feel about them. Our past lives may cause us to predict catastrophe or utopia or something in between for the future, but we inevitably expect something.

Our brains, some scientists argue, evolved for prediction. When I flick on the light switch, I expect the light to go on because I have learned that this gesture leads to illumination. In the morning, I pour milk into my oatmeal and expect it to taste as it always does. Predictability creates automaticity. Once I have learned how the light switch works, I don't have to think about it anymore. My reach for it is largely unconscious. The argument goes like this: In evolutionary terms prediction is what the brain has evolved to do because we learn about danger and remember to avoid it. Accurate prediction protects survival. We save our conscious thinking for surprises, for when the world does not go as planned.

Once in an early morning state of absentmindedness, I poured orange juice into my oatmeal instead of milk. The containers are the identical size and shape and sit beside each other in the refrigerator. My assumption that the liquid I had poured into my bowl was milk did not result in taste recognition of the orange juice as orange juice. Instead I tasted hideous milk. My breakfast routine was so determined by habit that although I knew something had gone wrong, I could not identify the liquid instantly, even though I have drunk orange juice every morning for years. Perception cannot be separated from either the past or the present context of experience.

Despite our predictive brains, actually predicting the future is problematic. Even excellent data and sophisticated Bayesian models fail us when we venture into the uncharted territory of the future. Think of the 2016 election in the United States. For all their sophistication the polls were wrong. For many, the result came as a shock, one far worse than mistaking a container of orange juice for a container of milk. In truth, the only certainty we have about the future is that it holds the secret to our mortality: when and where and how each one of us will die. And dying is not an experience any of us will remember.

I cannot speak with any confidence about the future of anything, including literature, although I am not predicting its demise, if only because human beings are creatures who use symbols and seem to crave stories in one form or another and quickly link events in our own lives into more and less coherent narratives. Every known culture has been a storytelling culture. Stories were first transmitted orally and served to bind a particular people with a shared history through common tales and myths. Written stories are much younger, but recorded stories in one form or another persist in every culture with a written language.

We tell ourselves stories about ourselves to make sense of ourselves. Paul Ricoeur, the French philosopher, called narrative "human time," a way to "yoke" experiences together in a temporal sequence and create relations among them. Time is an immensely difficult concept, but telling stories is one way to give events in time meaning. Stories imply causes. The plot of a life moves in one direction or another, and one event is viewed as determining the next. There are many ways to tell the same story, however. Narratives always leave out as much as they put in. But without memory, we could not tell ourselves any stories about the past. We could not fantasize about the future, or write novels about imaginary lives.

Memory, Mnemosyne, mother of the muses, is key to the art of literature. There are different kinds of memory. Once I have learned to ride a bike, swim, and read, the memory of how to perform these acts is coded in my body thoughtlessly. I no longer have to return to the laborious process of learning the skill. Eric Kandel, who was awarded the Nobel prize for his research, worked on memory in a sea snail of the genus Aplysia and discovered that the humble creature remembers and learns. Snails, rats, and dogs learn from experience through memory, but it is not clear they have autobiographical memories as we do. Does your dog conjure up pictures of running in the park last Thursday or fantasize about a trip that will take place next Friday? I suspect this human gift of recollection and projection is connected to representations that make stories and literature possible. People can represent in words or images what is not present. Caution is in order, however. Other mammals and birds dream, and scientists speculate that many of these animals dream in images, which must come from their waking experience. Are human dreams qualitatively different? Do the dreams of other animals have a narrative form? Do our dreams have narrative forms, or do we assign them a story after we wake up?

If narrative is universal to the human species, it will probably last as long as human beings do. The word *saga* in Icelandic means a long story in prose. It might serve as a definition of the novel. Novels are long stories in prose, and despite the genre's many historical jigs and jags, it has existed for centuries. There were ancient Greek novels and Roman ones. Lady Murasaki's *The Tale of Genji* was written around 1010. The cycle of connected stories in *The Thousand and One Nights* were probably first written down in Syria late in the eleventh century. The first part of *Don Quixote* was published in 1605, the second part in 1615. In 1666, Margaret Cavendish published *The Blazing World*, which some scholars have called the first work of science fiction. All of these long prose works predate the advent of the modern novel. The English and French novel bloomed in the eighteenth and nineteenth centuries and then took a number of interesting turns in the twentieth. Do we know what is happening to literature in the twenty-first? Fictional stories are everywhere in many forms of media, in film, on television, the Internet, in blogs and fake news, and they do not appear to be in danger of disappearing. Stories are thriving.

But what is fiction for? Why do people like reading stories that never happened featuring characters we will never meet off the page? We are the only animals on earth who have built libraries, study literature, and proclaim books good, bad, and mediocre. Why do writers write what they write? How does an author know how a novel's plot should develop? Where do fictional characters come from? They must come from life. That is all we have. The genesis of a work of fiction is often a mystery to the person who writes it. The title of an essay I wrote on the subject encapsulates the riddle: "Why One Story and Not Another?" In fiction, all the possibilities are open. The sun does not have to rise and set. The light switch might bring a rainstorm rather than a bright room. In a novel human beings can fly or live forever. Anything goes. So how does a writer know what is right and wrong?

Although any number of journalists and some reviewers have assumed that my novels are thinly veiled autobiographies, this is not the case. My books often surprise me while I am writing them. Characters rise up from unknown regions and begin to speak. Scenes grow as I write. Autobiographical novels and *romans à clef* exist, of course. Karl Ove Knausgård's *My Struggle* is a good example, but even he, a novelist who claims to have drawn only from his own life, does not actually remember the multitude of details he crammed into his life narrative. Few of us remember what was on our plate thirty years ago at a dinner party unless we were made sick by the oysters or one of the guests threw his baked potato at another guest. We forget the routine and remember the novel (which is how the novel got its name). The bad oyster or the flying baked potato, the unexpected, stands out in time. We remember what was emotionally potent.

But our autobiographical memories, the way we retain the past in the present, are foggy terrain. Our memories not only grow dim over time, they change. Freud used the word *Nachträglichkeit*, "afterliness," the idea that the present always informs the past. We cannot return to what was except through the lens of now. Memory scientists speak of *consolidation* and *reconsolidation*. Emotion consolidates memories—the amazement I felt when the baked potato landed on the dinner guest's head keeps it alive inside me—but the same memory is also subject to reconsolidation—change. We do not store memories in boxes in our brains and then remove them whenever we choose. The transformations of memory are complex and not fully understood, but it is well known that human beings may recall something that never happened or happened to someone else.

Rachel Aviv published an article about a gruesome case of misremembering in *The New Yorker* in June 2017. Ada JoAnn Taylor retains strong visual and tactile memories of smothering a woman to death. She confessed to the crime and spent nineteen years in jail before she was pardoned. She did not commit the murder. The police had shown her graphic images of the victim, pictures that remained in her mind and may have mingled with feelings of guilt to create a false memory. She is a person with a painful past, and she was perhaps more vulnerable than most to this form of memory distortion. But there is strong empirical evidence that every person's memory can be manipulated by social pressure. In 2011, Micah Edelson and fellow scientists at the Weizmann Institute published a paper in *Science*, "Following the Crowd: Brain Substrates of Long-Term Memory Conformity," in which they noted, "Participants exhibited a strong tendency to conform to erroneous recollections of the group, producing both long-lasting and temporary errors, even when their initial memory was strong and accurate." I suspect the mental imagery a person produces that conforms to what the crowd believes supplants the initial pictures. None of the people in the study wanted to misremember, but through the influence of others, their memory of the film they had seen and remembered clearly was forever altered. Autobiographical memories may be shot through with fictions.

In a 1995 essay called "Yonder" I wrote, "Writing fiction is like remembering what never happened." Twenty years later I returned to that sentence in another essay, "Three Emotional Stories," and elaborated on the idea. Why am I convinced that I am not inventing the story of a novel but unearthing it from memory? It is not, I hasten to add, because the events in my books actually happened. Further, I am not deluded. If a character in one of my books commits a murder, I know that no one has actually died. And yet, there is an important connection to be made between the dynamics of remembering and imagining, between past and future.

I am convinced that the labile realities of conscious autobiographical memory—the swarms of images we see in our minds accompanied by an emotional tone—and the act of imagining oneself in the future or composing a novel—which also generate mental images and feelings—are not distinct but part of the same activity. The novel and other forms of literature are the offspring of memory, and memory itself is subject to imaginative changes. When I remember the baked potato in the air, I have to travel back in time to the event at the dinner party, feel myself as I was then, sitting across the table from the victim, and recall my shock. I double myself in memory. I am here now writing in my study, but when I recollect that moment in the past, I am also there long ago watching the airborne potato. I know, however, that I am not identical to the young person I was then. I must become another to myself in order to remember. It is interesting to note that patients who have bilateral damage to the hippocampus, a part of the brain linked to both autobiographical memory and navigation, do not only have difficulties remembering—they also imagine poorly.

Novels do not pretend to be "true." So why do we read them? What does fiction give us that nonfiction doesn't? Can novels lie? Why do we care about them? When I am remembering what never happened, what am I doing? The truth I seek as a fiction writer is not a documentary record of the past. I am seeking emotional truth. The characters must behave, discuss, and think through their lives in ways that resonate for me as true. This truth has nothing to do with the nature of the events rendered. The characters could be gazelles with wings. Rather, my judgments are founded on a gut feeling, a sense of rightness and wrongness that guides me through a book. My feeling is conscious, but why I feel what I feel is not. I cannot explain why a character must die or why a plot must take one direction or another. That is unknown to me. But I know this: the novels I love, the books I carry with me through my life are all *true*. They are books that have made me see people and the world again from another perspective. They have changed my understanding of my own life. The novels I have forgotten are the ones that had no emotional impact on me. They were either so conventional that I felt I had read them before or they simply reinforced cultural truisms, and truisms are not truths.

When I write, I write for an imaginary other, an imaginary reader. Every story, every novel, is told or written for someone else. Language is at bottom dialogical. It happens between and among people. As the Russian theorist M. M. Bakhtin put it, "Every word is half someone else's." When I read novels, I am that other, the one who accepts the gift from the writer to me. Every book is invented, not only by the writer, but by its reader. We bring ourselves to books, our pasts, expectations, interests, tastes, prejudices, and limitations. Reading is a form of dialogue, an engagement with the textual other, words on the page that conjure a parallel world I actively imagine. For the duration of the book, I, the reader, am invaded by another consciousness, a narrator with whom I engage or disengage, whose rhythms become my rhythms, whose words are my words. The book's narrator becomes my internal narrator for as long as I choose to live inside the book.

Reading is a form of possession by another, and it is one that should not be taken lightly. Powerful books take control of our minds. They are not outside real life but part of life. And yet, through literature we are allowed to have experiences that will become memories, sometimes lasting memories, of events we might avoid if they were happening outside the novel. Would I want to witness the terrible murder in *Crime and Punishment*? Would I really want to run into Heathcliff walking across the moors? No. But inside what I have called the "aesthetic frame" of fiction I am not in danger of being physically harmed. This safety allows catharsis to happen. Why do we enjoy weeping over a novel but do not enjoy weeping over a dead friend? Why do people crave violent, frightening, and heartbreaking stories? These imaginative travels within the aesthetic frame can be emotionally and intellectually enlarging, can bring us excitement and high feeling without risk to life and limb.

The emotions stirred in me by Emily Brontë's *Wuthering Heights*, for example, that great novel that takes me beyond the human into the terror of natural forces I do not understand, a book with a structure so complex and diabolical I am stunned every time I read it are not feelings of safety. They push me beyond ordinary feeling. Books can be dangerous. They can threaten the status quo, shake us up, and turn us upside down. *Wuthering Heights* shocked its critics, most of whom believed it had been written by a man. One reviewer thought its author may have been a rough-hewn sailor. Repressive political regimes fear books. We know this from Nazi book burnings, from Soviet socialist realism—the prescribed mode of literary production under Stalin that gave us such literary works as *Cement*. We know writers were and are imprisoned and killed for what they write. Think of the Russian poet Osip Mandelstam. Think of Liu Xiaobo, the attack on Charlie Hebdo, on Danish cartoons, on *Huckleberry Finn* in school libraries in the United States, and the fatwa against Salman Rushdie. Hamsun's fascism or proto-fascism caused thousands of Norwegians to mail his books back to him. Literature worries people.

The outcry against the novel in eighteenth-century England was loud and vociferous. It was regarded as a pollutant that corrupted the minds of women and kept them from their duties as daughters, wives, and mothers by turning their thoughts toward sins of the flesh. The novel had a scandalous, masturbatory reputation and no doubt there were people, who, by some current definitions, would be regarded as addicted to novels. Today new technology, games, Twitter, Facebook, and the Internet in general are regarded as a cultural force that damages the minds of its users and has addictive power. When fear of new technology sweeps a culture, the alarm has sometimes included a new illness to explain it. In the nineteenth century, the advent of the train that caused human beings to travel at speeds unheard of before created a new diagnosis, "railway spine," which afflicted only people who had been in train accidents. Railway spine no longer exists, but Internet addiction does. It is a new sickness for a new age. I confess I am glad Internet addiction was not included in DSM-5, the recent edition of the *Diagnostic Statistical Manual of Mental Disorders*, the American psychiatric bible. I have a hunch Internet addiction will go the way of railway spine.

Is the future a place where reality will disappear and virtual reality will become the norm? Is the future of literature inhabited by robotic Internet addicts harnessed to their machines? Isn't that one of our frightening fantasies? And yet, isn't the novel also a form of virtual reality? I am not laughing off either compulsive reading of novels or Internet use. Both the novel and the Internet are purveyors of many kinds of fiction. If one takes fiction seriously, and I do, what one reads is important. We are not only what we eat; we are what we read. Reading becomes part of memory and imagination. Reading cereal boxes may be a good exercise for the child who is becoming literate, but later in life that list of ingredients will not develop his mind. The idea currently fashionable in the United States is that reading is a good in itself, that because children read too little, reading anything is a cultural victory, but this strikes me as dubious. What should we read now and in the future? It is commonplace to argue that there is good and bad literature, but how do we decide which is which? Is it always obvious?

I was educated largely on the literary canon, on a cultural consensus about what the great works of Western literature were at the time. I did not study Greek and Latin, but the mythos of classical greatness directed my reading. I dived for books I was told were important and worked hard to understand them. I do not regret reading Homer, Dante, Milton, Shakespeare, and Cervantes. I also read Holberg, Hamsun, Ibsen, Undset, Vesaas, Strindberg, and Nordic myths, tales, and sagas because I come from a Norwegian family and acquired a Nordic canon as well. It is also true that those canons of greats systematically excluded women with a few exceptions, as well as the works of writers who for racist reasons were not deemed significant enough to be part of the tradition.

The canon fell on bumpy times in the 1970s. It has since been revised in literature departments to include works that were once excluded. Many English students in universities are introduced to eighteenth-century writers, such as Delarivier Manley and Eliza Haywood, as well as the works of the former slaves Ignatius Sancho and Ottobah Cugoano, authors I had never heard of when I studied literature in college. Margaret Cavendish has found a place in both literature and philosophy departments after three hundred years of being ridiculed, ignored, or underestimated. These changes should be celebrated. And yet, we now live in a world where few texts are shared canonical texts.

Specialization has created a world in which conversations among educated people are fraught with difficulty because they do not read the same books. In an essay, "Excursions to the Islands of the Happy Few," I told a true story about sitting next to a neurologist on a plane. We chatted, and he told me about his fascinating work on Alzheimer's disease. During a pause in our conversation, he looked down at my lap and asked me what I was reading. I told him I was rereading Kierkegaard's *Either/Or*. He said, "Who's Kierkegaard?" I pretended not to be startled. After we had talked more about dementia, I asked him, "What do you think of mirror neurons?" Mirror neurons were discovered in macaque monkeys in the early nineties. They were and are a controversial topic among neuroscientists. He looked at me blankly and said, "What are mirror neurons?"

What does specialization mean for the future of literature? If a highly educated person, a doctor doing important research, doesn't know who Kierkegaard is and has never encountered mirror neurons, does it matter? Before World War II, there were privileged Europeans and Americans (by Americans I mean South and North Americans, not just citizens of the United States) who had read the same books of literature, philosophy, and science. There was still an idea of the educated man, and I do mean MAN, although there were a few women among them. Men of a certain class had access to elite educations. Niels Bohr read Goethe and Dickens with great passion. Einstein read Cervantes and Dostoyevsky and Madame Blavatsky. Sigmund Freud could recite Homer in the Greek by heart.

We cannot return to that world, nor would we want to. Knowledge has exploded and our access to it has become far more equal. And yet, are there certain texts within certain cultures that lots of people should read? Would this create greater cohesion among us as we wander into an unknown future? Undergraduates at Columbia University still read great books for a year. They begin with Homer, Aeschylus, Sophocles, and Plato. Augustine, Dante, and Cervantes follow. The year ends with Virginia Woolf. The only other woman on the list is Jane Austen, although some scholars believe that Homer could have been a woman or a group of women and men.

The past lives in the present, which informs our idea of the future. Ideas can be both insidious and omnipresent. You don't have to encounter them in books to be influenced by them. What has become clear to me is the degree to which Plato, for example, has shaped thinking in the West. Even if you have never read a word of him, your mind has been shaped in his image. Platonic thought became part of Christianity, and Christianity, even for non-Christians, has directed our thoughts for centuries in the West. Plato banned poets from his Republic. The reasons for the ban are complex, but his suspicions turned on his theory of forms. For Plato the real isn't available to our senses. It is hidden from bodily understanding. It is a static perfect world of truth. Poetry, and we can add fictions of all kinds, with their seductive sensual power, threatened to lure people away from this truth. Many contemporary physicists are Platonists. The "real" in physics rests on mathematical truths, not on human experience. I will not take this tangent further, but it helps to frame the question of a single writer's influence on contemporary thought. I think it is better to confront Plato on the page, to read and think carefully about the philosopher's words than it is not to read him and walk around ignorant of the manner in which that writer has *literally* helped "make up your mind."

The modern novel has long been associated with women, and women have long been associated with the body, emotion, and nature, the stuff that has been deemed low, messy, dirty in opposition to the high stuff, the mind, intellect, and culture, which are associated with men. Plato famously thanked heaven he was not born a woman or a slave. Aristotle described women as inferior beings and deformed males. I admit that I love reading Aristotle. I return to him often, but I am acutely aware that the Greeks, Aristotle among them, were misogynistic and their legacy is alive among us. The mind/body split haunts contemporary ideas just as it dominated Greek thought. It has haunted our literature for centuries and will continue to do so unless we actively counter its ongoing influence.

We are not, I believe, made of two stuffs, mind and matter. Our minds do not mysteriously hover over our bodies and somehow control them. I am not a Platonist or a Cartesian. Women are no more natural than men, but that truth does not prevent bias, does not alter the fact that messy corporeality is associated with femininity. There are still detractors of the novel itself, people who regard it as a form of light entertainment for women because women are its most ardent consumers. Real men read nonfiction. They chew over historical facts and explore the secrets of nature. And if real men read fiction, they read fiction by men to give it the comforting stamp of masculinity, to toughen up a weak, feminine, emotional, oh-so-sensitive form. And further, if real men are passionate about literature and consider themselves gatekeepers of seriousness and high culture, they are often driven by explicit or implicit prejudices against work written by women. And we women are not free of those biases either. The canon with its greats, among which women are scarce, cannot help but encourage in women feelings of inferiority, self-hatred, and sometimes despair.

Why, I often wonder, does it never stop? Why are books by women still disparaged or held to false standards? Why, for example, are books by women criticized if their protagonist isn't "likable"? Is Raskolnikov likable? Is Madame Bovary likable? Where did this criterion come from? I never see this criticism aimed at male writers. Why do novels with intellectual references and complex ideas written by women meet with resistance while similar books by men are championed as erudite and deep?

Social psychologists speak of precarious masculinity—the notion that although femininity is perceived as a stable, unchanging fact, masculinity must be proven over and over again. Masculinity is not a passive state of being. Having testicles and a penis and an Adam's apple are not enough. Keeping up masculinity requires constant action: eating steaks, not arugula salad; reading books by men, not women. It is odd that precarious masculinity should affect the reading of literature, but it does. Reading fiction by women means giving oneself up to the *authority* of a woman, and many heterosexual men find their self-worth in recognition from other men, not from women. The idea of submission to a woman, even if it is only her words, is repugnant.

This is nothing new, but something new has happened to the study of literature. When I was in graduate school in English in the late seventies and early eighties, nearly all of the professors and most of the graduate students were men. That has changed. Katherine Binhammer, a literary scholar and feminist, writes, "It is not without note that the study of literature has become feminized at the same time as it has become devalued." Feminized simply means there are more women studying literature now than men. In the United States, other disciplines such as medicine, psychology, and law have met with the same fate. As soon as women enter a field in large numbers, its status plummets.

And this returns us to past, present, and future, to the fact that we often perceive the world through habit, that no reader's understanding is free of perceptual biases because perception itself is guided by unconscious inferences about how the world works. Perception is conservative. I tasted bad milk, not orange juice. We do not take in the world as it is; we actively create it from patterns of the past and they include conceptual constructs that form our imaginations. Artists who are women have to deal with what I call "the yuck factor," a broad cultural acceptance that the body is feminine and the mind masculine, the intractable idea that literature by women is somehow less and more than work by men—more emotional, more personal, more autobiographical, but also less intellectual, controlled, and universal.

I will give you a stark personal example of this idea at work. A number of years ago, my husband and I were interviewed onstage in Australia by a literary journalist. When he introduced us, he turned to me and said, "I guess we can characterize your work as domestic." He then turned to my husband and said, "And we can characterize your work as intellectual." After gaping at him in amazement, I explained that

I disagreed with his blithe assessment, but my point here is that these frames of understanding—women write about domestic life and men write about the life of the mind—become part of a reader's perception. They are cultural fictions that drive how we read fiction. The actual content of my work did not seem to have affected this man's view of my books in the slightest.

Is the future of fiction going to be inhabited by robotic Internet addicts harnessed to virtual-reality machines that feed them the same clichés about masculine minds and feminine bodies that have been around since the Greeks? It has become abundantly clear that the biases of programmers have affected artificial intelligence. We cannot blame the machines for the faults of those who design them. The ever-deferred future of literature is not to be found in the algorithms of machines, as much as they may regurgitate the deep prejudices of the culture. The future of literature depends on readers and writers. Stupid literature, whether it's eighteenth-century anti-clerical French pornography or contemporary romance novels featuring young women and billionaires or self-help books that endlessly remind readers to love themselves, think positively, and work at their relationships or mediocre novels championed as works of genius by reviewers who are intimidated by any work they don't understand or think that writing fiction should follow a rule book, will not disappear. Nor should we fall prey to the idea that great literature lasts, that it floats to the top like a drowned corpse. I suspect there are countless important works that have been lost, suppressed, or misunderstood, that there are many Margaret Cavendishes and Eliza Haywoods out there who have not been reread and revived.

To return to the fundamental question: Why read novels? Reading is a form of self-expansion and, while I am glad the neurologist on the plane knows what he knows, I have come to believe that flexibility of thought is not gained by narrow specialization, that accountants, financiers, neuroscientists, and carpenters can find not only pleasure but knowledge in the novel. It is knowledge that comes from deep engagement with another life and its particular realities. The abstractions of philosophy have given me much, but they do not replace the immersive life experience I have found in reading *Middlemarch*, *Moby-Dick*, *Night-wood*, *Giovanni's Room*, or that great philosophical novel or novelistic work of philosophy, *Either/Or*.

When literature is merely easy entertainment, it cannot change you for the future. It cannot pull you out of the conceptual framework and learned patterns of your life as you live it. There is nothing wrong with easy entertainment. I have a weakness for Hollywood movies from the 1930s, and they don't have to be excellent to satisfy my craving. Nor do I think that literature is cod liver oil to be swallowed every morning for your health. It can, however, be like orange juice in your oatmeal. What the hell is this? This tastes wrong. Sometimes we resist books because they require reorientation. They make us uncomfortable and confused. What is to be done? Let down your defenses. Breathe deeply. Be open to what might happen. Art is like sex. If you don't relax, you won't enjoy it.

There is some irony, I think, in the fact that transformative novels are precisely those that break down the truisms of a given culture that many have come to take for granted, the platitudes that tell us that novels by women are domestic and novels by men are intellectual. Such truisms are often tainted by the fear of the other, whether it's woman or Black person or Muslim. I cannot help noting in this context that the current president [as of 2017] of the United States does not read any books, much less novels, and our former president read many books, including novels. The absence of literature in Trump and its presence in Obama are significant. Trump's anti-intellectualism reprises an old populist melody with verses that strike out at pompous elites and stuffy, effeminate types who sit around and drink sherry while they discuss incomprehensible books. The crude cliché is politically useful and shared by many people who do not belong to the political right. The easy ridicule, however, disguises a simple fact: Reading novels means you are willing to immerse yourself in the complex realities of other lives. It means you are curious and willing to engage in a form of pluralism. For me, the best novels are those that push me to take multiple perspectives with sympathy.

To read is to surrender yourself to someone else, to share a consciousness with a narrating other or several others for a time. A highly cultivated and well-read neuroscientist friend of mine once told me that when he is swept up in a work of fiction, it is sometimes too much for him. He feels he is losing himself, that the book is drowning his own thoughts, and he must withdraw to recover himself. I found this confession fascinating. Reading fiction does entail a loss of self in the other, a giving up and letting go. For a malignant narcissist, such a loss of self is not possible. What matters is seeing one's self endlessly reflected back in the adoring faces of the spouse, friend, or crowd. There is no dialogue in this hall of mirrors. The other exists purely to inflate the self. The other is a tool, a thing, an it, a vehicle, not an interlocutor.

Extreme narcissism cannot be cured with literature, but it is time to recognize the power fiction has to create new spaces of possibility in a reader, to extend and enliven thought. The future of literature is about far more than adding volumes to the library shelves or becoming refined people who have read that great woman writer or group of writers, Homer. I am arguing that the experience of complex novels with their plural voices and multiple points of view, with their characters who suffer and celebrate, who travel and come home or just sit in a room pondering, who are kind and cruel—these imaginary people can and do move us elsewhere in relation to real others. The foreign becomes familiar. Reading novels is not a solution to our political miseries. For that, organization, active resistance, and hard rhetoric are required. But we need stories, too, good stories with nuance and ambiguity that disturb our habits of thought.

Fictions can lie. The culture is shot through with corrosive fictions, with prejudicial narratives that circulate and entrap people and infect their ideas about what the future will or should be. I am not naïve. Some of the novels I love most have been and still are for the happy few. Reading a novel is an intimate experience, which may be another reason why some men who proudly announce they don't read fiction are in fact frightened by it. There have been, are, and will be readers who find themselves enchanted and changed by a truth discovered inside a book of fiction, inside a book that doesn't simply repeat cultural platitudes. There were, are, and will be people who open a book, read it, and by the time they reach the last page discover that they are no longer who they were when they began. And the book will live on in the reader's memory, not word for word, not exactly as it was written. It will mutate and change inside the person who read it, as all memories do, but its emotional power will remain, and it may shape her or his imagination for years to come. It may change the reader's ideas and feelings about how the world works and how she or he chooses to live in it.

2017

TRANSLATION STORIES

A German friend of mine once commented that I was lucky to have read the famously difficult philosopher Edmund Husserl in English rather than in the original. When I expressed surprise, he looked at me and said, "The translator had to make a decision." I laughed, but his insight has remained with me as brilliant shorthand for the difficulties that face the translator.

I have translated a few texts in my life—most recently something by the Norwegian poet Cecilie Løveid, whose work I have long admired. The poem, written in the first person, is about the fifteen paintings that comprise Gerhard Richter's series *October 18, 1977*, which is to say, the poem itself is a translation of a visual, emotional, and meditative experience into words. The painter, Gerhard Richter, created the canvases from newspaper images related to the radical terrorist group the Red Army Faction (RAF). When I first saw Richter's blurred renderings of the black-and-white photographs at the Museum of Modern Art in New York, I found them so moving and complex, I had to close my eyes every once in a while to keep my balance. I wrote about them in an essay called "Gerhard Richter: Why Paint?"

I'm not sure I did the Løveid poem justice, and I have second- and third-guessed decisions I made. The poet helped me. She even rewrote a line for the English translation.

My translation of a poem about paintings that have their origin in photographs of real people, three of whom—Andreas Baader, Gudrun Ensslin, and Jan-Carl Raspe—died in a high-security prison in Stuttgart on October 18, 1977, and another member of the group, Ulrike Meinhof, who had hanged herself earlier, reflects some of the murkiness that surrounds the very notion of translation. Arguably, Richter's paintings of photographs are visual translations, twice removed from their living subjects. Distance and ambiguity are vital to their effect, which are then reimagined with new forms of ambiguity in Løveid's poem, and are different again in English, a language with another rhythm and a more ample lexicon. The resonances possible in a language with relatively few words such as Norwegian do not exist in a vocabulary-rich language like English. The poetic possibilities in the two languages diverge.

Translation studies is an academic field that takes up questions of theory as well as application. For some time now there has been an ongoing debate about the philosophy and politics of rendering a text from one language to another. The two opposing positions have become known as "domestication" versus "foreignization." In his book *The Translator's Invisibility* (1995), Lawrence Venuti argues that domestication, rendering a fluid translation that reads "well" in the second or "target" language, can be a form of violence to the original or "source" text, a way of gobbling up its foreignness. The question turns on the problem of ethnocentrism versus ethnodeviance. Should a translation become *us* or should it remain *them*? This is not a new problem.

Friedrich Schleiermacher (1768–1834), the German theologian and philosopher, advocated for what would now be called foreignization. In a famous lecture, "On the Different Methods of Translation," he argued that there are only two fundamental approaches: "Either the translator leaves the author in peace as much as possible, and moves the reader toward him. Or he leaves the reader in peace as much as possible and moves the author toward him." (Translation by Susan Bernofsky.) Schleiermacher believed strongly in the first strategy, and he spoke from a position of authority. His translations of Plato are still read. I have repeatedly come across the fact that Gregory Rabassa adopted the Schleiermacher approach when he translated Gabriel Garcia Marquez's *One Hundred Years of Solitude*. I loved the book and the translation, but I had no idea he was an advocate of "foreignization." The Schleiermacher dichotomy is no doubt conceptually useful, but I have long been wary of poles. Is it always possible to know which acts of translation are foreignizing and which are domesticating?

Did I domesticate Løveid? I wanted the poem to sound "good" in English, but my reinvention couldn't be described as either "literal" or "free." I didn't want to betray the poem by adding words, for example, which would have made it sound more "natural" in English and at times given it a rhythmic flow that the original Norwegian has and my translation may lack. But isn't translation also an act of feeling, of the apt word that arrives suddenly from the translator's closeness to the text? Isn't it true that the "rightness" of a decision can often be explained only afterward, and sometimes not even then? It seems correct to say that I sometimes domesticated and sometimes foreignized the poem, that the two strategies coexist in the translation.

A poem is made only of words, but the reading of a poem is not made only of words—reading is an embodied act of felt rhythms and sounds and meanings in a person who lives in and is of a culture. That culture, of course, is not outside or inside the person but both at once. Habits and gestures vary from place to place, but they are embodied in cultural actors. And language is an expression of culture and of person in dialects and idiolects, in platitudes and original phrases. There is no private language. The other inhabits every word we think or speak. And language itself is translating experience into words for another, even when that other is one's self. After seeing Richter's *October* paintings, I had to try to translate what happened to me in front of them into a language my English reader could understand in the form of an essay. While translating Cecilie Løveid's poem, I was also trying to feel an experience embedded in her Norwegian words and convey it in English.

The translator is a reader who knows her source and target languages, and presumably something about the cultures of each, but she is also a person with a specific history, a person who breathes and eats and farts and thinks and finds some jokes funny and others not. The translator is not a machine. Although they have improved considerably, machine translations of the kind one encounters on Google Translate are often so egregious they become Computerese, which is to say, nonsense. I plucked an example from the Internet for a book I wrote on the mind-body problem, *The Delusions of Certainty*, which includes a critique of a model of the mind used in artificial intelligence research, now referred to as classical computational theory of mind (CCTM). I lifted the sentence translated by computer from a brief biography of Simone Weil in French: "The strength and clarity of his thought mania paradox grows logical rigor and meditation in then ultimate consequences." Foreignization as word salad. Computerese decodes and translates language by the disembodied method. The machine doesn't feel its choices. As I argue in the book, "If language were a logic-based system with a universal grammar that could be understood mathematically, then we should have beautiful computer translations, shouldn't we?"

Translation does not lend itself to the binary rigors of 0s and 1s. Then again, there are joys to be found in literal transfers from one tongue to another, as nimbly demonstrated in Fran Ross's 1974 novel, *Oreo*, reprinted in 2015 by New Directions. The book, itself a hybrid carnival of languages that mingles Yiddish, Ebonics, and the high diction of Academic-speak, follows its half-Black, half-Jewish heroine, Oreo, as she looks for her white Jewish father, a quest that mirrors the Greek myth of Theseus's journey into the labyrinth. On her way, Oreo meets Scott Scott, an American boy obsessed with the world's babble who speaks multiple languages in precise English translation. She has caught him on a French day. "Ten-eight," he says for eighteen [*dix-huit*]. "What is this that this is that you are so formal?" he asks her. [*Qu'est-ce que c'est que . . .*] "As his mother exploded from the kitchen with the tray of hors d'oeuvres, Scott rushed over to her, 'Permit me. The outside of works—*me*, I them will carry.' He took the tray from her. 'Rest you on that chair-long there.'" To which I say, adding to the mix, *wunderbar*.

Translation, more and less literal, is a form of intimate reading that calls for interpretation at the deepest level, which subsequently becomes a dynamic reality of ongoing choices. Husserl's writing is so dense and sometimes so opaque, the translator may inadvertently relieve the reader of what remains ambiguous in the German. I have often looked at the poems of Olav H. Hauge, a Norwegian poet I love more than any other, with the thought of translating them, but after working on a line or two, my inadequacy slaps me in the face, and I stop. Indeed, the impossibility and possibility of translation exists simultaneously, a seesaw of ups and downs. In an essay: "Emily Dickinson's Poetry: On Translating Silence," Margarita Ardanaz, who has translated Dickinson into Spanish, writes, "Emily Dickinson feels very comfortable on the edge of meaning itself." Dickinson's poetry is so radical that her first editors, Mabel Loomis Todd and Thomas Wentworth Higginson, domesticated both her English and her punctuation. The project of restoring Dickinson to herself is ongoing.

Some texts are much harder to translate than others—those with culturally laden comedy, eccentricity of expression, philosophical flights of a blurry character, puns, and, of course, irony. And yet, sometimes a translation choice opens up thoughts in a reader that might have remained closed in the original.

I discovered such an opening while I was working on a lecture in 2011. I was to deliver the 39th Annual Sigmund Freud Lecture in Vienna, and, although I had been reading Freud for many years, I had been reading him in English in the Standard Edition translation by James Strachey. When I sought out the German versions of the texts I was quoting, I discovered something interesting. In "Remembering, Repeating, and Working Through" (1914), Freud discusses how an analyst should deal with the patient's "compulsion to repeat." Strachey renders the German this way: "We admit it into the transference as a *playground* in which it is allowed to expand in almost complete freedom . . ." (my italics). The German word is *Tummelplatz*. There is no English equivalent. *Playground* suggests children, but *Tummelplatz* is not a place only for the young. It is a place of commotion, hurry, and lots of action. Freud also refers to the zone of transference between analyst and analysand as a "field of struggle" and a "battlefield." There is abundant evidence that he was not thinking of children playing when he used the noun *Tummelplatz*. Strachey's translation is an example of domestication. Had he used many English words to describe one German word, which I think Schleiermacher would have supported, Strachey would have rendered ponderous what is not and lost the lilt of Freud's prose altogether. He made a choice.

Playground was the word D. W. Winnicott, the English psychoanalyst and pediatrician, read when he encountered Freud's text. He had no German. And, although he never mentions it—he rarely cited the sources of his inspirations—Winnicott's theory of play was surely sparked by his reading of Freud's essay in English. There are further clues in Winnicott's work that demonstrate his close reading of the translation, including his use of specific phrases taken directly from Strachey's translation with few changes. Had Winnicott read *Tummelplatz* and not *playground*, who knows whether he would have come up with his rich theory of play that revised Freud's "intermediate region" of the transference as "potential space," a space that is neither inner psychic reality nor the external world. In my lecture, later published as an essay, I discuss Strachey's translation choice and pay homage to both the original and its translation that became fertile theoretical ground in the mind of an important reader like Winnicott. I called it "Freud's Playground."

An astute description of translation can be found in an essay by Paul Ricoeur: "Just as in a narration it is always possible to tell a story in a different way, likewise in translation it is always possible to translate otherwise, without ever hoping to bridge the gap between perfect equivalence and perfect adhesion. Linguistic hospitality, therefore, is the act of receiving the word of the Other into one's own home, one's own dwelling." ("On Translation," translation from the French by Eileen Brennan.) Translation is a way of welcoming the foreigner. It is a way of saying, "Come in and make yourself comfortable."

But the reader of a translation is also a foreigner, taken into unfamiliar houses and down streets that look nothing like home. When I think of all the books I could not have read without translation, all the experiences I would have had to forgo, all the thoughts that would never have occurred to me, all the places that would be forever lost to me, I shudder. My ongoing reading of Husserl may have been made lighter by some of his translators, but unlike Freud's German, Husserl's German is far too daunting for me to understand. And "his" English is quite hard enough. Some of the translations I read when I was young, Constance Garnett's *Anna Karenina*, for example, have been much maligned, but my first reading of Tolstoy's novel was passionate nevertheless. With some notable exceptions, translations grow old, and new ones replace them.

My own work has been translated into more than thirty languages, most of which I cannot read. I know some of my translators, but many of them I have never met. Some of them send me questions. Others don't. But they have all taken me in, and they have all interpreted and reinvented my words in their work. I often return to the King James translation of the Bible, that translation by a committee—forty-seven scholars, according to those in the know. Many of its decisions, accurate or not, have become rooted in English and marked us who speak the language forever. I have always loved the passage from Exodus, "I have been a stranger in a strange land." Writers, readers, and translators have all made that trip in one way or another. We have all been strangers in many strange lands.

2018

THE SINBAD VARIATIONS:
AN ESSAY ON STYLE

1. Her Sinbad: The First Voyage

I open the book, and she is inside it telling me stories.

Scheherazade is telling stories. Learned, clever woman, she is telling her husband stories to keep herself alive, to keep her head on her shoulders. The stories are her seduction, her power, her breath. *Listen to this one. This one is even better than the one before.* He is listening. I am listening. She stays alive one night and then the next night and the night after that. She is the voice in the dark telling me stories.

She is going to tell him about Sinbad the Sailor, but first, she tells him about Sinbad the Porter, weighed down by the loads he carries on his head in the scalding sun. "I carry heavy loads for light pay." Poor, panting Porter rests his weary body on a bench outside a rich man's house and sings.

The other Sinbad hears the song, and the first Sinbad meets the second Sinbad. There are two Sinbads: one poor, one rich. One will listen to stories. The other will tell stories. As he listens to the seven stories of the seven voyages, the poor man will get richer. One Sinbad gives the other Sinbad gold.

As he listens to his wife's voice in the dark, the husband will learn. He will become richer in knowledge. He will change. The wife's knowledge will become the husband's knowledge. One Sinbad becomes the other. Fortunes change.

Scheherazade said: *And then Sinbad said*, You must know, my noble guests, and you, O honorable porter, who bear the same name as myself, that I inherited a large fortune from my father and then I squandered it until I had almost nothing left, and so I set out to sea.

One day after weeks of sailing without seeing land, we happened upon a beautiful GREEN island and disembarked. We wandered about in the foliage, lit fires to cook our meals, washed our linens, and then, THE ISLAND CONVULSED.

This is the exciting part. Isn't it interesting that we all like to listen to stories about disaster? The story goes on in Sinbad's voice: We fell to the ground, and the captain shouted: SAVE YOURSELVES! THIS IS NO ISLAND! IT'S A WHALE! COME ABOARD! The whale LEAPT and SHUDDERED and then SANK INTO the SEA. Men DROWNED. But thanks be to Allah, I was saved by a piece of hollow wood, and I clung to it for dear life. All night and all day and all the next night, I BATTLED the sea and the wind and the fishes that bit my feet until I came to an island and dragged myself up its steep cliff.

Bruised and cut, I fell into a SWOON. I knew nothing. After countless hours, I woke up.

Poor, panting Sinbad. Hungry, alone, lost, he HOBBLED across the land and spotted a beautiful mare tethered to a stake and a man with her, a groom, who took the starved Sinbad into a cave and fed him. Thank Allah in heaven! Reversal of fortune! Sinbad lives!

As it turned out, the mare belonged to a king named Mihrajan, and this is the groom's story inside the story inside the story: *Every month at the new moon*, said the groom, *I bring a virgin mare down to the shore, tie her up, and run to hide in a cave. Before long, a sea horse springs from the deep onto the shore and mates with the mare. He does not want to leave her, but she is held fast and cannot escape. When I hear his whinnies, I run from the cave and drive him back into the sea. The mare becomes pregnant and, in time, she drops a foal worth a fortune.* When the groom stops speaking, Sinbad resumes his tale.

I, Sinbad, visited King Mihrajan and became his confidant. He preferred me to all others and loaded me down with treasures. Before long all the business of the kingdom had to go through me, and while I was in this foreign land, I saw and learned many wondrous things.

One day I was standing on the shore and a great vessel entered the harbor and began to unload its goods. "Is there anything else aboard ship?" I asked the captain.

"Yes," he said, "but those goods belong to a man who drowned at sea, Sinbad the Sailor."

"I AM SINBAD THE SAILOR!"

"Liar!" he cried, because he could not believe that a dead man was alive. But when I supplied him with details about the CALAMITY that only he and I could have known, he exclaimed again. "Allah has given you a second life!"

And that is how, said Sinbad the Sailor, I made my way home again to Baghdad, bearing with me in the hold of the ship great riches.

Sinbad falls SILENT.

And the listeners marveled at the tale.

And the porter marveled at the tale. And Sinbad the Sailor gave Sinbad the Porter a hundred pieces of gold and begged his namesake to return on the morrow.

And the next day Sinbad returned to Sinbad's great house, and he and the other guests ate and drank and listened to the music of lutes until they were sated and drowsy.

"And then, my husband," says the woman's voice in the dark, "and then, listen to what I have to tell you. Sinbad begins to tell another story, one more astonishing than the first . . ."

2. Rhyming Sinbad: The Second Voyage

And so, my friends, I lived a life of peace,
And yet, my itch to travel did not cease.
I bought a vessel and again I went to sea
To quench my curiosity
About the lands I'd never seen before.
We sailed for many weeks and went ashore
To trade and sell our goods, and all went well
Until the cruelest blow of fate befell
Me while I rested on the verdant ground
Of a deserted island we had found.
I slept soundly as a sweet wind blew
And woke to find them gone! No ship! No crew!
Sinbad the Sailor, left behind and lost!
I threw myself onto the earth and tossed
And raved and groaned and nearly went insane.
At last, I stopped. Your helpless cries are vain,
I thought, regrets won't change your destiny.
I wandered for a time, then climbed a tree
To get a look at what was there and spied
No one, just sky and earth and foaming tide.
But then I saw it, vast and white and round;
What could it be, that nameless, gleaming mound?
I clambered down the tree and made my way
To where the dome-like, hulking structure lay,
That oval thing with no identity.
And while I pondered on this mystery,

The sky turned dark; the sun had disappeared.
Above, I saw a flying form I feared,
A giant bird I'd heard about: a Roc.
My next deduction will not be a shock;
I'd stumbled on the mammoth creature's egg!
It came to nest on top of me; its leg
Was thick and gnarled and, frankly, frightening.
Now act, I thought, before it takes to wing.
I used my turban as a ready rope
To tie me to the monster's foot in hope
That when it flew, I'd also soar away.
I lay awake until the break of day,
And then it screeched and rose into the sky
And dropped to earth so fast I thought I'd die.
It left me stranded on a mountain peak,
A craggy, barren place, so harsh and bleak,
I moaned and wept again! And there were snakes!
Almighty God, I prayed, my mistakes
Are grave, and this ordeal I shan't survive!
I won't escape these vicious snakes alive!
And then I swooned and lost all consciousness.
No man can bear to suffer such duress.
But life is strange, and Allah chose to save
Me yet again. It's true I had to brave
More twists and turns on Fortune's winding road,
But hear! On that terrain I found a load
Of precious diamonds fit for twenty kings.
I traded them for goods and other things,
And bought my passage safely home to you.
I swear that every word I've said is true.
Tomorrow night, I'll tell another tale
To stupefy, delight, and turn you pale!

3. Academic Sinbad: The Third Voyage

Abstract

The Sinbad narrative is composed of a series of ten movements, each of which contributes to the story's overall structural identity. The Sinbad anatomy allows for the dissection of a single voyage, in this case, the third, according to the necessary unfolding of a sequence of events, which are common to all seven voyages and establish the characteristic dialectical tension of the Sinbad narrative as a dynamic of loss and recuperation, dreaming and wakefulness, near-death and resurrection. The particular adventures of the hero in the third voyage are here construed through the model of the ten narrative movements, without which Sinbad would not be Sinbad.

Keywords

Quiet, forgets, sea, lost, survive, fortune

1. *The hero embarks upon or returns from an earlier voyage and lives a quiet, opulent life of ease.* This inactive, unadventurous life at home frames all the voyages and serves as a contrast to what follows. After the seventh voyage this state of peaceful, luxurious living becomes permanent.

2. *The hero forgets the trials and tribulations of his previous voyage.* In order to travel again, this amnestic state is necessary and therefore precedes every voyage, with the exception of the first and the seventh that bracket the Sinbad text, which is itself bracketed by the larger text of *The Thousand and One Nights*. The text does not elaborate upon this memory loss in any detail, except that past adventures are often compared to dreams. Some form of amnesia antedates adventure in voyages two through six. During the ad-

ventures themselves, forgetfulness also punctuates the story and takes the form of swoons and a subsequent loss of consciousness, sometimes for several days. Memory loss serves as the indicator of narrative lapses—what cannot be contained in the story itself.

3.   *Hero voyages abroad with compatriots at sea and all goes well for a time.* In this phase, the hero visits many lands, increases his knowledge, and his trading business thrives. These facts are simply stated without detailed descriptions, as there is no opening in the narrative structure for long discourses on contentment.

4.   *The ship is lost.* With element four, the possibility of narrative variation is created. Elements one through three serve to establish the pacific ground for what must follow: disaster. With each subsequent voyage, the storytelling stakes are raised, that is, this element—loss of ship—should change in particulars. In the third voyage, the ship is overwhelmed by an army of apes, who carry the merchant sailors ashore and then depart with the vessel.

5.   *The hero has near-death experiences but survives his comrades.* This element is necessary to establish the hero, Sinbad, as blessed by fortune. In all seven voyages, many of his fellow sailors perish, and he is left alone with only chance and his wits to guide him. In the third voyage this element takes two forms: a hungry giant and a huge snake. A black giant with fiery eyes, tusks, deformed lips and ears murders the ship's corpulent captain, roasts him on a spit, and devours him in front of the horrified company of sailors. This is followed by the gourmandizing of another man the next day. Although the men band together and blind the giant with a hot poker, there are further deaths among the sailors when they attempt to flee on a raft they have constructed. The blind giant and a female cohort throw boulders at the raft, and subsequently only the hero and two others manage to escape. Sinbad's two comrades are summarily eaten by a snake, leaving the hero as the sole survivor.

6. *The hero despairs and laments.* The grief phase of the narrative is needed to establish Sinbad's humanity and bind him to the reader as, not godlike, but mortal, despite his unusual gifts for evading death. Distraught and alone, he is tempted to capitulate, but inevitably does not. In the third voyage, Sinbad contemplates suicide but, citing the preciousness of the human spirit, decides against it. At some moment in the despair sequence, he may lose consciousness. Time vanishes, and its movement cannot be articulated or included in the tale.

7. *The hero eludes death by an act of cleverness.* Sinbad shares this trait with the countless trickster figures in folklore, as well as with Odysseus. Although the hero may be buffeted by fate, he must also display an ability to outwit adversaries or think quickly in a desperate situation. In the third voyage, the hero fashions a wooden suit that prevents the snake from ingesting him.

8. *The hero recovers and augments his fortune.* Restoration follows the death-defying adventures that take up most of the textual description. The still-alive but abandoned hero is saved by a passing ship or is provided with one by new compatriots. He wakes from his nightmare, and the monsters and horrors of his adventure begin to take on an unreal quality, as if they had been a dream. In the first and the third voyages, the hero literally regains his lost fortune through a recognition scene (Homeric echoes). A ship's captain believing Sinbad to be dead is still carrying his valuable cargo and returns his goods to him, riches that are then usually increased by the booty he has acquired during his adventure.

9. *The hero returns home.* This phase, like the three elements of the preface phase, is related with great brevity and described in similar language near the end of every voyage. Sinbad arrives, bearing rich

cargo, is reunited with family and friends, and returns to his original state of peaceful luxury.

10. *The narrative frame is expanded at the end of the tale, and the reader is returned to Sinbad's house and the ritual storytelling.* Through this device memory becomes story. The survived past enters the present of the telling as entertainment for guests, which echoes the pleasures of the reader who has just taken in one tale and is ready for another.

Discussion

The Sinbad narrative is constructed as a sequence of necessary repetitions, which depend on the serial recitation of the ten defining movements, each of which is crucial to the dialectical tension of the story as a whole between amnesia and memory, dreaming and waking, loss and recuperation, despair and joy, abroad and home. Technically, the mechanics are eternal, that is, circular, and there is nothing in the form itself that augurs an end. Narrative closure is arbitrary because the end of one story can inevitably be the beginning of another. Therefore the Sinbad narrative, which relates a fantasy of immortality through the adventures of a hero who refuses to die, is structured as a perpetual motion machine.

4. Inner Sinbad: The Fourth Voyage

How did it begin? Vague stirrings in the belly, yes, always that. I would ask myself, what is it, this feeling? No, not the lamb or the grapes, not the memory of the lutes from the night before, not the perfume in my nostrils, but all of it, sweet and dull and familiar. She, too, dull, her face stupid and swollen in the morning light. Yes, it began like that, and I have felt it before, the same restless need to stop the wheel from turning as it always turns, day and night, day and night and the moon growing and waning in her predictable rhythms. And then the memories of other skies, of winds and standing at the bow of the ship, fat with my goods, my treasures. Why did I forget the torments? They dissolved to nothing. Traitor soul.

Bassora was cloudless that day. The sea smells . . . kelp, salt. The deck under my feet and the quiver of pleasure. I am master of all this, I, Sinbad, and the shouts from the men as we sail out. Bartering well. Oh yes, clever devil. One night, worlds away. What was that instrument? What did they call it? Its high whine, but those days have merged now . . .

It was the storm that changed everything, the heaving first, then the thunderous booms of wood cracking at its seams. Men bellowed, howled as they dropped. I was drowning, choking, and then a plank from the hull, broad and rough, but floating. We seized it, half-dead. The hours of terror, holding on, paddling. How many were we? I can't remember. It was still night when we beached and slept on the sand, indifferent to the rough grains, our torn clothes, the blood from our wounds, our hunger. I slept. Dreamless hours of nothingness.

The building seen first in the morning as the sun rose pink—a tall structure above foliage and trees. The men seemed to come from nowhere, a crowd of silent black men who surrounded us before we were fully awake. The odor of the hall. Meats? Oils? Herbs? My disquiet then, a tightness in my throat, quickened breath. Their naked monarch on his high throne. His unintelligible eyes. And they brought us the curious-looking meats on large platters in silence, meat for starving men. And why didn't I eat? What prevented me? Was it the king's face, that empty expression? I did not eat. But my comrades ate and ate and ate in a gluttonous stupor, bit, chomped, chewed, drooled. Oh, the dreadful sounds of smacking, moaning, and sucking in my ears. What enchantment, what herb had wrought this? Before me their skins ballooned; my fellow travelers turned into fleshy monsters, unbearable strangers, and with each bite, their minds shrank. I watched as they turned into speechless imbeciles, gnawing at bones. They brought the ointments then, didn't they? After hours of gorging, my bloated comrades allowed themselves to be greased with a thick yellow unguent. And I, a frail ghost, withdrew, and no one seemed to see me. And how was it I knew that my shipmates would be eaten raw? A blank in time? Yes, a blank.

I understood, but my horror and hunger had made me dizzy. I have lost the moment of knowing.

My bloody feet moving forward, away. I walked. Breathed and walked. On the eighth day, I saw the men. O joy, the first real food and the sound of my own language like a balm, and the bed where I slept, a stone's sleep. The motion of the ship, my cradle, as we sailed to their king. And then, yes, the luck of the saddle. Imagine, they had no saddles in that country, horses but no saddles, and, with this ignorance on their part, I made my fortune. Those good, sunny days. At the king's command, I married her. She had everything, my wife, money and beauty and a musical voice I liked to hear in the morning and long into the evening.

There is no story when the seas are calm, no story when the marriage goes smoothly, when life moves along day to day.

His calm voice droned on about the law of the land. No one was exempt. How was it possible? Barbaric, unjust custom: Why bury a living spouse with a dead one? Fate turns in circles, around and around. Oh, why had I left home? Her dead face on the pillow, and they would bury me alive with her. Insane law.

The sound of my wails in my ears as they tied me with ropes. The indifference in their eyes. Lowered into the well. Seven loaves of bread and a jug of water, my only accompaniment. Seven loaves, seven seas, seven voyages. Sinbad, seven times, Sinbad.

The corpses, old and new. Bones, rotting skin, and stench. What madness was this? The memory of that underground, of life with the dead—my ululations in the murk—and then, the change . . . Sinbad as beast, barking dog in his prison beneath the earth. I killed them as they came into the hole, the living dead, and I stole their bread and water. I killed them to go on living. And I stole their gold and their goods and their clothing, in case I found my way out. Jewels on skeletal fingers and hung around necks, a nightmare of glittering fragments as I lie here, remembering. But then it wasn't I. Not I, not me, no words for that bestial being driven to live, just to live, just to be alive.

I woke to the sound of its breath and then heard its running feet, another animal alive in the cavernous room, and I chased it through a fissure in the rocks into the light and found an exit.

I came home. I, Sinbad, with a name again, with a voice to speak again. Repetition. Home again. I came home again to tell the story again. I came home again, but not for good, not yet for good . . .

5. Cinema Sinbad: The Fifth Voyage

OPENING CREDITS
A series of brilliant abstract images in undulating colors—shades of blue, green, and yellow, but also reds, oranges, and streaks of black that evoke motion, water, excitement, and peril, followed by a monochromatic blue screen.
  Dissolve to:

INT: SINBAD'S HOUSE, MEDIEVAL BAGHDAD—NIGHT
We see an ornately decorated room with burning incense and glimmering oil lamps. Guests lounge on tapestry cushions in violets and reds with

gold accents as servants bring in silver dishes heaped with fruits, dates, and steaming meats. An old man with a white beard, Sinbad, rises from his chair, and the room falls silent.

SINBAD

And so it was, my friends, that the good life at home began to feel monotonous. Yet again, I felt a yearning for the open sea, for salt and wind and adventure. I set out on my fifth voyage.

EXT: AT SEA—DAY

A turbaned younger Sinbad with a short brown beard stands at the bow of a ship, wind rippling his clothes. Cobalt blue sky, a few cumulus clouds, turquoise water.

EXT: CROWDED, VIVIDLY COLORED, NOISY MARKET—DAY

Sinbad is trading goods. He grins at the FOREIGN MERCHANT and bows deeply. We see him receive a heap of gold coins.

EXT: BEACH OF AN ISLAND—DAY

A view of the ship anchored near a broad white beach. Deep green palm trees and foliage stick up from beyond the sand. Flanked by several trees is an immense pale pink egg, surrounded by the tiny figures of several men. Camera zooms in for closer shot:

FIRST MERCHANT SAILOR

Any thoughts?

SECOND MERCHANT SAILOR

Better safe than sorry!

Second merchant pulls out his sword and begins to slash the egg. His comrades join in. A thick yellow liquid oozes from the cuts in the egg's shell, leaking onto the bodies of the men, who look up with startled faces as a huge, wet, fledgling bird slowly emerges from the egg, and the cracked pink shell falls to pieces around them. A jagged eggshell cuts a merchant, who howls as red blood pours down his tunic, blends with the yolk stains, and turns orange. A man rushes the bird's leg and hacks at it with his knife. The bird emits a harrowing cry and falls to the ground. It flails as the men jump on it, cutting and hammering until the broken bird lets out a single last scream and dies.

EXT: SHIP'S DECK—DAY
The bruised, bloody, and yolk-stained men clamber onto the ship. Sinbad eyes them with a worried look. Suddenly, the enormous shadow of a bird falls over the vessel. Sinbad looks up at the sky with an expression of horror.

SINBAD

Rocs! Allah save us! You've killed their offspring!

Camera tilts upward to a view of the sky, where two gargantuan black birds fly with enormous boulders in their claws. One roc lets its weapon drop. Its trajectory is followed back to the ship, where the captain is at the helm shouting orders. The boulder just misses the ship. A giant wave smashes onto the deck. Men fight to hold on. Some fall overboard. The second boulder falls, hits the stern. The tiller splinters to pieces, crushing several crew members, who bellow in pain. Blood mingles with water as the ship sinks. The head of the captain bobs above the water, his face contorted in agony. He vanishes below the waves.

EXT: AN ISLAND BEACH—DAY
Sinbad, disheveled, exhausted, bleary-eyed, is hugging a wooden plank that washes up to shore. He throws himself onto the beach, closes his eyes, snores.
    Dissolve.

EXT: ISLAND—DAY
Sinbad, looking much restored, bites into a bright orange fruit. Behind him are blue, purple, and red flowers. Light green parrots chatter in the tree. A wide stream flows in the foreground. A crooked old man ap-

pears from between the trees and beckons to Sinbad to take him across the stream. Sinbad puts him on his shoulders and carries him across, but when they arrive at the other side the old man will not let go. He squeezes his thighs into Sinbad's neck. Sinbad gasps; his eyeballs bulge. The old man takes out a whip and beats Sinbad.

EXT: ISLAND—DAY
The old man sways back and forth on Sinbad's shoulders as he takes deep swigs from a gourd.

SINBAD (*tears streaming from his eyes*)
I am not a slave! You must let me go!

OLD MAN (*slurring his words*)
You will die under me, wretch!

With a single swift movement, Sinbad grabs both legs of the old man, throws his captor off his shoulders, seizes hold of a large rock, and smashes the old man with it. Blood and brains run onto the ground. The camera pulls back farther and farther into a long shot of the island.

SINBAD (VO)
For days he had tortured me, had pissed and shat on me. I saved myself by getting him drunk. May his bones rot. Some days passed. I knew not how or when I would ever escape and then, as luck would have it, I boarded a passing ship and traveled with the crew to the Sea of Pearls, where a fortune glittered before my eyes.

EXT: UNDERWATER—DAY
Turquoise surface of ocean seen from below.
Dissolve.

MONTAGE
Sequence of multicolored pearls underwater appear on the screen.

SINBAD (VO)

And I returned home, dear friends, on that same vessel laden with riches, and I lived a good contented life until one day . . .

Fade to Red

6. Hard-Boiled Sinbad: The Sixth Voyage

It was around one o'clock on a steamy afternoon in Baghdad when I got the urge. It felt like some no-good dame had just sidled up beside me in a bar with a pair of scarlet lips and those eyes that keep looking down at something that isn't there. Trouble can look pretty good. Still, I told myself, there have to be some missing brain bits in a guy who lolls around his eighteen-room shack counting his money and decides to throw it all up for a jaunt at sea. Too bad I was that guy.

The captain's name was Haroun, a lean-jawed, heavy-lidded customer, whose voice sounded like a clogged drainpipe. The crew seemed tough enough. Their faces looked like well-seared flank steaks and they smelled like fish guts. The ship sailed along as smoothly as a seasoned card cheat for eight days. I made a smart deal in port with a withered old boy whose fingers were so nervous they made me think of a troupe of down-and-out dancehall girls who never learned their steps. I should have known Haroun wouldn't make it. Behind that steely mug of his was a panicky kindergartener who howls for Mama when she walks out the door.

The sky had an iron tinge. The wind came up hard and loud, and I could hear the waves crack at the hull like a prizefighter gone berserk. Haroun's face went pale under his sunburn. His mouth dropped open. He let out a long croak and got religion faster than a nutcase at a revival. We were headed straight for an ugly cliff the size of Everest. I looked up. The rudder crumbled like one of those dry little biscuits at a ladies' tea.

Things weren't pretty after that. A lot of underwater praying went on, most of it useless. A few of us managed to drag our carcasses up onto the rocks, but the place had nothing to offer, except more rocks. Rubies, emeralds, diamonds, gold, silver, the works. But those goodies can't do much for men who have holes in their bellies and aren't going anywhere. One by one, my pals dropped out of the competition, permanently. The last three succumbed to a gut ailment that made dysentery look like a bout of flatulence. After I had tucked them in for their everlasting naps, I got sore, I mean really sore. I'd been marooned before. I'd played the sucker before. But this time I was in deep. I started to dig a pit I could roll into when the big man in the sky gave me the final shove.

With my mitts full of sand, I thought I saw something. My eyes caught a few hundred shards of light about ten yards up the crags. Water, not ocean water, a river headed straight into the rock. It was a chance. Not a good chance, but a chance. With a boat, I could follow it. The raft I built looked about as sleek as an unshaven, unzipped drunk taking a snooze in the gutter, but then I wasn't aiming for maritime elegance. I loaded my handicraft with the biggest and best baubles, grabbed a couple of planks for oars, and pushed off. The thing moved all right. I felt like I'd been shot out of a .38. I ditched the oars quickly and threw myself down flat. The raft smacked the boulders on either bank. My ears exploded. Lights shuddered over my head, then blackness, then light again. The tunnel narrowed. Boulders jutted on either side. I cursed myself. A flash of pain sliced through my head. I saw sparkling circles, round and round, a blast of nausea just above my ribs, and then nothing.

It's hard to say how long I was out. It felt like a year, but between my shaky eyelids I saw blue. Then a face poked into the scene. It looked friendly enough, if a little pointy and bug-eyed. You're still dreaming, Bub, I said to myself. But the mouth on the face began to jaw and words came out of it—something about him being a farmhand. I was lying on my back in a meadow. Woozy, I arranged my elbows and pushed. No hallucination: A couple of yards ahead my raft was tied to the riverbank along with every last bag of stones. After my farm buddies had come up with a lamb sandwich, a smoke, and some new duds, I guessed I could pass for human. The island went by the moniker Serendib, and its king was one of those silky types with a drawl that made me think of a cat slinking past a window. The big guy had an errand for me in Baghdad, a neat little bit of diplomacy with the Caliphate. It came off without a hitch, and I toddled on home, to rustle around the old shack and study my rock collection. Some guys just get lucky.

7. Scheherazade's Sinbad: The Seventh Voyage

You're mine, Sinbad. Well, you're mine now, even though I listened to murmurs about you when I was a girl. The woman who dressed me in the morning and undressed me at night and fanned me in the heat before I slept had heard tell of Sinbad, and she liked to whisper in my ear about your adventures, and so when the time came, you sailed into my own stories, a man after my own heart, a man who lives by his wiles and his good fortune, a man who won't die, a teller of tales with seven lives, a life for every night.

I had to keep my king and master listening, after all, and for six evenings I had held him rapt with you, my dear, resilient character, reborn near the end of every voyage. From inside the story you couldn't have known that I was your breath and your voice. Even though every man is born of a woman, men like to forget this uncomfortable truth. Still, I am your mother, your author. My own travels have always been journeys into the minds of others—poets and philosophers, Sassanid storytellers and court gossips. But I didn't want my husband to grow weary of you, and so I knew the seventh voyage would be your last. After that, I would leave you to live out your life in comfort and the sweet slowness of old age. Your taste for adventure had turned bitter on your tongue, but you were bound by duty, as was I, and when the Caliphate called on you to venture out yet again to Serendib, you could only submit, despite the grief you hid with a smile when you left your family and friends.

I equipped the ship well and sent you off with gifts for the king of Serendib, treasures that made my husband's eyes shine—a scarlet bed and two others, a hundred silk robes, a vase of white carnelian, and more, of course. There was always more. You carried out your mission perfectly, as was to be expected, as the story demanded. That is part of the pleasure: the expectation that the tale will take a particular form. The sun shone down upon Sinbad the Sailor until the day the sky went dark and a storm shook the ship's hull and the rain fell hard and fast. When I saw my husband lean back and close his eyes, I moved from the third person into the first, Sinbad, and my voice changed and deepened as I spoke, so he would hear you speaking directly to him.

As the torrent fell, the captain climbed the mast to survey the land and sea and returned with a despairing face. Then he carefully opened his sea chest. From it he took a bag filled with a powder, sniffed a bit of this ashy substance, removed a little book from the chest, and began to read. The enchanted book confirmed his fears. We had drifted into waters near the Clime of Kings where fishes and serpents of a size unheard of elsewhere gobbled up vessels as if they were bits of kelp. And while we stood on the deck aghast at our coming fate, we felt the ship rise high up on the crest of a mountainous wave and then drop suddenly. An unearthly cry came from the deep, and I saw a sea monster before us. Then another, even larger than the first, and finally a creature so enormous its body parted the waters into two great shelves of sea. This last fish opened its jaws and, in a single gulp, consumed nearly the whole of our ship. The stern where I was standing lurched violently upward, and I leapt from the side. With the waves churning around me, I watched the vessel vanish into the black innards of the monster.

Sinbad, my husband liked hearing about these horrors. People do. I gave you a floating plank again, materials to build a raft again. Then I nearly sent you over a precipice to your death, but saved you at the last instant with a fishing net. You had to be fed and clothed again. I gave you a kind old man who offered you his daughter in marriage. I made you humbler, wiser, and even richer. The old man died, and you inherited his wealth. The winged men came to me all at once as part of the very last adventure, a small tale of hubris for my husband's benefit. Every spring, the men in that country grew wings and soared in the skies, and you took a ride with one of them and were so moved by the heights and your proximity to heaven, you called out to Allah. At the sound of the name, however, our birdman plummeted downward and you fell with him. I saved you again. Even kings do not control their fates. Accidents, sickness, wars intervene. We are not gods. But I am the storyteller, Sinbad, and I have kept you alive from one voyage to the next, and I have sent you home after each trip to sea. But you, my beloved creature, along with all the others, have kept me alive, too. The threat of death drove my words. We need stories to mold our worlds, to string our lives together with the wishes and ghosts and fantasies that do not stop until we die.

8. The Hypothetical Eighth Voyage: A Dialogue Between Wife and Husband

A: Why don't you and I write an eighth voyage for Sinbad? The formula is there. We could tweak it a bit if we wanted. It might be fun, an adventure in marital collaboration.

B: Can't be done. Eight is a pedestrian number. Seven, on the other hand, is magic: seven leagues, seven swans, seven dwarves, seven voyages. Even numbers can't compete with odd ones. Don't you think an eighth voyage would be inelegant? Numbers have personalities that must be respected.

A: I hadn't realized you were so conventional. Where is your insurrectionist Dada spirit, your love for blasting apart the expected? Why are you smiling? I know we could do it. Maybe it's time for you to pay attention to the ignored and stomped-upon number eight and bring out her somewhat withdrawn personality.

B: *Her* personality?

A: Don't tell me it isn't perfectly obvious to you that eight is a woman. Have you never studied the shape of that number? Those two round forms, one on top of the other, does that look like a man to you? Eight has a positively voluptuous appearance. There's an idea. In the eighth voyage, Sinbad becomes a woman!

B: That's not tweaking the formula. That's destroying it. As a woman Sinbad wouldn't be able to set foot on a ship.

A: In the sixteenth century there was a woman, Sayyida al-Hurra, who became prefect of Tetouan in Morocco and conducted piracy raids on Spain. So there you have a woman pirate. There were others, too. In the eighteenth century, there were multitudes of woman pirates. Well, multitudes may be an exaggeration, but lots of them. They disguised themselves as men and headed out to the high seas for plunder and infamy. What about this idea? Sinbad stays home after his seven trips, but his daughter dons men's clothing and takes the ship out for an eighth voyage. It would continue the narrative theme of survival because children and grandchildren and great-grandchildren are the route to a kind of immortality, aren't they? The circle of the generations, birth and death and then another birth?

B: Yes, I suppose that might work, but no piracy. Sinbad was an honest merchant, clever but not wicked, and his daughter must be *cut from the same cloth, a chip off the old block*. I like those clichés. The scissors moving across a piece of muslin, the knife whittling a block of wood . . .

A: Yes, I agree, but let's go back to the story. She needs a name. How about Sinbadia? That's a chip whittled off the old block, isn't it? The beginning writes itself. Sinbadia sets off with her crew and for a time all goes well. She makes piles of money, the weather is fair, and the winds are good.

B: And then one day, the wind stops blowing. The ship doesn't move. The sea is an unruffled pool for days on end. Captain Sinbadia feels the crew grow restless and unhappy, possibly mutinous. They begin to run out of food and supplies. Starvation is imminent . . .

A: That's good, but we need a supernatural element now. A leviathan or a roc.

B: Too many rocs already.

A: I love the rocs and their huge eggs. I love the fierce defense they mount to protect their fledgling rocs.

B: No rocs.

A: Okay, what do you suggest?

B: A giant, not any giant but a gargantuan man rising up out of the sea. He is so big he can wade into the ocean's depths, and it comes up only to his waist, and when he takes a breath, he changes the weather. His inhalations create a tremendous suction that pulls everything for miles around him toward his nose, and when he exhales, the winds blow at high speed. At first, when the creature is still at a distance, the unknowing crew welcomes the sudden breeze that pushes them in the direction they want to travel. The ship begins to move again, and the captain and her men celebrate, but the closer the monster comes, the stronger the gales, blowing first one way and then the other . . .

A: That's good. Your giant reminds me of the Goya painting *Colossus*. Over at the Prado, they're now saying it was painted by someone else, a man named Arsenio Juli who knew Goya, but the picture is wonderful whoever painted it, and maybe it inspired you unconsciously. Anyway, I like the giant. As the colossus nears the tiny ship, he breathes in and out, and his vast quivering nostrils create a whirlwind. The ship is tossed back and forth. It begins to groan and creak. Sinbadia and the men aboard the ship are terrified as the giant approaches, his massive form darkening the sky. The mast snaps in two, and then the monster picks up the ship in his mammoth hand and crushes it as if it were a . . .

B: A matchbox.

A: A matchbox? How about a cracker? Or a wafer, or maybe a potato chip to continue the chip business. Maybe the giant feasts on ships, no, on the crew. He has a taste for raw human flesh, gobbles down those poor men like so many sardines.

B: Fine, but the ship can't be crushed like a sardine. They're oily. A matchbox is wooden and hard and cracks as a ship would. We'd have to work on the metaphors, but let's say the giant munches on the crew. That's suitably horrible. Sinbadia watches the monster's blood-filled mouth open, and she looks into his maw and at his stained teeth, huge yellow bicuspids and molars framed by red gums. He licks his lips . . .

A: And our heroine leaps from his great lumpy tongue into the roiling waters below.

B: She grabs hold of a plank. Then she faints.

A: Faints?

B: Yes, she faints.

A: Women are always fainting in books and movies. Can't we keep her awake?

B: Sinbad is a swooning hero. Do you want to alter an essential part of the story? She is *in extremis*. The faint stands in for death—it's a corpse-like state, a small death.

A: I thought orgasm was the little death: *la petite mort*.

B: Are you trying to derail my thoughts? Do you want to turn Sinbadia's voyage into an erotic tale? That could be done easily, you know. Sinbadia the Sailor: the famous voyage of a bawdy wench whose lusts are legend, a bad girl with a taste for sin, a strumpet on the sea, a ribald, randy dame with an appetite for manly flesh. By the way, is that a new blouse?

A: Do you like it?

B: It shows off your beautiful little breasts. Shall we pause from our creative labors for little deaths?

A: Later, dear, later. Enough of sinning and badness for the time being. We have come to a crisis in the narrative, but not *that* kind of crisis. I accept that she has lost consciousness. She drifts ashore, where she wakes up on a beach, alone under a burning sun. Her body is battered and bruised, her clothes torn. She cries out for help but there is no answer . . .

B: In a movie, her clothes would be strategically torn so the viewer could savor her heaving breasts and long wet tangled hair as she lies seductively on the white sand . . .

A: This is not a movie, and we are not engaging in sexual voyeurism.

B: You started it with your idle talk of little deaths. Besides, all stories are voyeuristic. That's the pleasure of them, isn't it? The listener or reader experiences danger, misery, and passion from a safe distance. Children love stories, even gruesome ones, especially when they end well, as all fairy tales do, at least for the hero and heroine. *And they lived happily ever after.*

A: I am interrupting our discussion for a quotation test. It's relevant: "Reader, I married him. A quiet wedding we had: he and I, the parson and clerk, alone were present." Where is it from?

B: It's famous, that's all I know.

A: Charlotte Brontë's *Jane Eyre*, the first sentences of chapter 38. You never read that novel, did you?

B: No. I started it once, but it wasn't for me. What does Jane Eyre have to do with Sinbadia? Must you always wander off on tangents? Are we marrying off Sinbadia already? She hasn't even found her way off the island.

A: Tangents? Tangents? Who turned our heroine into a pornographic harlot lying on a beach? Did I do that? Isn't it possible to have a female protagonist who is not an object to be possessed but the subject who possesses, not a passive being but an active one? That's the whole point of the eighth voyage. She, Sinbadia, is the story, not the delectable tidbit the hero indulges in along the way, not the reward at the end of the story, not the thing that's sold off in marriage!

B: You're shouting.

A: I am not shouting!

B: Darling, where is your sense of humor? Don't you know when I'm teasing you? We're playing with a story. It's supposed to be fun.

A: There's no fun if it's not serious. There's no fun if the stakes aren't high. No one cares if the story is just a joke because comedy, too, must explore deep human themes. Think of Shakespeare. Think of *The Merchant of Venice*, a comedy that's also tragic. Think of Portia. She disguises herself as a doctor of law to argue in front of the court and save Antonio. No one in the play matches her brilliance.

B: And who is the undisguised genius of *The Thousand and One Nights*?

A: Scheherazade.

B: "And the king agrees to listen to her. She begins her story, and what she tells is a story about story-telling, a story within which are several stories, each one, in itself, about story-telling—by means of which a man is saved from death." Who wrote that?

A: Paul Auster. *The Invention of Solitude.*

B: You win the quotation prize.

A: We tell stories to stay alive.

B: We tell stories because without them there is no life that we can understand.

A: Our life together is a story or rather a collection of stories that we tell ourselves about ourselves, and we keep rewriting them as we go along. Your story of us is not the same as my story of us, however.

B: No, because we are different, and we see the world differently.

A: Still, we can agree on this: You and I are going to keep Sinbadia alive, so she can go home and tell the story to her children.

B: Where did the children come from?

A: At some point, my love, we're going to have to marry her off, you know, so that she can have children to tell her story to. That's very important. That's how stories stay alive.

B: Who's the lucky guy?

A: The husband, you mean? Oh, some kindhearted, docile character with a good sense of humor, a man who loves children; a writer, maybe. If he's married to an adventuress, it's best that he stays at home a lot, scribbling away in his notebook.

B: Someone like me.

A: Or me.

B: All right, she'll marry someone like us, and then maybe after her voyage and after she has her ten children—

A: Five, five children.

B: After she has her five children, Sinbadia will stay at home and write her memoirs about how she fought and killed the behemoth on the island, a furious beast with eight arms and eight legs and fingernails like knives, and discovered the treasure it was hiding in its cave, just before she was saved by a passing ship and fell in love with the writer who happened to be on board . . .

A: It sounds good. I like the eight arms and legs, but maybe she should have some affairs before she gets married. What do you think?

B: I think you're a devil.

A: But a nice devil, with a sense of humor.

B: Reader, she has affairs before she marries him, but then, once wedded, the two of them live happily ever after. Is that how it goes?

A: No, I'm afraid they fight.

B: They fight?

A: Oh yes, they fight all the time because they see the world differently, but then they forgive each other for being different and go back to writing their stories.

B: But they take time out for little deaths.

A: They take time out for their little deaths and for all the cuddling and jostling and slobbering that comes before their crises, because life is not worth living without those little deaths, the ones that we survive.

B: The End.

A: *La Fin.*

B: Are you insisting on the last word?

A: Yes, are you going to give it to me?

B: Yes.

2011

HE DROPPED HIS PEN

Jane Austen's *Persuasion* begins with a boring man reading a boring book: "Sir Walter Elliot, of Kellynch Hall, in Somersetshire, was a man who, for his own amusement, never took up any book but the Baronetage . . ." The catalogue of British nobility, "always opened" to the page on which Sir Walter's own aristocratic lineage is reflected back at him, serves as a neat summary of the man's repugnant narcissism, but it is also a brilliant introduction to a central problem of the novel itself, which turns on the power of words to move human beings to action. From the start, we know that the patriarch of *Persuasion* is a man of inaction, a person literally stuck on the same page.

And yet, it is in the Baronetage entry—ELLIOT OF KELLYNCH HALL—that the reader of *Persuasion* first encounters its heroine, squeezed between an older sister, Elizabeth, and a stillborn, might-have-been-heir younger brother, followed by another daughter, Mary: "Anne, born August 9, 1787." Six paragraphs later, the second daughter of Sir Walter and the now deceased Lady Elizabeth reappears: ". . . but Anne, with an elegance of mind and sweetness of character, which must have placed her high with any people of real understanding, was nobody with either father or sister, her word had no weight; her convenience was always to give way—; she was only Anne." The painful question of *Persuasion* is: How can the words of a person treated as nobody exert any power in the world?

For many of her contemporaries, Austen's title would have summoned the art of rhetoric, which Aristotle defined as "the faculty of discovering in any particular case the means of persuasion." But before the ancient philosopher, Austen's readers would probably have thought of the New Rhetoric, which combined classical rhetoric with the ideas of the eighteenth century and expanded it to all forms of discourse, including poetry and fiction. The New Rhetoric was not purely an art of oratory but also one of written texts. It addressed an expanding print culture and its growing numbers of literate consumers of books. In his influential *Philosophy of Rhetoric*, published in 1776, George Campbell, a Scottish minister and academic, made the argument for four distinct forms of discourse: those that please, convince, move, and persuade. Only those that persuade, however, result in action. In chapter 7 of his book, Campbell maintains that there is no persuasion without passion: ". . . when persuasion is the end, passion must also be engaged. If it is fancy which bestows brilliancy on our ideas, if it is memory which gives them stability, passion doth more; it animates them. To say that it is possible to persuade without speaking to the passions is pure specious nonsense. The coolest reasoner, always in persuading addresses himself to the passions in some way or other." For Campbell, reason is essential, but it is not enough to persuade.

By my count, the word *persuasion* in its various forms appears a couple of dozen times over the course of the novel. It pops up first in the second chapter when Anne has devised a plan for extricating her father and sister from the severe financial difficulties they have incurred by their extravagance. Notably, neither one of them has turned to Anne for help. Instead, they have sought out the family friend, Lady Russell, and it is she who "did, what nobody else had thought of doing, she consulted Anne." "If we can persuade your father to all this," Lady Russell confides to Anne, "much may be done." But when Lady Russell presents a modified version of Anne's course of retrenchment to Sir Walter and Elizabeth, they reject it out of hand. The impeccable logic of an argument will not sway those whose hearts are not touched.

I first read *Persuasion* when I was twenty. I have read it several times at various junctures in my life since then. Jane Austen's last finished novel has become the book of hers I love best, despite the fact that I find it more painful to read now than I did when I was younger. The first-time reader of the novel may rest assured it ends well, but the world of this book is different from that of *Pride and Prejudice* and *Emma,* with their sprightly if myopic heroines, whose sentimental educations and the tremors that accompany them take place in orderly, hierarchical milieus. As many critics have pointed out, the ground has shifted in *Persuasion.* Old money has given way to new money, aristocracy to meritocracy. The dull sentences printed in the Baronetage may transfix Sir Walter, but they cannot prevent his fall from grace: Kellynch Hall is let out to Admiral Croft of the navy, who, unlike Sir Walter, is most definitely a man of action. He has made his fortune in the Napoleonic Wars. A societal upheaval is under way, the private repercussions of which will eventually allow Anne the rhetorical opportunity she seeks because she will find herself in new company among people of greater understanding.

The central dilemma of the novel is this: At nineteen, Anne was persuaded by Lady Russell to give up the man she loved, Captain Frederick Wentworth, because he had "no fortune" and had "realized nothing." Lady Russell's argument was not irrational. The young man's future was uncertain. She gave her advice to Anne out of concern and affection. Further, there was nothing surprising about the fact that the young Anne Elliot *gave way* to her older friend. With a vain fop for a father and two shallow, selfish sisters, Anne had no one to turn to after her mother's death but Lady Russell, whom the narrator explains, with ironic poignancy, had "almost a mother's love" for her. Eight years later, Anne has suffered the consequences of her friend's persuasion: "an early loss of bloom and spirits." Her love for Wentworth, at least in memory, is undiminished. Both the constancy of her affection for her lost lover and her age, now well beyond the time most young women are married, mitigate against another chance for love. Austen presents Anne's loss as a gain in eloquence. Campbell defined eloquence as a way "to convey our sentiments into the minds of others in order to produce a certain effect on them." Time has made Anne eloquent.

"How eloquent could Anne Eliot have been,—how eloquent, at least, were her wishes on the side of early warm attachment, and a cheerful confidence in futurity, against the over-anxious caution which seems to insult exertion and distrust Providence!—she had been forced into prudence in her youth, she learned romance as she grew older—the natural sequence of an unnatural beginning." Anne has discovered the rhetorical argument to which her younger self might have listened, one that would have engaged her passions and persuaded her to act in spite of risk. Austen is far too subtle a thinker to frame Anne's earlier decision in terms of right and wrong. The narrator's use of the subjunctive tense "were her wishes" places the reader in a discursive dialectic between the later Anne and the earlier one. The more mature person can now eloquently argue the position her younger self never heard.

The aching sadness of Anne's story lies in that mantra of human regret, *could have been*. "How eloquent could Anne Elliot have been . . ." But her words are stifled because she has no interlocutor except herself. In her family and their circle, she has been assigned the status of Nobody, who says little or nothing because the mutual recognition required for social intercourse does not exist. Her own sister Elizabeth declares, "Anne is nothing to me." When Anne speaks, more often than not her words have no audience. "But nobody heard, or, at least, nobody answered her." "They had no inclination to listen to her." "They were not much interested in anything relative to Anne." Wentworth returns, now rich and determined to marry but still angry at Anne for her refusal. He has decided that her character is feeble and wants firmness. She had, he believes, fallen prey to "over-persuasion," and he treats her politely but coldly. "They had no conversation together, no intercourse but what the commonest civility required. Once so much to each other. Now nothing!" This *nothing* is far more devastating for Anne than for Wentworth. As the captain flirts with the adoring, eligible young ladies of Uppercross, the mortified Anne remains silent.

"No more fiendish punishment could be devised," wrote William James in his *Psychology*, "were such a thing physically possible, than that one should be turned loose in society and remain absolutely unnoticed by all the members thereof." Anne's day-to-day nonexistence comes perilously close to such fiendish annihilation. Every Jane Austen novel explores the complex realities of what James called "the social self," but in *Persuasion* the stakes are ontological. If you are not recognized by other people and not answered by them when you speak, what are you? If your words, no matter how cogent, are impotent before they are even uttered, are you a person or a ghost?

For Aristotle the art of rhetoric did not apply to women, children, slaves, or noncitizens. Their subordinate status in society meant they did not need to be persuaded of anything. They needed simply to be told. In the eighteenth century, women rarely spoke in public. Dr. Johnson's remark to Boswell in 1763 may stand as exemplary: "Sir, a woman's preaching is like a dog's walking on its hinder legs. It is not done well, but you are surprised to find it done at all." The casual cruelty of these often-quoted sentences should not be underestimated. The broader definition of rhetoric advocated by Campbell and others implicitly includes women because its devices could be used in a private letter, a thank-you note, a drawing room conversation, as well as in a novel or poem. The new often carries echoes of the old: In *Phaedrus*, Plato's Socrates says: "Is not rhetoric in its entire nature an art which leads the soul by means of words, not only in the law courts and the various other public assemblages, but in private companies as well?"

There are certainly garrulous women in the private companies of *Persuasion*. Anne's sister Mary chatters away, becoming increasingly insufferable with each subsequent word. Miss Clay is well spoken but ingratiating and duplicitous; Elizabeth cold, dull, and correct. And the eloquent Lady Russell, who is once described "as able to persuade a person to anything," suffers from enough class bias to distort her vision and therefore her advice. Without access to the motions of Anne's mind— her precise thoughts, astute observations, and tumultuous feelings—that come by way of the novel's indirect speech, the reader would not *know* Anne. For much of the book, she rarely speaks aloud. It is the narrator's intimacy with Anne's passionate inner being that allows the reader entrance to her pain. "Anne's shudderings were to herself alone." While the rest of the company, which includes Wentworth, dances, Anne obediently plays the piano with tears in her eyes. When Wentworth saves Anne from the strangling attentions of her two-year-old nephew by unfastening the boy's hands from her neck, Anne is rendered "perfectly speechless." Her agitation is so great she must retreat from the room in order to recover. She spends a lot of time recovering from bouts of high feeling and nervousness, and frequent episodes of blushing.

Arguably, all this inner turbulence, with some aid from her exposure to the sea air, contributes to the revival of an earlier, blooming Anne. "She was looking remarkably well; her very regular, very pretty features, having the bloom and freshness of youth restored by the fine wind that had been blowing on her complexion and by the animation of eye which it had also produced." Anne has traveled to Lyme, and at this moment she has just been seen and admired by an unknown gentleman. Moreover, Frederick Wentworth has witnessed the gentleman's openly appreciative gaze, which causes him to glance at her and communicate in that instant that he sees "something like Anne Elliot again." This moment of the wordless exchanges of glances among three people constitutes nothing less than a momentous turn in the narrative, which will open new rhetorical possibilities for the heroine: Before she can enter the conversation, she must be *seen*, must be acknowledged as a worthy member of the company of speakers. The admiring eyes of the strange gentleman, which, it turns out, belong to Anne's cousin, Mr. Elliot, heir to the family property, effectively transform Anne from Nobody into Somebody. In this silent play of back-and-forth gazes, Anne has been doubly recognized. She has been seen as an object of desire by Elliot and has been seen *again* by Wentworth. The unheard, marginalized, literally *unremarkable* Anne has moved from one place into another.

The family's misfortune, its displacement from Kellynch Hall, will become the vehicle for Anne's persuasive power. Had she remained at home and not traveled to Uppercross, to Lyme, and then to Bath, she would not have found herself among less genteel but more vigorous, kind, and open people—she would have remained Sir Walter's ignored spinster daughter, fixed in a state of perpetual mourning and acquiescence to her superiors, a woman stuck on the same lost page of her life. The brutal injustice of this possible fate reverberates throughout the pages of *Persuasion*, which appropriately reaches its climax in an argument, by which Anne's rhetorical skills are allowed to shine, and her eloquence turns *could have been* into *shall be*.

The argument, ostensibly about the relative constancy of women as opposed to men, is conducted between Anne and Captain Harville, another man of the Royal Navy, but the true object of Anne's speech is Frederick, who sits at a table in the same room writing a letter. After listening to Anne's crisply argued but fervent defense of women's attachment, Captain Wentworth *drops his pen*. What follows is one of the most memorable exchanges in the history of the novel. Harville notes that literature is dense with references to fickle women. "But perhaps," he allows, "you will say, these were all written by men."

Anne leaps through the door he has opened. "Perhaps I shall.—Yes, yes, if you please, no reference to examples from books. Men have had every advantage of us in telling their own story. Education has been theirs in so much higher a degree; the pen has been in their hands. I will not allow books to prove anything."

A book that begins with a book, which lists the lines of male (never female) heirs, comes around to other books, books that have been written mostly by men who have had every advantage, who have used the pen to charm, cajole, ridicule, and persuade for their own ends, often, I must add, at the expense of women who have gone and still go unheard. But we, the readers of *Persuasion*, are the recipients of another woman's consummate rhetorical powers. Her name is Jane Austen. Reader, he dropped his pen.

2016

THE ENIGMA OF READING

"*Wuthering Heights* is a strange inartistic story," an anonymous English reviewer wrote in *Atlas* in January 1848. "This is a strange book," commented another in the *Examiner*. "His work is strangely original," said a reviewer in *Britannia*. "*Wuthering Heights* is a strange sort of book— baffling all regular criticism," wrote a fourth in *Douglas Jerrod's Weekly Newspaper*. He continued, "yet, it is impossible to begin and not finish it; and quite impossible to lay it aside afterwards and say nothing about it." Strangeness was not a quality that led reviewers to recommend the novel Emily Brontë published in 1847 under the pseudonym Ellis Bell. At best, they treated the book as a flawed work by a gifted writer who might make something of himself after he acquired more polish.

A good number of the American reviewers responded to the book less charitably. They were morally outraged. "We rise from the perusal of *Wuthering Heights* as if we had come fresh from a pest-house" was the verdict from *Paterson's Magazine*. "It is a compound of vulgar depravity and unnatural horrors," wrote the reviewer in *Graham's Lady's and Gentleman's Magazine*. Edwin P. Whipple concluded his review of Bell's novel in the *North American Review* with this sentence: "Nightmares and dreams, through which devils dance and wolves howl, make bad novels."

It is common practice to look back at excoriating reviews of "classic" books and smirk with superiority. In large measure, this smug attitude is the result of having been handed a piece of cultural wisdom by the invisible makers of the literary canon, whose selections have found their way onto reading lists for high school and college English classes. The 1925 headline of the review in the *New York World* of *The Great Gatsby*,

FITZGERALD'S LATEST A DUD, is now infamous for its obtuseness. And yet, the very idea of a literary canon has been under fire for at least half a century. Whatever consensus there may have been in decades past about greatness has been replaced by warring political opinions. There is good reason to protest against the received wisdom of the canon makers who were blind to the work of writers who fell outside the strictures of their "taste," many women and most non-whites, although exceptions were made for an anointed few.

Moral outrage of one kind or another remains a common American response to literature. The portrait of Wolfsheim in *Gatsby*, for example, has long been condemned as anti-Semitic, a fact that might prevent its inclusion on a course list in 2020. Then again, the scholar Michael Pekarofski argues in the *F. Scott Fitzgerald Review* that Jay Gatsby himself is "a passing Jew"—an original thought. Cleansing literature of the taints of misogyny, racism, and xenophobia, not to speak of countless other ugly offenses against greater humankind, would quickly shrink our libraries to an alarming size of a few volumes blessed by those who have taken upon themselves the arduous task of literary purification. And yet, even profligate and sophisticated readers who open their hearts to psychopathic narrators murdering women or pedophiles stalking their prey may find themselves irritated and even revolted by particular texts for their lack of some element or elements deemed necessary for a "good" novel.

For several years in a row, I participated in a public book-club series in New York City. A group of writers read literary classics, discussed the works onstage, and answered questions from an enthusiastic audience, all of whom had prepared for the evening by reading the book in question. We read Jane Austen's works in a single gulp but also individual books, *Middlemarch*, *Anna Karenina*, *Portrait of a Lady*, and *Madame Bovary*. We did not read *Wuthering Heights*, but during one of those discussions, a writer I admire, who is widely celebrated as an author of unusual talent, let it be known that she "hated" Emily Brontë's novel. I cannot recall what I said in return. I may have mumbled some defense of the book but exactly what that was has retreated to a hidden corner of my mind. My interlocutor's condemnation was not driven by canonical snobbery or by moral purity concerns, but, if I remember correctly, by a repulsion for the general bombast of the thing, which echoed the sentiment of Mr. Whipple, who declared that dancing devils and howling wolves were the ingredients of "bad novels."

Although I disagree with my fellow writer about *Wuthering Heights*, I am fully aware of the vicissitudes of reading and the concomitant absurdity of turning books into stone monuments. Although Emily Brontë's only novel is now widely acknowledged by scholars as "a work of genius," the diversity of readings it has inspired is astounding. The book has been read from many different perspectives—Marxist, psychoanalytic, feminist, theological, as a response to the Romantic and Gothic literary traditions, as a psychological novel about abjection, personality disorder, and other psychiatric illnesses—to cite just a few. But there is also sharp disagreement among scholars as to what the book is actually *about*. Academics, by no means all of them in literature departments, have found an array of contradictory meanings in the novel. Emily Brontë is a Platonist. True forms exist beyond the illusions of this natural world in the realm of the soul. Others have claimed she was a Stoic. No, still others argue, she espoused a form of naturalism. She believed in God. She didn't believe in God. Her proximity to Methodism and its enthusiasm explains the intense emotions in the narrative. Many ideas, it seems, can find a home in the book. I ran across the following title in my reading: "Family Systems Theory, Addiction, and Emily Brontë's *Wuthering Heights*."

Depending on the critic, the novel's hero-villain, Heathcliff, the strange boy whom Mr. Earnshaw finds abandoned on the streets of Liverpool and brings home, is Irish or Roma or Black. His background and family story are never revealed in the text. The word *gypsy*, however, is used in reference to him as an aspersion, never as a fact. He gives a "dark" impression and has black hair, but critics must guess his origins, and guess they do. In her paper "Can the Subaltern Speak? Color and Silence in *Wuthering Heights*," Magda Hasabelnaby claims that the "less than human" portrayal of Heathcliff by one of the book's narrators, the family's servant and confidante, Ellen Dean, "supports our reading of him as a slave from Africa." This guess about his origins is important for her interpretation, which she specifically identifies as "post-colonial."

In this reading, Heathcliff is a creature created by white perception— "the object of the whites' 'gaze.'" Although he speaks in the novel, he is taciturn, and does not write his story or compose letters as some of the other characters do. The larger narrative is therefore a vehicle to silence him, and his death at the end signifies a restoration of white rule. "For the novel to end in harmony, the black intruder must disappear, and the whites, the original owners of the Heights must restore order and bring back peace and joy." The critic acknowledges ambivalence in the novel's portrait of Heathcliff, but she argues that this occurs despite Emily Brontë's "racist authorial control."

In his essay "The Cuckoo's Story: Human Nature in *Wuthering Heights*," Joseph Carroll gives the book a reading far removed from the social and historical considerations that animate Hasabelnaby. He calls on Darwin. He, too, notes Heathcliff's status as alien interloper. For Carroll, however, the strange boy is not the exotic other of European racism but an invader akin to a biological parasite: "Nelly introduces her story of Heathcliff by saying it is a cuckoo's story. It is, in other words, a story about a parasitic appropriation of resources that belong to the offspring of another organism." To put it more plainly: Cuckoos lay their eggs in the nests of other birds. The fact that Darwin's *Origin of the Species* was not published until 1859, more than a decade after *Wuthering Heights*, is of little importance to Carroll because Emily Brontë could avail herself of "folk" beliefs about nature, which apparently come close enough. He notes the strong role heredity plays in the novel, the transfer of physical and psychological features from one generation to the next, and frames the story through the Darwinian idea of fitness.

"The literature on *Wuthering Heights* is abundant and its incoherence striking," J. Hillis Miller wrote, echoing the reviewer in *Jerrod's*, who claimed it baffled "all regular criticism." Miller, a subtle and astute critic, argued in his essay on the novel "Repetition and the Uncanny" that there is no key that will open the door to the novel's secrets. "My argument is that the best readings will be the ones that account for the heterogeneity of the text, its presentation of a definite group of possible meanings which are determined by the text but logically incompatible." Although his argument has been cited and summarized countless times by other scholars, the search for logical coherence continues. Reading through the fantastic variety of opinions on the book's meanings is dizzying. But what is this strange, baffling book, and why does it generate so much controversy about how to read it? No critic has ever domesticated *Wuthering Heights*. I think Miller is right. It is useless to try to beat the novel into submission. It will not comply.

I first read the novel when I was thirteen in a house in Reykjavík, Iceland. My father was researching the sagas, and my mother, my three sisters, and I were along for the adventure, which in my case turned out to be as much an internal adventure as an external one. It was summer. The sun never set, and I read one novel after another with greedy joy: Austen, Twain, Dickens, Dumas, Balzac, and the Brontës, among others. My two favorite novels of that summer were *Jane Eyre* and *David Copperfield*, stories about two mistreated orphans, whom I loved as I loved myself, with an acute identification I have retained into my old age. I loved the experience of reading *Wuthering Heights*, too, but the book and its ferocious beings with their biting, slapping, pummeling, and altogether bloody ways frightened and mystified me at the same time. I had a strong sense that in this book, right and wrong, good and bad, angels and devils had been mixed up together, and extricating one from the other was useless. The novel held a nameless mixture of dread and excitement that has been circulating in my bloodstream ever since.

The story did not provide a character with whom I could safely identify. It had no moral anchor, no David or Jane to pull me through to the end. Even the early readers of the novel who didn't instantly condemn it for depravity had a sense that they had been thrown out of a familiar moral universe. "It is humanity in its wild state," wrote the reviewer in *Britannia*. Its characters "show no trace of ideal models." In 1949, the critic Melvin Watson was similarly puzzled: "What may be the moral which the author wishes the reader to deduce from the work it is difficult to say."

I read *Wuthering Heights* to my daughter, Sophie, when she was eleven. Long after she could read to herself, I read to her at night. We chose books that she might find difficult on her own. I hesitated to read the novel to her, but she begged to hear it. I told her it was a strange, complex, and frightening book, different from Charlotte Brontë's *Jane Eyre*, which we had read before. I told her anytime she wanted me to stop reading, she should tell me. We were well into the story when she said, "Mom, Heathcliff and Catherine aren't very nice, are they?" I said they most definitely were not. She was silent for a few seconds, and then said, "But Mom, they love each other so much! Keep going!" This "not very nice" quality continues to trouble readers, some of whom condemn the characters for immorality. The following are short excerpts from a long, civil, and interesting conversation on a popular online discussion forum.

Jacqueline: I often wonder how Heathcliff, whose acts are often mean spirited bullying, is often seen as a Byronic hero . . .

Lucinda: I feel sorry for Heathcliff in the way Nelly Dean does (I think she's often the spokesperson for humane values in the story and underestimated).

Alecto: Catherine and Heathcliff are wild things, driven by instinct and passions, almost the embodiment of the nature they live in . . . They're beyond right and wrong . . . does a lightning feel remorse for the tree it burns? I actually very much empathize with them and always find boring most of the other characters and especially, self righteous Mrs. Dean verging on the annoying.

Lucinda: I have to say that I think any character's being seen as "beyond" good and evil is a very dangerous one, just as it is for real people (I expect Hitler felt he was beyond good and evil as do other psychopaths).

Teresa: Catherine's selfish nature was the result of being pampered and spoiled and catered to, whereas Heathcliff's was the result of abuse.

Lucinda: Well, Alecto, fascinating as I find your points, we must agree to disagree, I think. I don't think any character should be placed above ethical notions. Sadly, given the damage that their obsessive behavior causes, I don't see Cathy and Heathcliff as truly loving one another at all; they're obsessed, but it's selfish possessiveness on his part for sure, and conventionally patriarchal . . .

This preamble to my own reading of the novel is intended as more than a series of anecdotes about old reviews, literary politics, good writers with whom I disagree, the wildly diverse views of scholars, my first encounter with the book in Reykjavík many years ago, my eleven-year-old's response, and ethical debates among contemporary readers. My intention is to introduce *Wuthering Heights* through the phenomenology of reading—the first-person experience of ingesting a text—which I believe is intimately linked to the problem of *Wuthering Heights* itself and its now well-established reputation as a baffling riddle that remains unsolved.

Reading is a strange business, after all. Whether the text in question is a science paper or a novel, it is, rather like a virus, dead until animated by the body of a host and, although the words of a book or paper are always the same, the bodies, situations, experiences, and biases of its readers vary. The interpretations of Hasabelnaby, Carroll, Jacqueline, Alecto, Teresa, Lucinda, and me and Sophie as children represent different views of what the book is about and how it should be read. Plural readings of any text are inevitable, but this particular book is rather like a bomb, which, when ignited by its readers, explodes and sends a thousand fragments flying in all directions. To say that is not to preclude the possibility of judgment or to render all readings equal, it is rather to acknowledge that a text literally reverberates with the pulse and breath of its reader, her character, emotional makeup, and readerly capacities. The more baffling and ambiguous a text is, the more heterogeneous its interpretations. Every reading is wrought in the space between text and reader.

It is important to stress that while a person reads, her internal narrator, the voice each and every person carries in her head, is temporarily suspended, taken over by the voice or voices of the book. It is possible to stop reading and think over what has just been read, but it is not possible to have one's own voice and the narrative voices of the book running at the same time. Because language is dynamic, shot through with multiple meanings that cannot be fixed, meanings that are made and remade among people in specific contexts and at particular historical moments, there is no final reading of any complex literary work. The words on the page do not change over time, but readers do. Many critical readings of books seek to fix or stop meaning. The postcolonial reading and the Darwinian reading, to return to the two papers briefly mentioned, may have uncovered pieces of the truth about *Wuthering Heights*, but each one traps the text inside a ready-made box, neither of which can contain this particular novel.

As I have argued repeatedly, human beings engage with a book, especially a novel, with an intimacy that does not pertain to most other inanimate objects. Reading is a form of ordinary possession of one person by another. While it is being read, the story is infused with the traces of another living human being, who is not there physically, but the author's breath and being are present in the rhythms and meanings of the words on the page, which are literally embodied in the reader—incorporated into his biological being—a mixing of the two. John Dewey had a beautiful expression for this, "organic clicks." Books register not only as articulate thoughts in the reader but as excitement, shock, sorrow, surprise, pleasure, relief. Not until the reader returns the book to the shelf does it regain its status as a mere thing, and even then the story may live on in him as a memory, recalled not as a long recitation of serial sentences, one after the other, but as images and feelings the work has left behind it. A beloved book remains in the reader as a ghost, with both conscious and unconscious resonances.

I have read *Wuthering Heights* at regular intervals over the course of my life, and it has never failed to seduce me with the same urgency it had when I was thirteen. Although my mature self is now so fat with reading that I am obese compared to my young self, the emotional power of the book is undiminished, and while reading it again I found it difficult to withdraw from the occupying voices of the text to meditate on them and give them the scrutiny they deserve. The word *wuthering* describes my reading experience well: I am blown hard, destabilized, even uprooted at times, but always pushed in a single direction—toward the book's end. The novel's first narrator, the urbane, repressed outsider, Mr. Lockwood, defines *wuthering* early in the novel:

> Wuthering being a significant provincial adjective, descriptive of the atmospheric tumult to which its station is exposed in stormy weather. Pure, bracing ventilation they must have up there, at all times, indeed: one may guess the power of the north wind, blowing over the edge, by the excessive slant of a few, stunted firs at the end of the house; and by a range of gaunt thorns all stretching their limbs one way, as if craving alms of the sun.

Luxuriant descriptions of weather abound in the novel. Wind and air and sky are ever present as are the changing seasons that buffet, freeze, warm, hide, and reveal rock and moor and heath and birds and animals, including human animals. The shifting atmospheric tumult in *Wuthering Heights* cannot be described as the novel's *setting*, that word so dear to the hearts of junior high school teachers who treated novels as theaters with backdrops against which the *characters* appear in relief as they go through the motions of the *plot*. The novel's storms do not obey the boundaries of character, setting, and plot. They do not obey the boundaries of person and environment, self and other, or even human and rock. I think this explains in part why the book both excites and distresses many of its readers.

The novel shreds not only the established conventions for realist fiction of its time, but the organizing categories for thinking about how the world works. This wuthering story refuses to carve up the world into accepted categories. Its rich metaphorical movements seem to shudder with a version of panpsychism, the belief that mind or spirit, *Geist*, is in and of everything, but then again, perhaps this is simply what the natural world is—alive. Near the end of the book, Heathcliff says of the dead Catherine, "What is not connected with her to me? . . . I cannot look down at the floor but her features are shaped on the flags! In every cloud, in every tree—filling the air at night, and caught by glimpses in every object by day, I am surrounded by her image!" Forms of turbulence disfigure and reconfigure the book's human creatures as well as its trees. Rage, envy, humiliation, hate, and love break out in thunderous cries, windy howls, and rains of tears.

Catherine describes Heathcliff as heath, uncultivated ground, "an arid wilderness of furze and whinstone." In contrast, she speaks of her love for Edgar Linton and her decision to marry him in the clichéd, sentimental terms of romantic love. She tells Nelly defensively, "I love the ground under his feet, and the air over his head, and everything he touches, and every word he says—I love all his looks, and all his actions, and him entirely, and altogether. There now!" Heathcliff is something else again for Catherine—"he's more myself than I am. Whatever our souls are made of, his and mine are the same, and Linton's is as different as a moonbeam from lightning or frost from fire." The two worlds of moonbeam and lightning, of civilized and uncivilized, of heaven and hell, of domestic order and cultivated manners at the Lintons' Thrushcross Grange and wild nature and chaos at the Earnshaws' Wuthering Heights, constitute a much-discussed opposition that occurs throughout the book. At the same time, there is no keeping the two apart. The characters move between one place and the other. They tread the same ground. They marry one another and have children who mix the two families and are bound by emotional attachments, money, and memory.

Notably, the novel's "visible" action takes place only in the geography of the Heights and the Grange. Whatever occurs beyond this territory is hearsay, rumor, or enveloped in a kind of narrative fog. Mr. Earnshaw's adventure in Liverpool when he discovers Heathcliff is a tale he brings back with him, but its precise details are fuzzy. When Heathcliff runs off, he leaves the world of the book behind him and, after he returns, the reader never discovers what happened to him. His posture suggests to Ellen that he may have been in the army, but that is not certain. He has become a rich man, but how? No one knows. Lockwood's life in the city is another cipher. What he did before he arrived or what he does when he leaves the remote region play no part in the novel. His narration picks up only when he returns to the district. His life beyond it amounts to little more than vague references to "town." Isabella Linton's flight from the area and her life once she has left it are similarly unfocused. The moors, not the people who live on them, determine what falls inside and outside the story. The place with its shifting winds and weather and seasons may be described not as a setting but as the novel's dominant living character. Its breath and pulse and temperature are omnipresent. The story's speaking creatures belong to that larger natural body, a body that harbors human beings and animals and flora within it. When someone moves beyond its borders, he or she becomes wan and indistinct and falls outside the narrative.

The body of a book is made of words only, but *Wuthering Heights* confounds the reader with its own words about words. The role of speech and written texts inside the novel may also be described as wuthering, windy ventilations of a human kind, which can't be separated from the respiration of the place itself: "a golden afternoon in August— every breath from the hills so full of life, that it seemed whoever respired it, though dying, would revive." Inspiration, breath, exhalation are all expressions for spirit, and they recur through the many levels of narration. "And that wind sounding in the firs by the lattice. Do let me feel it—it comes straight down the moor—do let me have one breath," cries a delirious Catherine not long before she dies.

She begs that the window be opened, that she be free for a moment from the walls that close in on her, that hold her locked inside them. Gales blow through the narrative, but there are lulls, too. Calm descends on the landscape for a time, part of a variable continuum of seasonal weather replicated in how the story is told and in the moods of the characters. "Catherine had seasons of gloom and silence, now and then; they were respected by her husband, who ascribed them to an alteration in her constitution, produced by her perilous illness, as she was never subject to depression of spirits before. The return of sunshine was welcomed by answering sunshine from him." Ellen describes a dialogue of moods between spouses, a changeable human climate.

The weather of words whirls and blows in various directions, depending on who is speaking and where she or he is standing at the moment. The perspective often shifts violently. There is no unanimity, no final authoritative voice in *Wuthering Heights*, moral or otherwise. Like a telescope, the narration zooms into intimate scenes and action, and then withdraws, sometimes abruptly, as if to remind the reader that this is a story within a story, and there is a teller of the tale. But the teller of the tale changes, too, and the collective, anonymous speech of gossip blows through the book as well, words that travel from one mouth to another without identified speakers and become part of the linguistic atmosphere that eventually settles into regional stories or lore that include, by the end of the novel, sightings of the phantom lovers Heathcliff and Catherine roaming the moors.

Who is speaking? Who is who in this story? When does one person become another? These are not idle questions.

"Nelly," Catherine says, "I am Heathcliff."

But what or who is Heathcliff? The wilderness of furze and whinstone is there in his name, but so is cliff—a steep face of rock or earth or ice—a precipice, an edge over which one could take a fall. In a dream Catherine recounts to Nelly, she finds herself exiled in heaven, a "miserable" place, and she longs to fall back to earth, to Wuthering Heights, to heath and cliff and moor. "Is Mr. Heathcliff a man? If so, is he mad? And if not, is he a devil?" Isabella asks Nelly. What it means to be Heathcliff is a central problem of the novel, and what or who he is turns on the problem of the narration itself, on the telling of the story and how the reader understands that telling.

As the chief narrator, Ellen or Nelly Dean looks on at a raging, desperate Heathcliff and feels she is not in the company of a creature of her "own species." At another moment, she scolds Isabella for calling Heathcliff "a monster." Nelly is adamant: "He's a human being." In fact, Nelly describes Heathcliff in multiple ways. She insists he is a human being. She depicts him as an animal, "He gnashed at me like a wild dog," and as a demon, "It appeared to me not Mr. Heathcliff but as a goblin." And is this creature also Catherine, as Catherine insists he is?

How could the narrative as a whole endorse Nelly's view of Heathcliff as merely human or bestial Other or supernatural demon when she herself either cannot make up her mind about him and/or has different views at different times in the story, views that may depend on whom she is speaking to at the moment? Isabella's hatred of Heathcliff, her belief that he is not human, is so passionate that Nelly is shocked. Is she rebuking Isabella for extremity or for the content of her sentiment, a sentiment Nelly herself has shared?

When Nelly recalls Heathcliff's initial appearance at Wuthering Heights, she refers to the boy as "it." Is this a narrative tactic to enlist the reader into a racist view of the child, a subhuman being, as Hasabelnaby believes? Don't Nelly's fluctuating descriptions of Heathcliff necessarily create doubt in the reader's mind? Doesn't any final judgment rest heavily on the reader's own beliefs and prejudices? Isn't this precisely what explains the highly variable scholarship on *Wuthering Heights* and its missing key or logic? There is abundant evidence to support many perspectives on the story.

It seems to me that Brontë enacts a strategy very much like the one the Danish philosopher Søren Kierkegaard advocates—she throws the reader back on herself or himself. Kierkegaard was writing away in Copenhagen while Emily Brontë was writing away in West Yorkshire. He published *Works of Love* under his own name the same year she published *Wuthering Heights* under a pseudonym. But during his writing life, Kierkegaard published many works under pseudonyms. He hoped the ironies produced by his "poetic personalities" would throw the reader "back onto himself," would press him into a moment of decision, would change his life. Brontë ensnares her reader in similar ironic puzzles. What am I as a reader to think? Who or what is Heathcliff? Are he and Catherine really one immortal soul? Are they both mad? Are they natural beings? Søren Kierkegaard died in 1855 at forty-two. Emily Brontë died in 1848 at thirty. The two geniuses are linked in my mind, not only by the time period they shared but by the consuming passion and intellectual complexity of their baffling texts.

Heathcliff appalls Lucinda of the online forum for legitimate reasons.

He is brutal. He manipulates Hindley out of his property, hangs Isabella's spaniel (the dog is rescued by Nelly), and terrorizes his own son—just a few of his many crimes. Still he fascinates and attracts Alecto as a force of nature: "Does a lightning feel remorse for the tree it burns?" She links him to Catherine and prefers the wild couple to the tediously conventional and moralizing Nelly. Is it possible to come down on one side or the other? What does it mean that this child interloper, Heathcliff, becomes Mr. Earnshaw's favorite child, a child he prefers to his own flesh and blood: Hindley and Catherine? Is this an "unnatural" attachment on the part of the father, a cuckoo's story, or does he see qualities in the boy that are genuinely admirable? The reader has no access to Earnshaw's narration. His brief speeches offer no glimpse into an explanation of his love for Heathcliff. But Catherine's passionate adoration of her adopted brother repeats her father's infatuation. Why does she love him? If we believe her, she is he. Self-love and her love for Heathcliff are one and the same. Is this a shared narcissism, spiritual love, or something else? They both have a penchant for violence. When asked by her father what he wants him to bring her home from Liverpool, she requests a whip. She gets Heathcliff instead.

Readers such as Hasabelnaby and Lucinda have put their faith in Nelly, the servant who is also a quasi–family member, a "foster sister" to Catherine's brother, Hindley. They have adopted Nelly as a narrator-guide to the book's broader meanings. Depending on the reader's perspective, Nelly Dean's racism and/or her "humane values" reveal the secret of the narrative perspective as a whole. From their perspectives, *Wuthering Heights* is either a racist or a humanist text. Heathcliff is also brutalized and dehumanized by Mrs. Earnshaw, Hindley, and the Lintons as a dark other, "a gypsy brat." And Nelly does stand up for what she calls "common humanity" and decency, and she condemns violence, but she says, "People who do their duty are always finally rewarded," a nice thought but patently untrue, at least in this world. A reader's alliance with Nelly requires that large parts of the book be shucked off in order to squeeze it into the desired box. The structure of Emily Brontë's narrative is diabolical, a trap for the reader, which makes such readings impossible. It is constructed as a mystifying polyphony made up of voices in conflict. The book itself is a storm that wuthers every careful reader into doubt. To choose a position or fixed meaning is to be sucked into the novel's vortex.

Lockwood, the stranger who is wholly ignorant of the goings-on at Wuthering Heights and the Grange, begins the story well after most of it has taken place: "1801—I have just returned from a visit to my landlord—the solitary neighbor that I shall be troubled with." The reader understands that she is reading someone's diary from that year. Before long, Ellen Dean will take over the narration from Lockwood, but inside both his and her narrations are other speakers who take over from them, and they speak and write as if all temporal and spatial remove have evaporated.

The dialogue supposedly remembered by Lockwood seems to occur in a textual present, not the immediate past. No one remembers and records events in a diary with such exactitude unless he is *fictionalizing* his account. Contemporary memoirs often use this device to the same purpose—long dialogues are included in these books, supposedly remembered by the author word for word. Realism is jettisoned for the novelistic conceit of *immediacy*, an immediacy that is possible *only* in fiction or in the play-by-play of a sports announcer or the breathless narration of a journalist at the scene of an event. Lockwood's diary and Ellen's story occur in both the narrator's and the reader's *now*. The reader and Lockwood are also privy to Isabella's long, desperate letter to Ellen while Ellen is presumably telling the story. The letter itself contains verbatim dialogue and descriptions of precise action that make the reader forget she is reading a letter and not a blow-by-blow account in the present. Blow-by-blow can be taken literally in this case because the action is violent. The reader is not listening to Ellen or reading Isabella's letter but watching scenes play out in front of her imaginative eyes. Nevertheless, at decisive moments, the reader is abruptly pulled out of this temporal illusion and carried back to Lockwood, who is sitting in a room listening to Ellen talk.

At the end of chapter 7, the reader "hears" Heathcliff speak to Ellen:

"Let me alone, and I'll plan it out: while I'm thinking of that, I don't feel pain." The words that immediately follow in a new paragraph yank the reader back to another present time. Ellen says, "But Mr. Lockwood, I forget these tales cannot divert you." Lockwood, whose *role as listener* echoes the role of the *reader as listener*, insists, in a childlike manner, that the storyteller continue the tale even though it's eleven o'clock at night. "I am interested in every character you have mentioned more or less." He does not say "every person," despite the fact that he has met some of the "characters" in the flesh at Wuthering Heights. For Lockwood, the eager listener, the real people have become characters in Ellen's tale, just as they are, of course, for the reader who holds Emily Brontë's novel in her hands.

But Lockwood is not the only one who construes life as a fiction. Ellen confronts Heathcliff after he has married Isabella: "You cannot doubt that she has the capacity for strong attachments, or she wouldn't have abandoned the elegancies, and comforts, and friends of her former home, to fix contentedly in such a wilderness as this with you." To which Heathcliff responds, "She abandoned them under a delusion, picturing in me a hero of romance, and expecting unlimited indulgences of my chivalrous devotion. I can hardly regard her in the light of a rational creature, so obstinately has she persisted in forming a fabulous notion of my character, and acting on the false impressions she cherished." Isabella mistook Heathcliff for a Romantic hero.

Jacqueline puzzled over why so many readers had fallen into the trap of thinking of the bullying Heathcliff as a "Byronic hero." Isabella's first version of Heathcliff, the one she falls for, has lived on in readers' fantasies and in movie versions of the book. The dark, brooding lover is a persistent and popular cliché, and he didn't die out with nineteenth-century fiction. He has been reincarnated over and over as a hero in films and in the contemporary genre also called "romance," which inevitably mines the erotic fantasies of its readers. The romance genre runs on titillation, a quality wholly missing from *Wuthering Heights*. Heathcliff rejects the role of dangerous but sexually arousing hero. Isn't his rejection also a note to the reader? He did not play the part, he tells Nelly. Isabella foisted it upon him. This is hardly the speech of an "it," of an inarticulate dog or a stroke of lightning. Heathcliff is dispassionate, shrewd, pitiless. During their first encounter, Heathcliff impresses Lockwood as "very intelligent on the topics we discussed." Indeed, Heathcliff's extended speeches betray his insight, his quick penetration of most situations, ironies included. This is not the discourse of a beast. Is it the discourse of a dancing devil?

Heathcliff understands that Isabella's quixotic fantasies have blinded her to what was always in front of her eyes. She has been infected and addled by Romantic stories. The fact that Heathcliff has taken advantage of her temporary insanity for his revenge scheme is cruel, but is it irrational? And where does the reader find herself? I feel pity for Isabella, but I also share a piece of Heathcliff's contempt for her, at least in the textual moment, that is, *when he is speaking*. Isabella Linton's infatuation with Heathcliff, noted by other characters but never "acted out" in the narrative for the reader, is a weaker reverberation of Catherine's infatuation with Isabella's brother, Edgar Linton: "I love the ground under his feet" and "the air over his head." Like gossip and rumor, fanciful fictions are abroad in the land, traveling like the wind. Their consequences are fatal inside the book. For careless readers outside the book, they may be fatal, too, leading them to cloak the characters in their own dreams, wishes, and truisms, their own conventional desires for a romantic hero, or convictions about our "common humanity" or "nature," including "human nature," as brutal, alien, and indifferent.

In chapter 10, Lockwood again longs for a continuation of the story, "Yes," he says, "I remember her hero had run off and her heroine had married." Lockwood's fictional characters are not the living persons whom Nelly knew intimately. They are creatures of Ellen's story and remain one step removed from him, exciting but remote. And then, at the beginning of chapter 15, a curious narrative shift occurs. Lockwood begins to narrate and explains to the reader that he will go on with the story, which he has now heard from Ellen in its entirety, but *he will tell it in the housekeeper's voice*: "I'll continue it in her own words, only a little condensed. She is on the whole a very fair narrator and I don't think I could improve her style." Lockwood is now both ventriloquist and editor. His voice and the housekeeper's are indistinguishable as he retells with some omissions what she has told him *in her words.*

This merging of voices is not simply a matter of calling upon the reader's suspension of disbelief. After all, to continue the narrative as Nelly *telling* Lockwood the story would have been a reasonable authorial choice, but that is not the choice Emily Brontë made. Instead, she chose to collapse the border between the two narrations. The reader is now listening to Lockwood *writing* as Nelly Dean. The book is his book. In chapter 17, after Lockwood has taken over the story and is wearing his Nelly mask, his pseudonym, and the reader has again become lost in *her* narration, *Nelly* again addresses Lockwood (the man who is acting, or rather, writing, her part): "But you'll not want to hear my moralizing, Mr. Lockwood: you'll judge as well as I can, all these things; at least you'll think you will, and that's the same." You, Mr. Lockwood, will imagine you can judge "these things" as well as I can even though *you did not witness them.*

Nelly, now appropriated by Lockwood, seems to be asserting the superiority of her judgment by mocking the man listening to her. Because he is her superior in station, she assumes that he falsely believes he has a more sophisticated understanding of the story. Until the unification of narrators, Lockwood, the outsider from town, remains *like* the reader outside the story listening to Nelly Dean narrate. He is one step removed from the action, at least technically. When he usurps her telling into his own written text, the two effectively become the same person, a doubled narrator. *He is she but a little condensed.* He, the outsider, takes one step further inside, closer to the action, and in the process, Lockwood, the author, has changed sex and class. He has become the female servant.

Lockwood's role now mimics the *author* of a fiction as much as the reader of it. He is a person who writes in the voice of another "I"—the disembodied voice of the page. He is the writer who becomes another person for the duration of a work of fiction. *I am you.* Lockwood is not Emily Brontë, however. Emily Brontë wrote behind the masculine or sexually ambiguous mask of Ellis Bell, a mask she used for her poems that were published in 1846. *Wuthering Heights* was composed between October 1845 and June 1846. E. Brontë/E. Bell is the author of the author, Lockwood. E.B. is the "I" who spawns Catherine, Heathcliff, all the others, and breathes life into the novel: "I am Heathcliff."

For years, I have been thinking about the novel's opening, which reaches a climax in the third chapter. It serves as an entrance to the book and implicates the reader in the novel's complex structure and its multiple collapsing boundaries. The attentive reader is initiated into the uncanny depths of *Wuthering Heights* and its proliferating meanings.

Chapter 1. Lockwood, diarist and narrator, has let a house in the neighborhood, the old Linton place, Thrushcross Grange. In the first paragraph, he makes the flippant comment that he has found himself in "a perfect misanthrope's heaven," which immediately evokes Satan's line in Milton's *Paradise Lost*, "The mind is its own place and in it self / Can make a Heav'n of Hell, a Hell of Heav'n." Heaven and hell are continually referenced and often inverted over the course of the novel, as in Catherine's dream of falling from misery in paradise down to paradise on earth, Wuthering Heights, which is most definitely not a paradise. Above the door to the house is an inscription from Dante's inferno: "Abandon all hope, ye who enter here." Catherine's world is the world upside down.

Lockwood gives an account of Heathcliff's surly manner, the unremittingly sour, muttering servant, Joseph, and a description of the house. The reader also learns that Lockwood has fled town on account of his attraction to a nameless young woman and his subsequent and perverse failure to act on it. He has fled to stew in this remote part of England. Our narrator, it seems, is frightened of and confused by his own feelings. While at Wuthering Heights, Lockwood is attacked by dogs, has a drink with his host, returns home, and remarks that he is amazed at how sociable he, who believes himself to be unsociable, is in comparison to his landlord.

Chapter 2. Because his dining plans have been foiled at the Grange, our narrator returns to the unsociable Heights with its brutal canines and meets Cathy number 2, who was born to the first Catherine just before she died, and Hareton Earnshaw, Hindley's son, neither of whom is remotely sociable. It begins to snow. The snow becomes a blizzard. Lockwood wants to return to the Grange with a guide, but no one will oblige him. Our narrator is again attacked by dogs, suffers a nosebleed, and ends up staying at Wuthering Heights for the night.

Chapter 3. Rattled and nauseated by his ordeal, Lockwood is led upstairs by the servant Zillah and put in a room. Inside he finds a chair, a clothes press, and "a large oak case" with a window. He opens the case to discover a sleeping couch and the window's ledge that doubles as a desk. Lockwood pulls the doors shut and "feels secure against the vigilance of Heathcliff and everyone else." *Lockwood is locked in wood.* The name has been noted as meaningful, and some critic has probably noticed the obvious fact that the name is *enacted* in the text itself, but I have not come across it in my reading. Lockwood finds himself in a room within a room. Lockwood and the reader of *Wuthering Heights*, his double, are introduced to the complicated archaeological structure of the book's narrations, one voice inside another, through a fragmented hallucinatory experience inside a closed wooden object that opens and closes like a coffin or a book.

Inside this odd book-coffin-like piece of furniture, Lockwood finds actual books, mildewed volumes, but also the changing name of its former occupant, Catherine, who has inscribed herself into the wooden ledge in three variations—Catherine Earnshaw, Catherine Linton, and Catherine Heathcliff: "And then, a glare of white letters, started from the desk, as vivid as spectres. The air swarmed with Catherines." The name, itself a ghost or trace of a living hand, is not only scratched into the paint, it dances unmoored in the claustrophobic space. Lockwood discovers "a testament," a religious text, opens it, and inside he finds more Catherine.

Detached sentences, commentary, and a caricature of Joseph, as well as diary entries, are written in the book's margins and between the lines "in faded hieroglyphics" "that covered every morsel of blank the printer had left." Catherine's account of herself is marginalia "scrawled in an unformed childish hand." Her text both runs parallel to and invades the authorial religious text of the book Lockwood has found. Catherine has squeezed herself into the space allowed, an apt introduction to a girl whose energy and life force cannot be accommodated within the conventional forms available to her and whose changing names reflect the constrictions imposed on women whose names change according to the man to whom she owes obedience—father or husband.

The margin and blank spaces that remain are the perfect evocation of the place the literary woman is forced to occupy, the woman whose words must dance outside the tradition of masculine authoritative texts, the canon, the woman who finds room for herself in the narrow spaces along the edges or between the lines of "real, serious" work. This feminine space was largely inhabited by decorous ladies, who never competed with the big boys but contented themselves with pleasing, moralizing verses or well-mannered novels. Despite Charlotte Brontë's mythologizing of her sister in her problematical, if well intended, preface to *Wuthering Heights* composed after Emily's death, which turned the novel's author into a wild, brilliant, but untutored and naïve talent, I suspect her comment about finding and reading Emily's manuscript of poems is true.

> Of course, I was not surprised, knowing that she could and did write verse; I looked it over and something more than surprise seized me—a deep conviction that these were not common effusions, nor at all like the poetry women generally write.

Like her author, Emily Brontë, whose poems sold two copies after they were published, the young Catherine may write herself into the limited space that is available, but what she writes is not at all like what women generally write. It is not common, and it is not well behaved. It is a story of insurrection that subverts the pious, religious testament that fills the center of the page. But Catherine's marginalia, her text inside the text, also serves as an efficient introduction to the ongoing allusions and references in the novel to multiple authoritative texts sanctioned by tradition, both biblical and literary, texts that over the course of the novel are often misquoted, parodied, or perverted.

Lockwood reads Catherine's diary scribbled inside a book while inside a piece of furniture that opens and closes like a book, which is part of his own diary narration inside Emily Brontë's novel.

The text he reads is neither childish nor unformed. It is vivid, immediate, and complete with dialogue, some of it rendered in Joseph's thick Yorkshire dialect. The text, like all the texts inside *Wuthering Heights*, is less a diary entry than a reenactment, a peephole into the past, which is immediately present, its characters fully alive. The scene Lockwood reads takes place on a Sunday not long after Mr. Earnshaw has died. Because bad weather has kept them all from church (just as the weather has kept Lockwood from returning to the Grange), Joseph forces Catherine, Heathcliff, and a ploughboy to submit to a three-hour at-home service in the freezing garret while seated on a sack of corn. After this lengthy ordeal, Joseph inflicts on the children more holy punishment: a period of pious silent reading. Catherine rebels, throws the religious book, *The Helmet of Salvation*, into the dog kennel. Heathcliff follows her example. A "hubbub" ensues.

Lockwood ignores the printed text and instead absorbs himself in Catherine's secondary hieroglyphics. The dueling texts mirror the double narration of the novel as a whole—Lockwood and Ellen Dean. Further, the two narrations, Catherine's story and the religious work with its bellicose title, will merge in the narration of the dream that follows. Lockwood gets sleepy, and just before he dozes off, he notices that the printed text, the official version of the book in his hands, is a pious discourse entitled "'Seventy times Seven, and the First of the Seventy-First' delivered by one Reverend Jabes Branderham, in the Chapel of Gimmerton Sough." Lockwood falls asleep and dreams.

The reader of the novel moves from Lockwood's reading, during which Catherine's voice has taken over his, to his dream, which makes good use of what Freud called "day residue," elements taken from the day before and recombined in the logic peculiar to dreams. Lockwood is trying to get home through the snow with Joseph, but a detour occurs, and the reader moves from one memory scrap—snow, desire to return to the Grange—to another scrap—the last words that met his eye, Branderham's sevens. An anxiety dream follows, which plays out as Lockwood's personal revision of the story Catherine recorded in her diary.

Lockwood and Joseph find themselves in a chapel listening to the endless droning of Reverend Jabes Branderham, who is delivering a sermon on unpardonable sin in 490 parts. One of them—Joseph, the minister, or Lockwood—is guilty and will be "*exposed and excommunicated.*" In the dream, tormented by the tedium of listening, Lockwood, like Catherine, rebels, screams at the minister to stop at once and end his torment. This act of insurrection exposes him as the guilty party. Neither Catherine in her diary nor Lockwood in the dream feels guilty about being bored, but the wheels of sanctimonious religious authority have been set in motion, and excommunication—being thrown out of the sacred space of the chapel into the margins, the space filled in by Catherine in the testament—is to be his punishment.

Branderham's sevens refer to two biblical passages, which are not mentioned in Brontë's text, but which many of her readers surely knew. The first is Genesis 4:24: "If Cain is avenged seven times, then Lemech seventy-seven times." The second passage is Matthew 18:22. Peter asks Christ how many times he has to forgive a person who has sinned against him—seven times? Jesus answers, "I say not unto thee, until seven times; but until seventy times seven." I am not an expert on biblical sevens, but Jesus is obviously recommending much forgiveness over just a little. The cleft established is between Old and New Testaments—revenge versus mercy. The Branderham of the dream, however, is unforgiving. It ends in a melée of vengeance among the congregants as the minister loudly taps "on the boards of his pulpit," the sound of which catapults the dreamer, Lockwood, back to his closeted space and an awareness of the fir branch rattling against the lattice is responsible for the noise of the ruckus in his dream. He sleeps again.

Because the nightmare that follows occurs inside the "oak closet," it disrupts the border between Lockwood's waking and sleeping states.

My own most terrifying nightmares have inevitably taken place in the room where I was sleeping. Because the location of my body in the dream and the actual location of my body in the room are one and the same, waking provides no instantaneous end to the dream's frightening content, only further confusion. It is impossible to separate waking reality from dream. Inside the nightmare, Lockwood again hears the fir bough knocking its cones against the outer room's window, a fact he had already verified while awake. In the dream, he decides to leave the closet to stop the noise and discovers he is *locked* in because "the hook is soldered into the staple." Panicked, he breaks the window with his knuckles to reach the branch. Instead of a pine branch he finds himself holding an ice-cold little hand.

The limb of a stunted fir configured by the wuthering north wind has metamorphosed into a human limb. Catherine's girl ghost, the author of the liminal text inside a book that contains Branderham's sermon, appears at the window or limen of the casement. She calls herself Catherine Linton, not Earnshaw. She wants to be *let in*. Later in the novel's narration, but earlier in narrative time, before Catherine Linton dies, she is also at the window. She desperately wants to be let out, not in, to feel the breath of the moors upon her. The problem of inside and outside, locked in or locked out, recurs throughout the book. Catherine locks herself in at the Grange and refuses to eat. Nelly discovers the second Catherine is visiting Linton, Heathcliff's sickly son with Isabella, at the Heights and confines her to the Grange under threat of telling her father. Heathcliff locks the second Catherine in at Wuthering Heights to force her into a marriage with the stunted, tubercular Linton.

Lockwood sees the first Catherine's face obscurely at the window and is terrified. He writes that he was seized "by the intense horror of nightmare." To free himself from her grip, he scrapes her wrists on the broken glass and her blood runs all over his bedclothes inside the casement. The dream blood is another bit of day residue. It recalls Lockwood's nosebleed earlier in the evening. He promises to let her in if she will let go of him. She does. He yanks his arm back inside the broken window and, as a fortress, he piles books in front of the hole, plugs his ears, unplugs them, and hears that she is still moaning. The moaning and scratching continue. The pile of books moves. Lockwood, paralyzed with fear, shouts in his sleep.

The ghost's bleeding and moaning refer the reader back to Branderham's text delivered in the Chapel of Gimmerton Sough. In chapter 10, Nelly mentions a sough, a drainage channel, in a parenthesis "(for very soon after you pass the chapel, as you may have noticed, the sough that runs from the marshes joins a beck which follows the bend of the glen)." As a verb, *to sough* means to make a moaning or sighing sound, a rushing, rustling, or murmuring that applies to human beings and animals but also to the wind through the trees or to the sound of moving water. *Gimmer* is a local term for a young female sheep. One thing or kind runs into and blurs with another, running water and running blood, but sounds, too. Human beings and animals moan and sigh, but so do rushing water and the wind in the trees.

Just as the name Lockwood resounds with a theme of closing and opening in the novel, Branderham, which contains the word *brand*—an identifying mark burned into the bodies of livestock and/or criminals, slaves, and prisoners—carries with it ongoing meanings for the novel. A brand is a sign of *ownership, possession*. Heathcliff's zeal for domination and possession is nothing short of maniacal. The abused child wills himself to power. He seizes the whip Catherine longed for to become master of Wuthering Heights. He treats Lindley, his wife, and his son as chattel. Because he is a man, an able, intelligent man, Heathcliff can come and go, travel unaccompanied, pile up riches, own property. A woman has no such freedom of movement. A woman of Catherine's class is caught, locked inside domesticity.

Catherine's desire for the whip, her lust for dominance, and her desire to topple authority cannot be fulfilled in this world. Her need for mastery takes another form. She has cut her names into the casement, inscribed her patronymics, the signs or brands of the paternal line, Earnshaw and Linton, but she has also inscribed the name *Catherine Heathcliff*, a person who did not exist in her lifetime, the product of an imagined union, a fantasy. Is Catherine Heathcliff the masculine other that is also her "self," the thwarted self she longs for, a self that did not and could not exist in the body she was given, which, when ill and dying, she refers to in Platonic language as "a shattered prison"? She has inscribed herself into Branderham's pious text in a story that includes her throwing a pious text literally *to the dogs*, a gesture Heathcliff *imitates*. She leads. He follows. It is by means of this story of rebellion, a text written in the blanks of a book that survives her, that Catherine *brands* herself into Lockwood's reading and dreaming mind. This is authorial power. I possess and master you, my reader, and my story is so potent, it reappears even in your dreams.

There is a Catherine Heathcliff in the novel. Catherine Linton, née Earnshaw, is the mother of Catherine Linton 2, who marries Heathcliff and Isabella Linton's son, Linton Heathcliff. The offspring of that marriage, who first appears as a whining pathetic boy and grows into a stunted, selfish, sickly young man, whom Nelly refers to both as "a puling chicken" and "a changeling"—dies not long after the forced marriage, conducted while Catherine 2 is under lock and key and engineered by Heathcliff to gain power over her and her father's property. Notably, in order to lure Catherine 2 into sympathy for the cringing, self-pitying Linton, Heathcliff *edits* his son's love letters to her, as Lockwood claims to edit Nelly. Heathcliff condenses Linton's missives to Romantic clichés that do not betray their author's true character. The ironies, attendant to the problem of authorship in the novel, wind in and out of one another in a tangle as perplexing as the intermingling of the two families' names. In the course of his narration, Lockwood confesses his own attraction to Catherine Heathcliff and then reflects on the danger involved should he have acted on it: "I should be in a curious taking if I had surrendered my heart to that young person, and the daughter turned out to be a second edition of the mother!" The last thing he needs, it seems, is a second "Book of Catherine," even if significant changes to the text have been made.

Wuthering Heights itself falls into two halves. Many critics have viewed the second half with the generation that follows Heathcliff, Catherine, and Edgar Linton as a diluted or thin-blooded version of the first.

The second Catherine marries Hareton Earnshaw in the end, whom she has taught to read and write. Her knowledge of letters lifts Hareton out of the illiterate servitude he has been forced into by the loss of his inheritance to Heathcliff. This last marriage completes a circle of names by restoring another Catherine Earnshaw to the story, but the meanings of this circle are unclear.

I do not think there is a single key to the secrets of the novel or that any reading can contain its richness, but there is a dream logic at work throughout the text. The more one looks, the more thematic overlaps one finds. By dream logic, I am not joining Charlotte's ranks and consigning Emily to the "wild workshop" of the "rustic" and "moorish," nor claiming that she was a writer driven solely by her unconscious. Rather, I am saying that the text is evidence of the writer's openness to the uninhibited play of a magisterial imagination, which drew from both unconscious and conscious knowledge. I am convinced that writing fiction and dreaming partake of similar processes, which uncover profound emotional depths in elaborate imagery. Unlike a dream, however, a novel can be *edited*. Both powerful dreams and powerful novels can last a lifetime.

Catherine says to Nelly, "I have dreamt in my life dreams that have stayed with me ever after, and changed my ideas; they have gone through and through me, like wine through water and changed the color of my mind." The first Catherine will have more power when she is dead than when she was alive, if not as an actual ghost, as a text. Later in the novel, the reader discovers that she has predicted this turn after her death: She tells Nelly that although she may pity her mistress now, the tables will be turned. "I shall be sorry for you. I shall be incomparably beyond and above you all." Catherine's will to power cannot be accomplished except in death. In chapter 3, she is resurrected in Lockwood through his reading of her mutinous text, which then turns into his dream. She haunts him. Dead, Catherine has become that single entity that is also plural, a "swarm," which summons bees, or better, locusts—one of the seven biblical plagues. In the Gospel of Mark, the demon says, "My name is Legion: for we are many." This Catherine is, or these Catherines are, letters on a page that move through and through her reader and turn up as images in his dreams. Catherine runs through him like wine in water or blood in water, staining the color of his mind and the mind of the reader of the novel along with him.

The circling linguistic movements of this hallucinatory chapter are astonishing. As I, the reader, hold *Wuthering Heights* in my hands and read Lockwood's diary, Lockwood holds Branderham's book with Catherine's diary running alongside and into the printed book in his hands, and he reads. While locked in this room inside a room, this room of competing texts, one inside the other, which metamorphose into a dream-room with a bleeding ghost, Lockwood deploys *books* to wall himself off from his gruesome visitor. This pathetic gesture verges on the comic and might be interpreted as his gradual emergence from the dream accompanied by increasing lucidity. The reader tells himself it's only a book. I'm just reading. The dreamer wakes, and says, thank God, it was only a dream, only a figment of my imagination.

But here in the casement of chapter 3, the borders between the real and the imaginary, natural and supernatural, center and margin, authority and rebellion, between waking and sleeping, between death and life, between author and reader, male and female, self and other, human and animal, between inside the book and outside the book bleed into one another. They are not kept separate. The barriers between them do not hold. After he yells in his sleep and explains the dream to Heathcliff, Lockwood witnesses Heathcliff throw open the window and plead with the dream figment, the ghost: "Come in! Come in! Cathy, do come! Oh, do—*once* more! Oh! my heart's darling, hear me *this* time—Catherine at last!" But there is no beloved revenant beyond the opened window, just bracing ventilation, just wind and snow that rush in from the outside.

Lockwood is the last person to let Catherine in. The reader already knows he is uneasy about letting anyone into his inner sanctum. The man wants to be removed from the social world. Although the novel's critics have often rightly noted Lockwood's unreliability and errors of judgment, he shares a desire for solitude with his author, Emily Brontë.

She was a deeply private person who loved reading and writing and apparently hid her poems even from intimate family members, her sisters. There is a fierce irony in Lockwood's desire to be alone. His stirrings of attraction for a young woman, which he resisted, have landed him not in a peaceful bucolic heaven, but in a rural hell—a provincial wilderness populated by uncouth brutes, vicious dogs, the specter of another young female who scares the living daylights out of him, and a landlord who howls out the window—a man who, although seemingly in command of his senses, appears to be convinced the dead walk.

This startling chapter is surely an evocation of the imagination itself, of reading and dreaming, and the mental images generated from them, as a condensed preview of what is to come in the novel, a chapter that brings the reader inside its multiple ambiguities. Texts are phantoms, after all. The body of the author is nowhere to be seen, but the written word is our chief mode of communion with the dead. All readers are possessed by multiple ghosts. And once texts have been digested, they live on in us, not only in waking thoughts, but sometimes in our dreams, in the spontaneous nocturnal fictions we all make.

Wuthering Heights is an intense, passionate, and ruthless novel. This is what many of its early reviewers, countless readers, and many scholars over the years have felt—with disgust, horror, and pleasure—and have tried to explain or explain away. They have dismissed its dancing devils out of hand. They have built rigid theoretical edifices, both simple and elaborate, many of which crumble under pressure, and they have come with their own moralizing or romantic or ideological fictions that have swayed them into reading what is not there or what is only partly there. This is common enough. Readers of all sorts suppress complexity and substitute their own platitudes to avoid the discomfort of uncertainty.

Every time I have read the novel, its story has seized me by the throat and led me panting to its end. I am hardly alone. And yet, I know it's a book, and I know it is a book that knows it's a book. It is an object that opens and closes and can be put away on the shelf. But *Wuthering Heights* wields within it a ferocious philosophy, one that rescinds the very idea of fixed category. I think this is why the book has refused to settle for me, and I have returned to it so many times. Because the borders between one thing and another, and the border between the words on the page and me, are continually faltering as I read, the book will not rest quietly in what I call *myself*. It runs through and through me and continues to change the color of my mind.

2020

LIVING THING

What happens to a person when she or he looks at a work of art? Is the work outside the person or inside the person as a perceptual representation?

If the art can't be located in the world, then there is nothing for us to talk about, no reference, no point of return. For something to be art it has to be a thing that can be shared. Dreams and hallucinations are not art. And yet, if the art doesn't enter the spectator, if she doesn't register its presence, then it may as well be no-thing as far as she is concerned.

And when night falls on the museum, when the lights are turned off in the living room and the family has gone to bed and the painting hangs alone on the wall or the artist has left the studio for the day and no one is there to see the thing, is the art inert, a potential but unrealized object? Yes, I think it is—unless it is remembered. Memory is another form of presence, more fragile than immediate perception, akin to dream and hallucination and prone to distortion.

And yet, art always lives much longer in a person's memory than in perception. When I leave the museum, the gallery, the living room, if I take the image with me, it has become mine. And, as time goes on, the artwork changes. The image carried in the mind is rarely identical to the one seen yesterday, last week, a month ago, twenty years ago.

Should I mourn the inaccuracies of my memory? Human beings are not cameras. If I remember a work of art, it is because some quality of it survives in me as a feeling or a thought, as a color, an expression, or a detail that I continue to wonder about. Some aspect of the thing moved me, and to be moved by art means to be in one place before seeing the object and then finding oneself in another place afterward.

Art is haunted by a quality of aliveness, a strange animation the spectator feels in her muscles that tense or relax, in her breath that stops suddenly or is extended in a long exhalation, in the memory that leaps suddenly to mind, perhaps one she hasn't recalled in many years.

And then there is the question: Why? Why do some objects move this viewer and others leave her cold? What is great art? How can we tell?

There are works of art that have been anointed as great, works made by our art heroes, sanctified by cultural consensus and media attention. Dutiful spectators troop through the museums to genuflect for a moment before them and then hurry past the paintings and sculptures by unknowns. The viewers feel personally enhanced by their proximity to the "priceless" and the "beautiful." They take pictures of the pictures and pictures of themselves with the pictures.

Not one of us is immune to the sway of greatness. A work on the sidewalk does not command our interest in the way a work in the Louvre does.

The expectation of greatness becomes part of the experience of greatness. This is how human perception works. But remember that Vermeer died in 1675 and his work remained obscure until his paintings were reseen and rethought in the middle of the nineteenth century by the scholar and art critic Théophile Thoré, alias Willem Bürger. And remember, too, that the best canvases by the Italian baroque painter Artemisia Gentileschi, who died about twenty years before Vermeer, were attributed to her father—even those she had signed—and it was not until well into the twentieth century that a few art historians began to believe what should have been obvious all along. Prejudice is literally blinding.

Aren't we all influenced by the hierarchies the busy art historians have erected for us? Don't we all look a little longer at the objects pre-approved for our worship?

But what about the artists buried from our view?

Sometimes we find the lost and the unseen and the undervalued. I often wonder how many there are who have not been found and seen and valued.

Time is required if one wants to see what is there. When I take time with a thing that provokes or interests or soothes or irritates me at first glance, decide not to leave it but to stay with the object, then "it" begins to become "you." If I look long enough in the silence of that encounter, I have discovered that I see what I hadn't seen before, that various aspects of the animated thing emerge into my consciousness to be puzzled over, and sometimes thoughts appear that I didn't know I could have. The patina of "greatness" and the seduction of the "big name" fall away because the art has become a particular experience, one that cannot be contained in an adjective or a proper noun.

I am not interested in art that I can understand easily. I am only interested in art that keeps me wondering. For me art is not a problem to be solved. Great art is a cloud of unknowing.

The particular experience is always located between the viewer and the work of art. It is always made and lived between them.

Some of us carry around a host of paintings and sculptures and installations in our memories, not exact replicas of the works we saw, perhaps, but mental images that in turn generate rigorous thought or laughter or empathy or the itch of the uncanny or swirling half-formed sentences or long conversations over dinner or scholarly papers or novels or new works of visual art or even birthday greetings.

Art cannot be fixed to a single location because lived experience is not left behind in the room where the object rests unseen at night after the museum has closed its doors. The art object travels in many bodies in multiple forms and it speaks and writes and sings in many languages. It is a living thing.

2019

VISITING ST. FRANCIS

I don't know what will happen to me once I'm in front of the painting, but I know that if I let go of my expectations, if I open myself to the experience of looking closely, I may be surprised by what I discover. We are all creatures of habit, and most of the time we forget to look closely. Before we even have time to think, we size up a thing, a place, or a person instantly and then move on. Anticipation is often a form of prejudgment, after all, and sometimes it distorts what is right in front of our eyes. No one is free of these prejudgments. They help us navigate the world, but as I walk toward the building on East Seventieth Street that houses the Frick Collection, I tell myself that once I'm inside, I can take my time with the picture. Art is there just to be seen. All I have to do is look.

I've studied a number of the paintings that hang on the walls inside the white mansion where the robber baron Henry Clay Frick once made his home in Manhattan, but as I take the steps, I have a single canvas in mind: *St. Francis in Ecstasy*. Giovanni Bellini painted it late in the fifteenth century. I know it's an exalted work, but I've neglected it. I've never read anything about it. All the better. I haven't been told what to think or feel. I take several deep breaths, pull open the tall, solid door, and step inside. I hear the clamor of conversations, see people milling in the hall, and worry that the museum is too crowded, but once I have secured my ticket and have walked down the hard marble floors of the hallway and have turned right, I step into what used to be Mr. Frick's living room, and I feel my shoes sink into the carpet. It's quieter here. People are speaking in low voices. The dark wood-paneled walls and the three tall draped windows on either side of the room that let in diffused light are grand but comforting. I hear a man and a woman quietly speaking Italian to each other. I hear the word *bellissima*.

As I make my way toward the Bellini in the center of the wall to my left, I notice several people gazing up at the painting, which I guess is about four feet tall and four and a half feet wide. I find a spot to stand. I watch two older women pause to look at it for eight or nine seconds and then move on past me. A man is standing close to the canvas, his collar up, his thinning brown hair almost the same color as his jacket. I station myself to the right of him. I see the rather small figure of Saint Francis in the foreground. I see the tiny donkey behind him in a meadow, his ears pricked up, as if he is listening. But I let myself feel the colors of the big, peculiar landscape first—the many shades of green in delicate foliage, curling vines, and grass, the deep and medium browns and ochres of branches and slender tree trunks and fallen leaves and the saint's cassock, and the many shades of cool pale turquoise in the steep rock cliff. The whitening blue-green makes me catch my breath. I take in the strong hit of cerulean blue sky at the top of the picture and the white clouds that interrupt the color as they float above a walled city. I think to myself: This isn't one place; it's three places—the rocky mountain zone of the saint, the green meadow of the donkey, and the remote city on high.

I take out my notebook and begin to write. The man standing in front of me leans toward the canvas. I admire his attention and wish he would leave at the same time. I hear two people speaking French as they pass behind me. The jutting stone face of the mountain rises above Francis and dwarfs him. As I focus on his body, I straighten up, inhale, and expand my chest. I realize I'm imitating the saint's posture, that I've become an involuntary mirror of the figure in the picture. I write in the notebook: "turned to his right, eyes and chin lifted, sharp slender nose, mouth open, cowl fallen backward, chest open—transfixed." His hands are extended to either side of him in a gesture of reception, his upper body radiant in soft light. He looks awed but calm. There's nothing wild or frightening about this man's ecstasy. I'm afraid to stick my nose right up to the canvas. Instead, I lean forward, hoping I look inquisitive, not aggressive. I want to see his right hand. I think I can make out a tiny

MOTHERS, FATHERS, AND OTHERS 193

red spot. Stigmata. He has the wounds of Christ. One slender bare foot sticks out from under his robe.

The man in front of me leaves just as my discoveries are mounting. I spy a little rabbit looking out from a crevice in the wall to the left of Frances. I'm stupidly proud of finding the rabbit. I discover a heron not far from the donkey perched at the edge of the cliff that becomes the meadow. I make out another little bird far to my left. St. Francis and the animals. I remember stories. Birds came to listen to his sermons. He once tamed a vicious wolf. Didn't hundreds of larks swoop down from the sky as the saint was dying? I study the rock formations, and I seem to see hands, paws, hooves, and claws. I wonder if the painter intended to make this allusion. I begin to draw their forms. There are three of them bulging from the thin layers of shale.

A plant with nine small blooming flowers grows just behind Francis. I draw it quickly and then draw the wooden trellis to the right of the plant, the jug that stands in front of it, and the inclined desk behind it, on which rests a skull with no jawbone and a book. As I draw, I feel as if I am touching each thing, tracing its outlines with my hand. I look up and think to myself that the Bible is the color of dried blood. Then I spot the monk's sandals lying under his desk. He's left his cane or walking stick behind him, too. It rests at an angle on one of the trellis rungs. The sandals and the stick are poignant. As I continue to look at them, I have a keen sense of ordinary life and ordinary death. Everything that is alive will die. Our things often outlive us.

And then I imagine the story. Francis is sitting at his desk reading. He closes the book of scripture and turns around because he feels the tug of a presence behind him. He forgets everything. He doesn't think about his shoes or his cane. He stands up and walks out of his little enclave. After he has taken a few steps, he stops. He turns his face toward the light of God. The word *grace* comes into my mind.

I'm writing the story down when a guard approaches me. "You can sit if you like, ma'am." He nods at a tall plush green chair decorated with pom-pom fringe right in front of me. His kind voice has jolted me out of the painting, and I realize I haven't heard or seen anyone for some time.

I thank him and sit down. It feels good to sit and lean back in the chair. I'm no longer facing the painting, and I let my eyes move across the room. I absorb the cobalt blue behind Holbein the Younger's Cromwell and the green drapery behind his Thomas More. I stare at the chinoiserie lamp with fringe on a round table directly in front of me. The voices of the other visitors are suddenly audible again. It's as if I've been away. I stand up and turn toward the canvas again.

It seems to me now that there are three invisible light sources shining on the painting: one for the city, one for the field where the donkey and heron have paused, and one for Francis. It occurs to me suddenly that the source that illuminates the saint is not inside but outside the canvas. It begins somewhere to the right far above and behind me. I imagine that I am in that light, too. A curious thought.

Before I walk out of the room, I check my phone. I've been in front of the painting for two hours. It doesn't seem possible. I'm not thinking in sentences. I'm between worlds. I know that it takes a while to withdraw from a painting. I walk into the hallway and hear the percussive clicks of footsteps on the bare floor. Instead of heading to the coat check, I turn left and walk into the enclosed garden. Late afternoon sunlight comes through the opaque glass ceiling above me. I seat myself on a stone bench adjacent to the room I have just left and listen to the rush of water from the fountain. My eyes land on one of two black frogs that shoot thin arcs of water from their mouths. I crane my neck and look back at Bellini's painting through the window behind me. I see it from a distance now. I feel a small pinch of grief. Grief for what? Am I sad to go? Have I suddenly remembered the brutal politics of here and now? Or is it time, the time represented by the skull? Saint Francis will stand there fixed in wonder as long as the painting lasts. I push myself off the bench and retrieve my coat. As soon as I open the door, the wind blows into my face. I hear a car horn, the squeal of a truck stopping, and make my way toward the Q train.

2019

BOTH-AND

Louise Bourgeois did not become famous until after she had turned seventy. It seemed unlikely at the time that she would continue making art for nearly three decades, but she did. I was twenty-seven when I saw the retrospective at the Museum of Modern Art in 1982. I am now sixty-five. I will say this: Although the young woman I was then had been a feminist since she was fourteen and found herself amazed and inspired by the work in that astounding exhibition curated by Deborah Wye, she had to strive and observe and suffer and get older to understand the degree to which the perceptual expectations for a work of art made by a woman in our culture conspire to smother, if not kill it, especially if the work takes on questions of sexual difference, the body, emotion, and autobiography directly.

On the heels of her first big success ushered in by the MoMA exhibition, Bourgeois offered a founding myth for her oeuvre in *Artforum* the same year, a project that presented a tale of jealousy, sex, and betrayal guaranteed to attract attention: *Child Abuse*. Louise's father carried on an affair with her young English governess, Sadie Gordon Richmond, an affair that was tolerated by Louise's mother. From the project: "I am a pawn. Sadie is supposed to be there as my teacher and actually you, mother, are using me to keep track of your husband. This is child abuse." Notice the use of the present tense.

The sensational story also deflected attention from her life after childhood, her marriage to the prominent American art historian Robert Goldwater, her three sons, and her psychoanalysis. Bourgeois denied that she had ever been in psychoanalysis, but she had begun seeing Henry Lowenfeld in New York for years of intense therapy in 1953 and maintained contact with him until he died in 1985. She did not disguise her interest in the subject, however, a subject in which she was supremely well read. Psychoanalysis served not only as an explanation for her depression, anxiety, and aggression but as a rich and shaping mythology for her own work. I am using *mythology* to mean a grand narrative of origin. It was a word Freud himself used for drive theory in his *New Introductory Lectures on Psychoanalysis* (1933). He called it "our mythology."

I do not believe Bourgeois's childhood story is false or that she wasn't tormented by her memories. Rather, I think she was conscious of the story's usefulness as a frame for her work. From the outset, what she presented as confession was a double game, both a revelation and a mask, at once sincere and ironic. The artist's narrative of the family romance has been startlingly effective. It is endlessly repeated in the press, in catalogues, and in scholarly articles and books. Her interviews and now published writing, including her writing about her psychoanalysis, have been windows for interpreting her life and art. Bourgeois interpreted herself in her analysis with the aid of Lowenfeld's interpretations and her own reading in psychoanalytic theory, and she made art that relates to these insights. Then more interpreters came along and interpreted and reinterpreted further.

"Bourgeois says that 'pain and pleasure are merged in hysteria,' indicating that she understood that hysteria 'is a substitute for orgasm' . . . I am arguing that Bourgeois's art is conspicuously and deeply rooted in her penis envy." (Donald Kuspit, "Symbolizing Loss and Conflict: Psychoanalytic Process in Louise Bourgeois' Art.")

Just as in Freud's case history of Dora, the "nature of her disposition was always drawn toward her father." (Philip Larratt-Smith, "The Return of the Repressed.")

"The threat is associated with the pre-Oedipal mother, appearing in our nightmares and in psychotic delusions as a two-way goddess: having produced her child she can gobble it up again." (Paul Verhaeghe and Julie De Ganck, "Beyond the Return of the Repressed: Louise Bourgeois's Chthonic Art.")

"She did have an analysis. It 'cured' her of nothing, nor should it have done. She used it to become an important artist. The talismanic precept of psychoanalytic treatment is 'where id (unconscious) is, there ego (conscious) shall come to be'; for Bourgeois it was where id (unconscious) is, there shall a sculpture (consciousness) come to be." (Juliet Mitchell, "The Sublime Jealousy of Louise Bourgeois.")

"Bourgeois's writings not only expand the archive of psychoanalysis but transform it. In particular she brings feminine aggression to the forefront of psychoanalysis, making this the main theme." (Mignon Nixon, "L.")

Louise Bourgeois has become the gifted patient for the psychoanalyst who cares about art, as well as the serious art critic well versed in psychoanalysis, and a deliciously clever one at that, but caution is in order. The artist was a trickster who delighted in puncturing pompous balloons.

Her preferred weapon was a needle.

Louise Bourgeois spoke and wrote with a bluntness that disarmed her many interlocutors and continues to disarm her readers. Sample quotes from the volume of her writings published under the title *The Return of the Repressed*:

"My father has betrayed me with other women, but my mother has never betrayed me."

"To eat to kill to devour to come to kill the mother to incorporate the father to take his strength and to be killed as punishment."

"I am the cutter who cuts everything."

"I break everything I touch because I am violent. I destroy my friendships, my love, my children."

"If you leave me, if you abandon me (to Robert) . . . if you separate me from you, I will kill, I will kill your children. To Jerry. Medea."

Strong stuff. Her writing inscribes and re-inscribes violent fantasies many people would not have the courage to record, but by doing so Bourgeois takes her reader into a primal theater of memory that turns the personal into the universal and *elevates* her particular story to myth. This is hardly a humble or victimized position. Medea does not sneak into the above passage by accident. In the Greek myth, Medea is so enraged when her husband, Jason, leaves her that she murders their children. The spider Bourgeois repeatedly insisted was the image of her mother, whose work was repairing tapestries, resonates not only with Arachne in Greek myth but with the spider woman-mother-goddess figures in the myths of southwestern American Indian tribes and the formidable Teotihuacan Spider Woman of pre-Columbian Mexico, the goddess of creation itself. Robert Goldwater was an expert on what was then called "primitive art." No one will convince me that the artist wasn't aware of every one of these resonances. One myth is deftly woven into other myths.

From an interview with Stuart Morgan, 1988:

"When you talk of killing the parents, are you talking literally or metaphorically?"

"I never talk literally. Never, never, never. You do not get anywhere by being literal. You have to use analogy and interpretation and leaps of all kinds."

There were no murders in the Bourgeois household, but myth often turns on vengeance and murder. In *Totem and Taboo*, Freud's originating myth is the murder of the tyrannical father. His sons gang up on him, kill him, and eat him. Parricide begets the incest taboo begets society. Women are mere pawns in the Freudian story. Pater wants all the girls for himself. In her work *The Destruction of the Father* (1974), which she made the year following her husband's death, Bourgeois retold the parricide myth, making it both personal and feminine. *The* tyrannical father is *her* tyrannical father.

In an interview with Donald Kuspit: "At the dinner table, my father would go on and on, showing off, aggrandizing himself. And the more he showed off, the smaller we felt. Suddenly there was a terrific tension, and we grabbed him—my brother, my sister, my mother—the three of us grabbed him and pulled him onto the table and pulled his legs and arms apart—dismembered him, right? And we were so successful in beating him up that we ate him up. Finished. A fantasy. But sometimes the fantasy is *lived*."

Someone goes missing in this telling of the story. It should be "the four of us"—Louise, her mother, and her two siblings who gobble up the father. She told the story several times. It changed. Her mother is sometimes present, sometimes absent. Her mother sometimes tries to appease the husband-father, sometimes she doesn't. Of course, fantasies can have several versions. There is no real carnage being remembered. What is certain is that in the Bourgeois myth, daughters get to be cannibals, too.

The emotional dramas of a middle-class French family take on epic proportions in the artwork. The sculpture is not a literal depiction of a man being eaten by his children (and perhaps his wife) but a work that captures violent feeling in anatomical forms suggestive of a mouth and mastication. The strange Bourgeois maw with its mess of animal bones and casts made from meat is unsettling. As Elisabeth Bronfen writes in the essay, "Contending with the Father: Louise Bourgeois and Her Aesthetics of Reparation," "the dark recesses, shadows and folds suggestively open up a mental site," that which cannot be "rendered visible." The story as told to Kuspit is the stuff of black comedy—the man is pulled apart like a well-cooked chicken. I can almost see the wicked glint in the artist's eyes. No doubt she remembered her place at the dinner table and her father droning on, but the fuel for the artwork turns on felt rage in present memory about a dinner table routine in the past and a fantasy generated from it.

All fantasies are lived. They are part of human experience, but when someone uses a specific fantasy to make art, it is *lived through again in the work*. This is true for all art-making—for novels, poems, music, paintings, and sculptures. The object, whatever it is, seems to take on an organic reality, which, during the process of sculpting or writing, partakes of the artist's living embodiment, but as John Dewey stresses in *Art in Experience* (1934), an art product is not something that is pressed out of the artist's insides to the outside world. An artist is always interacting with her materials and her environment. The artist's search is not for literal truths but for rendering emotional and intellectual truths in the thing she is making, a thing that answers her feeling, gets it right, and then can be abandoned. The artwork is not the fantasy, although it may represent it in one way or another.

And yet, the mythical dismemberment suggested by *Destruction of the Father* is rooted in a personal and broader cultural reality, in a real father's vain ramblings at dinner, but also in his assumption of paternal power as socially *legitimate*. Any child, wife, or other peon who has watched a long line of patriarchs hold court (at the family table, in boardrooms, or at dinners after art openings) with the smug expectation that the assembled underlings are there to smile and nod in admiring silence as he yatters on knows what strangled fury means. They also know that interrupting, speaking up, or complaining will be met with outrage. How dare you question my authority?

To say that Louise Bourgeois seized hold of her own narrative in 1982 is a gross understatement, and yet, this action came late. After many years of observing the machinations of art institutions, more and less unnoticed from the inside, she not only understood what was at stake, I think she felt liberated and deserving enough to grab the opportunity when it came. Bourgeois, as Robert Storr makes clear in his monumental monograph, *Intimate Geographies: The Art and Life of Louise Bourgeois*, knew everyone who was anyone in that world—famous artists but also museum moguls, including Alfred Barr, who in 1929 became the first director of MoMA and played a role in the workings of the museum until 1967. In 1951, he bought her *Sleeping Figure* for the museum's collection.

Bourgeois showed her work, was reviewed, and yet she was not regarded as important. "There are a lot of people but nobody hears me" (January 4, 1959). Storr, who knew Bourgeois well, argues that she was to some degree responsible, that she shrank from opportunities out of fear. "*The absolute refusal to grow up disguised under / the refusal of success*" (circa 1959, italics in the original). She was born a girl to a dominating father who had wanted a boy in a world that preferred boys. Exactly how does one separate the personal story from the social one? Several times in her writing Bourgeois refers to having been born a girl as having been "gypped." Culture-psyche-soma cannot be cut with a knife into three parts and boxed. When she was interviewed before 1982, she did *not* share personal stories about childhood suffering. "No one likes the crying ones or those in trouble," she wrote in 1951 at age forty. "So keep your chin up, and be a prima donna." Louise Bourgeois was savvy about the biases of art reviewers and critics. She knew that women artists were repeatedly reduced to their personal lives.

The sculptor Eva Hesse, whose career was as short as Bourgeois's career was long, complained that critics continually discussed her life, not her work. Hesse was on one of the last Kindertransports that took Jewish children out of Nazi Germany in 1938. She was reunited with her immediate family in the Netherlands. They later moved to New York City. Her parents divorced. When Hesse was nine, her mother killed herself. The artist had a traumatic childhood. And she was a woman, a beautiful woman who died at thirty-four and never grew old.

In 1965, Hesse wrote, "A singleness of purpose no obstructions allowed seems a man's prerogative. His domain. A woman is sidetracked by all her feminine roles from menstrual periods to cleaning house to remaining pretty and 'young' and having babies . . . She also lacks conviction that she has the 'right' to achievement . . . I dwell on this all the time." Eva Hesse did not have many years to work it out or work it through. Bourgeois did.

However hampered by self-doubt she may have been when she was younger, Bourgeois was an intensely ambitious, competitive woman whose art had not been given its due, and she was acutely aware of how the institutional art machine churned. I suspect that the full-blown mature prima donna with a MoMA retrospective and many years of analysis behind her aggressively embraced *the personal* to silence in advance the inevitable whining that women's art is confessional and autobiographical even when it's not confessional and autobiographical. She beat them to the punch. By announcing the story of child abuse, she fulfilled perceptual expectations and defeated them at the same time.

That the body, emotion, and nature have been associated with passive femininity, and the mind, reason, and culture with active masculinity is a given in the Western tradition. Sexual difference has long been part of the ongoing and still fiercely debated psyche-soma distinction, which has also cut the human body into two parts: masculinity has taken up residence in the head and femininity in the body from the neck down. The hierarchy is vertical, up over down, high over low. Bourgeois played with this cultural anatomy and her viewers' expectations, using cultural biases about female and male bodies to subvert them—turn them inside out or upside down or blend them until they are neither one nor the other but indistinguishably both. She robbed psychoanalytic thought but was hardly limited by it. She greedily digested bits and pieces of other artistic traditions, including Paleolithic, pre-Columbian, and Egyptian, to create her own sacred objects and images. Look at *She-Fox*, 1985.

Bourgeois ruled over her own mythical world: "I can create / my own artist world of omnipotence and fantasy." Three centuries earlier, another artist and thinker, Margaret Cavendish, wrote in her preface to her fantasy fiction, *The Blazing World*, "Though I cannot be Henry the Fifth or Charles the Second, I endeavor to be Margaret the First . . . rather than not be mistress of a world, since fortune and the fates would give me none, I have made one of my own." Artists of all kinds withdraw into self-made worlds, inside of which they may reign as potentates, but for women the struggle to be *seen* as rulers from the outside has been far more difficult than for men. Further, women were and are punished for ambition, are still expected to bow to male authority and sit quietly at the table. Aggression, anger, and dominant behaviors in women still inspire "backlash"—social psychology's word for punishment. A paper in the *Journal of Occupational and Organizational Psychology* (2010) by Olivia O'Neill and Charles O'Reilly, "Reducing the Backlash Effect: Self-Monitoring and Women's Promotions," found that if confident, dominant women "self-monitor"—turn on and off their masculine qualities depending on the situation—they do better, get promoted, etc. By self-monitoring, the authors appear to mean a kind of hyper-self-consciousness that allows women to change faces when needed. Women, it seems, must be masters of disguise.

In her 1929 essay "Womanliness as Masquerade," the psychoanalyst Joan Riviere writes about a successful, intellectual woman who, when in the company of men, hides her accomplishments behind a feminine facade. "Womanliness therefore can be assumed and worn as a mask both to hide the possession of masculinity and avoid the reprisals expected if she was found to possess it—much as a thief will turn out his pockets and ask to be searched to prove that he has not stolen goods. The reader may now ask how I define womanliness or where I draw the line between genuine womanliness and the 'masquerade.' My suggestion is not, however, that there is any such difference, whether radical or superficial, they are the same thing."

"We are all vulnerable, we are all male-female," Louise Bourgeois wrote.

I am convinced that by the time the artist was in her sixties she felt freer to wear her authority, her masculinity, openly. But she also felt freer to announce her vulnerability, her femininity, openly. She told Amei Wallach, "I became a sculptor because it allowed me to express—this is very, very important—what I was embarrassed about before." Was she embarrassed about her need, dependence, and pain, or her ambition and aggression, or was it both? I suspect it was both.

Femininity and masculinity mingled as Bourgeois played freely with the cultural masquerade in art and in life to create high tensions of multiple ambivalent meanings. The work is never embarrassed or ashamed.

Femininity and childhood have been continually linked in Western culture as conditions of shrunken intellect and dependence. This was particularly true for women of the middle and upper classes in the eighteenth and nineteenth centuries. The Victorian doll-wife and the Angel of the House are familiar iterations of the same persona. And yet, the dependent child lives on in the adult, in every adult, in memory that is more feeling than a specific autobiographical image. "You do not get anywhere by being literal." The literal is small, particular, detailed, and bound to facts. The figurative can fly free of those concrete constraints. Louise Bourgeois suffered, and she documented her suffering. The characters in her story have the names of real people who correspond to an actual time and place, but they are also continually abstracted into grand archetypes—Mother, Father, Child, Sister, Brother, Wife, Husband.

It would be interesting to know how her legacy would have been different if her critics had had less personal material to plumb. It is well known that the artist suffered from depression, had somatic symptoms and mood swings. She was a gifted, succinct writer, and I am grateful for the texts that have been published, but the fact that she was a woman and not a man continues to skew readings of her work, and those readings often fall into the mind/body or male/female schism. I worry that by overemphasizing her misery, some of her critics have reduced the artist to the bottom half of the binary.

Bourgeois worked at a fevered, arguably hypomanic pace in her late life. She sped up as if to compensate for lost time. The fear, fury, and pain in her work cannot hide the wit, humor, and irony that also acted as forceful engines in her artistic output. Although her earlier work was not humorless, her work got funnier as she got older. And yet, her potent sense of the comic is mostly missing from the many psychoanalytic interpretations of her art I have read.

Donald Kuspit, for example, founds his interpretation of Bourgeois's art on Freud's highly dubious notion of penis envy. "As so many of the works suggest, Bourgeois had body image problems. They had to do with the fact that she had no penis—that she was not a man—thus her implicit penis envy and explicit appropriation of the penis, to make herself into a man, indeed to bespeak her inner masculinity." I dare say it is Kuspit who is obsessed with penises. Penis envy was critiqued by Karen Horney when Freud was still alive and later by Clara Thompson in the early 1940s. Thompson argued that women did not envy male genitalia but male social power (to which I say Amen). While meaning to be expansive, Kuspit is unforgivably *literal*. What is "inner masculinity" if not an appropriation of the power that accrues to men in the culture as a result of genital difference? In his essay "The Phallic Woman," he interprets Bourgeois's statement "The phallus is the object of my tenderness" through a famous photo by Robert Mapplethorpe taken of the artist with her penis sculpture *Fillette*: "She triumphs over the phallus, completely and unequivocally dominating it; it is her phallus, however ugly and unsavory its appearance."

The poor critic who waxes eloquent about Bourgeois as a hermaphrodite appears to be blind to the real and terrible vulnerability of male genitalia that dangles exposed outside the body. And he accepts without question the absurdly important symbolic role the phallic has gained in the culture. Bourgeois's *tenderness* exposes both truths—the penis is an easily assailable body part that must be protected from harm, and its metaphorical cultural inflation into omnipotence is ridiculous. This is irony, irony about power.

Philip Larratt-Smith's reference to Freud's famously bungled Dora case and the young patient's focus on her father also appears to be without irony. Many volumes have been written on Freud's inability to recognize what was really going on with "Dora." "In this celebrated failure, Freud provides an example of what not to do in terms of technique," writes Lou Acosta in his book *A Rumor of Empathy*. Acosta is one in a large chorus. The fact that Dora became a pawn in her father's extramarital affair, a fact that parallels Bourgeois's own situation as a girl and her rage at both her parents over Sadie, is worth noting. Larrat-Smith recognizes the connection but not Freud's notorious misreading of this patient.

Squeezing Louise Bourgeois's art into Jacques Lacan's "pre-Oedipal mother" and that theorist's almighty "phallus" requires a delicate touch and a recognition of Bourgeois's skepticism about Lacan's willful obfuscations. In an interview with Storr, she said she "distrusted" Lacan and linked him to the seventeenth-century theologian and rhetorician Bossuet: "They gargle with their own words." (Storr's translation from the French.) This is both succinct and true. Bourgeois does evoke a terrifying mother, and she plays with phallic meanings, but she doesn't play straight with either one of them. Paul Verhaeghe and Julie De Ganck write, "After returning from the borders of the Real via the pre-Oedipal stage back to the normal level, meaning the Oedipal stage of sexuality and gender relations, the quality of her work, compared to that before the 1950s is much higher—the confrontation with the fringes of madness seems to have proved fruitful." Isn't this an easy narrative masquerading as complex theory? I do not know De Ganck's work, but Verhaeghe is a subtle thinker, sensitive to social influences and its influences on the collective psyche. The treatment of Bourgeois by the authors, however, is reductive.

Bourgeois read Melanie Klein. In 1968, she made the following note: "(see and quote Melanie K.)." Many commentators on Bourgeois have turned to Klein, who gave the world an aggressive baby with primitive "phantasies" and a part-object, the breast. The good breast soothes and feeds. The bad breast isn't there when you need it. In *Love, Guilt, and Reparation*, Klein writes, "Love and hate are struggling together in the baby's mind; and this struggle to a certain extent persists through life and is liable to become a source of danger in human relationships." Bourgeois's art is full of breasts and breast-like forms. Kleinian fairy tales? Mignon Nixon subtly unearths the connections in her book *Fantastic Reality*. Melanie Klein's furious baby with a death wish may well uncover pieces of the truth about Bourgeois and her work, but again, humor and irony disappear in the process.

Juliet Mitchell's insistence that the artist was never "cured" by analysis may be true, although one begs to know exactly what "cure" means. Her careful analysis of sibling rivalry also captures an aspect of Bourgeois's work that had been neglected before, but her idea that sculpture takes the place of ego, which she equates with consciousness in Freud's famous formulation "where id was there ego shall be" is too simple. In *The Ego and the Id*, Freud also wrote, "The ego is first and foremost a bodily ego." This bodily ego is not always conscious. The act of making sculpture is not purely conscious.

Psychoanalytic thought played a significant role in the intellectual armature of the artist's work. No doubt about it. What I am arguing here is that every one of these interpretations is too narrow and too sober. These writers miss the dance, humor, irony, and fun in the woman and in the art. They forget that this was a person who made "the scene" in New York in the 1980s after her smashing success at MoMA. She was photographed by Mapplethorpe, with Andy Warhol, and was out in clubs with the designer of the moment, Andrée Putman. I once saw the prima donna myself as she paraded chin up through the Pierre Matisse Gallery with a line of young male acolytes trailing behind her. Genuine Louise? Masquerade? No difference between them?

Many writers on Bourgeois have cautioned about taking the artist at her word. She herself said, "An artist's words are always to be taken cautiously." Nevertheless, she integrated words into some of her art. Her words are not all hiding out in her private diaries or in public interviews.

"A man and a woman lived together. On one evening, he did not come back from work. And she waited. And she kept on waiting. And she grew littler and littler. Later, a neighbor stopped by out of friendship and there he found her, in an armchair, the size of a pea" (*She Lost It*, 1992).

How not to laugh?

"I HAVE BEEN TO HELL AND BACK. AND LET ME TELL YOU. IT WAS WONDERFUL." (Inscribed on an embroidery, 1996.)

"Later he died right in his factory of refinement. / Everyone worth talking about cried and cried. Of / course no one could see his soul, not even his wife. / But they said his body was dry and they think he was a puritan." (From the illustrated book *the puritan*, 1990.) According to many, the dead puritan was Alfred Barr.

A psychiatric point: *People who suffer from major depression do not make art.* Despair does not lend itself to making art. Bourgeois's fallow period corresponds to the time when she was in intense analysis for depression. She may not have been "cured" by her analysis, but I do believe the years she spent working through her painful reality helped her to recognize her anger and her fear of it. "(To Lowenfeld this / seems to be the / basic problem) / it is my aggression / that I am afraid / of."

And that fear of aggression was not purely personal. It was also social. For European and American women of her class during that period—perhaps even more acutely then than now—aggression was not only forbidden, it was often turned inward on the self, disguised as self-laceration and depression. Art moves in the other direction: it is the inward turned outward. Bourgeois created visual and verbal parables for volatile feelings with heavy doses of reflection and the irony that results from that reflection. As she put it herself, "A steady rage can be productive." Severely depressed people are not enraged. They are listless.

Further, Louise Bourgeois was able to embrace without apology an adaptive grandiosity that gave her personal saga the immensity of myth. Years ago I stumbled across the term *adaptive grandiosity* in an astute essay by the psychoanalyst Peter Wolson in *The Psychoanalytic Review* (1995). Wolson writes, "The artist needs adaptive grandiosity to create." Without an inflated sense of one's own importance to the world, it is impossible to make art and keep making it. Wolson recognizes that this inflation is a fragile business, and that it can easily become "maladaptive," but he also understands its necessity for creative work. The obvious grandiosity that informs her art is not part of the psychoanalytic discussions that I have read. Louise Bourgeois had adaptive grandiosity. She became Louise the First.

My own psychoanalysis has unleashed me into my work in ways that were not possible earlier in my life. Despite the Romantic notion that "madness" is a well from which artists draw inspiration, I have seen too many talented psychiatric patients stymied, not released, by their illnesses. Depression is especially deadening. Plain old neuroses aren't helpful for making art either. Freedom is what is needed. *Sublimation* was Freud's term for channeling threatening or aggressive erotic drives into something else—including works of art. Louise Bourgeois used and reused *Sublimation* as a title for her artworks. One of them, a fifteen-page book, includes this text: "the symbolic action / can take many many / forms, some people will / become perfectionist / in whatever they are / doing / or they can write a story / or they can work on / the house." Because Bourgeois played again and again in her work on "the house," woman as house, *Femme Maison*, body as house, wife-house, housewife, cells as jails, as biological elements, as lairs, lures, caves and hideouts, the wit is self-referential.

Bourgeois repeatedly argued that her art was a mode of survival and sublimation. There is no reason to disbelieve her. Indeed, many artists working in various forms would tell you the same thing. I would say the same thing about writing fiction. The English psychoanalyst and pediatrician D. W. Winnicott quoted James Strachey who noted that Freud "used the word 'sublimation' to point the way to a place where cultural experience is meaningful, but perhaps he did not get so far as to tell us where in the mind cultural experience is." That may be a task too large for anyone, but Winnicott located cultural experience *between* the person and the external world in what he called "potential space"—not quite me, not quite you. He also called it the "intermediate area." He coined the term *transitional object* for the blanket or toy a child clings to as a thing that is not completely her but is not her mother either. The child is the one who gives the thing meaning. She invents it, and that invention gives her new control over a precarious world. In "Transitional Objects, Transitional Phenomena," Winnicott writes: "The place of the object—outside, inside, at the border." This quotation from Winnicott, not unlike a pithy bulletin from the pen of Louise Bourgeois, serves as a brilliant spatial description of her work.

Winnicott was a less gloomy thinker than Freud. In Freud, sublimation redirects destructive erotic urges. Winnicott revises the concept into play, and play requires freedom. He believed play is essential to a person's growing up, but that play continues through a lifetime. He believed that some of his patients had to learn how to play because they had lost or had never gained the capacity. He believed that play fulfilled a necessary creative urge that is part of every person's life, not just the lives of the especially gifted. All artists play. They may play desperately. They may play for their lives. They may play because they feel they have no choice, but what they are doing is play nevertheless. Their work is play embodied in the object. This is what Dewey means when he writes, "The artist has his problems and he thinks as he works, but his thought is more immediately embodied in the object." For Winnicott, the artist creates a transitional object between herself and the outside world. Neither Dewey nor Winnicott say the following. I say it: *In play, the person establishes an umbilical connection between self and world.* The artist carves out her work in intermediate space.

From the beginning to the end of her career, Bourgeois addressed the push and pull of intimate human relations, the bonds formed, as well as the separations, breaks, or cuts that occur in the zone between people—a space that is not the self and not the other, but a third thing, which can include confusions of self and other, displacements of self onto the other, and various illusions as well as insights. In psychoanalysis this zone is called transference, and it takes place between patient and analyst, and during the treatment the analyst may become mother, father, sister, brother, or someone else who is important to the patient. "Robert is suddenly cast in a new role— / Instead of being a taboo brother figure—he / becomes a mother figure . . ." There is also counter-transference, from the analyst to the patient. I do not think *transference* and *countertransference* can be cleanly delineated—one affects the other. They blend.

And this third between-zone is not limited to the analytic encounter. Both Freud and Winnicott regarded it as part of everyday life. Winn-icott's play theory is a reimagining of transference as much as sublima-tion, something I have written about in detail in an essay called "Freud's Playground" in *Living, Thinking, Looking*. Here I want to emphasize the free play of Louise Bourgeois's art located "*inside, outside—at the border.*"

I do not know if Bourgeois read the French phenomenological phi-losopher Maurice Merleau-Ponty. Whether she did or not, his idea of *intercorporeality*—that human relations take place between and among bodies, that we perceive and understand others in embodied ways that are not conscious—serves as a door into her work. Simple examples of human intercorporeality include smiling when someone smiles at you or the sudden urge to yawn after the person across from you yawns. "It is a simple fact," Merleau-Ponty writes in *Phenomenology of Perception*, "that I live in the facial expressions of the other, that I feel him living in mine." This phenomenon has more recently been understood through mirror systems in human and some other primate brains.

Well before a person can speak or have articulate thoughts, she is awash in sensations and feelings that come from inside and outside her, and those feelings take on meaning in the repetitive back-and-forth of her primary social relations. Bourgeois imagined, depicted, and compli-cated the story of embodied human reality in ways no artist had done before her, and she conceived of it as necessarily relational, between people. "She always thought of her works as the portrait of a relation-ship," Jerry Gorovoy said in an interview. Gorovoy was the assistant, manager, organizer of daily life, and an intimate friend of the artist for thirty years. She referred to his work with her as "mothering."

The dynamic of relationship in the artworks continually moves between merger and separation, inside, outside, at the border. In her *Personnages* sculptures (1945–1955), she created fragile, lean, abstracted bodies from brittle wood she somehow forged as living isolates that ache with confused longing for one another. She later used soft plaster and latex and hard materials that nevertheless turned round and pliable under her guidance. The late works she called *Cells* combine both hard and soft in large spaces that explore forms of confinement and enclosure and borrow the shifting logic of dreams. After all, in our dreams, bodies sport impossible outcroppings, the dead speak, and a supposedly familiar house (home) becomes a strange place with extra rooms and mysterious doors. When we wake up, if we remember our dreams, we make stories of them.

"Seamstress, mistress, distress, stress." Bourgeois used this text in a work on cloth and as the title of a sculpture with hanging clothes. The wordplay moves toward reduction, toward the root. And the four words become a story if we know the story.

Going back to the root in time, to origin. For Bourgeois, entanglements and separations hark back to beginnings—to an *unremembered, mythical* past in fetal life and infancy, as well as a remembered childhood. No one remembers being a fetus or being born, but the blur of bodies in the story of human life is most dramatic in pregnancy. In its late stages, pregnancy is literally one body inside another body, a both-and condition all placental mammals share. This two-in-one formation clearly fascinated Bourgeois. Over and over, she drew and sculpted figures of mother-with-fetus or -newborn, and these images are often touched by magic. A soft sewn mother figure sits under a bell jar as her newborn flies outside her body still attached by the placental cord. Umbilici of one form or another recur—hair, threads, strings, and yarn winding or spiraling in and out of and around bodies. The pink fabric and thread-stuffed maternal and newborn bodies of *Do Not Abandon*

Me repeat the still-attached theme. The two are uncut, still united by the placental cord.

The world of childhood of
dependency, of the hearth which is not
yet the world of reality (1959)

Bourgeois's images of erotic coupling and merging, of gestation, and of birth are not yet the world of reality. They draw on the wondrous to create an anatomy of desire, dependency, desperation, tenderness, brutality, and the comic, which describes maternity in all its darkness, light, and fog. Her treatment of the subject is unprecedented.

It wasn't until the 1960s and '70s that a new female body burst into the art foreground to challenge the traditional, often static representations of women—the nude, the Madonna, or their reiteration in modern art that was innovative in style but did not alter the meaning of the iconography—woman as a passive, receptive thing for man's use. "Picasso and his women" has become an art institutional cliché. Imagine a show called "Louise Bourgeois and Her Men." Picasso's formal innovations did not include revisions of male/female artistic conventions, nor do they temper his works' frequently overt misogyny redolent of active sadism. I love Giacometti's sculpture, and his work clearly influenced early Bourgeois, but his women are fixed in place. They stand. The men walk. David Sylvester argues in his book on Giacometti that the women were modeled on street prostitutes—women waiting. The fetishism of the Surrealists turned women into lifeless mannequins decorated with signs of masculine perversion. The Surrealists also influenced Bourgeois, but she slapped back hard at their shallow jokes and knowing nods about "woman."

Feminist artists hoped to reconfigure and overhaul the womanly body and its narrative space. The artists did it by pushing against perceptual expectations. They used surprise to reorient their audiences. Look, she's moving! Their strategies were different, and they didn't always work. Perception is far less flexible than most people imagine. We are creatures of habit and predetermined patterns, which are not conscious, but they direct what we see nevertheless. There are innumerable artists who might be mentioned, but I will limit my examples.

The work of Carolee Schneemann, always poorly understood, startled viewers with its insistence on the woman-body as agent-subject. She used her own naked body to explode the nude. Schneemann wanted to push the female figure in art to action.

Ana Mendieta often used her body-self to vanish into landscapes, to lose outline in relation to the surrounding material, to blur the distinction between self and world until no lines can be drawn around an anonymous female body. Outline, absolute thresholds, and clean division may be said to describe modern Western culture since its early partial codification during the Scientific Revolution, a codification that has become increasingly rigid over time.

The artist Betye Saar borrowed brutal stereotypes of Black American femininity and juxtaposed them with conflicting images to force the spectator to look again and look hard. I am thinking of the power of such works as *The Liberation of Aunt Jemima*.

Adrian Piper turned herself into a man of ambiguous race, "The Mythic Being," and haunted the streets of New York City between 1973 and 1975: "I am everything you most hate and fear." The multiple levels of subversion implicit and explicit in this action are profound.

Although the work of these artists, among that of many others, was marginal to the "art world" and even sometimes to feminism (infighting, purity tests, and ingrown racial and class prejudice are hardly new to the political/artistic left), I believe feminist art created a multiform disturbance to stereotypes deeply embedded in dominant cultural perceptions, which on hindsight can be seen to have prepared the ground for what we are reliving with differences now. The fact that MoMA, despite its entrenched resistance to art made by women, owns works by all these artists, and Adrian Piper had a major retrospective in 2018, are indicative of the change.

Bourgeois actively supported causes for women artists and knew that feminism helped create a receptive audience for her 1982 MoMA retrospective. "The feminists took me as a role model, as a mother," she said. "It bothers me. I am not interested in being a mother. I am still a girl trying to understand myself." However ambivalent she may have been about mothering young feminists, there is no artist I can think of who has explored the maternal with more wit and depth.

In 1941, she made two ink drawings of a woman giving birth. She had adopted a son, Michel, in 1939 because she was worried that she would be unable to conceive, despite the fact that she had been told by a physician that there was nothing wrong with her. After the adoption, the artist gave birth to her son Jean Louis in 1940, and a year later to her second biological son, Alain. The images correspond to the time of her birth experiences. Robert Storr reproduces both images along with a Jean Dubuffet canvas of childbirth dated 1944. Dubuffet's painting was made while under the influence of his fascination with what he called Art Brut, or raw art, which he defined as "art executed by people untouched by artistic culture." For Dubuffet this included untrained artists and children, but the movement grew out of art produced by the insane.

Storr connects Bourgeois's imagery to the hallucinatory art of mental patients, but he does not comment on her depiction of birth as such or the fact that the subject is missing from the canon of Western art. The Dubuffet canvas is a rare exception. It resembles a child's drawing more than any psychiatric patient's, and its doll-like, blank-faced mother, legs akimbo, is not in the process of giving birth. The birth is over. The bodies are not joined. The infant lies outside the mother; the two bodies are delineated isolates. The canvas is dead: two marionettes lie on a bed. Dubuffet's image is as remote from the realities of the wet and bloody convulsions of human birth as possible. There is nothing *raw* about it. This is birth painting as defensive act. It is the birth painting of someone who cannot implicate himself in birth. I was never a fetus. I was never born.

In the Bourgeois drawings, the newborn emerges. In one as a small being; in the other as head only, a fantastically large head, the size of its mother's, which turns her into a vertical mirror image reminiscent of a totem pole. The maternal face in both drawings is concentrated, thoughtful, slightly pained, but it is neither anguished nor triumphant—this is mother as thinker, as sage. It is birth recollected in tranquility.

Almost four decades after Bourgeois's birth drawings, Judy Chicago began work on her *Birth Project*. In 1985, after Chicago had completed the project, she told the *Chicago Tribune*, "I started looking for images of birth, and I didn't find any. There were almost no birth images in the history of Western art." I have had exactly the same experience. A Google search for birth in Western art calls forth—nothing. Despite this Google nullity, exceptions exist, such as Frida Kahlo's 1935 image of herself giving birth to herself. Nancy Spero made birth art in the 1960s, and some of Dorothea Tanning's remarkable sculptures strongly suggest birthing, but before that, natural birth is almost entirely missing from the Western canon. And yet, *it is an absence that is almost never commented upon.* Judy Chicago is one of the precious few to have done so.

There is a bombastic quality to Chicago's birth paintings and needlepoints that for me, anyway, misses the ordinary and intimate realities of pregnancy and birth, as well as its strangeness. Someone begins to grow inside you—is you, of you, and then isn't you anymore.

Bourgeois made many works of art that *suggest* parturition and many others, especially late in her life, that depict it. *Nature Study*, a sculpture from 1986, is a spiral, from which emerges a hand holding a small adult female body, which makes me think of Hans Christian Andersen's Thumbelina—the tiny maiden born of a wish and magic. Bourgeois made many works under the same title, including a number of proud, headless, multibreasted beasts—maternal deities that resemble the *She-Fox*. Among my favorite explicit birth images are the red gouache drawings exhibited in 2008 at the Royal Botanic Garden in Edinburgh made only three years before she died, paired with botanical teaching drawings collected by John Hutton Balfour during the nineteenth century, under the common title *Nature Study*.

Together the lush, charged gouache drawings present a narrative of human origin—first, a menstruating girl, followed by diagrammatic, awkward male-female pairings—bulbous woman, often with extra breasts, accompanied by skinny man, his small, thin penis erect—then images of uterine space; headless, legless pregnant body; newborn emerging from vagina, and massive dribbling breasts paired with howling, tiny, helpless being. A couple of the Bourgeois Lilliputians are hanging on to a gigantic breast for dear life. I laugh out loud every time I look at them—mother's breast as helium balloon. But they are also poignant. The perspective in these drawings is a newborn's, not a mother's. Another drawing of a hanging infant in pink gouache, not included in the book, but in the 2017 MoMA exhibition, combines the ridiculous and the poignant to a degree that strikes me as ineffably brilliant. The drawing is called *Self-Portrait* (2007). Artist as newborn.

Inside, at the border, and finally outside is a nice description of the gestation-and-birth story. Bourgeois created one sculpture and drawing after another that may be called intercorporeal. She understood, however, what Merleau-Ponty searched for in his philosophy but was never able to find. Despite the fact that the philosopher used pregnancy as a metaphor and arrived at an overarching concept of universal mingling he called "the flesh" in *The Visible and the Invisible*, he could never root his theory in the fact that we all begin inside another person's body, and that no understanding of human embodiment can ignore this obvious fact. Bourgeois presented the entanglements and relations between and among human beings as rooted in our beginnings inside another person, a body-subject.

The amnesia that has accompanied this reality in the history of the West is frankly stupefying. As an old woman, Louise Bourgeois burrowed unembarrassed into the maternal body with a freedom and glee that explodes countless stereotypes, stereotypes that remain stubbornly with us. Bourgeois's maternal is not the body of a sterilized Madonna, but it is not the body of Mother Earth or Mother Nature either. Mother Nature as unthinking slug of fertility has haunted many feminists who have regarded "biology" as the enemy of freedom. They have fallen into the trap of thinking that biological processes are somehow alien from psychic and social processes. This is not true. Bodily systems are also relational and contextual. In her work Bourgeois creates a borderless mélange of body-mind-world.

In *Fantastic Reality*, Mignon Nixon emphasizes the fact that the artist created a space for maternal subjectivity that is missing from psychoanalysis, which has often been so focused on the baby that the mother vanishes as an active subject. In her 2017 paper "How Psychoanalysis Lost the Birthing Body: Commentary on Balsam," Nancy Chodorow points out that although there were analysts who wrote on the importance of the birth experience, it nevertheless went missing from the field. Rosemary Balsam "excavated" these "silenced" writings in an address she gave on childbirth to the American Psychoanalytic Association in 2012.

Birth has been suppressed from the Western art canon, suppressed in psychoanalysis, and in much of philosophy until recently. Bourgeois loved the umbilical cord as an image of human connection, but she, along with everyone else, forgot the placenta. It was long the great forgotten organ of gestation, not only in art but in science, too. In medical texts, the growing fetus is often depicted as if it is somehow unattached to the maternal body and to the placenta. But Bourgeois repeatedly drew fetuses inside bodies illustrating attachment and dependence. One image called *Maternal Man*, penis outside, fetus inside, is a work on which I have been able to find no commentary whatsoever. Perhaps I missed it. She also depicted infants emerging from a mother's body; and those entirely outside it, but still clinging, holding, or resting near it. Sometimes the mother is whole, sometimes just part, often torso only, but these images are never sanguine evocations of "Mother Nature." They are complex investigations of merging domains with no stark dividing lines—body, psyche, culture, but also human, animal, and plant.

The attempt to link Bourgeois's fertility and birth works to the Balfour botanical drawings is at once reasonable and unreasonable. Bourgeois loved playing with plant and human forms as metamorphoses—tendril is like umbilicus is like hair; branch is like arm, leg, and finger; pod is like sack, but also like testicle is like pocket is like uterus; "The woman and the sack / the sack becomes a tube / it's a river / it's a sack, it's a pocket, it's a house /"

There's a witty drawing at the Tate called *Tree with Crutch*. The title literally describes what the viewer sees.

A series of red flower drawings are titled *My Own Voice Wakes Me Up*. This is not what the viewer sees.

Another drawing, *Turning Inward*, shows a pregnant female figure with cord-like hair winding around and in and out of her—hairy, umbilical, botanical attachments that can be cut.

The metamorphoses that recur in her sculpture and drawings, however, have little in common with the history of pedagogical nature drawing that dates to the Greeks and reached its zenith during the Enlightenment in images of exactitude intended to aid scientific classification. I have a Victorian medical illustration of a brain on the wall in my study that looks strikingly like a cross between an eggplant and a pepper, but every discrete part is precisely rendered. The Balfour botanical drawings include uterine-like sacs and phallic protuberances, but they are didactic forms. The impulse in Bourgeois is the opposite of these pedagogical images—she blurs the divisions between one and the other and breaks down conventional perceptual borders and categories.

One could say her work creates a visual ecology, which explores the relations and overlaps among organic forms. This includes parasitic and symbiotic relations and multiple kinds of interdependencies, to which she assigns complicated meanings and in the process destroys conventional taxonomies. Bourgeois explored interdependence through forms that have broad collective meaning. Uterus as house, enclosure, or container and its link to pods is familiar, after all, but the artist's execution of the associative links can be radical. *Single III*, for example, a stuffed sewn body from 1996, is a double-headed armless being with breasts, penis, and ball-testicle but also head-like forms, which appear between the humanoid creature's legs. The sculpture disrupts the viewer's expectations of single versus double being and female/male, but it also forces her to look more closely at what could be a multiple birth, common in other mammals, much less so in human beings. The spectator is forcibly pressed toward abstraction but not across its limits. Because expectations are shattered, meanings proliferate. Bourgeois created many armless bodies. It makes me think that for such a creature an embrace is impossible.

Perception is conservative. We fit what we see into known patterns and explicate accordingly. In writing about art, critics often retreat to the known theory, story, or stereotype. This is true of every field, but pat explanations are worrying. Louise Bourgeois's art is unembarrassed about the body and procreation, but it also partakes of the rigorous, abstract, and intellectual. It is no accident that in a culture of ferocious dualism—mind and body divorced—an artist who is also a woman would generate defensive postures in some of her critics, who go to great lengths to rehabilitate standard perceptual categories that reinforce the social hierarchy of male over female.

Donald Kuspit may be unaware of his hostility for an artist he professes to admire. When he discusses Bourgeois in an essay for *Artforum* "in the Surrealist context," he refers to her as a "handworker rather than a literary artist." In saying Bourgeois is a "handworker" "who models or shapes or let us say 'masturbates' it [the art object] to find the phallic in it," he creates an image of L.B. as thoughtless little crafts lady getting off on her homemade dildos. This thought is made even more curious by the fact that titillation is a feeling wholly missing from this art. Imagine a critic writing about Picasso's canvases as vehicles for wanking.

In his introduction to the gouache birth drawings he titled "Mother Nature," Philip Larratt-Smith reproduces a series of dizzyingly various quotes by the artist, on which he makes no comment. He follows this list of epigraphs with a personal story. He witnessed Bourgeois hastily roll up her gouache pregnancy images just before a childless woman entered the room. She explained that she didn't want her visitor to see them because "She's an old maid, poor devil." He heard her intonation. I did not, but he assumes her comment was made without irony. He then notes that "motherhood is central to Bourgeois's conception of herself" and offers standard psychoanalytic thoughts about maternal fusion and paternal division, followed by quotes from Freud's essay on the uncanny and the "womb-tomb" link. "Confronting her mortality," Larratt-Smith writes, "Bourgeois reverts to the primary images of the passage into life, which, like the uncanny double of the mirror-image, announce the inevitability and proximity to death." While it is true that thoughts of ending may prompt thoughts about beginning, these images of fetus and newborn scream: I am alive! What shape or stroke in these pictures alludes to death? I do not see them.

Larratt-Smith quotes Freud's reference to the uterus as the "former home of all human beings." This is surely true, but the father of psycho-analysis was, frankly, obtuse about the maternal, a fact that was much discussed by object relations theorists and revised accordingly. Freud remains an innovative and brilliant thinker, but his obsession with sons and fathers in Oedipal conflict, male genitalia as norm and female gen-italia as the image of castration, coupled with what was probably an unrecognized fear of maternal power, creates a ragged blind spot in his thought. It is a blind spot hardly unique to him.

In a 2010 essay, "Through the Eye of the Needle," Frédérique Joseph-Lowery is sharp about the artist's verbal and visual puns, but she stresses Bourgeois's immense personal suffering to a degree that prompts her to write the following sentence: "Louise Bourgeois died a few weeks ago and long, long ago." I beg to differ. She did not die before she died. No one does. And the artist worked like crazy well into her nineties. What-ever the metaphorical meaning of this early "death" is supposed to have, it's ridiculous. Moreover, it's insulting. But the agonized woman, victim of her own story with Father and Mother, fits nicely into the paternalistic narratives the French have repeatedly employed to discuss female artists, and the convention is so ingrown, it has become invisible.

On the popular front, Jonathan Jones wrote in *The Guardian* in 2014, "Louise Bourgeois is a comforting artist. She told stories about the human psyche that could be easily understood. She has the same easy narrative meanings and bold unproblematic images as establish-ment heroes down the ages have tended to produce. As time passes her images will fade when compared to the real nightmare of modern art." *The real nightmare of modern art?* Admittedly, cultural journalism is often a lazy enterprise given over to intimidated mediocrities who don't know what they're talking about. What is personally comforting to Mr. Jones appears to be the erasure of female genius by adopting a patron-izing tone he seems to hope will mask an impoverished intellect. It is all so tediously predictable, so neatly framed by perceptual expectations. The woman has risen up and out of her place and needs to be knocked back into it.

And yet, why does it matter? We who write about the artist are all handmaidens to Louise the First. I think it matters because the Bourgeois master narrative, now repeated ad nauseam, must be treated with caution. She knew that the female artist who embraces the body, emotion, and autobiography in her art is routinely denigrated. She knew that such art inevitably conjures the uncomfortable nether regions of the feminine associated with the personal, private, and domestic—with menstrual cycles, housecleaning, having babies—but also with sexual desire, natural reproductive processes, and the discomfort, even revulsion, that attend to this blurry bodily terrain in the culture. She knew the reprisals that "masculine" women face and the disguises needed to fend them off. She played with all of these expectations. She played ferociously but also delicately. She was free and restrained, informed by strong feeling and by stringent thought.

The life and the work of every artist are entwined, but all forms of representation partake of distance. The artist sees the object unfold, a thing that rises out of you, is related to you, but is *not you* either. And it is precisely the distance, the ultimate otherness of the artwork that provides relief and satisfaction during the process of creating it. Art is the "I" that is also "not-I." It is "the alien familiar," as I have dubbed the act of writing in the past. This phrase works equally well for visual art. Over the course of art-making, the "I" becomes a "you," an other, but it is also always made with an other in mind, not a real other, but an imaginary one. In this way all art is the portrait of a relationship.

Far from providing her viewers with art that is easily interpreted, comforting, and neatly encapsulated by a story, Bourgeois is a dancing insurrectionist of ambiguity, merger, and blurred borders. She is neither feminine nor masculine, but deeply invested in sexual overlap, in the both-and. Bourgeois is a both-and, not either/or artist, and her emotional range is wide, not circumscribed. She soothes and alarms, weeps and then bursts into raucous laughter. She stumbles, and she leaps. She is vulnerable one moment and malicious the next. I am frequently bewildered by the promiscuous mingling of sincerity, passion, irony, comedy, and puns in her work. Her intellectual acumen, her strategic brilliance, and her masterful analysis and mythologizing of her own life in her work surely exploited her memories and the profound emotions that accompanied them, but the feelings were not only painful feelings, and they were always distanced and abstracted by ideas embodied in the objects. And it is this distance and the rigor involved that has often been left out by her critics.

It seems to me irony increases with age. That is my experience at least. Irony is difficult by its very nature because in it meaning is doubled, sometimes tripled and quadrupled. The word did not appear in English until the sixteenth century, a version of the Latin *ironia*, derived from the Greek *eironeia*—simulated ignorance. Socrates was the great ancient simulator of naïveté, a sage whose pretense of simplicity exposed his interlocutors as fools. Women are rarely acknowledged as masters of irony. The cultural bias that identifies reason as masculine applies equally to irony, for which reflective self-consciousness is an essential requirement. Dogs and babies don't have it.

I will end with the *Sainte Sebastienne* drawings and its sister series, *Stamp of Memories*. They were made between 1990 and 1995 when the artist was in her eighties. She also made a sewn sculpture of the saint figure. Which adjectives apply to these works? Ridiculous, weird, satirical, poignant, uncanny, baffling—all of the above? According to legend, Saint Sebastian was martyred during the reign of Emperor Diocletian, a period of Christian persecution. Over time, the saint became a staple of the art canon. Tintoretto, del Sarto, Mantegna, Messina, and El Greco are among the artists who portrayed the youthful Sebastian, who was frequently depicted tied to a tree or a post with one or two or several arrows piercing his gorgeous, nearly naked body, a drooping loincloth strategically placed to cover his genitals—an iconography shot through with homoerotic desire.

Every art history student can recognize Sebastian instantly. He is the saint whose expression betrays no agony about having been penetrated by arrow or arrows. Instead, he gazes heavenward with a look of preter-natural sweetness, if not pleasure. By the nineteenth century, the render-ing of St. Sebastian had hardened into little more than cloying soft porn.

Bourgeois's ironic treatment of the Sebastian iconography is hilari-ously subversive. Her saint is a woman, and her form is not borrowed from the idealizations of art history's many nudes. In her rendering, Sebastian becomes Sebastienne, a nod to her own name. The daughter, Louise, is named after her father, Louis. In the *Stamp of Memory* series that employs a version of the same figure, the sexual difference of the full names is efficiently erased by the initials L.B., which are stamped or branded all over the character's body. The patriarch is inscribed in the child's name and into her flesh. Make your meanings, but bet on the fact that they will multiply.

Bourgeois transforms the sexy ephebe of art history into a pregnant, peripatetic, armless, sometimes headless, comic self-persona. When the character is not decapitated, Sebastienne or L.B. sports various elaborate hairdos/hats/baskets on her head. The allusion to a mode of transporting goods in many parts of the world—always by women—fixes the creature firmly in female territory. And in her hair-hat-baskets she sometimes carries a traditional sign of fertility, the egg—three of them, one for each of Bourgeois's children. When this persona has a face, she wears a mysterious smile. Is the artist mimicking the unconcerned expression of the pierced beautiful boy in the paintings? Is this a smile of satisfaction, of self-containment, of irony? Sometimes a cat face shadows her own as the arrows skewer her bloated body from both directions—neck, breast, side, genitals, thigh, shin, and navel. The arrow of the St. Sebastian paint-ings that came to serve as a thinly disguised symbol of the penis is re-imagined in Bourgeois as multiple, depending on its location: weapon certainly and penis, but also umbilical cord.

These pictures are funny, but they are hardly reducible to a joke. They twist the rigidly conventional imagery into something altogether new. The drawings collapse private, sociological, art-historical, and philosophical meanings into one another, while preserving ambiguities among them. Sebastian is the saint of plague. During times of contagion, the faithful call upon him for protection. Because I have been writing this essay during the 2020 COVID-19 pandemic, I cannot help but wonder if Bourgeois was also thinking about plagues—about AIDS perhaps, which she lived through as it ravaged New York City in the eighties. Then again, perhaps these drawings conjure a metaphorical plague—the endless diminution by ridicule of femininity in general. When irony is rich, it is never simple.

These images beg to be looked at but also to be read carefully. The artist relished her mental acuity and delighted in the density of her myriad references that retain but also soar beyond autobiography. With Louise Bourgeois, it is safe to assume that she was and is still running well ahead of most of her critics.

Our Sainted Lady of the Arrows appears to be in a great rush. Where is she going? The figure is headed to her right, apparently indifferent to the attacks from invisible enemies. Literate people understand time in space according to the direction of their reading. For both English- and French-readers, the motion from past to future is represented in space as left to right. The artist has sent her character, Sebastienne, alias L.B., into the past, not the future. The prima donna is headed chin up in the direction of psychoanalysis, memory, and the land of beginnings—of gestation, birth, infancy, and childhood—into the world of myth and its many stories of our origins.

2020

WHAT DOES A MAN WANT?

Misogyny is derived from the Greek *misos*, hatred, and *gune*, woman. I have come to recognize misogyny in my own life, its verbal slaps, sputtering rage, seething contempt, and disgusted looks. The misogynist also kicks, punches, strangles, rapes, throws acid at, stones, mutilates, and murders women. It's a strange hate, if you think about it, because every human being was born from a woman or a person with female reproductive organs. After birth, an infant is usually nursed by its mother or another woman and in many cultures is raised mostly by women. Unlike other hatreds of one group of people for another group of people—the enmities of difference that turn on tribal identity, religion, class, race, or geography and may explode into wars, acts of terror, or genocide—women belong to all states, castes, classes, religions, and tribes.

Although there is general agreement that misogyny has taken and still takes different forms in different cultures and has been more and less acute during certain historical periods, there is no consensus about its origins, how or why it develops, or exactly how it works. Interestingly, the word does not appear in many book titles in English, although it has been popping up more frequently lately. I have read every book devoted to the subject I have been able to track down. I am at once puzzled and grieved by multiple theories that try to explain why I am the object of hatred. I do think of myself as a woman, and hate hurts.

Misogyny belongs to patriarchies, and it carries a demand for womanly behavior. It is built into ways of being in a hierarchal culture, and it infects everyone's thoughts, words, gestures, and acts. Whether patriarchy was always with us is a matter of contention. Scholars have a tendency to project their own worlds backward in time. Hunter-gatherer societies were organized according to a sexual division of labor but appear to have been far more equalitarian and peaceful than was once assumed. A number of scholars have posited that with agriculture and an end to roaming, collective life became more hierarchical. (See Dyble et al., "Sex Equality can Explain the Unique Social Structure of Hunter-Gatherer Bands, *Science*, 2015.) These days, patriarchy has swallowed up most of the world. For a female creature of the Western tradition, the condemnations of her sex by male sages over time into the present have the force of a hammer that has pounded to admonish, blame, and punish her as variously evil, polluting, dangerous, demonic, sexually insatiable, asexual, weak, conniving, childlike, emotional, passive, but always intellectually incapacitated and inferior to men.

The Book of the City of Ladies was published in 1405. In its opening pages, its author, Christine de Pizan, sits in her library and wonders plaintively, "Why on earth it was that so many men . . . have said and continue to say and write such awful damning things about women and their ways." Why indeed? Why does it never stop? Misogyny in the West has turned on the rather weird idea that women are more *natural* than men, which is related to the old mind/body problem. Man is mind and culture. He thinks. Woman is body and nature. She can't think and has babies. "She [woman] is more carnal than man, as is clear from her many carnal abominations," write Heinrich Kramer and James Sprenger in *Malleus Maleficarum* (1486). They are explaining why women are more vulnerable than men to becoming witches.

Misogyny is on the rise around the world. Facilitated by technology and the shifting political weather, misogyny has found its voice in online invective, its lurid online imagery in decapitation, dismemberment, and rape, and in real violence in the world.

A right-wing thug murdered a counter-protestor, Heather Heyer, by running her over with his car in Charlottesville, Virginia. In her book on misogyny, Gail Ukockis quotes the editor of the neo-fascist *Daily Stormer*, who called Heyer "a fat, childless, 32-year-old slut."

The British writer, director, and producer Danielle Dash reported her experience on Twitter to Amnesty International: "The violence," she said, "is at the intersection of everything that I am—for example—'I am going to rape you, you black bitch. You have the misogyny, and you have the racism and you have the sexual violence all mixed up into one delicious stew of cesspool shit.' " Dash's anonymous Twitter person seems to be suffering from a schizophrenic confusion of self and other. He has dumped his own misogyny, racism, and sexual violence into the object of his hate.

Before Elliot Rodger murdered six people in Isla Vista, California, he wrote a 137-page screed of retribution for his sexless existence, the first phase of which was ridding the world of rival men who had had the sexual experiences he felt were owed to him. The second phase was a "War on Women." Rodger was literally up in arms against the "hot beautiful blonde girls" he had seen near the Alpha Phi sorority house in his town—"all spoiled, heartless, wicked bitches." Spoiled, heartless, and wicked for not wanting him.

Scholars have jumped in to explore burgeoning misogyny online, as if it is unique. The technical speed and easy anonymity of the Internet are new, but machines are not hateful. They do not write texts, tweet, or seek out others who share their spleen against women. The vituperation is old. The avaricious Eve eats of the tree of knowledge first. Pandora opens her "box." As a child, I heard the following platitude uttered repeatedly in a joking, friendly way among adult men: "Can't live with 'em. Can't live without 'em." I gathered they meant women are trouble but they needed them. They referred to women as if they were another species.

The Greek poet Hesiod wrote his *Theogony* in 730–700 BCE. His paradise is a world without women where men live in harmony with the gods. After Zeus punishes Prometheus for his gift of fire to mankind, the supreme god's vengeance takes the form of the first woman, the first of a "race" of women. In *Works and Days*, Hesiod's hot, beautiful girl, Pandora, is described as "an evil you want to embrace," an early version of the wicked bitches Rodger lusted after. Pandora opens her pregnant jar and gives birth to woe—evil and death fly out of her container. In *Myth and Thought Among the Greeks*, the anthropologist Jean-Pierre

Vernant noted, "The dream of a purely paternal heredity never ceased to haunt the Greek imagination." If men could only reproduce alone, so many torments of life would be eliminated.

Vernant also cites Aeschylus: "It is not the mother who gives birth to what we call her child: she only nurses the germ sown in her. The one who gives birth is the man who impregnates her." This usurpation of female birth is a constant theme in Western misogyny, which might be summarized as: it may look as if pregnancy and birth are all about women, but they're really all about men. In the *Symposium*, Plato evokes many kinds of pregnancy—natural female pregnancy that results in a child, the pregnancy of desire for another person fulfilled in love, and spiritual pregnancy, the highest of all: the pregnant mind of the male philosopher gives birth to an idea, no taint of the body involved. Aristotle, who was fascinated by actual reproductive processes in animals, knew both male and female were needed for procreation. He proposed that in human beings each sex contributed its own kind of sperm to the process. For Aristotle, it was the male sperm that implanted *soul, form, animation* into the passive *matter* of the female. It was this soul, this masculine force and form that gave the fledgling being life and movement.

There are no images of natural birth in Greek art, only supernatural births. Athena arrives fully grown from Zeus's *forehead*. The art textbook I knew as a young person, H. W. Janson's *History of Art*, first published in 1962, still standard, is dense with female nudes, Madonnas and babes, crucifixions, battle and deathbed scenes, but no births. Until 1987 there were no women artists in Janson. When you think about it, this is astounding.

In Hindu painting there are images of women giving birth. In many cultures pregnancy and birth are "seen," not hidden. There's a pre-Columbian figure of a woman in an elaborate headdress giving birth. The famous Venus of Willendorf is not pushing out a child, but she is the image of plump powerful fertility. In 2011, a shard from an Etruscan vase was discovered in Poggio Colla not far from Florence in Italy. On it is the image of a squatting woman. An infant's head emerges from between her legs. But Etruscan culture was not Greek culture, and it is

Greek civilization that has been an obsessive point of reference for centuries in the West, a tradition haunted by the dream of paternal birth. Birth is ordinary, as ordinary as death, part of the cycle of life. Every one of us was cut from the body of a mother after birth. Omission can be annihilation. What is missing tells a story. Women and slaves were not part of public life in ancient Greece. Although the entire system was dependent on their labor, they were out of the picture.

Versions of the Aeschylus seed theory, which turns woman into a container for masculine generation and effectively eliminates her from the "real story" of procreation, have come and gone with various theories about reproduction. There have long been two conflicting ideas about how human beings are generated—epigenesis and preformation. Despite his insistence on the life-giving qualities of male sperm, Aristotle promoted epigenesis. The embryo evolves over time and develops new features that weren't there to begin with. In the seventeenth and eighteenth centuries, preformation theory was popular. The entire being was present in semen as a miniature man or homunculus, who just needed a warm enclosure to get bigger and bigger. There were "ovists," too, those who believed the person was already fully present in the female egg. These theories were riddled by religious and metaphysical debates, but how we become what we are and what makes us that way remains an explosive issue with profound ethical and political meanings. Misogyny then and now turns on questions of sexual difference, on bodies and how they grow, and what the feminine and masculine signify in our world.

Is misogyny about the female sex, female genitalia and reproductive organs, or is it about gender and femininity? Punishment for insufficient masculinity or femininity or for blurring the lines between them remains fierce depending on where you live in the world. Surely transgender people in the United States, especially transgender people of color, have felt the lash of misogyny and misogynoir, as the scholar Moya Bailey named the latter, as, or more harshly than anyone else. The attack on Danielle Dash is an example of misogynoir—when racism and misogyny overlap and thicken hatred.

What exactly is femininity? Is it a performance, as Judith Butler argued? Surely much of what we do unconsciously and consciously is an embodiment of gender. I cross my legs on the subway or keep them squeezed tightly together, but when I'm home, I happily sit with my legs apart. My folded legs are a defensive womanly posture, a learned code of behavior I rarely think about. Although feminist scholars have distinguished between sex, a *biological* category, and gender, a *social* category, there is controversy among them about what this distinction means and whether it is helpful. In popular discourse, the word *sex* has all but been erased and has been replaced by the word *gender* to cover all versions in a fluid understanding of many forms of sexual identity and desire.

In the original division between sex and gender, sex stood in for *body* and *nature* and gender for *mind* and *nurture*. The nature-body half is *biological* and is supposed to represent a fixed, unchanging division of male versus female while gender is a *social* construct. But an examination of the "nature" half of this equation reveals that human development, even before birth, is variable and dependent on many factors during the months of gestation. There are a number of trajectories a human embryo can take and there are outcomes that do not fit neatly into one sex or the other, including an intersex infant. Most often, however, the newborn is recognizably female or male.

Embryology is extraordinarily complex and much remains unknown about the story of fetal development that takes place during a woman's pregnancy. I have always thought the unknown is as important as the known because it prevents the certainty that can become dogma. Sexual difference turns on reproductive difference, and Western misogyny has been and still is obsessed with the difference. Trans men can and have given birth to children, but they do so with intact female reproductive organs.

Male birth has been part of countless mythologies all over the world. As a child, I liked the story about the Norse trickster god, Loki, who changes himself into a mare, seduces a giant's stallion, gets pregnant, and gives birth to Sleipnir, a steed with eight legs. But this mythical birth involves shape-shifting and sex change.

The Greek fantasy skipped over women altogether or elevated intellectual labor over natural labor. The dream of taking gestation away from the female animal lives on in the idea of an artificial womb as a scientific brainchild. In 2017, media made much of an innovation called a "biobag," a bag filled with artificial amniotic fluid, oxygenated by an artificial umbilical cord, which had kept fetal lambs alive for weeks. (See Partridge et al., "An Extrauterine System to Support Extremely Premature Lamb," in *Nature Communications*, 2017.) The bag has the potential to serve as a superior incubator, which might keep extremely premature infants alive. It was loudly advertised in the headlines, however, as *an artificial womb*, which it most definitely is not.

Artificial intelligence has nurtured the wish to transcend corporeal reproduction by delivering children born of mental effort for decades. Like Zeus, the scientists will generate conscious offspring from their thoughtful foreheads, no female bodies required. The eagerness to avoid female reproduction often takes on a fantastic quality in AI circles. Ray Kurzweil, a tech guru who predicts the golden future of the Singularity, is a prime example: "In the future," he writes, "we will do therapeutic cloning, a very important technology that avoids the *concept* of the fetus" (my italics). By cloning replacement parts when they wear out, perpetual life will be ensured. Kurzweil does not want to die. Of course, cloning new human beings from scratch would dispense with not just the *concepts* woman, uterus, and fetus, but the actual things to which these concepts refer. The wish is old. Let's forget the woman.

Gestation involves far more than a fluid-filled bag or the concept of the fetus. The ongoing mysteries of actual organic gestation become vividly apparent while reading embryology papers: "Molecular cross talk at the feto-maternal interface occurs between many different cell types" begins a 2015 paper by Gendie E. Lash in *Cold Spring Harbor Perspectives in Medicine*. The metaphor *cross talk* appears again and again in these papers to cover interactions that remain unknown. The precise mechanisms of these "conversations" have not been discovered, but lots of cellular signaling and negotiation take place during pregnancy between maternal cells and the fertilized ball of cells that may or may not form an embryo and placenta.

Lash's conclusion is typical: "Many layers of communication are required for the successful establishment and continuation of a pregnancy, which are likely often unique in humans. Although not all of the molecular communication signals are fully understood [an understatement], we are starting to understand the cellular components of this communication and establish tools for their greater study." A lot is going on in the maternal body, and for it all to work out this much is certain: the placenta is essential. And the placenta is the least understood of all human organs. It has been called forgotten, ignored, overlooked, mysterious, underappreciated, and even the "Rodney Dangerfield of organs."

How can a human organ go missing in plain sight? The afterbirth has always been part of birth and in many cultures is treated with reverence as a twin or double of the infant. Much has been written about the medicalization of pregnancy and birth and the tendency to turn a woman into her reproductive organs as if they do not belong to her. Think of all the headless charts and images of the fetus without umbilical cord or placenta or even uterus that track its growth as if the mother were wholly uninvolved in the process; but even in feminist literature the placenta is often forgotten. The placenta grows along with the fetus. I gave birth once. My daughter, Sophie, was born in 1987. I have no memory of my placenta. It must have been whisked away. It dies when its job is done, but there is something flabbergasting about the amnesia that has haunted this organ until recently. Now the Human Placenta Project has been launched, and the great mediating organ of pregnancy is finally getting some respect.

Contemporary misogyny in the developed world includes fundamental misrepresentations of the maternal role during pregnancy. Gestation is a dynamic process during which a diploid cell may eventually develop into a nine-month fetus through the successful parallel development of the placenta, which is a fetal-maternal organ, formed from both fetal and maternal cells and attached to the mother's uterus and to the fetus by the placental cord. Fetal waste goes directly into the mother's bloodstream. The placenta orchestrates the delivery of hormones and nutrients and, by the end of the first trimester, it serves as a maternal-fetal blood barrier. Amniotic fluid is thought at first to be generated entirely by the mother's plasma, but later fetal urination and swallowing contribute to the volume of fluid, which subsequently shrinks during late pregnancy as the fetus gets bigger. The fluid contains growth factor, which scientists guess contributes to the development of the fetus, but they don't know how it does this.

The placenta appears to control the migration of cells from mother to fetus and fetus to mother, a phenomenon called microchimerism. In Greek mythology, a chimera is a fire-breathing she-monster with a lion's head, a goat's body, and a serpent's tail. In biology, it's an individual, an organ, or a body part that has tissues of different genetic constitution, *a blend, a mix*. Scientists once thought the cell traffic indicated accidental leaking from one into the other, but that is not the case—the cell migration is part of pregnancy. When the news of microchimerism arrived in 2012, *New Scientist* carried the headline: SON'S DNA FOUND INSIDE MOTHER'S BRAIN. *Smithsonian* went further: BABY'S CELLS CAN MANIPULATE MOM'S BODY FOR DECADES. In *Science*: BEARING SONS CAN ALTER YOUR MIND; and my favorite, in *Science News*: THE ALIEN WITHIN: FETAL CELLS INFLUENCE MATERNAL HEALTH DURING PREGNANCY (AND LONG AFTER). How these cells influence maternal health is not yet known. The cells may play a role in improving the mother's immune function; they may also have a role in some illnesses.

But the idea that male DNA might be in a woman's body, which turns her into a female-male DNA mixture, a monster blend, stole the headlines—Alien invasion! Oh my God, the woman has a man in her! Cell traffic in the other direction has not been touted. Man with Mom's DNA! But what the headlines demonstrate is a general alarm and surprise about male-female DNA mixtures, which is, after all, the essence of human reproduction: the two in one. The general hysteria turned on the fact that male fetal DNA had entered the mother's brain, her mind—that sanctified locus of *ideas* far from the lowly uterus.

I am making this little introduction to gestation and the placenta simply to point out how hard it is to divide maternal and fetal domains, a division fraught with metaphysical, ethical, medical, and political questions that relate directly to misogyny. The placenta is an organ between mother and fetus that facilitates both corporeal separateness and their continual overlap. What researchers feel sure of is that the placenta can have dramatic effects on long-term gene expression and disease vulnerability in both the mother and her child. A woman's fetus is highly susceptible to environmental stimuli, which can affect gene expression; that is, a gene can be turned on or off depending on what's going on around it. Contemporary epigenetics studies changes to DNA that affect how genes are expressed but do not alter the underlying DNA sequence.

Before scientists knew about the specifics of these epigenetic alterations, Conrad Hal Waddington coined the term *epigenetic* in 1942 to explain how an organism unfolds. In *The Evolution of an Evolutionist* (1975), he described the epigenetic as "a developmental process whose course is steered by the combined action of the whole genotype and the impinging environment." In her 1983 Nobel Prize speech for genetic studies she had done in the 1940s (better late than never), Barbara Mc-Clintock called the genome "a highly sensitive organ of the cell." This is an apt description. The genome acts only in relation to, never independently of, its cellular surroundings. Environmental stimuli during a woman's pregnancy that can affect gene expression include everything from what's happening at the immediate cellular level in her body to what she consumes every day for lunch to her mood caused by money worries to the toxic air she may be breathing or the contaminated water she may be drinking.

Human development is a complex, dynamic process in which the genome plays a crucial role, but it never functions in isolation, only in context. The genome and its cellular milieu are completely interdependent and further dependent on what happens to the organism as a whole. The very idea of *nature* versus *nurture*, *innate* versus *acquired*, looks like folly from this perspective. The sex/gender distinction that treats nature and environment as separate entities may be useful at times, but it distorts the motion of actual human growth, which is not arbitrary or shaped exclusively by either nature or nurture.

Many philosophers of biology and scientists working in molecular genetics agree that the nature/nurture opposition is both useless and misleading when it comes to thinking about organismic development. Other fields such as behavioral genetics and evolutionary psychology insist the nature/nurture divide is legitimate; the two halves can be parsed, and in these disciplines nature is usually thought to have the upper hand. I think the distinction between nature and nurture is not only false, I think it is ideological, a division suffused with misogyny and fantasies of masculine control of reproductive processes.

Sir Francis Galton coined the jingle "nature versus nurture." He also coined the word *eugenics*, "well born." Influenced by his cousin Charles Darwin's theory of evolution, Galton was convinced that superior, accomplished men—white men, of course—were achievers by nature. His book *Hereditary Genius* (1869) set out to prove it well before the word *gene* was invented. Smug racism and sexism permeate the book. It was Galton who produced the first twin study and set in motion the eugenics movement that would reach its catastrophic climax in the Holocaust. Eugenics was scientific, and, as it developed out of Galton, it was founded on Mendel's discoveries made while breeding pea plants, coupled with IQ tests that supposedly measured innate ability—the natural hereditary goods delivered from one generation to the next. Eugenics was huge in the United States. Both right-wingers and progressives embraced it. Forced sterilization laws were passed. Its early victims were thousands of psychiatric patients and those deemed feebleminded, imbeciles, or morons. Sterilization in the United States did not stop after the Nazi horrors. It targeted poor women. In the fifties and sixties, those women were disproportionately Black. After the 1970 Population Research Act was passed, it is estimated that twenty-five percent of Native American women capable of bearing children were sterilized. A significant number of them were either pressured or tricked into the procedure.

Although religious dogma continues to direct the lives of many people, the authority of science has equal, if not greater, power, at least among those who regard themselves as secular forward-thinking citizens of the world. Despite the fact that the word *science* is an umbrella for many disciplines that may run on contradictory assumptions, work on innumerable hypotheses, and make discoveries that are contradicted by later discoveries, or sometimes by earlier discoveries, which have been found to be superior to later ones, public faith in scientific findings remains high. The interesting question to ask is which science are we talking about? Eugenics was based on science, on scientific testing and impressive statistical innovations. Although eugenics is often referred to as a pseudo science, this distorts its status as a serious discipline of the time. When science echoes a cultural truism, a notion that is dearly held by the public, it inevitably has advantage over the science that bucks it. Science that reinforces dreams of masculine birth by suppressing the role of the mother in gestation or turning her into Aeschylus's container for a precooked, predetermined seed is as powerful today as ever.

The preformation fantasy, and the misogyny hidden within it, is so widespread it passes mostly unnoticed in the public imagination. An article in the *New York Post* from 1990 summarizes the popular view: After conception, "the result is a single nucleus that contains the entire biological blueprint for a new individual, genetic information governing everything from the length of the nose to the diseases that will be inherited." The now ubiquitous phrase "It's in the DNA" is a way of saying that the trait or quality being discussed cannot be changed. "Your Genes Make You You" is the message delivered on a site called Gene Account. The billion-dollar company 23 and Me, which offers "Health and Ancestry Service," trumpets the same message, "Know what makes you, you." The genome is you.

In a 1987 article before the launch of the Human Genome Project, a *New York Times* science reporter, Robert Kanigel, reached for biblical myth to encapsulate the grandeur of the scientific mission: "In a new understanding it promises to give humans about themselves, the genome project also raises philosophical questions going back to Eden and the Tree of Knowledge: Can we know too much? For it would place in human hands the actual blueprints—in unremitting, look-it-up-in-the-dictionary detail—for how they grow, how they differ among themselves and from other animals." Kanigel enthuses on the new world opening at Walter Gilbert's Harvard lab, where "researchers today explore not just living animals but the molecule that makes elephants elephants and humans human—the master molecule, DNA." Metaphors matter. *Master* is derived from the old English *mægester*—a man having control or authority, a teacher or tutor, master of the house, a master key, master and slave, the master race. The master masculine molecule dictates the course of life.

The geneticist and philosopher of science Evelyn Fox Keller has written brilliantly on the "master molecule" and its ancient resonance. In her book *The Century of the Gene*, she writes, "In this cellular version of the Aristotelian cosmos, the nucleus [which contains DNA in eukaryote cells like ours] is the sufficient cause as Aristotle posits sperm to be." DNA has taken on the role Aristotle and many who came after him gave to sperm—form and soul. And it has taken on contemporary religious significance. Writing for a Vatican publication on the neurosciences in 2007, Enrico Berti connects DNA to Aristotle's animating soul, form. He did not come up with this thought. He borrowed it from the biophysicist Max Delbrück. Physicists have long harbored Platonic ideas about how the universe works. Although Berti is forced to admit that DNA is, in fact, "matter," a natural thing, he asserts, "the sequence of its components, which distinguishes a plant from an animal and from a human being, and even a human individual from another, is a formula, that is a form." DNA has turned into *the soul*. The link to Aristotle is explicit. The assertion of masculine mastery over the feminine, of the mind-soul over body-matter, is implicit.

DNA as an abstraction, as information, as the code of life, as a new twist on the Aristotelian soul has taken hold of the public imagination in astounding ways. The idea that the code, the letters or symbols, can be separated from materiality, the bodily stuff that is the genome, gives it a higher, Platonic spiritual reality, one that can be divorced from mere flesh or matter. Therefore the genome holds the secret to the real you, a disembodied essence or authentic self, which is preformed in the zygote at the magical moment of fertilization, before the cells have multiplied, before implantation in a woman's uterus, before the gradual parallel development of fetus and placenta inside a whole, not piecemeal, person.

The DNA fantasy excludes the temporal reality of gestation. It excludes the woman and Waddington's "impinging environment." It excludes all the changes that are part of her new corporeal reality in pregnancy, during which her cardiovascular, renal, endocrine, immune, and metabolic systems all change. Exactly what happens to her nervous system, no one knows, but there seem to be detectable changes, such as gray matter reduction in her brain. Pregnancy is not equivalent to a uterus. It is not a uterus that hosts a predestined DNA soul. It is an active process of ongoing metamorphoses in the mature maternal body, which initially accommodates a traveling cell ball and the "cross talk" between it and her cells that may result in implantation in the uterine lining, after which those cells may develop into fetus and placenta and grow to term. And these myriad changes are sustained by the woman's overall homeostatic reality, her whole being, during which the placenta serves as crucial negotiator. Homeostasis is the continually shifting adjustments an organism makes to stimuli inside and outside of itself. Iris Marion Young described the pregnant condition well in her essay "Pregnant Embodiment: Subjectivity and Alienation." She writes, "Although she does not plan and direct it, neither does it wash over her, she is this process, this change."

One might imagine that early and contemporary work in epigenetics would have undermined the your-genes-are-you message and rendered the old nature/nurture opposition moot. As the philosopher of biology John Dupré writes in "Causality and Human Nature in the Social Sciences" (2009), "The crucial explication of epigenetic phenomena is that it finally lays to rest that the nature and behavior of an organism was somehow inscribed in the sequence of nucleotides in its nuclear DNA." But it has not been laid to rest. The genome is vital to human becoming, but it is not a prescripted, predetermined plan. It is not a dictator of human traits. Ideas die slowly, and old ideas infect new ideas. The imaginary genetic blueprint has been invested with a soul-mind, a mysterious masculine spirit with a master plan that commands biological matter to do his bidding. The Greek dream of masculine birth survives: "It is not the mother who gives birth to what we call her child: she only nurses the germ sown in her."

In their 2017 paper in *Genetics*, "The Evolving Definition of the Term 'Gene,'" Petter Portin and Adam Wilkins write, "Genes are not autonomous, independent agents." Portin and Wilkins are writing about the changing concept of the gene and how to think about discoveries in the field, but they aptly describe the stubborn fantasy that genes are autonomous, independent little men giving orders, chief officers in a Central Command. No one personified the gene more vividly than the zoologist Richard Dawkins in his popular book *The Selfish Gene* (1974). He turned genes into competitive, horny little heroes steering their "lumbering" human machines or "robots" over evolutionary time, as they hopped from one machine to another across generations. This metaphorical masculinization of the gene keeps the fantasy of paternal heredity alive. The woman, pregnancy, and birth are incidental to the *real* story. (I have sometimes wondered if Dawkins's belligerent atheism might not be explained by the fact that he already has a version of an eternal soul—genes.)

It is not surprising that DNA as master controller has been coopted by the anti-abortion forces in the United States and elsewhere to claim the authority of science, and pro-choice forces have done a bad job countering the faux biology. The following is taken from the Family Research Council's online site, which describes "The Best Pro-Life Arguments for Secular Audiences": "The DNA includes a complete 'design,' guiding not only early development but even hereditary attributes that will appear in childhood and adulthood, from hair and eye color to personality traits." By assigning a godlike role to genes, the "right-to-life" forces have adopted science in their service and effectively denied the reality that a female body is crucial to fetal development. The "person" is there from the start. But genes do not code directly for traits, not even for height and eye color. Although single genes have been identified for some diseases, such as PKU or Huntington's disease, most complex diseases or traits involve untold numbers of genes and countless environmental factors. No one knows which genes may be involved in schizophrenia, depression, or intelligence—despite many claims (and headlines to go along with them) to have located such genes in the past. The idea of the human being premade in the fertilized ovum reinforces the notion of mother-container.

The gene that circulates in the popular mind is a fiction, and it is a fiction kept alive not only by media outlets but by kinds of science that I believe advance a hidden misogyny that is not surprisingly often accompanied by hidden racism. In 2018, the prominent psychologist and behavioral geneticist Robert Plomin published a blog in *Scientific American*, which he summed up with the following: "The nature-nurture war is over. Nature wins hands down." (Plomin is a Galton fan.) That same year, he published a book for a popular audience called *Blueprint: How DNA Makes Us Who We Are*. "Nice parents have nice children because they are all nice genetically," he writes. Plomin's world plan is to give infants a DNA test *at birth* and use it to plan their education according to their genetically scripted futures: "Genetics is by far the major source of individual differences in school achievement, even though genetics is rarely mentioned in relation to education." Plomin wants education tailored to everyone's "personal" abilities made apparent in the genetic test taken as soon as the babe has left its mother's vagina.

Plomin's Brave New World is founded on a gene that has little to do with the gene of molecular genetics or epigenetics; it is a statistical marker for genetic influence based on twin and family studies and more recently on polygenic risk scores for diseases and traits, the scores you can purchase from companies such as 23 and Me, scores that have been criticized for not being replicable, for false positives, and for bias. These scores tell you nothing about what genes *cause* a trait or disease. No one knows whether the genetic variations or single nucleotide polymorphisms, SNPs, identified in Genome Wide Association Studies are truly involved in a disease or trait, only that a statistical association between these SNPs and people who have the trait or disease in question has been established. The connection is made possible by sophisticated data technology and statistical analysis. Despite attempts to be scrupulous about methods, if environmental factors creep into the calculations, the numbers are rendered moot. In a commentary written for *Evolution, Medicine and Public Health* (2019), Noah Rosenberg, Jonathan Pritchard, and Marcus Feldman voice their concern about how these scores will be interpreted. "We show," they write, "how genetic contributions to traits, as estimated by polygenic scores, combine with environmental contributions so that differences among populations in trait distributions need not reflect corresponding differences in genetic propensity." Two papers in *eLife* published in 2019 cast doubt on studies based on polygenic scores and height. The original research found the polygenic scores from southern to northern Europe did increase, which supported the idea that height is largely genetically determined. However, when applied to a newer and larger database, the UK databank, the apparent proof vanished. Shamil Sunyaev, a computational geneticist at Harvard Medical School, who took part in one of the *eLife* studies, summed up the problem neatly in *Quanta Magazine*, "New Turmoil Over the Effects of Genes" (April 24, 2019): "Maybe the Dutch just drink more milk, and this is why they are taller. We can't say otherwise from this analysis." Despite the many critiques of polygenic risk scores that predate his book, Plomin refers to these scores as "fortune tellers."

Plomin barely mentions epigenetics and has nothing to say about fetal development, nor does he mention either sex or race in his book. He was, however, one of fifty-three academics to sign the notorious "Mainstream Science of Intelligence" letter published in the *Wall Street Journal* in 1994 that supported the conclusions of Richard Herrnstein and Charles Murray's *The Bell Curve* and their elaborate IQ statistics about racial differences. I have read that long, boring, and controversial tome and am hard-pressed to understand how anyone could read it without regarding it as a racist tract. Herrnstein and Murray employ the statistical gene as a vehicle for their claim that social policy intervention intended to help people does not affect human outcomes: "The technically precise description of America's fertility policy is that it subsidizes birth among poor women, who are disproportionately at the low end of the intelligence distribution. We urge generally that these policies, represented by the extensive network of cash and services for low income women who have babies, be ended." Notice that in their thinking the circumstances of the pregnant woman play *no role* in her or her infant's health or fate. This is not only politically pernicious; it is biological nonsense.

The political meanings of Plomin's *Blueprint* were not lost on all of the book's reviewers. The right-wing *National Review* read its political meaning accurately and praised it highly. In the journal *Nature*, under the headline "Genetic Determinism Rides Again," the historian of science Nathaniel Comfort called the book "a roadmap for regressive social policy." Comfort is keenly aware of the history of eugenics and intelligence research and its rabid racism. He does not mention the misogyny that drives this ideology, however. It is less obvious. Plomin fits neatly into a long Western narrative that turns the woman into an empty container, a germ or gene carrier. As with Enrico Berti, the spokesman for Vatican science, the story of woman hatred seems to be hidden between the lines.

It is easy to identify misogyny in a phrase such as "fat, childless, 32-year-old slut" and the misogyny and racism in "black bitch." It is much harder to locate misogyny in what is not there—in the absence of birth in the Western canon of painting, in the missing placenta, or in scientific findings and impressive genetic data that suppress the role of environment and gene expression in human development, first inside another person and then outside that person in the world. Absences matter. Dangerous ideas are hiding in plain sight. Avoiding the biology of gestation comes at a heavy price.

Pregnancy is a chimeric state, and the chimera is still a terrifying animal because it involves mixing. Is it one or two? Is it one person early on and then two later? Is it three with the transient organ of the placenta? How do we understand the overlap, one with the other, and the fact that they cannot be severed during the process without mortal danger to both mother and fetus? These dynamic processes belong to the pregnant woman. She is the process, the change, and the accommodation. By avoiding the ambiguity and complexity of actual biology and the continuous merger that is nurture-nature, the guiding illusion of dry science, a science of statistical calculations and correlation coefficients in eugenics and in polygenic risk scores, is that reproductive processes can be *controlled* by an immaterial, abstract reality above and beyond matter—which that pregnant masculine mastermind Aristotle called *form*.

Understanding something about the complexities of pregnancy is useful because it helps skewer the agendas that lie beneath not only headlines but some scientific agendas. It does not tell us what drives the intense need to annihilate the woman. It does not tell us what a man wants. Is this urge for control "womb envy" as the psychoanalyst Karen Horney called it? In "The Flight from Womanhood," she writes, "When one begins as I did, to analyze men after a fairly long experience of analyzing women, one receives a most surprising impression of the intensity of this envy of pregnancy, birth, and motherhood."

Commenting on her work with people in New Guinea, far from the story of the West I have been exploring, the anthropologist Margaret Mead noted, "It is the men who spend their ceremonial lives pretending it was they who had borne the children, that they can 'make men.'"

In *Symbolic Wounds*, Bruno Bettelheim argued, "We are hardly in need of proof that men stand in awe of the procreative power of women and that they wish to participate in it."

In *Sigmund Freud: Life and Work*, Ernest Jones reports that Freud once asked Marie Bonaparte, "What does a woman want?" (*Was will das Weib?*) Freud also noted that paternity is fraught with doubt. How do I know it's mine?

Nancy Chodorow understood men's hatred of women as a need to repress the feminine in themselves (*The Reproduction of Mothering*, 1979/1998).

Jessica Benjamin argued that for some boys the intense need to separate from their mothers turns into contempt for the entire sex (*The Bonds of Love*, 1985).

David Gilmore identifies ambivalence at the core of misogyny, a man's unconscious wishes to return to the succor of the "omnipotent mother" accompanied by a resistance to those same wishes and a drive for autonomy (*Misogyny*, 2001).

In *Hiding from Humanity: Disgust, Shame and the Law* (2004), the philosopher Martha Nussbaum has linked misogyny to human feelings of disgust for signs of our mortality, disgust directed at both female secretions and the male fluid that enters a woman's body in heterosexual coupling, semen, the old womb-tomb connection. I daresay that in the contemporary West semen is regarded as cleaner than menstrual blood. In making her argument, Nussbaum cites the important work of the anthropologist Mary Douglas, who wrote about bodily thresholds, their waste products, and their link to societal borders and categories.

The political theorist Jacqueline Stevens roots kinship rules in male pregnancy envy in her 2005 paper "Pregnancy Envy and the Politics of Compensatory Masculinities." "The only reason men need kinship rules and elevate genetic information to mythic status is because the penis is lacking in its ability to physically give them children." Stevens recognizes that the gene has achieved a "mythic" status in contemporary culture. She wants to remake the rules entirely.

Many contemporary popular treatments of misogyny do not discuss human reproduction. They emphasize power structures that reproduce themselves and keep women in their place. This is vital, but Christine de Pizan's question still resonates. Why? She was reading men and getting depressed about their attacks on women. The attacks still come from men but are hardly limited to them. Many women harbor hostile feelings about their own sex. In the United States, this hostility seems especially strong among white women, who no doubt identify with their male partners and cling to their racial status, but the question still lingers. Why the hate?

The lack of male power in procreation has been compensated for in a ritual that has existed in many and still exists in some parts of the world—the couvade. The father is subject to various taboos and restrictions during the mother's pregnancy, and he imitates the pains of labor. Couvade syndrome, the symptoms some male partners of pregnant women develop—nausea, vomiting, back pain, cravings, and more rarely a swelling belly and breasts—seems to be especially prevalent in developed countries. The symptoms inevitably subside after the birth of the child. Would having a formal ritual lower the incidence of couvade syndrome?

The explanations for the phenomenon range from the psychoanalytic (envy of the mother or rivalry with the fetus) to the biological (the hormonal shifts that occur in expectant fathers), but exactly how and why these endocrine highs and lows occur isn't at all clear. Full-blown pseudocyesis, or hysterical pregnancy, has also occurred in men. The closeness to a pregnancy or the wish to be pregnant are manifest in bodily changes in men that mimic those of women—another form of the chimera. Couvade syndrome further helps to undermine the habitual divide made between nature and nurture. How does a disembodied wish make a man's breasts grow? Wishes are not disembodied; they are instantiated in the nervous system and no doubt in other systems as well. Hormones fluctuate in relation to a person's experiences. Human gender mixing and fluidity is not about minds isolated from bodies or social constructs as separate from natural processes. What people often think of as external is also internal. The experiences of a beloved other become our experiences as well. Couvade syndrome is psychobiological, and it is sociopsychobiological, a mingling of categories we isolate into three separate realms, which are not, in fact, separate realms.

From these various distinct and overlapping perspectives, misogyny is a widespread hatred that necessarily mingles with other emotions— envy, fear, disgust, desire, love, and need for a powerful figure, from whom everyone was born, and without whom the human infant would not survive. The intense craving for the mother is turned into disgust or rejection. Absolute dependence on her can turn into the dream of absolute independence from her, all women, and ideas of the feminine in general. It can become vengeance. Human beings explain their hatreds and fears in many ways and spin elaborate rituals, taboos, myths, and ideas, including scientific ones, to explain and/or justify them, which in turn affect the wider community and are handed down from generation to generation and are then revised, altered, and often reincarnated over time. "It is not the mother who gives birth to what we call her child."

Misogyny has been justified in various historical discourses that are by no means uniform, but the arguments for the badness or stupidity of an entire "sex," which is so various in its other attributes—class, ethnic, racial, or gender identity, not to speak of size and shape and physical strength and education and personality and interests—inevitably revolve around sexual difference in reproduction, whether the female is construed as an inverted male, a creature wholly distinct from the male, or as doomed by evolution to various traits from coyness to an innate ineptitude for physics and mathematics. Physics and mathematics must belong to the masculine side of things, as they represent the high and dry mental birth of the Platonic variety, with its codes, formulas, and forms, not the low, wet, corporeal kind of birth that remains necessary for species survival.

The ancient split between psyche and soma that mirrors a cultural hierarchy of man over woman remains with us, more and less disguised. Study after study has demonstrated that people devalue the intellectual labors of women, whether in the arts or the sciences or business or some other endeavor. The late Ben Barres, a neuroscientist who did groundbreaking work on glia cells in the brain, lived as a woman until he transitioned to a man when he was forty-three. In a 2006 editorial in *Nature*, he took a strong stand against the women-are-doomed-by-evolution-to-be-worse-at-science position loudly advocated by the former president of Harvard, Larry Summers. In an interview with *The Harvard Crimson* (January 19, 2005), Summers acknowledged that his declaration that research had demonstrated an innate difference in aptitude between men and women in science was taken from Steven Pinker's book *The Blank Slate* (2002), another text that heralds twin studies, IQ scores, and the statistical gene, and hides its ideology behind cheerful prose. (In the book, Pinker vigorously defends his late friend Richard Herrnstein of *The Bell Curve* from charges of racism. This seemed to go entirely unnoticed by the press.) Barres published important scientific work as Barbara and important work as Ben, but after his transition, he noticed that he received far more "respect" as a man, especially from those who knew nothing about his transition. "I can even get through a sentence without being interrupted by a man," he wrote. But a lack of respect is not hatred. When do these emotions turn into hatred?

A well-known scientist told me a story about a university cocktail party she attended shortly after she was hired at her first academic post. She decided to wear a simple black sleeveless dress that suited the occasion. Soon after she arrived at the event, the man who was head of her department stomped over to her and barked in her face, "Next time you attend a gathering of the faculty, I expect you to be properly dressed!" She was shocked. Did the man know why he was enraged? I doubt it. He was angry, perhaps disgusted by the uncovered arms (he may have desired them), and he had the power to act on his feelings, however irrational, without worrying about reprisal. Was she the evil he wanted to embrace? What is fascinating in this little story is that the man appeared to be motivated by genuine moral outrage.

As a young woman, I had several encounters with young men who, after I had told them I was not interested in romance or physical relations or whatever it was they were after, lashed out at me with such fury, I was rocked backward on the street or in my chair or wherever I happened to be at the time. After I had gently indicated that a shared coffee was as far as our relations were going to go, one of those suitors became incensed and launched into an enumeration of my physical flaws, which memorably included "a permanent sneer" on my upper lip. He declared he was crazy to have been interested in someone so wholly inadequate in the first place and stormed out of the café. I felt shocked but also puzzled. He, too, behaved as if he were morally outraged.

Moral outrage is the emotional fuel of misogyny, but what exactly is the crime here? In the case of the scientist and her boss and me and the angry suitor, we were held morally responsible for the desire the sight of us apparently evoked in the men. I have never met a heterosexual woman who blamed a man for her own lust, who believed he must assume the burden for what *she* felt. That woman may exist, but she is far more rare than the men who deny responsibility for their own feelings by dumping them onto women. This confusion of self and other is so peculiar that when I was younger I simply couldn't integrate it into the larger story. Neither of these incidents resulted in sexual assault, but the feelings the men displayed are by no means irrelevant to sexual violence.

These responses are, as is repeatedly pointed out, about power. Peons of various kinds exist at and for the pleasure of the rulers. And their rule must be seen as legitimate, not fraudulent, otherwise it could have no moral authority. It thrives on collective consensus. In 2010, Tyler Okimoto and Victoria Brescoll published a study in *Personality and Social Psychology Bulletin*, "The Price of Power: Power Seeking and Backlash Against Female Politicians." They found that when presented with a biography of a state senator described as "power seeking," which had been assigned either a male or female name, significant numbers of the participants, *both men and women*, responded with feelings of "moral outrage (i.e. contempt, anger, and/or disgust)" toward the woman but not the man. The authors explain that the imaginary woman was punished for power seeking because it implied a lack of "communality." By defying her assigned role as a soft, nurturing, helpful, deferent, caring female, she outraged potential voters.

The authors do not use the word *mother* or *maternal*—social psychologists seem to avoid saying it—but, in fact, the fictional senator violated the standards expected of the "good mother," and there is nothing more outrageous or criminal in our culture than a mother who instead of doting on her children is out for herself. How dare she put herself forward and seek power? Has she lost her mind? Studies suggest that women are equally complicit in these angry feelings at women who betray their given role, although one study I read found that women who identify themselves as feminists seem to escape this punitive rage at the archetypal bad mother. Consciousness helps.

The human newborn is far more dependent on its caretakers than other mammals who grow up faster. Think of the foal that only minutes after birth can stand up on its rickety legs and begin to move. For the first year of life, the human child has no such freedom of movement. He cannot survive without constant care from the people around him. He needs another extra-uterine year to develop, a year during which babies are often strapped to the bodies of their mothers or fathers or aunts and uncles or grandparents, fed, carried, rocked, and entertained. This slowness of maturation may well be part of the explanation for why human beings are capable of such immensely complex social interactions with others. Human beings have produced thousands of different languages and a host of societal arrangements that are remarkably varied. There are a few indisputable facts about our species, however. We are all born from another person. Without sustained early care, we die, and it is not just food and protection from the elements we need. If we are deprived of early emotional connection to important others, we, like other mammals, do not thrive. Deprivation, trauma, and many forms of stress affect brain development and gene expression.

Raising children is vital work, but unlike gestation and birth, it is not just women's work. In her book *The Mermaid and the Minotaur*, published in 1976, the psychologist Dorothy Dinnerstein proposed that by rearranging child-rearing practices, we could change the story of misogyny. The middle-class model of mother as lone caretaker and the father as breadwinner had distorted familial relations. Dinnerstein was rightly criticized for universalizing this model. Fathering has changed. Holding, rocking, singing, kissing, hugging fathers are far more visible in the United States now than when I was a girl. Sexual equality laws and paternal leave in Nordic countries have had positive effects on family life, but misogyny has not disappeared from that part of the world. In fact, these countries have a higher level of intimate partner violence when compared to other countries in Europe. Some have suggested this is because reporting is higher there, but others insist the numbers are sound. The irony may be that calls for greater equality create greater levels of moral outrage and backlash.

The irrational demand that fuels misogyny is like the double image found on a coin. On one side is the perfect, caring, sacrificing, loving *natural* mother—a being who does not and has never existed. Flip her over, and you find her evil twin, the rejecting, selfish, *unnatural* mother who seeks power. The irony is that mothers are already powerful, not always but most often the source of food and succor in infancy. The fact that there are men who mother has had little effect on the idea that mothering is female. The idea remains stubborn. The absence of mothering of one kind or another means peril. And that scary, potentially abandoning mother must be punished. She is the source of male and female moral outrage. Human beings, all human beings, are caring and rejecting, kind and cruel, generous and selfish, admittedly to varying degrees. But ambivalence is a feature of much of our intimate emotional lives. A woman doesn't have to be a mother to be punished. In fact, being "childless" can be a synonym for "selfish." All women are expected to act on this cultural imperative: the absurd demand that I, the woman, exist only *for* you, the eternal man-child—to soothe, placate, feed, hold, admire, and adore you. And if I do not perform this part to your full satisfaction, I am a spoiled, wicked, heartless bitch—a witch. The oaths and punches and kicks that come my way are well deserved.

When my niece was three, she said to my sister, her mother, "You know what's funny, Mom?" "No," said my sister. "Sometimes I love you so, so much. And other times, I hate you!"

All intimate relations are complex mixtures of emotion, of love and hate, but patriarchal structures in the West have enforced a prolonged infantile fantasy in many men, especially those at the top of the heap or at the top of their particular heap, that women, like the mythical Eve, were made *for* them. The idea that they were once inside a woman, and that a woman's body was instrumental in *making* them, has to be suppressed in mythical cultural ideas, which bleed into what is supposed to be stripped of all myth—parts of science. And if male heterosexual desire for women enters the picture, the need to embrace the mixed angel-demon creates a poisonous emotional stew.

When gender subversion, racism, class, or other factors are added to the patriarchal stew, it becomes all the more deadly. And the people we call women—a diverse lot to be sure—may also become ingredients in the concoction, to protect themselves from punishment, to align themselves with men or their status on the societal ladder (don't rock the boat/stand by your man) or to placate themselves with a delusion: that they are by nature kinder, gentler, sweeter beings.

I am a white woman in the United States. I live comfortably from my writing. I am intensely aware that my whiteness and my class have afforded me status *for free*. And yet, as people have long understood in hierarchal societies, trouble meets those who refuse to stay in their "places," who rebel against the obsequious, ingratiating roles they have been assigned, wherever they may find themselves on the social ladder.

In her book *Down Girl: The Logic of Misogyny* (2017), the analytical philosopher Kate Manne does not pursue the fantasies of male birth in myth or science or the often hidden complexities of maternity that I believe buoy and reinforce misogyny, but she distinguishes it from sexism and extensively analyzes misogyny as "the law enforcement branch of a patriarchal order." Manne does not tell many personal stories in her book, but in a footnote she reveals that as a schoolgirl she was strangled by a boy who came in second in a spelling bee she had won. The rage starts early.

If cutting the woman out of the picture or pretending she isn't there doesn't work, if ignoring what she says or denigrating her accomplishments as inferior doesn't work either, then the angry policeman arrives on the scene with a big club. This is Manne's central point about misogyny. Law enforcement is not vigilantism. It lives on a collective notion of legitimate rightness. Over the years I have acquired a more refined sense of smell for misogyny's particular odor. When a woman claims authority for herself or is recognized by others as an authority, then she risks punishment. Her authority is better tolerated if she shows communality, if she softens her knowledge with smiles, deferent, pleasing looks, or, even better, gives lots of credit to others for her work or declares herself really, really lucky.

Authority comes from the Latin *auctor*: master, leader, author, *originator*. We have made a circle and arrive back at the fantasy of male birth. The author originates, gives birth to ideas and to words, the Platonic birth that belongs to men. The author is the father who finally gets to be a mother. He expels superior thoughts or a superior book from his higher mind, a mind innately designed by nature to populate the earth with his beautiful offspring. In his book *The Autobiography of a Transgendered Scientist* (2018), Ben Barres shared a story about his young self, Barbara Barres, which resonated with me. A math teacher told Barbara she couldn't possibly have solved the equation she had, in fact, solved. Her boyfriend must have helped her. Barbara didn't have a boyfriend and was distressed by the accusation, but she didn't blame it on sexism at the time. She just felt wronged.

Since I was in high school, my writing life has been haunted by the same accusations. It is extremely odd to be told repeatedly that a man either produced or must have had a hand in papers and books that you have written quite alone. When a girl or woman is falsely accused of claiming a boy's or man's work as her own and is plainly hurt and distressed, no further action is needed on the part of the policeman. Although Barbara insisted she had done it herself, she was put in her place. I have been put in my place many times because although I denied the accusations, I was so startled and upset that I fulfilled the accuser's expectations: My visible pain secured my punishment. I was put in my place. All is well, and business can go on as usual.

The girl or woman who insists on her authority is the one who inspires "inappropriately hostile responses." This is how the British classicist Mary Beard summarized the caustic abuse she and other feminists have received on social media. She has met her detractors head-on and often with humor. Beard mentioned a tweet from a man who promised to "cut off [her] head and rape it." I couldn't help but notice that the body part he hoped to violate was Beard's *head*, one plump with a formidable intellect. Head rape is the perfect metaphor for the man's wrath, which is aimed at what Beard has upstairs. Her obvious authority, the kind perceived in the culture as high and dry, on ancient Rome no less, does not go down well with patriarchy's law enforcement units. It is important to note, however, that Beard's power plays a role in her response. She is a well-known, highly respected academic with a popular following, and her status gives her a public forum. Her resilient personality has also allowed her to laugh at the idiots. The power of comedy to wither the proponents of misogyny has been and remains vastly underestimated.

Like the anonymous note, online invective partakes of a freedom face-to-face encounters between strangers usually don't. It is harder to scream, "I'm going to cut off your head and rape it" at a conference or public event. Inappropriately hostile feelings may nevertheless be on the loose. I recall being loudly hissed at by a member of the audience for a polite challenge to a male interlocutor during a public conversation. I pretended I didn't hear it. On many occasions, after giving a lecture, I have faced an inappropriately angry man who has a comment he seems to believe will crush me instantly. These supposedly devastating verbal weapons are usually dealt with easily, but I continue to be amazed by the flimsy quality of the arrows.

I have also had the truly strange experience of being interviewed about my work onstage in front of large audiences by several men who did not ask me any questions about my books (including a man who moderated a discussion after I had received an honorary doctorate for my work in art and science). Instead, these several men rattled on about themselves or other writers and thinkers and their various meandering interests. When I calmly stopped them and reminded them of the subject at hand—my work, my book, my award for my work—I was met every time with the man's flushed, surprised, humiliated, angry face.

In an e-mail exchange some years ago, one of my European publishers declared that my novel *The Blazing World* had obviously "been written for women," and he would market it as such. I wrote back and explained that this was not the case. I did, after all, know my own intentions. I wasn't angry at him. I just wanted to clarify my position and explain the ironic meanings and structure of the book. But as we wrote back and forth, he grew more and more irritated until he finally exploded at me. "I refuse to be treated as a schoolboy" were his exact and revealing words.

The elevation and recognition of a woman's authority is often interpreted as the denigration and erasure of the man and his authority. The woman doesn't have to do or say anything that impugns the man's dignity. It is enough for her to be an authority on something or other, to be a generator of thoughts, ideas, books, or plans and assume that position. Acknowledging a woman's authority induces shame in many men—a terrible emotion. The heterosexual man who looks up to a woman's authority is shamed by the act itself. He feels emasculated, humiliated, like a schoolboy, a miserable child being corrected by his mother.

My personal stories are small in the big picture of misogyny, but in this exploration of the subject, which is by no means complete—there are many open questions—I have tried to show that what is missing from the picture also counts, that the dream of a purely paternal heredity has never stopped haunting the West, and that dream is bound up with ideas about authority, origins, procreation, and creativity of all kinds that are woven so deeply into modes of thought and ways of being in the culture that they are often invisible. Misogyny is a bad dream. It is an ugly fantasy about power and control, and it distorts truths about shape-shifting, dynamic human beings, about how we grow and mingle with one another, and how we spawn both people and ideas.

2019

SCAPEGOAT

There is a small monument to Sylvia Marie Likens in Willard Park in Indianapolis, Indiana, not far from a house that once stood at 3850 East New York Street, where they beat the girl with a police belt, a fraternity-style paddle, and a curtain rod, where they lowered her into scalding baths, pushed her down stairs, rubbed salt in her wounds, forced her to drink urine and eat excrement from a baby's diaper, where they dehydrated and starved her and put out cigarettes on her body, where they branded words into her abdomen with a burning poker, and where they finally killed her.

Movies have been made about her. True crime stories about her have appeared regularly over the years. Several novels have been based on her story. One of the defense lawyers, Forrest Bowman Jr., wrote about the trial many years later and published a book in 2014. Kate Millett, artist and scholar, author of *Sexual Politics*, built cage sculptures about Sylvia and wrote *The Basement: The Story of a Human Sacrifice*, in which she tries to make sense of it all. Part true story, part cultural-philosophical-feminist critique, part novel, Millett's book includes the running thoughts of victim and perpetrators, an effort to capture what the author imagines happened from the inside, but for me there is something wrong with this ventriloquism, and the imaginative intrusions fail. In *House of Evil: The Indiana Torture Slaying*, the journalist John Dean doesn't try to make sense of it all. He tells a story, and he reports: "Child after child, when asked to explain why he or she participated, said simply, 'Gertie told me to.'"

The Indianapolis Star, October 27, 1965:

A mother of seven children and a 15-year-old boy were arrested on preliminary charges of murder last night after they were implicated in the death of a sixteen-year-old girl who had been tortured and murdered. Investigators said a sister of the victim told them at least three of the woman's children took part in some of the beatings while the victim, Sylvia Marie Likens, was bound and gagged.

Arrested were Mrs. Gertrude Wright, 37, and Richard Hobbs, 15, 310 North Denny Street. Another teenage boy was being sought. [Later reports would identify the woman as Gertrude Baniszewski.]

Detectives said Hobbs admitted to beating the girl "10 or 20 times" and carving the words "I am a prostitute" on her stomach with a needle.

The Indianapolis Star, October 28, 1965:

The 16-year-old girl was systematically beaten and tortured over a three-week period by at least 10 persons, probably more, police said.

The Indianapolis Star, April 30, 1966:

A weeping Jenny Likens was led from Criminal Court Division 2 yesterday as huge photographs of the fantastically mutilated nude body of her sister were shown.

From the Trial Transcript Testimony of Jenny Fay Likens:

Q. Did Sylvia eat at the table with you when you had meals?
A. Not all the time.
Q. When you first went there, did she?

A. Yes.

Q. In what way?

A. I don't know they kept saying she was not clean and they did not want her to eat at the table.

. . . .

Q. What did you see and what was said?

A. She [Gertrude] said, "Come on, Sylvia, try to fight me."

Q. When did this happen, Jenny?

A. In September.

Q. When did—where did it happen?

A. In the dining room.

Q. What did you see and what was said?

A. Well Gertrude just doubled up her fist and kept hitting her and Sylvia would not fight back.

Sylvia Likens was not Anne Frank, a girl who hid with her threatened family in an attic, wrote brilliantly about her life, and died in a Nazi death camp, Bergen-Belsen, because she was a Jew and had been designated unfit to live by the authorities of the Reich. She was not Mary Turner, who bravely spoke out against the lynching of her husband, Hayes Turner, and was then lynched herself in Lowden County, Georgia, during what is now called the "Lynching Rampage of 1918." The mob disemboweled Mary Turner and then stomped on the eight-month fetus she was carrying, under the watchful eyes of another mob of several hundred white people who had gathered to watch. Likens's death did not ignite protests, political writing, and activism as Mary Turner's death did and still does. Likens was a poor white girl in a poor white neighborhood in Indianapolis. Deprived as she was, she was still a white Protestant in the United States. Her story isn't easily swept into the narrative of a just cause. It is not obviously political.

The forces aligned against Sylvia Likens were not the fearsome powers of the state and a malign ideology of racial purity. The mother of seven, Gertrude Baniszewski, was not carrying out anyone's orders.

When academics turn to the Likens case, it's Millett's book that interests them, the author's fascination, obsession, and analysis, not the facts of the actual murder. In "The Basement: Toward a Reintroduction," Victor Vitanza begins his essay with a warning. He will not "paraphrase" Millett but include direct quotations from the book: "Hence this discussion contains explicit descriptions of sexual violence." He calls Millett's style "paraorthodox." His essay is clearly not intended for the uninitiated. In *Murder: A Tale of Modern American Life*, Sara L. Knox doesn't discuss the news coverage of Sylvia Likens's torture and death, although her subject is the role murder has played in the postwar United States. Instead, she devotes many pages to *The Basement*. The destroyed body of a particular girl, a body Millett cannot take her eyes off, is a blur in Knox. As I read, I paused to look at the spelling of the criminal's proper name; a typo perhaps? Throughout her text, Knox misspells the last name of Likens's torturer as Gertrude *Baniewski*. The s and the z have gone missing. (Victor Vitanza, *Sexual Violence in Western Thought and Writing: Chaste Rape*, New York: Palgrave Macmillan, 2011. Sara L. Knox, *Murder: A Tale of Modern American Life*, Durham, NC: Duke University Press, 1998.)

What's her name? You know, the monster woman with a Polish last name who murdered that girl in Indiana? Kate Millett wrote about her.

The scholarly third person frequently serves as a hideout from horror. "All in all, intensive research on violence can be straining when one is emotionally involved, and detachment remains important." This sentence appears in a paper called "Studying Mass Violence: Pitfalls, Problems, and Promises" in the journal *Genocide Studies and Prevention* by Uğur Ümit Üngör. Exactly how detached should one be? Reiterating the details of the torture and murder of just one person, Sylvia Likens, is more than "straining," even though a woman and a gang of kids do not qualify as a mass. There is a leering fascination attached to the Sylvia Likens case, a queasy merger of moral outrage and titillation. To write about it is to become a vicarious participant in the girl's victimization and humiliation. I am doing it now, writing about it, and to what purpose? The story has the tawdry outline of a horror film, and the crimes against Likens, although not all explicitly sexual, reek of shameful urges, veiled excitement, and sadistic sport of an erotic kind. Prurient voyeurism still clings to the case like cheap cologne to a crowd of people in an elevator. And the stink does not go away.

During the trial, it became clear that Sylvia had not been officially or technically "raped." According to the coroner who examined her body, her labia and vagina were swollen from external assaults, but her hymen was intact.

How the world has worshiped at that absurd threshold: the border between female purity and impurity, between cleanliness and filth.

The surname of the accused woman was subject to considerable confusion. In the early days of news coverage, she was identified as Mrs. Gertrude Wright, but soon became Gertrude Baniszewski. In the trial transcripts, she is sometimes Baniszewski and sometimes Wright, depending on who is talking. At sixteen, the girl who would grow up to become the only adult in the Likens case charged with murder dropped out of school to marry John Baniszewski, an Indiana policeman. After ten years, four children, and assault and battery from Officer B., Mrs. B. divorced him and married a Mr. Gutherie. Gertrude's metamorphosis into Mrs. G. lasted only four months, and the surname evaporated with the man. She returned to Mr. B. As far as I have been able to tell, the two never remarried, but before their alliance came asunder for a second time, she gave birth to two more children. Gertrude lifted the name Wright from her post-Baniszewski, much younger paramour, Dennis Wright, who beat her badly enough to send her to the hospital twice, fathered her seventh child, and then absconded.

Whatever legal niceties might have been involved in determining the name of the accused woman, the courts and news organizations finally settled on Baniszewski as the name that met the standards of legitimacy.

Six of Gertrude's children, who ranged in age from eight to seventeen at the time of the murder, were the legal offspring of Baniszewski, who was himself a finger in what has been called "the long arm of the law," but which in the Likens case turned out to have the reach of an amputee. Gertrude's baby, who went by the first name of his vanished father, was not officially Dennis anybody, as he had, by no fault of his own, arrived in the world a bastard. It is helpful to recall that in 1965 in that neighborhood in Indianapolis, children born out of wedlock did not sit well with the neighbors. No doubt the eyes of the neighbors spawned the fictional character known as Mrs. Dennis Wright.

Gertrude was not the only Baniszewski to be charged with homicide. Every one of Officer and Mrs. B.'s children hurt Sylvia Likens but only two of them were tried for murder: Paula and John. Paula, the oldest, pregnant after a misadventure with a married man, assaulted Sylvia with such ferocity on one occasion that Paula broke her hand. While on trial for her life, Paula pushed a new life into the world, a girl she belligerently named Gertrude. John Jr., twelve years old when Sylvia died, and two neighbor boys, Richard Hobbs and Coy Hubbard, were also tried for Sylvia's murder. The three Baniszewskis, Hobbs, and Hubbard were all convicted, but none of them was executed. Gertrude served the longest sentence, twenty years. She became a model prisoner and was known to her fellow inmates as "Mom." After the three Baniszewskis were released from prison, they all changed their names, as did Officer Baniszewski, who had not taken part in any of the household torture.

When my mother read about terrible crimes in the newspaper, she used to say, "No sane person could do such a thing." Gertrude Baniszewski's defense lawyer, William Erbecker, articulated the same sentiment in court: "She's not responsible because she's not all here." He then tapped the side of his forehead with his index finger to emphasize that the problem lay in that part of the woman's body. The deputy coroner of Indianapolis, Dr. Arthur Kebel, who had examined Sylvia's corpse at the house, testified in court that when he had first seen the body, he had guessed the damage was the work of "a madman." After perusing the photographs of the dead girl in court, he said, "If I had nothing to see except these pictures, I would say only a person completely out of contact with reality would be capable of inflicting this type of agony on another human being." He said "person," not "people."

The lone gunman who "snaps" and begins firing his weapon in a church, synagogue, or school, and the sadistic psychopath who secretly stalks his prey are easier to keep at a comfortable distance by reason of mental illness than any group, small or large in number, that turns on its victim(s) with rabid fury. What about the underage mob that came and went at 3850 East New York Street in Indianapolis under the direction of a thirty-seven-year-old woman?

In *La psychologie des foules*, 1895, translated a year later as *The Crowd: A Study of the Popular Mind* in English, Gustave le Bon proposed a theory of the "group mind," an unconscious force created by a contagion of feeling that quivers through its multiple individual parts to become a single mental reality. "*The crowd is credulous and readily influenced by suggestion.*" In the grip of this *contagion mentale*, a person enters a kind of hypnotic trance. His conscious personality vanishes, and he moves to the rhythms of the greater whole. Crowds, le Bon's theory goes, are impulsive, irritable, irrational, volatile, and morally righteous. They become, he maintained, like those beings who are insufficiently evolved—"women," "children," and "savages."

Gabriel Tarde, another French scholar of the period, was interested in how thoughts and feelings spread in populations. "What is society?" he wrote. "I have answered. Society is imitation." Imitation, Tarde believed, usually worked by underlings imitating leaders, not the other way around. It can move beyond an immediate group and be caught by others. Bandits, for example, "an antisocial confraternity," reinforce one another's "toughness" within the group, but those mores "radiate" beyond the circle too, working their way into those vulnerable to its seduction. (Gabriel Tarde, *The Laws of Imitation and Invention*, trans. E. C. Parsons, New York: Henry Holt & Co., 1903.)

On May 19, 1966, the jury found Gertrude Baniszewski guilty of first-degree murder. Not three months later the same year, on the afternoon of August 5, tenth-grade students at the Girls Middle School in Beijing attacked three vice principals and two deans. They threw ink on their superiors, crowned them with dunce caps, forced them to their knees, scalded them with boiling water, and beat them with nail-spiked clubs. After three hours of torture, the first vice principal, Bian Zhongyun, lost consciousness. The girls tossed her into a garbage cart. She died. Bian Zhongyun was the first teacher to be sacrificed to the Cultural Revolution in China. Fourteen days later onstage in a concert hall near Tiananmen Square, students from Beijing's Fourth, Sixth, and Eighth Middle Schools whipped and kicked twenty teachers in front of a crowd of thousands. One witness said they were beaten so badly "they no longer looked human." The children had been given permission. They had the state on their side. (Youquin Yang, "Student Attacks on Teachers: The Revolution of 1966," University of Chicago, *Issues and Studies* 37, 2001.) Does "Gertie told me to" constitute authoritative permission under the roof of a single-family house?

Gustave le Bon, creature of late-nineteenth-century science and its research into hysteria and hypnosis, believed in "suggestion," a traveling underground message that infects the crowds that fall under its spell, a form of enchantment explained in the naturalistic terms of the period. Tarde, who was also interested in crowds and crime, posited "imitation rays" that move through society. Imitation can be a form of somnambulism. "To have only received ideas while believing them to be spontaneous: this is the illusion to which both sleepwalkers and social man are prey." I think it's my thought and my action, but it's not. I am under the influence of contagious rays that have almost magical properties to sway my will.

If the ending were changed, the story of Sylvia and Jenny could be told as a fairy tale.

Long ago in the city of I., there lived a poor man and his wife and their five children. Try as they might, the man and woman could not make a living in town, and when only a few coins remained in the family purse, they decided their only choice was to leave the children behind and try to make their fortune with a traveling carnival. Their oldest girl had married and lived with her husband, and their boys had a home with their grandparents, but the two youngest daughters, Sylvia and Jenny, had nowhere to stay. Sylvia was a pretty, obedient girl, who liked music and dancing. She helped her mother keep house and watched over her little sister, Jenny, who wore a brace on her leg and walked with a limp. The man and woman watched their money dwindle and prayed they would find lodging for their girls.

One summer day, Sylvia and Jenny wandered into the street and met a merry, mischievous girl named Stephanie who took them home with her. After the sun had set and his daughters had not returned, the man went out looking for them, discovered their whereabouts, and knocked at the door of a tall, broken-down house. An ugly, haggard woman appeared, and the man took fright, but when she spoke to him, her voice was sweet and mellifluous, and he no longer felt afraid. He asked after his daughters, and the woman told him her name was Gertrude and she had seven children of her own. Soon the two had struck a bargain. For twenty dollars a week, Gertrude agreed to watch over Sylvia and Jenny as if they were her very own. Father and mother bade goodbye to their daughters, went on the road, and promised to return before the autumn leaves fell.

Now, this Gertrude was a powerful witch. When the money she had been promised didn't arrive, she beat Sylvia and Jenny. When the money came in the post the next day, she beat them anyway. But as time went on, the witch turned all her wrath on Sylvia because she could not bear the sight of her youth and beauty. The witch cast a spell over the house so that everyone inside its rooms felt the same hatred she did for Sylvia, everyone, except Jenny, on whom the magic did not work. But when the children from the neighborhood entered the house, they too fell under the charm. The witch and the hexed children hit Sylvia. They laughed at her. They called her a slut, gave her crumbs to eat, and made her sleep in the basement on the floor. And Jenny with her lame foot was too afraid to say or do anything.

It is at this moment that a white dove flies through a small window and speaks, or a fairy godmother appears suddenly with her wand to grant three wishes, or a strange little man waddles into the room and asks our heroine to guess his name, but while Sylvia lies weeping in the basement of the terrible, enchanted house, no one comes, and she dies.

Most people want stories that make sense. The evil witch is banished or killed. She melts. Virtue rewarded. Justice done. Wishes granted. Moral lesson learned. Plucky hero fights like mad, defies all the odds, and survives. Music soars. Applause is heard. Standard cultural narratives are already there waiting for us. We pick them up, dust them off, and apply them when they come in handy. Beowulf, Cinderella, Odysseus. Stories are spun for meaning. They locate cause and effect. One thing leads to another, step by step. What is the *cause* here? A spell is akin to a hypnotic effect. In the old movies I watched as a child, the evil hypnotist would say, "You will obey my every command."

Marie Baniszewski was eleven years old when she testified in court about the murder of Sylvia Likens.

Q. Tell the jury what happened.
A. Mom had scalding hot water running and she told Sylvia to come up from the basement and Mom putted her head under the hot water.
Q. How did she hold her head?
A. By the neck.
Q. By the neck?
A. Yes, sir.

Q. Was there any soap on her head at the time?

A. No, sir.

Q. How long did she hold her head under the faucet?

A. Mom did not get to hold her head under there very long because Sylvia was hysterical to get away.

Marie lit the match to heat the poker they used to brand Sylvia. Was she afraid? Just following orders? Hypnotized by her mother's authority? Did she catch the violence around her as one catches a cold, tuberculosis, the plague? They were all in on it. They slapped, burned, kicked, punched, and laughed. There was a lot of laughing and giggling.

Emotional contagion is alive and well in science. Mention of hypnosis, however, is mostly avoided. Mimesis, that old word, to mimic, imitate, is built in to the species.

Primitive emotional contagion: "The tendency to automatically mimic and synchronize facial expressions, vocalizations, postures, and movements with those of another's and, consequently to converge emotionally." (E. Hatfield, J. Cacioppo, and R. L. Rapson, *Emotional Contagion*, Cambridge, UK: Cambridge University Press, 1993.)

Newborns imitate faces. Parent-infant "synchrony," coordinated timing between caretaker and baby, from biological rhythms to symbolic exchanges, is a much-studied subject these days. "Developmental outcomes of the synchrony experience are observed in the domains of self regulation, symbol use, and the capacity for empathy across childhood and adolescence." (Ruth Feldman, "Parent-Infant Synchrony: Biological Foundations and Developmental Outcomes," *Current Outcomes in Psychological Science* 16, 2007.) Unconscious imitation begins early before a child speaks. Mothers and infants coordinate heartbeat rates. They are attuned, a unit of reciprocal, mirroring gestures and feelings and sounds and glances.

"The reader should note that for this analysis, the non-rational, non-symbolic transmission of emotional states among individuals is treated as an aspect of *information transit* among populations." (James

K. Hazy and Richard E. Boyatzis, "Emotional Contagion and Proto-organizing in Human Interaction Dynamics," *Frontiers in Psychology* 6, 2015.)

I see you. I imitate you. I feel what you feel. Think of smiles and yawns. And what about violence?

The epidemiologist Gary Slutkin: "Violence is a contagious disease. It meets the definition of being a disease and of being contagious—that is, violence is spread from one person to another . . . This paper intends to clarify how violence is acquired and biologically processed." (National Academy of Sciences workshop, 2013.)

"Social contagion accounted for 61.1% of 11,123 gunshot episodes in Chicago." The study covered the years between 2006 and 2014. (Ben Green, Thibaut Horel, and Andrew Papachristos, "Modeling Contagion Through Social Networks to Explain and Predict Gunshot Violence in Chicago, 2006–2014," *JAMA Internal Medicine* 177, 2017.)

The neuroscientist Marco Iacoboni writes, "The missing link between the compelling social science studies on the contagion of violence and the model of such contagion as an infectious disease is a biologically grounded mechanism. A recent neuroscience discovery, a type of brain cell called mirror neuron, may provide such a missing link." ("The Potential Role of Mirror Neurons in the Contagion of Violence," National Academy of Sciences, 2013.)

The scientists lay out their facts. Human beings imitate. They converge emotionally. Traveling emotion is *information transit*. Violence is not *like* a disease. It *is* a disease. The confident number 61.1 percent has been divined by an elaborate statistical method. The biological mechanism, the brain machinery underneath it all may be a kind of neuron. But it can't be at work between violent attacker and victim. If the victim is like me, feels like me, how can I torture and murder her? The victim must be out of the imitation loop. The children mirrored "Gertie" (but not Sylvia) by biological mirror mechanism, an unconscious contagion, by which brutality travels via nonsymbolic information transit? Isn't this what hipsters in the 1960s called "vibes"?

The marchers in Charlottesville are chanting, "Jews shall not replace us." They are carrying torches. They are riled up, inflamed in their whiteness and their rage. James Alex Fields drives his car into the crowd and kills a counterprotester, Heather Heyer. The political meaning of this murder is not in doubt.

René Noël Théophile Girard died in 2015. A French native, Girard earned his Ph.D. at Indiana University in 1950. By 1965, when the police found Sylvia's corpse, he was long gone from the state. He never mentioned the Likens case in his work, although he would have found it pertinent to his thought. Like a number of his countrymen, Girard had a weakness for the bold theory, and he claimed to have unlocked the secret to human violence. It all starts with what he called mimetic desire. The term may be foreign but the phenomenon is easily recognized.

A three-year-old girl skips across the floor in her nursery school and notices a discarded hand puppet on the floor. She bends down, picks it up, and begins to play happily with the nodding, talking mouse at the end of her arm. Another child, who had glanced at the puppet a moment before but had not displayed an iota of interest, watches his schoolmate and finds himself seized with an overwhelming desire for the mouse. He rushes toward her, snatches the thing from her hand, and a puppet war ensues.

Old, dying Mr. F. parades his beautiful young wife in public. His heart is too weak to endure the shock of orgasm, but it is enough that other men look upon him with envy.

Sylvia walks into Gertrude's house. She is young, pretty, good-natured, and oblivious. Gertrude has asthma, eczema, and seven children. Does she look at the girl and want the impossible: her face, her youth, her innocence?

We are mimetic, imitators deep down. For Girard, all of culture, all social life is about imitation, but it isn't really the puppet or the trophy wife or the unmarred face that is wanted, according to him; the rival seems to possess some inner quality the other lacks, a shine of wholeness, a magical property that must be wrestled away from her or him at all costs. Viewed from the outside, the two are doubles, mirror images, locked in a contest of desire for what is missing, and that desire leads to vengeful rivalry, which, according to Girard, is contagious. It spreads through the community and can turn into violence.

In Girard's telling of this big story or myth, and stories this big are always myths, the epidemic can be relieved only by a scapegoat. The bickering, rows, and moral sickness that infect the group are transferred onto a vulnerable or marginal person, someone who has few or no defenders, a person who acts as a sponge to absorb the blame: the witch, the Gypsy, the Jew, the homosexual, the Black person, the Muslim, the immigrant, the epileptic, the beggar, the albino, the crazy person, the female candidate for president, the pretty girl on Facebook. The group does not know that this is what is happening. The group sincerely believes in the outsider's culpability. Without belief, the scapegoat mechanism cannot work. The chosen one deserves to be punished and, through punishment and death, through the sacrifice of the one, the community emerges cleansed and harmonious once again.

After an eleven-year-old girl hanged herself in my hometown in Minnesota, the rumor circulated that she had been harassed and bullied to death by her classmates. One girl in particular had been the ringleader. The law was never involved, but I remember the gossip that flew through the town, and I remember that the eager telling of the tale was followed by silence and a sense of awe at how terrible it was—a dead child.

Every myth explains too much, but that doesn't mean there aren't truths to be found in the story. Girard's grandiose explanation for human violence unearths part of the truth. Sylvia Likens was a scapegoat.

"This is the chill of an evil essentially collective, social, cultural, even political. It is the site of an old crime, old as the first stone, old as rape and beatings: it is not just murder, it is a ritual killing." Kate Millett doesn't mention violence as contagion, or Girard's theory, but she wants to get hold of the story's essence and calls it "a ritual killing." She wants to unearth something true. What does this story mean? How can ritual killings take place without ritual? Or did the woman, the matriarch in that broken-down house, invent rituals from old stories she had heard? "You branded Stephanie and Paula and I am going to brand you." This sentence attributed to Mrs. B. is repeated several times during the trial.

Gertrude Baniszewski was the adult, the leader of the band, the authority in her little world, and she was no longer attached to a man, a higher authority in our world. She was no longer "under his thumb," as the saying goes. No man was making love to, impregnating, or beating her up anymore. Is her dominant feeling humiliation or does she feel a sudden surge of power or both? "To teach her a lesson," Mrs. B. said when asked why she "disciplined" Sylvia. "To teach her a lesson."

There is a picture: a grainy photograph of Gertrude Baniszewski in the newspaper, a gaunt, scowling visage fit for a Grimm brothers' ogress. She had chronic asthma, and she chain-smoked. During her trial testimony she denied everything. The children had lied to police, had lied on the stand. She moaned about her illness, the drugs she had to take, and how tired she was. She was lying down. She was asleep. She slept through the horrors. The kids must have done it.

There is another picture: a photograph of Sylvia Likens smiling with her mouth closed because she is missing a front tooth her parents couldn't afford to have replaced. She lost it in an accidental collision with her brother years before. Her eyes are large and lit with vivacity. An article in *The Indianapolis Star* a week after her death reported, "friends said she was 'shy' and she was 'the odd one in the family.'" Someone probably described her in this way. "Odd one"? Who were these "friends"? Sylvia was born between two sets of fraternal twins. She was literally the "odd" one, a singleton. Her nickname was "Cookie." She liked to roller-skate. Her favorite band was The Beatles. She was careful with her clothes. She washed and ironed them herself. Her father testified that she had made money ironing for a Laundromat. "She was very good at

ironing," he said. Her mother testified that she was "orderly." She went
to church. She owned a Bible. She was clean. The latter facts came out in
the trial, no doubt to prove that she was not a loose tramp but a good,
clean, churchgoing, Bible-owning white citizen. And yet, the information
about her personality is so scant, all that can be summoned to mind is
a smiling vacancy.

From the Trial Transcript of Marie Baniszewski:

Q. What kind of a girl was she before she was beaten up?

A. A real nice girl.

Q. Was she nice to you?

A. Yes, sir.

Q. Was she nice to the other children in your family?

A. Yes, sir.

Q. Was she nice to your mother?

A. Yes, sir.

Q. Did she work or help around the house?

A. She always got home before us kids and would straighten up our
bedrooms and the downstairs.

I recognize that girl from my own childhood in small-town Minnesota:
the nice, helpful, cheerful, orderly girl, willing to serve, the girl who did
not make trouble or made as little trouble as she could, the girl who
folded her hands on her lap in church and endured the intense bore-
dom of sitting through the service without complaint. This is how Sylvia
struck Marie, anyway, as "a real nice girl." Marie probably liked coming
back to a straightened-up bedroom. And yet, "the real nice girl" is also
a blank, a type, a nobody.

I was ten years old when Sylvia Likens died, the same age as Marie,
the girl who lit the match to heat the poker they used to brand the
naked Sylvia, who was tied up, gagged, and held down by Marie's
brother John and her sister, either Stephanie or Shirley. Marie lied stubbornly on the stand to protect her mother, got confused, cried, "Oh,

God, help me!" and, after that, slowly began to break under the prosecutors' examination.

"I know one thing," Marie said to the prosecutor, "Paula was very jealous of Sylvia." "Did she say that?" he asked her. "No," Marie answered. "You could see it in her eyes." Did they kill her because she was "nice" and "clean"? Was Sylvia an affront, a constant reminder of what the family had lost or was constantly in danger of losing—respectability? The other side of respectability is shame. Shame is not guilt. Shame is what you feel when others look down at you with contempt. Guilt is what you feel when you have internalized the morality of the larger society to which you belong and your conscience prevents you from behaving cruelly to others. Paula, pregnant and shamed, was her mother's eager, violent enforcer.

The sickness that infects the house on East New York Street cannot be located in a single room or in any one of its residents nor can it be found in the neighborhood kids who come and go freely, in and out, in and out. Like an infestation of vermin, it swarms up the stairs, disappears into floorboard crevices, and crawls inside walls. The whole house is sick with fever, except the girl they have singled out and her sister who drags around a brace on her left leg from infant polio and does nothing, perhaps because she feels there is nothing to do.

From the Trial Transcript of Jenny Likens:

Q. You were perfectly free to go and tell anybody you saw, weren't you?

A. Yes.

Q. You could've told the neighbors about this if you wanted to, couldn't you?

A. I could've. That don't mean I wanted to die though.

When Sylvia is dead and the police officer arrives at the house, Jenny whispers in his ear, "Get me out of here, and I will tell you everything."

From a message board, **Watching True Crime Stories: General Discussions.**

Serene 196936: I am sorry but I have no sympathy for Jenny Likens. I know that's harsh but I dont

Shar 001: . . . I would have taken Jenny Likens to the side and slapped her iin [sic] the face! She wasn't some emotionally disturbed 4 year old, you know? I tell yo this my Daughter and her friends age 10 could have gang ed up on those bastards I know this by heart someone you love, your own sister.

The two discussants, true crime watchers, hate Gertrude and Paula and Ricky Hobbs and Coy Hubbard and the neighbor kids who participated in or watched the crimes take place, but they also hate Jenny. They hate her passivity. Sylvia was passive, too, but she is the victim. If Jenny had really loved her sister, she would have acted. Serene and Shar have immersed themselves in the details of the case. They are emotionally involved. They have read the books. They "appreciate" Kate Millett because she is as "passionate" about the Likens murder as they are. The story is a vehicle for their moral indignation. Moral indignation feels good. The imaginary slap serves the imaginary Jenny right. What kind of person looks on while her sister is kicked and burned and used as a living effigy?

From the Trial Transcript of Jenny Likens:

Q. Alright, did you—how many operations did you have on your leg?
A. Approximately six or seven.
Q. When was the last one?
A. When I was thirteen.

Jenny Likens's polio was not an old story muffled in the amnesia of her babyhood. It was an ongoing drama of hospitalizations. I can only speculate on how this affected her will to act. It was Sylvia who had been her protector.

In September, the girls met their older married sister, Dianna Shoemaker, in a park. They told her that they had been hurt and beaten. Some credit Dianna with alerting social services. Some have speculated that Jenny made the call. According to the trial transcript, the call was anonymous. Some unknown person made a report that there was a child with "open running sores" at 3850 East New York Street. In response, a public health nurse, Mrs. Barbara Sanders, paid a visit to the house. Gertrude informed the nurse that the person she was looking for, the one with the sores, was Sylvia. Gertrude had kicked Sylvia out of the house because Sylvia did not mind and did not take care of herself. In this version of events, Sylvia is not a clean, orderly girl. Sanders recalled "Mrs. Wright" saying that Sylvia had "matted," "dirty" hair and running sores on her head because she did not wash. Sylvia had called Mrs. Wright's daughters prostitutes in school, but Sylvia was the prostitute who solicited men in the street. Mrs. Sanders testified that "Mrs. Wright" had claimed her own children were "good children, went to church on Sunday and were not in any kind of trouble and she did not allow them to play with the neighborhood children, she pretty much kept them at home so she knew where they were and so forth . . ." The nurse seems to have believed this story, and there was no further investigation.

In her book, Millett remembers the Midwest in those days. She was born in 1934—more than twenty years before me—in St. Paul, Minnesota, an hour's drive from my town of Northfield. Millett identifies with Sylvia intensely in a way I do not. "Because I was Sylvia," she writes. "She was me. She was sixteen. I had been. She was the terror of the back of the cave, she was what 'happens' to girls. Or can. Or might." Millett also knows she is not Sylvia, admits that the girl often vanishes for her as an imaginative object, but the connection remains. The rigidity of the moral code for girls was matched by the joyous need to condemn the easy make, floozy, tramp, tart, hussy, slut, bimbo, moll, whore. "Aren't nubile young females responsible in some complicated way for the sexuality they exude?" Millett writes.

"Decency" had a stressful punitive quality for girls in my world, and it was no doubt worse in Millett's early life. I felt it. Simply reaching sexual maturity brought suspicion in its wake, especially from older women, a suspicion not directed at boys, a suspicion that you were already guilty of something, even before you knew exactly what you were supposed to feel guilty about. But that code began to loosen in my teenage years—idea winds blew across the country and they hit the plains, too. "The double standard" became a phrase.

And the terror at the back of the cave? The stiffening awareness that arrives with a man's footsteps behind you on the street, the endless stories of rape and brutality meted out by familiars and strangers alike. Millett blames Sylvia's death on "faith, a series of beliefs, systematic beliefs." The hatred and shaming of women is alive and well—the threats are everywhere, to rape, behead, hack to pieces feminist bloggers—but when does religious, moral indictment become torture-murder?

Feeling and belief mingle. Belief opens the door to violence, but it may also serve to justify violence after the fact. Irrational hatred attaches itself to ideology. It isn't just emotion that is contagious, after all. Ideas are caught, too, carried from one person to another, and ideas are used to shore up "identities." There is no identity without perceived difference. I define myself against you. I am the pure, uncontaminated not-you.

Gertrude tells the nurse that *her* children are not running wild with the neighbor kids. She doesn't even let them *play* with the neighbors. *Gertrude's* children are pure of mind and body. They are in church every Sunday. They are never in trouble. It's that girl, the boarder, Sylvia, the repository for all that is unclean: for literal and metaphorical filth, dirty hair and dirty mind. Gertrude's intolerable feelings of shame have been dumped onto Sylvia. Gertrude performed "Mrs. Wright" for the nurse.

She acted the part of the good, vigilant, orderly mother, the upright moral citizen who forbids, disciplines, draws a hard line, and brandishes a Bible. To what degree did she believe in this role? Sylvia is the target of furious, if perverse, righteousness. Isn't the same dynamic at work among some white evangelicals, who spew hatred for dark foreigners of all kinds whom the zealots have loaded up with their own misery and shame?

Nancy Chodorow writes about the psychoanalyst Melanie Klein: "Many of the major political events, crises, and controversies of our time can only be understood if the operation of rage, splitting, projection, and introjection is taken into account. For example, political and cultural demonization of the enemy is psychologically based on projection and introjection, in which all good resides in the nation, the ethnos, the group, and all bad resides in those who are not part of this group. Splitting bad from good . . . underpins all virulent racism, nationalism, ethnic conflict and attempts at ethnic cleansing or genocide. Splitting may also be used to ward off elements that are threatening because they are too attractive." She mentions misogyny and homophobia—"attractions and desires that are too anxiety laden to be contained within the self." (N. J. Chodorow, "Melanie Klein," in *International Encyclopedia of the Social and Behavioral Sciences*, Oxford, UK: Elsevier Science, 2001.)

Larry Craig, former U.S. Republican senator from Idaho, vocal opponent of gay rights, supporter of a 2006 amendment to the Idaho constitution that bans gay marriage and civil unions, is arrested for soliciting gay sex from an undercover cop in an airport bathroom.

"On the campaign trail, you called yourself a nationalist. Some people saw that as emboldening white nationalists . . ." Yamiche Alcindor, one of the few Black women in the White House Press Corps, asked President Donald Trump on November 7, 2018. He cut her off. "I don't know why you'd say that, such a racist question." Swerve and dump.

In her testimony at the trial about her conversation with Nurse Sanders, Gertrude draws a pathetic self-portrait. She recalls the sad condition of her face at the time: "I was wearing sunglasses when I was up because my eyes were swelled and matted quite a bit and my face was swelled and it was raw to the point where it was starting to bleed here and there." The word *matted* again, the same word Sanders remembered Gertrude had used to describe Sylvia's hair—*matted*. Paula chopped off Sylvia's hair in uneven hunks. Gertrude pushed her head under scalding water. No soap in the hair. Who and what is matted?

Every one of the actors in the story was poor and white. Sylvia and Jenny's parents did not fit the description of a fairy-tale couple, but they weren't a spectacularly wicked pair either. The girls' mother, Elizabeth Likens, had been arrested for shoplifting. She and her husband had been separated. Lester Likens had trouble keeping a job. They moved a lot, fourteen times in the sixteen years of Sylvia's childhood. They hit their children. The corporal punishment of children seems to have been a matter of course for everyone involved in the case, one that supports an argument for contagion. Reading the trial transcript, I had the impression that neither the lawyers nor the defendants seemed to believe spankings and whippings were not acceptable punishments. Violence directed at children was *natural*. The neighbors heard Sylvia screaming for weeks. It was just part of the auditory atmosphere.

The Likenses and the Baniszewskis belonged to what would later be dubbed "the precariat," people who live from hand to mouth and have far too little financial security to predict their material futures. They make do. But precarious circumstances and hardship do not lead directly or even indirectly to the brutal torture and murder of a teenage girl.

In his book *Facing the Extreme: Moral Life in the Concentration Camps* (1991), Tzvetan Todorov meditates on heroism, sainthood, and acts of caring that took place among people in the camps who had been brutalized and had every reason to feel hopeless. He describes ordinary acts of kindness to others under extraordinary circumstances, the sharing of food, for example. "Here again," he writes, "we find a limit beyond which sharing was impossible, simply because hunger and thirst were too great. Once these were even minimally satisfied, however, it seems some shared and others did not." He cites Eugenia Ginzburg, who wrote a memoir of the eighteen years she spent in Stalin's prison and labor camps. In her book, she remembers "an old convict [who] brought her some oat jelly he had lovingly prepared but would not eat himself. He was happy just to watch her enjoyment." I look at your pleasure and it fills me with pleasure—the kind version of mirroring, of empathy. But under conditions of scarcity, of near-starvation, what is it that makes one person hoard food and another share it? Todorov is explicit that caring is to be distinguished from group solidarity and from sacrifice. "Caring," he writes, "is its own reward, for it makes the giver happy."

Who are the people who share and who are the people who don't? How does one know who is who? I have never lived such deprivation. How can I know if I am one or the other? And yet, isn't it also true that I have been selfish at some moments in my life and generous at others? I have acted bravely, and I have been a coward. Todorov also describes individual acts of kindness and generosity on the part of guards and others in positions of power, people who were during the same period responsible for monstrous acts. What are we? Isn't this the ultimate question, the question that is terrifying? Do we know? When are we deluded? What about the sadistic urges that everyone feels at one time or another? When do urges become acts?

I remember a girl in my third-grade class with long, unwashed hair that fell in strings across her face, strings she pushed out of her eyes over and over again. It was a tic. She always made herself as small as possible. She sat with her head down and when her fingers weren't in her hair, they were pressed protectively against her chest as if she were expecting a blow at any moment. When she was called on in class, she whispered. Mostly, I pitied her, but there were times when my sympathy for her paralyzing timidity vanished, and I felt an urge to slap her across the face and shout, "Speak up! Speak up!" I did not hit that girl or yell at that girl, but where is the threshold between thinking and doing? Is it when permission has been given? Is it when a soaring feeling of moral righteousness makes it right and proper to slap? "I would have taken Jenny Likens to the side and slapped her iin [sic] the face!"

"In any case, the condemned man looked so like a submissive dog that one might have thought he could be left to run free on the surrounding hills and would only need to be whistled for when the execution was due to begin." (Franz Kafka, "In the Penal Colony," in *The Complete Stories*, trans. Willa and Edwin Muir, New York: Schocken Books, 1988.)

"Revolution is not a crime! Rebellion is justified!" "Dare to think! Dare to act!" The teenagers were wild with their enthusiasm for Chairman Mao, quoting from the Little Red Book, singing on the buses that carried them from place to place. The fire was in them, a need to purge the pollution of bourgeois thinking from the bodies of the ideologically impure. Slap. Beat. Kick. Burn.

"Because children are often physically vulnerable, easily manipulated, and susceptible to psychological manipulation, they typically make obedient soldiers." (Human Rights Watch, "Coercion and Intimidation of Child Soldiers to Participate in Violence," www.hrw.org/en/topic/childreno39s -rights/child-soldiers.)

No one helped Sylvia. No one performed an act of caring for its own reward. None of the children, as far as I know, slipped her food or water or treated her wounds, much less ran off to seek help for her. No adult who visited the house was softened by sympathy either. An adult neighbor, Mrs. Vermillion, who lived at 1848 East New York Street, testified that she had seen Sylvia with a black eye Paula bragged about having given her. She had seen Paula throw hot water in Sylvia's face and rub garbage into it. She had heard Gertrude say she hated Sylvia. Mrs. Vermillion testified that Sylvia had "looked scared," that she didn't seem to care whether she lived or died. Mrs. Vermillion did nothing. The family pastor, Roy Julian, visited the house several times, a man whose testimony at the trial demonstrated not just his willingness to swallow lies about the nasty Sylvia but his tacit approval of severe "correction" for wayward children, an approval that hung over the neighborhood like a lowering cloud.

Sylvia's "difference" in that house was not a class, ethnic, religious, or ideological difference. She was not in the Baniszewski family, not blood, not Gertrude's child. Not mine. Theirs. This was perhaps enough. "Come on, Sylvia, try to fight me." But Sylvia did not fight back. Girls did not stage fights in the little world of my Northfield childhood. Wounding words, cruel gossip, hurtful notes left in lockers, hateful phone calls were routine. The occasional slap happened, but the only real violence I witnessed was among boys. Girls do fight in other worlds, however, and they take pride in defending their turf. They have a moral code that gives them permission.

"Sharon explains how the ferocity of Sophie's temper meant that she quickly got the better of the other girl; Sophie had quickly knocked her opponent unconscious and then dragged the girl by the hair to a nearby parked car, smashing her head through the windscreen. Sharon laughs because she can see how horrified I am by the story and in a vain attempt to reassure me, she emphasizes that girls don't fight as much as boys." (Gillian Evans, *Educational Failure and Working Class White Children in Britain*, London: Palgrave Macmillan, 2006.)

The neighborhood children came and went in the house, an intermittently violent horde Gertrude pretended she monitored closely while she was playing her alter ego, "Mrs. Wright."

During the trial Gertrude was asked about the child traffic by her defense lawyer.

Q. Did you ever tell them to stay away?
A. Yes, I did many times. I would try to lock the doors and
   Paula would—you know chase them out or chase them away

because—I mean I was to the point where I could not stand noise or anything anymore. It was, I just could not take it anymore. I had everybody's children.

But Sylvia was the only child forced to eat the family's demons. "It is always possible to bind together a number of people in love," Freud wrote in *Civilization and Its Discontents*, "as long as there are other people left over to receive the manifestations of their aggressiveness."

A worn face crusted with sores in the mirror, old before its time. Memories of a man's flying fists visit every room. A belly swells with the inevitability of another life. Slut. An infant squalls. Wheezing. Laughter. Cigarette smoke. Young voices inside and out. The screen door opens and slams shut. And the undefiled border blooms with seductive promise as she sings to herself and carefully irons her blouse for school.

The only letter the woman they called "Gertie" had the strength to impress with a burning needle on the girl's body is the capital letter *I*. Then she gave the task to her lackey, Richard Hobbs, who finished the job but needed help spelling the word *prostitute*. "I am a prostitute and proud of it." The crime of sex work was written onto Sylvia Likens's body, but to whom did that wandering "I" belong? Who owned it? Is this the problem? Who is "I"? The irony is fierce. The frenzied effort to blame and brand the other, to build a wall between self and other, collapses. What is "me" and what is "you"? But the commonality is visible only from the outside. Girard writes, "The proper functioning of the sacrificial process requires . . . the complete separation of the victim from those beings for whom the victim is a substitute." (*Violence and the Sacred*, trans. Patrick Gregory, Baltimore: Johns Hopkins, 1977.)

Gertrude Baniszewski had been pregnant thirteen times. Six of the pregnancies ended in miscarriage. Paula's pregnancy had become obvious, but it was Sylvia they insisted was with child. Over and over they told her she was pregnant, and once, after someone belted her in the stomach, Sylvia grabbed herself around the middle and said, "My baby."

Who's who in this game?

Once Gertrude had looked ahead toward the fuzzy but hopeful geography of the future, a place reached by means of one thing only: sexual allure. Without education or money, this was a girl's ticket to Somewhere through Someone, but that ticket is as dated as a package of meat. This is a contagious thought, surely, an idea that survives in a culture of female beauty worship that may easily take on a quality of desperation. Gertrude was sixteen when she married John Baniszewski, exactly Sylvia's age; Sylvia, who but for a missing tooth was hale and whole and perfect when she first came to stay in the house and her future had not yet been written.

But it's very late in the story now, and the woman must admit to herself that the girl's traveling carnival parents might return any day or the law might get wind of the indoor blood sport that has been so popular at 3850. What reasonable explanation can be given for the child's ruined body? She does not even "look human anymore." The game has become war. The woman dictates a letter to the girl for her parents. Obediently, the girl writes, "Dear Mr. and Mrs. Likens." The woman is blind to the mistaken mode of address. Is she panicked or seized by some other fundamental confusion? Who is writing? The woman invents a tale about roving boys with whom the girl had sex for money, boys who then beat her and cut the sentence into her, a ready narrative stolen from the tabloids, and the girl writes this down, but the girl's hand no longer belongs to her. The pencil moves across the page and forms the letters of the words: "I have done just about everything I could to make Gertie mad and cost Gertie more money than she's got. I've tore up a new mattress and peed on it. I have also cost Gertie doctor bills that she can't pay and made Gertie a nervous wreck and all her kids." The letter is not signed.

No, Gertrude Baniszewski was not a clever criminal who plotted the perfect crime. She was not one of those steely psychopaths of fiction so admired by millions of readers and moviegoers. She did not outwit or outthink anyone, but the absurd letter reveals her malignant narcissism nevertheless. It's all about Gertie all the time. She is the queen of 3850, despot for the moment, the one who gives orders: Take a letter. And there is never any evidence of guilt. Gertrude's crowd is a small one, but it's a crowd nevertheless. And this is the woman into whom all the suspects' identities have merged. The monster criminal is a hydra with many heads. The criminal is Gertie-and-the-kids, a collective nervous wreck acting in concert like a swarm of bees or a flock of geese, and Sylvia, the scapegoat, is part of them, too, isn't she? Isn't her body the site of their cast-out demons? Who is having the baby?

Is this the fable I have been looking for? Politics writ small?

In *I See Satan Fall Like Lightening* (1999), René Girard writes, "The torture of a victim transforms the dangerous crowd into a public of ancient theater or modern film as captivated by the bloody spectacle as our contemporaries by the horrors of Hollywood. When spectators are sated with that violence Aristotle called 'cathartic'—whether real or imaginary it matters little—they all return peaceably to their homes to sleep the sleep of the just."

When the task of the lynch mob is finished and the mutilated body of the Black woman or Black man hangs from a tree, a calm descends on the frenzied throng of whites and unanimity reigns.

After the rally, after the full-throated joy and venom of "Lock her up!" or "Send her back!" the crowd disperses and they climb into their cars to drive home appeased and smug that justice has been done.

I do not think the gang at 3850 would have tortured a boy, not a white, straight, healthy boy, anyway. No, it had to be a girl in this particular hierarchy in this particular story at this particular time and place, in which a brutal morality of feminine purity serves as the whip that transforms the clean, obedient, passive virgin into the filthy, rebellious, actively malevolent whore.

In the last hours of her life, Sylvia tried to run from the house, but was dragged back by Gertrude and, later, she tried to alert the Vermillions by scraping a shovel on the basement ceiling. Mrs. Vermillion testified she heard "hollering" and "scraping noises" from the basement next door the night before Sylvia died, that she and her husband went out to investigate and threatened to call the police. They did not call. The scraping sound stopped. Close your eyes. Plug up your ears. It will go away.

From *The Indianapolis News*, May 2, 1966:

The sobbing sister of Sylvia Marie Likens today quoted her as saying, "Jenny, I know you don't want me to die. But I'm going to die. I can tell."

John Baniszewski, Coy Hubbard, and Richard Hobbs were convicted of manslaughter with varying sentences from two to twenty-one years. All three were released after eighteen months in a reformatory. Paula, convicted of second-degree murder, was paroled after serving two years. Not long in a country with the largest prison population in the world, but the punitive lock-them-up-for-everything-and-anything policies and their barely disguised racism that resulted in the mass incarceration of Black men did not begin until the 1970s. And this is a white story, so the youngsters who committed these acts were treated as children, not monsters.

The house at 3850 East New York Street was demolished in 2009, but before then it was a featured destination on Historic Indiana Ghost Walks and Tours. "Explore the undead underbelly of Indiana's most haunted places with Indiana's most accomplished professional paranormal investigators." Sylvia Likens is surely a ghost, with or without "professional paranormal investigators." She lives on in the stories and in the books and in the true-crime watchers and in me because the case is fascinating and terrifying, and because I do not think it is as aberrant or unusual as is comforting to believe.

"The people of the world do not invent their gods," Girard wrote. "They deify their victims."

For some, Sylvia Likens is a martyr to the cause of ending child abuse. Thou shalt not torture and murder children. To others she is a saint—not a real one, of course. The girl wasn't even Catholic, and miracles are required. And yet, the torture she endured seems to qualify her for some status beyond ordinary mortal. Saint Agnes was stripped, thrown into a brothel, and tortured. Legend has it that they cut off her breasts, which in the iconography she sometimes carries on a plate. St. Agnes's faith was resolute, and her hymen remained unbroken.

One of Sylvia's fans online, MichaellovesSylvia, wrote, "I'm not an overly religious person but Philomena has always been my favorite saint and she is the one I most closely associate with Sylvia." It seems that this third-century Greek princess refused the advances of Emperor Diocletian and was sentenced to death. She died at thirteen, her virtue intact, but she was awfully hard to kill. Time after time, angels intervened to save her life, but their ministrations did not prevent her horrific pain. She was lashed bloody, cast into the sea to drown, shot full of arrows, and finally died when they chopped off her head. They say her grave was discovered in 1802. Inside it were her tiny brittle bones and a small vial of dried blood.

People like stories that make sense. Virtue rewarded. Poor Philomena may have left this earth headless, but the angels carried her broken body up toward the firmament, and, as they ascended, a celestial choir sang harmonies never heard before by human ears. Down here among the living, things are not so simple. The scapegoat mechanism is churning away among us. I feel it and I see it in others. Girard writes, "Each person must ask what his relation to the scapegoat is. I am not aware of my own, and I am persuaded the same holds true of my readers. We have only legitimate enemies." I must ask myself. Was the timid girl in my third-grade class enacting exactly what I most hated in myself—my own fear of authority, my own failures to speak up when I should have? The crowd gathers at a rally or it forms online. It bellows with one voice. It has its reasons. It is rife with pious feelings and honorable proclamations, and then it turns on its victim.

2020

ACKNOWLEDGMENTS

Not long after I had come upon *Mothers, Fathers, and Others* as a title for this collection of essays, I realized I had inadvertently robbed the anthropologist Sarah Blaffer Hrdy, whom I quote in this volume. In 2009, she published *Mothers and Others: The Evolutionary Origins of Mutual Understanding* (Harvard University Press), one of Hrdy's many books and papers I have read and admired. My addition of *fathers* alters her title, but now that I am conscious of the theft, I would like to acknowledge her title in mine as a tribute to her work.

The two essay books I published before this one included many pages of footnotes. Although I chose to forgo formal references in this collection, I have embedded citations in the text itself and included others in brackets. If not strictly conventional, the strategy is practical. The sources are given, and the reader who wishes to pursue a thought or idea further knows where to go.

THE
FORTUNE IN YOUR HAND

THE
FORTUNE IN YOUR HAND

Elizabeth Daniels Squire

BELL PUBLISHING COMPANY

NEW YORK

Originally published as *The New Fortune in Your Hand*.

Copyright © MCMLX, MCMLXVIII by Fleet Press Corporation
All rights reserved.

This 1989 edition is published by Bell Publishing Company,
distributed by Crown Publishers, Inc.,
225 Park Avenue South, New York, New York 10003,
by arrangement with Fleet Press.

Printed and Bound in the United States of America

Library of Congress Cataloging-in-Publication Data
Squire, Elizabeth Daniels.
　The fortune in your hand.

　Bibliography: p.
　Includes index.
　Reprint. Originally published: New York :
Fleet Press Corp., 1960.
　1. Palmistry.　I. Title.
[BF921.S63　1989]　　133.6　　　88-33347
ISBN 0-517-66987-0

h g f e d c b a

CONTENTS

INTRODUCTION

"Consciousness of our powers increases them."
—Vauvenargues.

Why should you want to read hands? Probably you have picked up this book because you are curious about the kinds of things that are likely to happen to you—"what is my future?"

Perhaps you are interested in self-knowledge or in human nature or in patterns and symbols that appear in nature and art and were given special meanings by ancient religions and superstitions.

At any rate, if you take up the study of hands—beginning with your own—you will be opening the door to a number of intriguing corridors to knowledge. To begin, hand-reading can help you to know other people—and yourself, too.

A common first question may be about money: Are you likely to make a fortune on your own? Could you hold on to money if you inherited it? Or are you one of those persons to whom worldly possessions are not really very important? Do you have what it takes to attract "good luck"? Or will you always work hard for every advantage you gain? It's fascinating to check the readings in your hand against actual experience in the past, and then estimate the future.

If you are married, you may be surprised to find how much more you will know after reading your hands and your mate's—more about some of the ways you get along best, and more about some of the areas that invariably spark an argument.

If you are single, it may interest you to discover that many of the dates who attract you most have hands roughly alike.

Or your interests may be deeper and you may want to acquire enough self-knowledge to find more inner harmony. Reading many hands and seeing how your problems compare with other people's problems seems to help with that.

Also, if you make a study of hand-reading, you'll discover that even casual glances at the hands of new contacts will give clues about how best to approach each person.

If you want to win the support of someone with large hands and long, knotty fingers, you'd better have all the facts ready. He'll want to know the details and study the whole situation before he makes up his mind

If you've ever heard families discuss whether Willie or Mary takes after Mother or Father, you'll realize how much fun it can be to look at the hands and see what facets of character come from which side of the family. Sometimes a child's hands will differ from the hands of both his parents but will closely resemble the hands of a grandparent, aunt or uncle.

You can check any part of hand-reading against experience—for example, whether a child really behaves as much like a particular relative as his hand says he will.

While I doubt if anyone ever learned to read hands for self-protection alone, the fact is that learning to read hands is some protection against an amazing con game that is based on hand-reading. But more of that later.

I am not a mystic or a scientist but a reporter, and

the reader will find my attitude toward hand-reading is flavored accordingly. That is why I keep referring him back to his own first hand experience. With an art that has been used for centuries as a tool of folk psychology, his personal experience will be a more fitting guide than my recommendation. (That is not the only way hand-reading has been used and judged, but it is one common way.)

It strikes me as amazing that some people scoff at hand-reading without trying it or bothering to find out about it, and equally amazing that others believe in it without bothering to find out anything about it, even going to hand-readers they know nothing about and then believing every word these unknown readers say.

As a reporter, I have been as interested in finding out about ways that hand-reading is used as in practicing it. That has required talking to people with violently differing points of view. For example, I had lunch with a self-declared witch and interviewed a police detective in charge of tracking down fortune-tellers, all in the same day. My doctor lends me medical journals that mention the use of hands in medical diagnosis. I talk to hand-readers who practice for their own enjoyment, wherever I go.

Letters I received while I was writing a syndicated column about hand-reading were a gold mine of information, too. And I've enjoyed the lectures given by the American Society for Psychical Research, an interest-group that includes scientists, people who believe they have extra-sensory abilities and others who just plain want to know more.

I have always wanted to find out whether things connected with hand-reading that are said to happen really do. After all, in life what is "supposed to happen" frequently does not.

One day, while helping to prepare a television script, I analyzed hand-prints and photographs of hands, an astrologer I had never met analyzed the birth-dates of the same people, and a hand-writing analyst prepared a report on their hand-writing. Then we compared reports for each subject. The reports were recognisably alike but not so alike that it seemed as if one analyst might have copied the other. Each enlarged on different facets of the personality. (There is, of course, more than one explanation of how this could have happened: the skeptic would say it was rigged; the ESP buff would say it was ESP; the occultist would say it was to be expected.)

But this made me more interested in the early connections among hand-reading, astrology, hand-writing analysis and other arts that the traditional occulist used jointly to judge a man.

That is not to say that the author of this book is a member of an occult religion. I am not. And that brings me around to a little-understood fact about hand-reading. There are four distinct kinds practiced in America today, each with a long tradition behind it. There is the occultist; the folk hand-reader, the member of a conventional scientific discipline, and the con-game artist.

Because this division is not generally understood, all hand-readers are generally assumed by the man in the street to be occultists; well-meaning hand-readers are amazed to find themselves arrested, while distraught people who wander in to see unknown hand-readers to ask for help are sometimes defrauded of their life's savings.

The member of an occult sect is practicing his religion when he reads a hand, for he believes there is a religious message in all natural patterns—notably the patterns of the stars, of the hands, of the whole body, of the handwriting, of taro cards laid out for the subject, and such. The beliefs of occult sects differ, but one belief seems to be common to all that I know anything about: An occultist would call this an oversimplification, I am sure, but in general he believes that the fact that natural patterns have interrelated meanings proves that the universe is not a product of chance but of a meaningful force—which is to say God.

There are evidences that religious hand-reading may have a very long tradition—that, in fact, it may have started in the Stone Age.

Some caves contain whole hand-prints that, perhaps, were left as a signature at a Stone Age religious initiation. Other hand-prints make it seem that some Stone Age men cut off finger joints and printed the record of this bloody sacrifice on cave walls.

Like the graceful prehistoric pictures of horses, bison, mammoth or woolly rhinoceros, hand-prints made with black pigment and red-ochre hand outlines can be seen in the cave of Atamira at Santillana del Mar, Spain, and in other European caves. Abbe Henri Breuil has written about these discoveries.

Some anthropologists believe Stone Age hand-mutilations and hand-printing were magic ritual, but because the cave men lived before written history, we still ask if cave magic or religion included hand-reading.

At any rate, methods of "reading" natural patterns—such as might be formed by lines on, and shape of, a hand—are as old as the oldest written records. (One place to find out about this is the 11th edition of the Encyclopaedia Britannica, under "Omens.") Clay tablets from the region near the Tigris and Euphrates rivers tell how priests in about 2800 B.C. read the livers of sacrificed animals to predict the future of King Sargon I by shapes and markings described as holes and paths, and by the position of these. Some of these "signs" are like those hand-readers study now.

And priests studied the patterns of the stars, and their star-reading led to later forms of astrology, whose language and ideas are still part of hand-reading. Today, palmists still name each part of the hand for a planet. For example the base of the thumb is the "Mount of Venus" and when it is large and rosy it is believed to reveal strong physical passion.

Certain designs had a similar meaning in more than one kind of early omen and in more than one part of the world. And certain favorable designs became charms to ensnare good luck. The circular line was meant to ensure good luck when it was used in a Babylonian or Hebrew devil-trap, for example, or an Egyptian ring amulet. Squares could be magically protective and were the true form for amulets among the Arabs and Persians and much used by other early peoples. (Many of these charms and omens are described by Sir E. A. Wallis Budge, of the British Museum, in his "Amulets and Talismans.")

The well-formed triangle was a good sign, seen for example in the shape of a torch flame or on a sacred bull amulet, or formed by the letters Abracadabra in an amulet to cure fever.

The out-of-the-ordinary mark or shape meant something remarkable for good or evil. The broken line signified the negative or passive, the unbroken line the positive or creative. (An example is the line-patterns used in the ancient Chinese book of changes, the I Ching.)

These same pattern-readings, and others equally ancient, are in recent hand-reading how-to-do-it-yourself books on my library shelf. A circle suggests you are creative; a square means protection; broken lines in your hand are read as negative signs (though no "sign" is read alone, and thus none is entirely negative or entirely positive).

A clear and balanced triangle of the head, life and fate lines is still considered "lucky." A wild and out-of-the-ordinary pattern of lines is a sign of something out of the ordinary in your makeup and possibilities.

These ancient signs, incorporated in hand-reading, certainly appear to be graphic reminders of a religious and magical heritage. The occult hand-reader is sure they are. He also will often tie in his reading with philosophy based on reincarnation. He may mention a connection between hand-reading and the Kabbalah. The hand-reader gives the subject religious advice along with the reading.

Sometimes the religious hand-reader calls himself a scientist—and this can be confusing. He means to imply, I gather, that he considers he is more truly on the path to knowledge than the member of a scientific discipline with a conventional diploma from a university—the biologist, say, or a medical doctor.

It muddies the issue, however, because in addition to occult hand-readers who call themselves scientists, there are also conventional scientists who study hand-patterns. For example, the study of the pattern of the tiny papillary ridges on hands and feet is called "dermatoglyphics," and the patterns have been shown to vary to a statistically significant degree between different racial groups and between members of the same group who are subject to certain diseases. Dr. Ruth Achs and Dr. Rita Harper have found a line-pattern useful in diagnosing birth defects. As you'll see when you read the history of hand-reading, there have always been doctors who used it for their purposes.

The Journal of the American Medical Association has pointed out that there is absolutely no connection between the way doctors read hands and the way other hand-readers work. While specific doctors may be interested in

WHEN THE MAIN LINES ARE ALL LONG AND CLEARLY MARKED— STRONG CHARACTER AND ABILITY TO MAKE THE MOST OF OPPORTUNITIES

LONG CLEAR HEAD LINE— BROAD INTERESTS

RING OF SOLOMON

HEART LINE

LONG, WELL-MARKED FATE LINE — CLEAR SENSE OF PURPOSE

Helen Keller

LIFE LINE

Here are signs of the ability to make the most of opportunities. They belong to Helen Keller, who has led such a remarkably useful and interesting life in spite of the fact that she can neither see nor hear. (Original length of print 7-1/4 inches)

occultism, there is in general no love lost between scientific and occult hand-readers. Yet to the layman it seems that some of the doctors' discoveries and the occultists' readings are enough alike to be interesting, as you'll see. That the two kinds of students are very different in their aims, however, there's no denying.

The third kind of hand-reader is the kind I have always thought of as the "black" hand-reader—because the reader aims to misuse hand-reading just the way the black magician aims to misuse other occult arts. He is the hand-reader who makes the headlines when he is discovered and arrested. Black hand-readers use the same methods of fraud in all parts of the world, police report, and like the religious hand-readers they seem to have a long tradition. They usually call themselves religious hand-readers.

In the Middle Ages, for example, one of the men who contributed to the Faust story was a wandering European mountebank, sorcerer and doctor who owned a trained dog or horse and contributed to the legend of the man who sold his soul to the devil. He had studied magic at Cracow and he practiced all of the "occult" arts including hand-reading, ritual magic, astrology, divination, alchemy and necromancy. One story says he was finally strangled by the Devil.

Perhaps he was typical of the worst sort of wandering hand-reader, if more colorful than most. The legend of Faust became more formidable than the man himself, for in his own time he was often regarded as a drunken braggart and a quack.

Even earlier evidence of the misuse of hand-reading is in the warning against dishonest hand-readers in the Indian Laws of Manu, dating from around 100 B.C.

The first step in the dishonest hand-reader's ploy is

to win confidence by telling things that are true. The black hand-reader's method of producing the impressive truth is variously described. A detective told me she believed these readers used shrewdness to estimate character and "played back" the information she let drop to make the reading more convincing. After you have learned to read hands, you may agree with my feeling that a good hand-reader could tell quite enough in a perfectly normal hand-reading to impress a gullible person, if he so desired.

At any rate, the black hand-reader implies that he has second sight, that second sight can come only from God and that therefore if he can "see" incidents in the past, he must be honest. It might help a person faced with one of these hand-readers to know that people who have studied extra-sensory perception say there seems to be no connection between honesty and E.S.P. Like intelligence, E.S.P. falls to the honest and the dishonest alike. Also, in my opinion, most hand-reading does not depend on E.S.P. —that being a fringe benefit.

Once the black hand-reader had persuaded you he was honest and had clairvoyant powers, he would say he could "see" a curse on something you owned. This curse, he would explain, caused all your problems. Then he would ask you to bring him various objects you owned so that he could test them to see which were cursed. If you had inherited money, it would eventually work out to be the money that was cursed. To remove the curse, you would have to allow the reader to burn the money. After you drew thousands of dollars out of the bank, you could watch while the reader put it in a burner and you could watch the smoke rise. The reader would vanish before you came to your senses and began to doubt if all that money had really burned. A case of this sort involving more than

$30,000 got quite a play in the New York newspapers a few years ago.

In an alternate ploy, the money is "cleansed" by sewing it into a package or the lining of your coat for, say, six months. The reader would have vanished by the time the subject discovered she had old newspapers sewn into her coat. (The subject is usually a woman—a widow, to be exact.)

If these con-games seem too transparent to work, remember that panic can make the most sensible-seeming person do strange things. I'm always reminded of a family story about my great-grandfather who rushed into the house, yelled "Fire! Fire!" and hustled his family out, then grabbed a valuable glass vase he loved and threw it out the window to "safety."

The fourth kind of hand-reader on the scene today is the modern equivalent of the folk hand-reader of earlier days. The only difference is that the modern hand-reader generally learns the art, to begin with, from a book rather than from oral tradition. The book he uses has typically been compiled from several sources including older folk hand-reading, bits of information culled from medicine and other science, new and old, and material that is also a part of occult hand-reading.

This half-book-half-folk hand-reading has been practiced in America at least since sailors on early whaling ships took hand-reading books on their long voyages to while away the time between whales. For-pleasure hand-readers may read palms for a lifetime and are often excellent. Many tea-room hand-readers are for-pleasure hand-readers gone commercial.

I have, however, received sad letters from folk hand-readers turned professional who have been arrested because they predicted the future for a price in an area where they didn't know it was against the law. Others have been propositioned to do things they considered dishonest. They reported that shady types asked them to report "success in real-estate investments" or a quick profit in some worthless stock, then became quite abusive when the reader refused. Evidently, dishonest promoters had sometimes dealt with more cooperative hand-readers.

The best hand-readers, however, are honest and read hands because they are interested in people or because it is their religion.

This book has not been written to expound any one theory of hand-reading. It is meant to be a simply written and clearly and amply illustrated how-to book for beginners. Some hand-prints and photographs are marked with the degree of reduction, so that it is possible to know the original size. Hand diagrams are reductions of exact tracings of prints. Dotted circles show areas of high padding on some diagrams.

The advanced student will be interested in the handprints but will find parts of the text over-simplified, I imagine. I have therefore included a bibliography at the end of the book for the student who wants to learn more so that he can read about whichever facet of hand-reading interests him the most.

As for the theories, the names of the parts of the hand make one of these obvious—that the hand shows the influence of the stars.

Another, propounded by Dr. Charlotte Wolfe, a British psychiatrist, is that hands reveal the state of the ductless glands and other physical conditions that are related to temperament.

Old-time hand-readers believed that the lines in the

hand could not be related to the way people used their hands. Manual laborers or craftsmen, they noted, have far fewer lines in their hands than dreamers or intellectuals do.

Now scientists know that traces of movement accompany thought. If you think about playing the piano, for example, your fingers move slightly—so slightly it is not even noticeable. You undoubtedly know people who make grand gestures as they talk—but all of us make at least slight, subtle gestures as we think, whether we realize it or not.

So the hands of dreamers have hundreds of lines while those of the craftsmen are more likely to have few lines.

Other theories about why hand-reading works are mentioned in the history of the art that follows.

The interesting fact about all the many types of people who have been seriously interested in hand-reading and set forth theories about it is that they all agree on one thing: Hand-patterns are meaningful and well worth a careful study.

In order to enjoy this old art, the reader has only to remember two things: First, that markings in hands are simply signposts indicating a probable direction, and that hands change, so it is foolish and unkind to predict inevitable catastrophes; second, that a knowledge of the how-to of hand-reading will not of itself make the reader an occultist or a scientist.

Hand-reading can, however, be an absolutely fascinating and fruitful study. It is also an antidote for the modern pressures that make each individual feel like a mere unimportant number out of a series in a computer. Hand-reading highlights the fact that each person—like each snowflake, each plant, each individual creation in the world—is marvelously unique.

Hands of Edward Steichen, noted photographer

Hands of Edward Steichen, noted photographer

CHAPTER I

HOW IT ALL BEGAN

"There is nothing in the three worlds for knowledge besides the hand which is given to mankind like a book to read."

—Hastha Sanjeevan.

There are hints that some meaning may have been attached to the designs found on hands since pre-history. There are those hand-prints on cave walls, for one example, and designs that could be copies of finger-prints in a Stone Age burial passage on an island off Brittany, for another. Was hand-reading practiced by early man?

Hand-reading's earliest origins are embroidered by myth, legend and tradition. It probably began in India long before written history. Indian tradition holds that the art of divination by all the limbs of the body, or Anga Vidya, was handed down by Samudra, the Sea God. The study of hands and feet was the most important part of Anga Vidya.

Tradition also holds that when Buddha was born (about 563 B.C.) he had marks on his feet that enabled sages to foretell his greatness. And people believed that Lord

16

Krishna (an incarnation of Vishnu come to help men in their sufferings) had special markings on his feet and hands.

Even today, Hindu hand-readers believe the appearance of marks such as those on the hands or feet of Krishna or the Buddha foretell a great destiny.

K. C. Sen, an Indian palmist, identifies the earliest documents on hand-reading as ancient Sanskrit verses or *slokas,* jealously guarded and kept from the public eye by Brahmin families in India. Cheiro, the seer so famous at the turn of the century, wrote that he was allowed to look at one of these documents. It was, he said, written in ink as red as blood on animal skins yellow with age.

Marks on the hands and feet of Buddha in the sixth century B.C. made sages aware that he would be a great man.

One of the earliest records of Anga Vidya, or study of limbs, is in the Ramayana—an Indian epic poem about the adventures of a hero and the patient faithfulness of his wife. This epic, comparable to the Odyssey, began to take shape in the third century B.C. and was passed on by bards.

Early Indian hand-reading was closely linked to astrology or the study of the stars to determine human destiny. Hand-reading and astrology even have the same patron deity, Lord Skanda.

Possibly from India, hand-reading spread throughout the ancient East. Later it reached Asia Minor and entered Europe about the time of Alexander the Great.

Gypsies, who are palm-readers by tradition, trace their tribes back to a village in Northern India, and their language is about one-third Sanskrit. Although some modern Gypsies rely more on astuteness and clairvoyance than on any real science of hand-reading, their palmist tradition clearly goes back to ancient India.

Hand-reading was well-known in Greece during the fourth century, B.C., reign of Alexander. Though brave as a lion and ready to rush into the bloodiest battles, Alexander revealed his concern about his future by a tremendous interest in all methods of predicting it, including, of course, hand-reading. First of all, his sword-makers were Gypsies—always skilled metal-workers and as we have seen, fortune-tellers. And secondly, Alexander spent two years in India attempting to conquer that country.

Aristotle, the philosopher who was Alexander's tutor, was supposed to have found an ancient Arabic document on hand-reading, written in characters of pure gold, on an altar to Hermes. Legend has it that he gave this document to Alexander. Probably Aristotle wrote a treatise on hand-reading because of Alexander's interest in the subject.

When Aristotle's hand was read for the first time, the story goes, his pupils were shocked by all the signs of weakness found in his hand. But Aristotle accepted the reading as truthful. He told his pupils that the faults read from his hands were the very ones he had struggled all his life to overcome.

Although much that Aristotle wrote on hand-reading may be lost, his book on physiognomy—including material on the shape, color and texture of the hands—is available today.

Most early Western books on the meaning of hands were parts of longer works on physiognomy, or the character and likely fate of men as revealed by the shape of the whole body. We have preserved in the West almost nothing written in ancient times about the lines of the hand. However, as you will see, the shape and size of the hands and fingers and the texture and color of the hands are the key to accurate hand-reading—and the reading based on lines must be tempered by the reading of the whole hand.

Aristotle does mention the meaning of lines in the hand. In *De Historia Animalium,* he says that long lines belong to long-lived people but that short lines mean shorter lives. He may even have written a special treatise on lines, though we have no record of it.

Later writers, feeling that Aristotle's name was more respectable than their own, tried to fill in the gaps in the philosopher's known works by adding works of their own that they attributed to Aristotle. For example, a fifteenth century German work, *Cyromancia Aristotelis* (Ulm, 1491), is a fascinating document typical of a later stage of hand-reading, though scholars do not attribute it to Aristotle.

Some of the oldest writings about hands are not directly concerned with lines and shape. Instead they are concerned with the idea that various parts of the body can reveal us for what we are. A wonderful document written by Melampus in 247 B.C. deals with the significance of the itching and twitching of various parts of the body. Without even stopping to think about it, we still associate certain characteristics with itchy fingers or twiddling thumbs.

Many intriguing passages in the Bible seem to refer to the idea that a man's likely fate may be shown in his hands. These passages also suggest that hand-reading was known in Old Testament days. For example:

—"Length of days is in her right hand; and in her left hand riches and honor." Proverbs 3:16.

—"He sealeth up the hand of every man; that all men may know his work." Job 37:7.

—"And he said, Wherefore doth my lord thus pursue after his servant? for what have I done? or what evil is in mine hand?" I Samuel 26:18.

Early physicians studied the whole man—mind and body—and therefore medical books sometimes included physiognomy as a way of determining a man's likely characteristics. Famous cures were sometimes based on a knowledge of a patient's mind and heart.

Erasistratus, an Alexandrian physician, was said to have cured a son of the King of Syria from a dangerous illness. The real trouble, Erasistratus decided, was that the youth was in love with one of his father's wives. The father proved to be so anxious to help in the cure of his son that he divorced his wife. The son married her in turn and was thereupon cured of his illness.

This frontispiece from a seventeenth century Latin book includes quotes from the Bible believed to endorse hand-reading. (Photograph courtesy of The Library of Congress.)

Galen of Pergamum, a second century physician to several Roman emperors including Marcus Aurelius, is said to have written about physiognomy, not overlooking, of course, a good deal of material about hands.

In contrast to India, where the lines of the hand were read from earliest times, the West in the second century entertained only a primitive idea of line-reading, regard-

During the Dark Ages, the meaning of the hands was linked with black magic. Thieves lighted the thumb of a mummified robber's hand to paralyze their victim's will.

ing it as a form of divination. Juvenal said that in his day upper-class women consulted astrologers while middle-class women went to hand-readers.

TRADITIONAL WITCHES' HAND

Arab doctors were influenced by the Greek and Roman. In the eleventh century, Avicenna—an Arab physician—wrote about the meaning of the shape and form of the hand in his huge book, *Quanoun Fi ul-Tibb* (Canon of Medicine). Translated into Latin in the twelfth century, this became the most important text in European medical schools and was used in France as late as the mid-seventeenth century.

Along about the twelfth and early thirteenth centuries, interest in physiognomy and all forms of hand-reading spread throughout Europe. Johannes Hispalensis brought out a document, probably of Arab origin, that he believed to be an exact translation of the one found by Aristotle on the altar of Hermes. And when Thomas à Becket didn't know what advice to give Henry II about an invasion of Brittany, he consulted a chiromancer or line-reader.

Starting in the twelfth century, more and more manuscripts (though we have only fragments of the earliest ones) were written about lines and special signs in the hand. Until then, as we have seen, almost all Western writings preserved were about hand shapes and had nothing to do with lines. Most of the manuscripts about lines and signs are semi-magical and are hair-raising to read—an early substitute for the murder mystery.

Here, for instance, are some gloomy suggestions from a manuscript dated about 1400 A.D.:

"If several lines go from the life line toward the thumb, the owner will be killed or endangered by fire."

"If tangled lines rise from the hollow of the hand, ending below the middle finger, death in prison is indicated."

"If a figure like an 'e' is found near the bottom of the hand, the owner will kill his father or mother or despoil a holy church. A woman with this mark will be a common strumpet."

Interwoven with all this superstition was a grain of truth that was winnowed by later hand-readers.

I have not found any mention of the mounts, those areas of the hand that are often bulging like little hills, before the fourteenth century. But most histories of palmistry claim that the mounts were studied by the Greeks at the time of Aristotle. This, they explain, is because the Greeks were admirers of energy, symbolized by high, firm mounts.

Even today, the mounts are named for planets—another example of the close link between hand-reading and astrology.

In the fifteenth century, when the art of printing was still new, the first book on palmistry was published—a wood-block book by Johann Hartlieb called *Die Kunst Ciromantia*. Slightly later the manuscript signed "Aristotle" appeared, and was accepted until quite recently by students of palmistry as truly the work of the great philosopher. Dr. Hardin Craig analyzed many of the thirteenth, fourteenth and fifteenth century hand-reading texts when he was editing a fifteenth century book by John Metham for the Early English Text Society. His analysis shows that Aristotle gave only his name—and that, involuntarily—to *Cyromancia Aristotelis*.

Just as hand-reading was growing more popular in Europe, twelve Gypsy dukes went to work in Germany about 1414 as spies for Sigismund, the Holy Roman Emperor. At first, these Gypsy dukes and their tribes were considered fascinating and exotic with their wonderful romantic music, wild and beautiful dances and their ability to tell fortunes. The fortune-telling was, of course, a valuable tool in their real trades. By comparing the questions asked by a variety of people, the Gypsies could get a pretty clear idea of what was going on.

When a statesman's wife had a Gypsy hand-reading, her questions to the Gypsy could reveal her husband's plans. For example, "Does my hand show I could be faithful to my husband if he left me for a year?" Or, simply, "Does my hand show a journey?"

The dukes were leaders of a large group of Gypsies who wandered through Germany and Italy. Their spying was soon suspected. Rumors that they were not only fascinating but dangerous preceded them into France. They were light-fingered as well as light-footed. Worst of all, the Church felt they stirred up old pagan beliefs among the faithful.

When bands of Gypsies arrived at the gates of Paris in 1427, they were politely but firmly asked to remain outside the city at La Chapelle St. Denis. But the people of Paris, probably feeling that exotic and dangerous visitors were much more exciting than people who were merely exotic, came flocking out of the gates to have their fortunes told.

To counter the Church's warning that they were inspired by the Devil, the Gypsy fortune-tellers explained that the Devil was afraid of silver and the sign of the Cross. If you frequently made the sign of the Cross over their hands with silver, they said, you would be perfectly safe. Naturally, the Gypsies kept the silver.

Undoubtedly, Gypsies made hand-reading seem more glamorous for a time, especially when they grew prosperous. Few realized that their prosperity was due to their role as spies for Sigismund. After 1437, without Sigismund's protection, they were condemned and treated with contempt. They were considered no better than godless bands of wandering thieves who were supposed to devour their parents and steal other people's children. This is why you won't find Gypsies mentioned at all in most histories of hand-reading.

For centuries afterward, the art of hand-reading was associated with the Gypsies' blackened reputation. Laws passed against the Gypsies made it illegal in many places for anyone to read hands, and even today, New York, Connecticut and several other states and municipalities have laws making it illegal to accept payment for fortune-telling.

Partly because of the Gypsies and partly in spite of them, hand-reading became more and more popular in the Middle Ages. Paracelsus, a controversial wandering sixteenth-century doctor with an inquiring mind, became so interested in hand-reading that he ranked it high among the sciences and called it the mother of the arts.

Paracelsus associated hand-reading with astrology and believed that the hand revealed, in one compact map, the astral signs also shown by the whole body.

He insulted traditional doctors with great fluency, and collected recipes from folk-medicine and probably from his fellow-wanderers, the Gypsies. That made him unpopular with doctors in his own time, but he denied the conventional medical world the pleasure of consigning him to oblivion, for he became famous for initiating the use of chemical medicines. He was also the first to mention the relation between goiter in the parent and cretinism in a child.

Since Paracelsus was a doctor and an occultist interested in astrology and folklore, he combined the main traditions of hand-reading. He never wrote a book explaining his whole system of hand-reading, however—he merely described it as the system used by the ancients. There were many books written about hand-reading in Paracelsus' time and later, including those by B. Cocles, Johann Indagine, Richard Sanders and Johannes Praetorius.

It was said that of fifty-five persons for whom Cocles predicted sudden death, only two were ungracious enough to die slowly.

Probably because hand-reading was still regarded as suspect, Johannes Praetorius gathered as many quotes as he could from the Bible to adorn the frontispiece of his seventeenth century book.

Scientific interest in the hands continued too, and we learn from Julius Spier that chirology was part of the curriculum of the German universities of Leipzig and Halle from 1650 to 1730.

In most places during the eighteenth century, men lost interest in hand-reading. In his preface to Spier's book, *The Hands of Children,* C. G. Jung wrote that the "rise of the Natural Sciences and with it of rationalism in the eighteenth century were responsible for the contemptible treatment and defamation of these ancient arts (astrology and hand-reading) which could pride themselves on a thousand years of history."

The eclipse was temporary, and by the 1800s hand-reading once more gained stature in the eyes of some of Europe's greatest men. Napoleon had his hand read and gave his name to the extra long, large index finger of the power-seeker—the "forefinger of Napoleon."

Honoré de Balzac, whose novels show such a profound knowledge of human nature, felt that hand-reading was one of the best ways to unravel the intricacies of the human heart.

About the same time, Alexandre Dumas, father and son, were friends and boosters of Adolphe Desbarrolles, who became known as the father of modern palmistry.

Desbarrolles, called "The Father of Modern Palmistry," reads a hand in his studio in Boulevard St.-Michel, Paris. (Photograph courtesy of the Library of Congress.)

He included in his system of hand-reading some conclusions of his friend Capt. Stanislas d'Arpentigny, who had spent years studying the shapes of hands.

Desbarrolles read character, the past and the probable future from the hands, but he wasn't a fatalist. He felt a man might change the direction of his journey through life through will power or help from others. He read the hands of many of the famous men and women of his day, including Pope Leo XIII, Napoleon III and the Empress Eugénie.

Although he was not a trained scientist, Desbarrolles sifted the evidence of what really worked in hand-reading. He was also interested in all the other sciences of character-reading and wrote a book on graphology.

Meanwhile, scientists were interested in their own kind of hand "reading." Francis Galton was one of those who wrote about fingerprint types and studied inheritance and racial variation in fingerprints. Harris Hawthorne Wilder and others studied the tiny papillary ridges of palms and soles. These biological studies, so far from the Gypsy's tent or the occultist's study, were the beginnings of the science of dermatoglyphics—which has only lately thrown some light on one of the ancient "signs" that palmists called a warning of a miserable or untimely end. But more of this later.

Not skin-ridges but hand-shapes interested Carl Gustaf Carus, personal physician to the King of Saxony in the mid-nineteenth century. Carus thought that evolution accounted for different hand-shapes.

Two principal types of hands were identified by Carus —the purposeful hand, best adapted to grabbing or holding on, and the expressive hand that uses the sense of touch to explore and learn.

Just as Desbarrolles inspired later traditional hand-readers, Carus had a great influence on Charlotte Wolff, a modern-day physician and psychologist who has made a study of human character as revealed in the hands.

Another scientist who became interested in the application of scientific method to hand-reading was Dr. N. Vaschide, a member of the French Academy of Sciences. He, too, worked to put hand-reading on a scientific basis, but his reward was ironic. While Dr. Vaschide was engaged in research, a fortune teller foretold every detail of his tragic early death.

The most colorful name in late nineteenth century hand-reading was that of Cheiro (Count Louis Hamon). Cheiro's career extended spectacularly into the early part of the present century. When he was quite young, his mother, who was a student of palmistry, saw from her son's hand that he had a strong talent for the occult sciences.

The young Cheiro began to study his mother's copious collection of books and went on from there to become one of the world's greatest hand-readers. He also studied graphology, astrology and numerology and could predict in great detail the course a life would take.

Cheiro called himself a seer. He was undoubtedly clairvoyant as well as deeply versed in all the sciences and arts of knowing human beings.

Vii Putnam, granddaughter of King Michael of the Gypsies, tells me that Cheiro was half-Gypsy, though it isn't generally known in non-Gypsy circles. Here is her account: Cheiro's mother was from a wealthy Irish family and his father was a Gypsy count. He was sent to India to study when he was about fourteen.

A person of tremendous magnetism, Cheiro was elected King of the Gypsies. (The Gypsies have a hereditary nobility but elect their kings). Not wishing to rule, Cheiro "passed the ring," as the Gypsy expression goes, to the next most popular candidate.

Cheiro, because hand-reading was still associated with the kind of Gypsies who told fortunes by hook or by crook, chose to refer to himself as a Greek count rather than as a Gypsy of noble birth. His rise to success was not only due to his own great talent but also because the times were ripe for the appreciation of a "seer."

In the early part of the nineteenth century, Indian philosophy began to be translated into European languages. The Romantic writers, artists and philosophers hoped to find, in Eastern ideas, all the mysticism and mystery that had been logically argued out of existence in the West. There was a wave of translations of the sacred books and literature of the East.

In 1875, the Theosophical Society was started to promote a moral philosophy that combined Hindu mysticism with Christian morality. The society launched its own publishing firm, which published (among other titles) a widely read book on Indian hand-reading by Mrs. J. Dale.

Educated people with open minds began to study psychic phenomena such as mind-reading and clairvoyance. In England, the Society for Psychical Research was started in 1882—the forerunner of all the groups studying extra-sensory perception. William James, the psychologist, was a supporter of such research.

Cheiro, the "Greek" count—handsome, young, intelligent and truly clairvoyant—knew Annie Besant, a founder of the Theosophical Society. He knew Swami Vivekananda, the Indian philosopher. And he read the hands of many great personalities, including Gladstone, Mark Twain and later Douglas Fairbanks and Mary Pickford.

Cheiro knew William G. Benham, the great American hand-reader, and wrote him a letter of congratulation upon the publication of the latter's book, *The Laws of Scientific Hand Reading*. While Cheiro was a mystic, Benham approached hand-reading as a lover of logic.

Benham became interested in hand-reading when he was about thirteen years old, and as he learned, he talked to all the professional hand-readers he could find. He was amazed to discover that these professionals knew only a few rudiments of the art. So he worked out his own methods and theory of hand-reading, using these rudiments plus experience, before he found such books as the *Révélations Complète* of Desbarrolles.

Benham became so interested in why hand-reading worked that he studied some medicine. He was a man with the large thumbs that show force of character, and he kept exhaustive files and records of his work. He started a hand-reading school that is carried on by one of his pupils, Florens Meschter, in New York.

Other hand-readers of note near the turn of the century included the Comte C. de St. Germain, who founded the National School of Palmistry in Chicago; Katherine St. Hill, who started the Chirological Society in England and E. H. Allen, who translated d'Arpentigny's book on hand-shape types.

By an ironical twist, contemporary Indian hand-readers began to study the European system because it was more advanced than their own for character reading. K. C. Sen includes a bibliography in his book *Hast Samudrika Shasta* that lists more European than Indian titles.

Influence was not entirely one-sided. The ideas of Julius Spier, a "psycho-chirologist," resembled the Indian as well as the European system. He thought the hands showed the character of our ancestry. Some Indians believe the hand gives a clue to previous incarnations.

Spier obtained such amazing results from reading character and past experience from hands that he aroused the interest of C. G. Jung, pioneer psychologist. Jung, in his preface to Spier's book published posthumously in 1944, wrote that "I have had several opportunities of observing Dr. Julius Spier at work, and must admit that the results he has achieved have made a lasting impression on me."

"I found an excellent teacher in Julius Spier," said Dr. Charlotte Wolff, whose *Studies in Handreading* explained how she remained interested in hand-reading while she became a member of the British Psychological Society. "I was inspired to continue my studies in hand-reading," she said, "not only by the discoveries which had been made in the field of graphology, but also by the psychoanalytical works of Sigmund Freud and C. G. Jung. I tried to apply to hand-reading the newly found knowledge of the unconscious with the light it threw on dreams, imagination and art."

To those who feel that searching for any truth in conventional hand-reading is like opening a Pandora's box of superstition, even serious scientists who have studied hand-reading seem controversial and "far out." Exceptions to this rule are the doctors and other scientists involved in dermatoglyphics. This study of hand-markings, with emphasis on the tiny papillary ridges of the skin, is based on such thorough and widespread research—including study of the palms of apes and of racial samplings of *homo sapiens* from all over the world—that it has not been branded as controversial.

In fact, Dr. Ruth Achs and Dr. Rita Harper use dermatoglyphics in a Brooklyn, N.Y. hospital to spot hard-to-find birth defects in babies whose mothers have had German measles during pregnancy. Theirs is strictly medical hand-reading.

Traditional hand-readers have also used hand-reading to diagnose illness or physical defects. But predicting disease is hardly a safe sport for amateurs, since the power of negative suggestion might actually help to cause disease.

But studies of skin-ridges, both by conventional scientists and by hand-readers such as Noel Jacquin, in England, have suggested a connection between skin-ridge patterns and non-medical characteristics, too.

Hand-reading is far from a finished, cut-and-dried science. There are different schools of hand-reading and different ways of approaching it.

Dermatoglyphics is so entirely scientific that it expresses hand-patterns in mathematical formulas.

Another view is neatly expressed by Dr. Wolff:

"The psychology of the hand is like medicine, an art as well as a science; and accordingly intuition plays a part in it. But intuition must not be confused with clairvoyance."

On the other hand, clairvoyants have produced fascinating readings. A true understanding of what clairvoyance is and how it works may turn out to be one of the major scientific discoveries of our age because of research now being done by parapsychologists all over the world.

Clairvoyance is not yet sufficiently understood to be reliable; sometimes it works, sometimes it doesn't. One way to checking its accuracy is through hand-reading. Thus we can gain clues to what is likely to happen to a particular person.

The great advantage of hand-reading is that you don't have to be a clairvoyant or a scientist to learn the most valuable lesson it has to teach—a true understanding of human nature.

*In general, inborn talents should be read from a right-hander's
left hand . (Original length of print 7-3/4 inches)*

Men whose work requires the same kind of temperament and talent tend to have the same general handshapes and types of line-markings. Compare this hand of Dik Browne, who creates the "Hi and Lois" comic strip, with that of cartoonist Charles Addams and that of comic artist Rube Goldberg.

(Original length of print 7-3/4 inches)

Artur Rubinstein took this print of his own hand without putting a pad under the center of the palm—which serves to show how high the padding tends to be on the hand of a musical virtuoso, so high that the lower areas in the center of the palm are difficult to print. (Original length of print 6-7/8 inches)

The musical hand like composer Dave Brubeck's has a highly developed Mount of Venus and Mount of Moon—thumb base and heel of hand. The knot, or pronounced joint, at the base of the thumb accompanies an excellent sense of rhythm. A naturally out-leaning little finger means a finely tuned ear.
(Original length of print 8-1/2 inches)

Producer David Susskind's hand is very firm, with a huge thumb and a well-marked verticle line up the center of the hand. If your hand is like this, you'll be continuingly successful —not through any fluke of good luck but because you are willing to work harder than most men can even imagine, in order to make the most of your talents. Note similarities with the hand of Patrick Dennis. (Original length of print 8 inches)

This hand shows an entirely different source of success. Moodiness, indicated here by numerous lines including some in grills on finger-mounts, can lend wonderful intensity and feeling to the work of a performing artist such as blues and folk singer Libby Holman. Often, the hands of famous people show that their most remarkable accomplishment has been to turn even their imperfections to advantage.

(Original length of print 7-1/2 inches)

The hand with all fingers held close together and the thumb held up near the palm belongs to one who likes to hold onto the old, tried-and-true ways and doesn't really enjoy change. Add lines that are marked in a clear and balanced pattern. Then add head and life lines joined into one line for about an inch under the index finger. With this combination, you can expect a clear spokesman for the conservative point of view— and, in this hand of Russell Kirk, conservative columnist and author, you have it. (Original length of print 7-3/4 inches)

CHAPTER II

THE HAND AT A GLANCE
OR A HANDSHAKE

"The face allows itself to be too easily controlled to be accurate in its findings——."

—Cheiro.

To start with, you already know a lot about hand-reading, though perhaps you don't realize it. For instance, you would hardly disagree with the ancient Indian sage who made this shrewd observation: "The hand should have one thumb and four fingers, and if there are any more, it is a very bad sign."

In this chapter I've reviewed some of the more general signs of character that you can use to size up people you meet. See how many of them you already know:

The general position of the hand reveals the open or shut personality.

A tense person will clench his hands or hold them tightly shut. He is unusually inhibited and difficult to know.

If you hold your thumb over your fingers, prize-fighter fashion, it is a sign of belligerence or determination. But when you hold it tightly folded under the fingers as if it had to hide and the fingers needed something to hold on to, it indicates a fear of life and a desire to give up.

Tense hands usually accompany abrupt, awkward gestures, as any actor knows. And at the same time, tense hands may go with a smiling, self-assured face and are thus the only clues we have to the person's real state of mind.

Thumb clutched under fingers shows a desire to give up. The open hand belongs to an outgoing person. These pictures are from an eighteenth century French palmistry book. (Photograph courtesy of The Library of Congress.)

Not long ago, a young girl ran away from home on the eve of her marriage—evidently in a highly wrought state. Later, a magazine printed a smiling picture of the girl, taken a short while before she ran away, to show that she had given no outward signs of nervousness. In this picture, the face smiles—but the hands are desperately clenched.

At the other extreme is the open flabby, dangling hand

that represents a person lacking firmness of character or a strong sense of purpose. When you meet him, you feel as if you are shaking hands with a cold fish.

The firm, sure hand, more open than shut, belongs to the outgoing person.

The size of a person's hands gives an immediate clue as to how his mind works.

If a person's hands are out of proportion to the rest of his body, look for something original or even bizarre in his character. Notice how many pictures of monsters have hands out of proportion to the body.

The hand that is in proportion to the rest of the body is about the same length, from the wrist to the tip of the longest finger, as the face.

Very small hands show immaturity. Small hands reveal a childlike quality—often charming—and a mercurial temperament. For this reason perhaps, small hands also indi- cate a wish to do things in a big way.

Large hands belong to analytical people and, curious as it seems, those who can do delicate, detailed or intricate work. Have you ever wondered why so many dentists have large hands?

The general shape of the hand gives a quick clue to the sort of person with whom you're dealing.

Practical people with a good deal of drive and physical energy usually have broad, muscular hands. People who have nervous energy and a more inward turn of mind have narrow hands. You'll recall that many of the saints in famous paintings have long, narrow hands to emphasize the importance of the inner life. This doesn't mean all people with long, narrow hands are saints, however. Some are pickpockets.

Artists almost always use the appropriate hand-type to show character in a painting.

It seems obvious that graceful hands symbolize a greater inner balance than clumsy ones. Brilliant people may have awkward hands, but clumsy, lifeless-looking hands usually indicate a lack of brilliance.

The hand with firm, high padding belongs to the person

Hand from wrist to longest fingertip is normally the same length as the face.

with lots of drive and a sure sense of his own abilities. It has been called the "lucky hand."

A flat hand belongs to the less confident person who has to work harder for what he gets. This doesn't mean he isn't talented and successful—merely that he has to work. But he has the energy to work, if his hand is also firm.

The thin, hollow hand—sunken like a bowl in the center but without high padding around the edges—is characteristic of the person who feels constantly defeated by bad breaks and who lacks the spirit to fight back.

A person with a solid, hard hand has lots of physical energy. And, as you might expect, a soft and spongy hand shows just the opposite. However, the man or woman with a soft hand and a large thumb may have plenty of mental energy, and this is a combination found in the hands of many persons with a high level of intellectual accomplishment. Eleanor Roosevelt has hands like these.

A flexible hand means a flexible mind capable of changing quickly from one train of thought or course of action to another. By "flexible," I don't mean to imply a lack of will or determination.

In a very flexible hand, the fingers can be bent back at right angles to the hand itself. Such are the hands of Alexander King. And many women lean their heads on their hands so as to bend their fingers back. They're the ones of whom it is said that "a woman's mind is cleaner than a man's because she changes it more often."

A stiff hand reveals a person set in his ways. When the hand is really stiff, the fingers won't bend back at all. If you've ever shaken hands with an old-time New England farmer, you know the sort of hand I mean (excluding, of course, the hand stiffened by disease or accident).

A skin as fine as a baby's suggests a delicately tuned person with hi-fi sensitivity. A coarser skin means an earthier person. Very coarse skin, as tough and wrinkled as the feet of a chicken, suggests a very coarse person— the kind for whom they invented "No Spitting on the Floor" signs.

Distorted, unbalanced looking hands show an odd, original mind. But before you jump to conclusions, remember that an odd mind might belong to a genius or a crank. George Bernard Shaw had such hands.

The outwardly balanced hand reveals inner balance.

The color of your hands may depend on the temperature of the room or a temporary mood. But when you notice a pair of deathly pale hands in a warm room, you can assume the person is suffering from anxiety or an illness. Hands that are not a "sick white" but merely pale indicate a lack of energy, or egotism. Pink hands go with a warm and happy nature. Reddish hands are the sign of an optimistic, ardent, intense and, sometimes, irritable nature. Yellowish hands indicate a nervous person who is inclined to brood.

Your health and moods affect the temperature of your hands. If you have a fever, your hands are hot; when you are fearful or anxious, your hands are cold. We've all heard the expression "he got cold feet." When a man has "cold feet," he also has cold hands.

If you already know these clues to character, you undoubtedly have a natural knack for hand-reading. If you haven't been looking for these easy clues, pick them out and see how much more you can learn, at a glance or a handshake, about your fellow human beings.

Though these clues are easy, they are important. Remember them as you learn the more technical parts of hand-reading.

CHAPTER III

HOW TO MAKE A MAP
OF YOUR OWN HAND

"You cannot clap hands with one hand."
—Chinese Proverb.

The easiest and most interesting way to read your own hands is to make hand-prints and then mark them according to your character and possibilities, as you discover them. This is the professional way to read other people's hands. Here is how it is done:

Use a red office stamp pad—not the sponge-rubber kind but the old-fashioned cloth-covered type. You'll also need a soft pencil and six or eight sheets of smooth white paper, typewriter size—the smoother the better.

Start with a clean, dry hand. Ink a quarter of your hand at a time on the red stamp pad, using a corner of the pad to ink the hollow in the center of your palm. Ink your fingers too. Place your hand firmly in a natural position in the center of a piece of paper and *leave it there* while you trace your hand, fingers and thumb with the pencil. Be sure to hold the pencil straight up while you make your outline of each hand.

If the center of the palm doesn't leave a print, make

48

another hand-print with a folded handkerchief under the center of your palm. Continue making hand-prints until you get at least two good prints of each hand.

To obtain the best results, make those hand-prints now before you read the rest of this chapter. Check the finished prints against your hands to be sure they show the correct shape and all lines show up clearly.

Now you're ready to read the "map" of your hand. You will notice that you naturally put your hand down each time in approximately the same position so that your fingers are the same distance apart. Here's how hand-readers interpret the position of your fingers:

—When all your fingers are close together, it indicates that you are cautious and conventional.

—If your fingers are wide apart so that your hands look like a starfish, your mind is quick and flexible.

—If your index and middle fingers are separated, you are an independent thinker.

—If your middle and ring finger are separated, you are basically unconventional.

—If your ring and little finger are separated, it means you are free in your actions and decisions.

Any finger that seems to draw the other fingers toward it like a magnet gives a clue to a quality that dominates your life. In general, if the other fingers lean toward the ring and little fingers, your life will be molded more by emotion and instinct. But if your index finger and thumb seem to draw the other fingers toward them, conscious effort will guide you. This latter hand-position indicates leadership.

In a serious, conservative hand, all the fingers lean toward the middle finger. If your fingers don't lean at all but appear spaced, yours is a balanced personality.

You can learn a lot about yourself from observing the

Your life will probably be guided by emotion and instinct if your fingers lean toward the little-finger side of the hand.

natural position of your fingers. Do you hold your little finger apart from its neighbors (freedom of action) and the index finger close? Perhaps you have Latin instincts and a Puritan conscience.

If your thumb is close to the fingers, you are probably a timid soul. But if it shoots out from the base of your hand and bends sharply in at the top like a claw, you are

DO YOU USE YOUR TALENTS?
— PATRICK DENNIS

HIGH "MOUNT" UNDER INDEX SHOWS AMBITION

HIGH "MOUNT" HERE SHOWS YOU WILL FIGHT TO FULFILL AMBITION

LARGE THUMB IN AMBITIOUS HAND — WILL TO ACCOMPLISH

patrick dennis   **HEAD LINE**

Conscious effort will likely mold your life if the fingers lean toward the index and thumb. This, plus other features, shows deliberate good use of natural talent.

supposed to be a rapacious or greedy person. Witches are often pictured with a thumb of this kind.

If your thumb is widely separated from your fingers, you have an open mind. If held close, you are cautious.

In large and important ways the hands are almost always the same. Both hands will be broad with few lines —the hands of action—or both may be narrow with many fine lines—sensitive, high-strung hands.

When it comes to details, however, the hands are never the same. The most-used hand, left or right, is the hand that shows your ordinary workaday abilities and feelings. The least-used hand shows subconscious motives, undeveloped potentialities, or faults that have been controlled.

The old saying that the left hand shows qualities you were born with and the right hand shows what you have done with these qualities is close to the truth. The saying errs, however, in failing to take into account the fact that both hands change. As you grow and live longer, your potentialities and long-term desires change just as surely as your ways of dealing with life, day by day.

The left hand shows natural leanings.

The right hand shows how you have learned to deal with your life.

Whatever shows in *both* hands is 100% you.

LEFT HAND PRINT SHOWS WHAT YOU ARE BASICALLY

HEAD   HEART

FATE

LIFE

MAIN LINES
CLEARLY MARKED

WHEN
RIGHT AND
LEFT HANDS
ARE DECIDEDLY
DIFFERENT,
CIRCUMSTANCES
HAVEN'T ALLOWED YOU
TO FOLLOW
YOUR NATURAL
BENT

HEAD

MAIN LINES
TORTURED LOOKING →

LINES CHANGE
AS YOU CHANGE

RIGHT HAND PRINT – SHOWS
WHAT YOU CAN DO, AS OF NOW →

HEART

FATE
BRANCH

MARS

FATE

If the main lines are not clearly marked in the most-used hand (in this case, the right), there are obstacles that have hindered development of your abilities.

CHAPTER IV

HAND TYPES

*"These types, like the separate breeds of the canine race,
cannot alter or modify themselves beyond a certain point."*
—Stanislas d'Arpentigny.

More than a hundred years ago, Stanislas d'Arpentigny
became interested in palmistry when a beautiful young
Andalusian Gypsy read his hand. Later he noticed that
his mechanical and scientific friends had knotty or square
hands while his artistic and poetic friends had smooth
hands with tapering fingers.

Continuing his studies, he developed the idea that there
are basic hand types which are related to basic character
types—and each of these types is so different from the
others that like separate "breeds of the canine race" they
can't be altered beyond a certain point.

D'Arpentigny's classifications are used in modern hand-
reading, though some changes have been introduced.
Here are the principal types:

THE CLUMSY HAND

Since you can read this book, you may assume that
yours is not an elementary hand that goes with a primi-

tive and undeveloped intelligence. You can recognize such a hand not only by its clumsy shape but its hard skin, stiffness and the few lines that are more like creases in the skin than actual lines.

You might think that hands like this are the result of manual labor. But hands that work hard year after year become calloused—never clumsy.

The Elementary Hand.

THE SQUARE HAND

Usually a broad hand with firm muscles, fingers of a rectangular shape and a square palm belongs to the decisive and active person whose thinking is down-to-earth. Such a person prefers to stick to tried and true traditions and customs until concrete examples convince him that new ideas or methods are worth trying. He has no respect for theories until he's seen them work. A farmer with square hands has no respect for new-fangled methods. An architect with these hands will prefer to design functional houses.

When fingertips are square (almost like a squared-off two-by-four board) they indicate an exaggerated love of

Square hands may have slightly rounded fingertips, but the fingers themselves are rectangular. The owner wants to know the truth, is often a scientist.

form. These very square tips are characteristic of builders and sometimes sculptors and architects.

The square hand is also called the "useful" hand because square-handers prize this quality the most in a person or object. These people are often too literal-minded. A boy shouldn't give a square-fingered girl a book of poetry but something she can wear or eat.

Fingers on a square hand are rectangular from base to tip, and the four sides of the finger are slightly flattened so that a cross-section would be square as well. The palm is generally square but the sides are not straight as a ramrod. In fact, the outer edge usually protrudes.

THE SPATULATE HAND

Perhaps your hand is more spatulate or flared. In its extreme form, this hand has what you might call stubbed fingertips that flare out at the tips like the spatulas used by chemists. The palm has an unusual shape—either the top of the palm or the bottom is broad, out of proportion to the rest of the hand.

This hand belongs to a person who combines a need for constant action with an original way of thinking. Such people are explorers of places or ideas. A dress designer with spatulate hands would be the one whose creations make you turn around and gasp. A general with spatulate hands would win battles because his strategy would take the enemy by surprise.

You will notice a hand that seems to be halfway between the extreme spatulate and the square. These hands belong to people who are original in a concrete down-to-earth way—often craftsmen whose work has great originality, tailors, for example. A writer with hands like this writes specifically, with many examples. The hands of such artisans may be nearly the same shape as square hands, and the flare in the fingertips is wider halfway up than at the extreme tip.

DO YOU LOVE ACTION?
— DENISE McCLUGGAGE

FIRM HAND— PHYSICAL ENERGY

SPATULATE FINGER TIPS —LOVE OF ACTION

WIDE AND HIGH AND FIRM BASE TO PALM—NEED TO TRY NEW THINGS

LIFE LINE

The spatulate hand denotes love of action. If the hand is also firm and highly padded, this love of action is a consuming passion, as it is with woman sportscar racer Denise McCluggage.

If you have a spatulate hand, be careful to use your originality in a constructive way; otherwise you will become a crank.

THE PHILOSOPHIC HAND

If your hand is philosophic, it is long and bony with knots at both joints of the fingers. The palm, which is fairly flat, usually contains many lines.

The person with a hand like this wants to examine every

The Philosophic Hand.

side of a question before he makes up his mind. Ask him a question he does not expect, and he'll answer, "Well—yes and no."

Although the man with the philosophic hand feels he is searching for the truth, he is contradictory and difficult to understand. However, he understands other people, and though he is reserved, he is usually tactful. He needs to get off by himself to enjoy the peace of solitude. He loves the quiet countryside and long hours of uninterrupted reading.

When this person makes up his mind to do something, he's as tenacious as a snapping turtle. He may stop to take another look at all sides of a problem, but then he'll start again. He has a restless and curious mind, and he's sometimes suspicious of others.

He likes to add up concrete, observed facts to get an abstract answer.

THE CONIC HAND

If you have a conic or receptive hand, you're a person to whom beauty is a tremendous inspiration. You're also a very impulsive person, a creature of whim and fancy. Conic-handed people will always try to make everything they touch as attractive as possible. Their main fault is that they would rather think about the ideal possibilities of life than face up to reality. But they are generally good companions, and when they are inspired, they are filled with infectious enthusiasm. They are fun to have at a party though they are not likely to stay to clean up. One warning to those of you who are conics: don't start more than you can finish.

Fingers in a conic hand taper to cone-shaped tips and are round like candles. The palm is slightly oval. Cleo-

ARE YOU BRILLIANT?
—ALEXANDER KING

FINGERS BEND
BACK AT RIGHT
ANGLE—
VERSATILITY

LONG LINE UNDER RING
FINGER—SPONTANEOUS
SELF—
EXPRESSION

HIGH PEAKED
"MOUNTS" UNDER
FINGERS—
LIVELY MIND

A conic hand belongs to a versatile person, easily inspired but without much persistence unless he has large thumbs. Other hand features shown here may enlarge on versatility.

patra probably had hands like these. Conic hands usually have small thumbs (when they have large thumbs, their owners find it easier to finish what they start).

THE PSYCHIC HAND

If yours is a psychic hand, you're far more interested in beautiful ideas and mysteries than drab everyday facts. The inner life means everything to people with this type of hand, which is long and narrow with delicate bones and pointed fingers usually so flexible that the tips can be bent back. The skin is very fine and delicate and it is sometimes glossy.

The princess in the fairy tale who woke up black and blue after sleeping on a pea buried under eight mattresses must have had a psychic hand in extreme form. We think of these hands as belonging to saints, poets and aristocrats,

The Psychic Hand.

but this isn't necessarily so. A saint with such hands would put more emphasis on faith than works.

THE MIXED TYPE

Unless your hand happens to be a "pure" type, which is rare, you have to be satisfied with the designation "mixed type." The person with a mixed hand, however, is more

SQUARE FINGERS
PRACTICAL IN LOVE
EVEN WHEN
INSPIRED BY
FULL MOON

CONIC FINGERS
ROMANTIC AND
IDEALISTIC IN
LOVE

versatile than the man or woman with "pure" hands. You have probably already decided that the trouble with these various labels is the lack of specific tests or measurements to determine exactly your type or mixture of types. Experienced hand-readers can spot the elements of hand type in a mixed hand, but there is a need for more scientific measurements.

More specific tests do exist that show you where your hand fits in the scale of classification. You will notice that the seven types range from broad, clumsy and fleshy hands to those that are long, flexible and over-delicate. Many modern hand-readers prefer to divide the types of hands between these extremes into three simpler classes, broad, balanced and long, and to deal separately with such features as the shape of the fingers, etc.

This is a satisfactory method of classification because with the help of a measuring tape, you know exactly which of the three types you are dealing with.

Measure your hand to see whether it is broad, medium, or long.

Medium Hand—The width of the palm (half the circumference at its widest point) is very slightly less than the length of the palm. The fingers are in proportion—the middle or longest finger is the same length from knuckle to fingertip as the distance between knuckle and wrist bone. The length of the long middle finger approximately equals the width across the top of the hand.

Broad Hand—The palm is as broad as it is long. The fingers are in proportion and frequently short.

Long Hand—If the palm is medium, the fingers are quite long by comparison. If the palm is long or at least half an inch longer than it is wide *(curved measure),* the fingers are either slightly long or *in proportion* to the rest of the hand. In these hands, the fingertips are often longer than the other two sections of the finger.

THE BROAD HAND

If your hand is broad rather than long, you have the necessary drive to finish what you start. Your watchword

Broad hands show an active, practical nature.

is common sense; you enjoy luxuries and work to get them. Your feelings are quickly aroused, but you are inclined to be steady and true. Your thinking is practical.

If your broad hand is quite small, you are at once practical, mercurial and imaginative.

If your broad hand is very firm, you love nature and would prefer an outdoor job.

If you wish to use your imagination in a practical way, your hand is firm and broad with many signs of imagination. The politician who makes a heart-rending appeal to the voter has a hand like this.

If you have a broad hand that is very soft, you love comfort more than action. You prefer strawberry shortcake to football.

If your broad hand is unusually pale, flabby and soft, and has fingers that are fleshy at the base but taper considerably toward the tips, you are a lover of physical comfort but not an advocate of common sense. You are a sensualist or a dreamer or both. Swindlers often have hands like this, usually dead white.

NARROW AND LONG

If your hand is narrow and long, you have a more thoughtful and inward turn of mind—though if your hand is also strong and firm, you may have as much drive and sometimes more determination than your broad-handed friends.

Long hands go with inquiring and sensitive minds. These hands usually belong to expressive people, especially if the hands are also flexible.

Narrow-handed people are inclined to be shyer than broad-handed ones, however. Their thinking is abstract or imaginative, and they are more sensitive. If you are going to insult someone, pick someone with a broad hand. The broad-handed person may punch you in the nose, but the long-handed person will be more deeply hurt and will remember and resent the hurt long after the broad-handed person has forgotten it.

Long, narrow hands go with a reflective, often introverted, mind.

The long, slender hand can be as materialistic as the broad hand, though not in a comfortable way. If the hand is tense, stiff, thin, dry, knotty and curves inward, look for other signs of miserliness. If it is very white or yellow and has a bent little finger, you should suspect envy and the desire for concrete possessions to bolster the ego.

The balanced hand shows a balanced temperament. The size helps us understand the subject.

The size of the hand is an important measurable clue to personality. Hands of average length are about seven and a half inches long, excluding the wrist. Men's hands may be slightly longer, women's hands slightly shorter.

THE SMALL HAND

A definitely small hand would be less than six and three quarters inches long (Gertrude Lindsay says less than a Size 6 glove for women). A hand under seven inches would be small on a man. If you are under twenty, your hand may be small because it is not full grown.

Does the size of the person make a difference? If his

AVERAGE ADULT HAND LENGTH—ABOUT 7½ IN.

With a small hand (7 inches or less for a man, size 6 glove or less for a woman), you think vividly, like to make big plans.

hand is out of portion, his personality is not balanced. The distance from the wrist to the tip of the middle finger should be the same as the length of the face. (Look out for receding hairlines—they throw this measurement off.)

THE LARGE HAND

Very large hands belong to people who are willing to be patient with small details and can do very intricate work. They are analytical and thrive on details. The next time you visit your watch-repairman, study his hands. People with excessively large hands are moody.

If you have small hands, you are likely to have more charm than depth and more cleverness and perception than stick-to-itiveness. You do anything well that can be done quickly or on the spur of the moment, but you become exceedingly bored with any job that is long and routine. You would love to plan a church fair but hate to account for all the money that is made. You love to make plans but prefer that others carry them out. You succeed most often through the quick sale but fail when you lose interest in a job before you finish it.

You nearly always see signs of imagination in a small hand. Many writers have small hands. Thus they can visit a foreign country for two days and then write a five-hundred-page book about their "impressions." They think quickly and intuitively, almost never analytically. The person with small hands seems precocious in childhood and young for his age in later life.

THE BROAD SMALL HAND

The small hand that is broad and firm is energetically vivid and impulsive. People with these hands are often artistic and carry out their plans better than folks with narrow, small hands.

The person with broad, small hands with conic fingers is impulsive and imaginative, though if his hands are soft he is indolent and a lover of luxury.

If your hand is narrow and small, it is even more intuitive than the broad small hand. You are usually so high strung you must be careful not to wear yourself out.

Balanced hands that are neither large nor small show a balanced nature, but the fingers tell us about personality and character.

THE FINGERS

It is sometimes difficult to classify the various types of fingers. Are they square with conic tips and just a hint of spatulate flare? Unless they are clearly spatulate, conic, pointed or square, you had best determine whether they are tapered or rectangular.

SQUARE FINGERS

Place your hand on a sheet of paper with your fingers close together. Make an outline of your whole hand. Now draw a line parallel to your little finger and another line parallel to your index finger. If these lines form two sides of a possible rectangle, your fingers indicate that you are a practical, matter-of-fact person. If your hands show other signs of imagination, you may be artistic, though you require symmetry or realism in your art. Even if the tips are slightly rounded, these square fingers on a broad, firm hand show an extreme love of the functional and utilitarian.

Square fingers on a long hand mean that a person is

more sensitive and thoughtful but still basically practical. He will express himself clearly more than inspirationally. Scientists frequently have square fingers.

If the little finger line and the index line slope together slightly, the fingers are still predominantly of the square type.

TAPERING FINGERS—
IMPULSE INSPIRATION

LARGE THUMB
UNDERLINES
DETERMINED
NATURE

FEW LINES—
ACTION
REPLACES
WORRY

LIFE
LINE

FINGERS WHICH FORM
TWO SIDES OF A SQUARE
WHEN HELD TOGETHER
——MATTER OF FACT
NATURE, PURPOSEFUL

SMALL THUMB
EMPHASIZES
IMPULSIVENESS

RECEPTIVE FINGERS

If your little finger line and the index finger line slope together quite noticeably, your fingers are receptive and you are an imaginative, often idealistic person.

On a broad hand these receptive fingers emphasize the enjoyment of all physical pleasures. If a person with such a hand wrote poetry, he would just as soon write an ode to a roast beef as a violet. People who love to cook usually have broad hands with receptive fingers, and such people are both less practical and more imaginative. They are not ethereal, however—they like their material comforts too much.

Receptive fingers on a long, slender hand indicate an appreciation of art, music, color and the beauties of nature. People of this type are otherwise less sensual in tastes than their broad-handed cousins. They would rather smell a rose than a roast beef.

The shape of your fingertips has a modifying effect on the shape of your hands and fingers. Square tips always indicate a love of form. Conic tips mean a bonus dash of idealism. Pointed tips are a sign of inspiration. Spatulate tips on any shape of hand indicate a love of activity and exploration of new places and ideas. On many hands the fingertips are not all the same shape. I will shortly explain the meaning of the shape of the tip of each finger.

FINGER LENGTH

The length of your fingers is also important. As I have pointed out, the average finger length makes the middle finger from tip to knuckle the same length as the back of the hand from knuckle to wrist.

SHORT FINGERS

Shorter fingers belong to people who think quickly and are impatient with details. Short fingers with smooth joints are characteristic of people who see the whole and have little patience with the parts. Fast thinking is their greatest asset. On the other hand, they often get into hot water by jumping to conclusions. If you are working from a palm

SMOOTH FINGERS—
ACT BY
INSPIRATION

SHORT FINGERS—
THINK QUICKLY,
INTUITIVELY

print, it is usually safe to class fingers as "short" if the middle finger is more than an inch shorter than the palm. However, this is not as accurate as measuring the backs.

LONG FINGERS

People who think in an abstract or analytical manner have long fingers. They like to go into details before they make up their minds.

They will read every word of a petition before they sign it. Particularly long fingers indicate such an extreme love of details that the whole picture is entirely lost. Those with extremely long fingers judge other people by details of manner and dress and are extremely meticulous. If their fingers have knots at the joints, they are more analytical.

Not only must they observe *all* the details, but they must test them.

If you plan a trip with a person with long fingers and knotty joints, he will spend forever deciding what to take and why. But once packed, he will be prepared for any possible emergency. He may be slow, but he is certainly thorough.

People with long, smooth-jointed fingers think more intuitively and therefore quickly than people with long fingers and knotty joints. They are instinctively graceful. They worry about details, however, and like "finish."

THE KNOTS ON YOUR FINGERS

You can find knots on any size or shape of hand. They always mean that the person takes longer to make up his mind or change it than the average person. Long knotty fingers on a stiff, long hand should warn you that you can't make this person decide anything quickly. What's more, you'll have an even tougher time trying to persuade him to change his mind once it's made up.

On the small flexible hand with short fingers that shows fast impulsive thinking in every other way, knotty fingers might be a balancing factor, adding a needed ounce of thoughtfulness.

The "first knots"—those nearest the fingertips—are called the knots of mental order or "philosophic" knots. They indicate orderly thinking. People with such knots accept nothing until they have proved it to their own satisfaction.

The "second knots" on the lower joints of the fingers are called the "knots of material order" and indicate a pragmatic, businesslike sort of person.

Smooth fingers without knots at the joints are characteristic of quick, instinctive or intuitive thinking.

KNOTS OF MATERIAL ORDER

WHORL PRINT ON THUMB TIP— WELL ORDERED THINKING, INDEPENDENT WILL

SQUARE PALM— ABILITY TO ORGANIZE YOUR LIFE

Knots of material order belong to the person who can organize the practical details of life. If this is an outstanding characteristic, it will be repeated in other ways.

Desbarrolles classed the combinations of knots and finger shapes as follows:

Shape	Leanings
Smooth fingers and pointed tips	inspiration divination
Smooth fingers and square tips	politics philosophy art based on nature practical planning

Knots on the joints nearest the fingertips, or "Philosopher's Knots," show order in ideas.

Smooth fingers and spatulate tips	great activity
	calculation
	mechanics
	administration
	art that depicts action
First knots and pointed tips	Utopianism
First knots and square tips	absolute justice
	useful work
First knots and spatulate tips	inventive realism
Second knots and pointed tips	inner struggle
	inspiration versus calculation

Shape	Leanings
Second knots and square tips	orderliness love of discipline
Second knots and spatulate tips	practical enterprise military tactics
Both knots and pointed tips	inspired inventions restlessness
Both knots and square tips	natural science history common sense
Both knots and spatulate tips	exact science physical activity the invention or running of machines exploration

Desbarrolles considered the conic tips half way between the pointed and the square. He called them versatile—a combination of the practicality of the square tips with the inspiration of the pointed tips.

THE THREE SECTIONS OF THE FINGER

The three sections of your fingers indicate the three spheres of interest for your particular talents. If your hand is long, your fingertips are probably your longest area. This section stresses your interest in ideas.

Long fingertips are characteristic of the mystic, the idealist, the intellectual or anyone who considers thought more important than action. The most sensitive and specialized nerves in the hand are located in your fingertips. The sensitive person adept at using his hands to explore and learn has the long tips. You usually see them on long

KNOTS BULGING AT UPPER AND LOWER FINGER JOINTS — YOU DON'T EASILY CHANGE YOUR MIND

MIDDLE FINGER OR "SATURN"—

LARGE THUMB STRONG WILL

COMBINATION OF LARGE KNOTTY THUMB AND KNOTTY FINGERS — STUBBORN AS A RUSTY HINGE

FROM BACK IN BALANCED HAND WRIST TO KNUCKLE EQUALS KNUCKLE TO SATURN'S TIP

LIFE LINE

SATURN

MUCH LONGER FINGERS SHOW LOVE OF PETTY DETAILS

hands, though they are found on all shapes of hands and always emphasize a strong interest in ideas. The fingertips of mental patients are often too long, showing that their own distorted ideas are more important to them than reality. However, unusually long tips are not a sign of insanity. The tip sections emphasize thought, and the sections of your fingers closest to your palm have an opposite meaning. If the lower areas are bulging and sausage-shaped in proportion to the other two sections, they emphasize sensuality, the desire for material comforts. People with fingers like this want the good things in life in large doses. If these lower sections are highly padded in the back but not large all the way around, they emphasize a love of quality. The gourmet fits into this category.

If the lowest sections are waisted, it indicates an inquiring mind and willingness to work hard. These sections are often slightly longer than the other two sections as viewed inside your hand. If they are noticeably long, out of proportion to the other sections, they indicate a very down-to-earth, materialistic nature.

The middle sections of the fingers are longest in the hands of people who emphasize practical planning. Metaphysics does not interest them as much as balanced checkbooks or the arrangement of their time to best practical advantage. If the middle sections look short in proportion to the other two sections, it's usually because the tips are long. If the middle sections are decidedly short in proportion to the other two, you know that the person is not balanced and lacks the ability to cope with life smoothly. The tip sections of the fingers are likely to be somewhat short in a broad hand. They emphasize the fact that the person prefers action to complicated brain work.

When all three spheres of interest are in balance, the three areas are in exact proportion to one another.

CHAPTER V

THE MOUNTS: KEYS
TO CHARACTER DEVELOPMENT

"Man will become better when you show him what he is like."

—Anton Chekov.

The hills and valleys of the hand and groups of lines that cluster in one part of the hand but leave another as smooth as silk show reservoirs of power or desire, or the combination of the two that may lead to fulfillment.

"Mounts," or special areas of the hand, are related to different facets of your character. They show what kind of instinctive energy you have and how you use it.

In some hands, each separate area has its own cushion of flesh. Therefore, these areas are called "mounts" even though they are flat as a pane of glass. Don't be confused by the traditional use of the word "mount." Here the name refers to the area, not to padding or elevation. A mount can be concave or sunken.

Look at Desbarrolles' picture of the mounts and you will see the kind of action depicted by each mount. On the elevation at the base of the thumb, you will see a boy and girl holding hands. This area of the hand is called the

Desbarrolles, an artist as well as a hand-reader, used this picture of mount meanings for his "Revélations Complètes." (Photograph courtesy of The Library of Congress.)

Mount of Venus, and it indicates warmth, vitality and sensuality.

On the outside heel of the hand, Desbarrolles has pictured a sailing ship. This mount is named Luna, or Moon, and is the index of imagination, mysticism and restlessness, hence love of the sea.

The battleground shown in the center of the palm is the Plain of Mars. If it is sunken like a bowl, and all the other mounts are low, you lack the spirit to struggle against adversity.

The part of the battlefield on the outside edge of the hand, and the determined-looking thinker standing on the line above the warriors are both on the Mount of Mars— the seat of endurance.

Under the index finger, in Desbarrolles' picture, is the Mount of Jupiter, where we read ambition and leadership marked by a picture of a king on his throne.

The picture of a miner under the long middle finger, on the Mount of Saturn, indicates the love of such basic and down-to-earth pursuits as mining, characteristic of the serious-minded, sober people with this mount large or heavily marked.

The muse plucking at her lyre under the ring finger tells us this mount shows flair and style, so necessary to the artist. It is the Mount of Apollo.

The Mount of Mercury under the little finger indicates the astuteness and fluency so necessary to the orator, and so Desbarrolles has pictured an orator there.

Modern hand-readers place aggressiveness in an active Mount of Mars at the base of the thumb just above the Mount of Venus.

(Other pictures on Desbarrolles' hand have nothing to do with the mounts. On the life-line, circling the Mount of Venus, we see the life span from the cradle to the grave.

On the thumb, we see Will paying no attention to Reason.)

Using a hand-print, mark with dotted lines any areas on your hand that have fleshy padding on them. Label each area: high, medium or low. This padding, if firm, shows physical energy. The amount of padding indicates the amount of energy expended in the direction of any given mount. For example, if the padding under the index finger

High padding on the mounts indicates physical energy.

is high and firm, you are actively energetic in your efforts to be a leader. You would lead a parade just as readily as you would write a letter to your senator. If you ran for senator yourself, you would be apt to direct your own very active campaign. The area of the hand where the high padding is shows how you use your energy.

If the padding is medium-soft, it indicates straightforward mental energy—the kind often found in people who are mentally alert but don't get much physical exercise. An intellectual leader would have this sort of padding on the Mount of Ambition. But flabby padding on the Mount of Ambition indicates love of luxury.

Groups of lines on mounts that are flat or low show nervous energy.

A flat or nearly flat mount covered with concentrations of lines is a sign of nervous energy. One clear, deep line or a balanced and well delineated group of lines mean that this nervous energy is being used to good effect.

Scrambled and faltering lines on a mount warn us that we've been using the quality of the mount in the wrong way. Often such lines reveal a part of our nature that has gotten temporarily out of control. For example, on the Mount of Ambition scrambled lines would show destructive pride. Remember, however, that markings change.

Vertical lines on a mount (they run in the same direction as the fingers) are a good sign unless there are more than three or four. But horizontal lines suggest obstacles.

If your hand is covered by a network of fine lines with the main lines clearly marked, you'll have to be a bit careful how you read them. The fine lines tell you that you are somewhat impressionable and high-strung, but don't interpret them to mean that you have scrambled lines on every mount. The strongest reading of such hands should be given to the most clearly marked lines.

A high mount covered with lines shows complex and passionate feelings and hence lack of control. On the Mount of active Mars, for example, it would indicate too much aggressiveness.

Patterns formed on a mount by papillary ridges of the skin reveal a great deal as to how you use the abilities indicated by that mount. Each of the mounts on your hand at the base of your fingers has a skin-ridge pattern called the apex of the mount. The natural place for this apex is directly under the center of the finger and approximately in the center of the mount. However, the apex under the little finger is apt to be closer to the inside edge of that finger.

When they are in their normal places, these apexes indi-

Usual position for the skin-ridge patterns called "apexes" found on the finger mounts.

cate a balanced use of the ability shown by the mount. If they are out of place they add to the significance of the mount toward which they lean.

Sometimes you will find other patterns in the papillary ridges of the skin, often in the shape of tiny whorls or bull's eyes. These may be on any mount in the hand. We'll see later how they add importance to the mount.

The mounts, then, show what kind of energy or drive we have and the general way in which we use it. You read the mounts under your fingers along with the finger. The mount indicates how much energy you have, your finger shows more precisely how you use that energy.

Most mounts are associated with one of the lines of your hand. This line usually has the same name as the mount and is related to it in meaning.

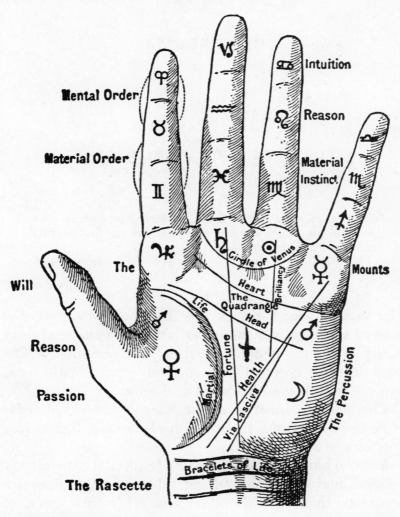

Principal lines are Life, Heart, Head and Fate (here called "Fortune"). Astrological signs on this old picture show the planets believed to be related to parts of the hand in the days when palmistry was combined with astrology.

CHAPTER VI

THE LINES OF YOUR HAND

"Chiromancie—old as the world, perfected by famous men and the most sublime geniuses—is so simple that a child can learn it in several days."
—Adolphe Desbarrolles.

The lines in your hand are like the words of a song—the tune of the song sets the mood just as the shape of your hands shows the general trend of your personality. The lines, like the lyrics of the song, tell more exactly what you are, where you're headed and why.

The general formation of the lines in your hand is far more important than the location of any one line or any special sign in the hand.

A broad hand is inclined to have fewer and more clearly defined lines than a long hand. More of these lines are horizontal than vertical in direction. When there are a lot of lines on a broad hand and many of them run up and down, the person possesses much of the sensitivity usually associated with long hands. Poets usually have broad hands with many lines.

A long hand usually has many more lines (also more vertical lines) than a broad hand. Also, there are generally more "faults"—breaks, chained formation, islands on the

lines or wavering lines. In a long hand where the main
lines are clearly defined, a few "faults" aren't serious,
though they do indicate some inner struggle. A large number of "faults" suggests that the person is oversensitive,
inhibited, nervous and unable to do all the things he wants
to do.

*Here's the hand of someone who doesn't let her worries over-
whelm her. There are many fine lines, but the main lines are
clearly marked.*

In general, women's hands have more lines than men's.
The man with many lines in his hand is a "thinking" man
rather than a man of action.

If you have a long hand with few but clearly marked
lines, you are almost as much a person of direct action as
your broad-handed neighbor.

You will notice in the "Table of Line Meanings" that few lines and average skin show more physical than nervous energy. This doesn't necessarily mean a lack of nervous energy, but does mean that if nervous energy exists **it** is translated directly into action.

A hand with few lines suggests concentration on the main issues.

Each line in the hand is related to the mount where it begins and ends. The two mounts and the clarity of the line determine its meanings. Therefore I will explain the mounts and lines together in the chapters which follow.

Incidentally, to be considered well-marked the lines

TABLE OF LINE MEANINGS

Fine lines	Subtle perceptions
Deep lines	Strong feelings, pronounced likes and dislikes
Few lines and average or coarse skin	More physical than nervous energy
Few clearly marked lines and very fine, delicate skin	Intuitive or intellectual energy consistently directed
Many lines	Nervous energy
Many lines, main lines well marked, others superficially marked	Nervous energy, constructively channeled
Main lines not much deeper or better marked than spider web of fine lines which cover the hand	High strung and impressionable person
Lines as above with very delicate fine-grained skin	Very sensitive person—you need calm
Main lines and many other lines all deeply marked	Deep feelings plus some inner conflicts
Lines as above plus high mounts	Passionate feelings
Lines as above plus flat or hollow mounts	Strong desires, more intellectual than emotional
Main lines badly marked with breaks, islands, chained formations	Nervous or physical strain, tendency toward hysteria when under pressure
Accessory lines wavering like wriggling snakes or forming scrambled, tangled groups	Nervous over-stimulation or run-down physical condition
Lines broad and marked like a trench in coarse skin	Undeveloped intelligence
Dead pale lines	Lack of energy
Yellow lines	Nervousness and inhibitions
Red lines	Strong feelings
Pink lines (if well-marked)	Healthy body and mind

*Fine skin with hundreds of tiny lines belongs to a person too
sensitive for his own comfort.*

must be clearly marked without breaks, islands or chains.
The lines of life, head and heart must be present and fairly
long, and if there are more than a few lines on the hand,
the line of fate must be present, too. (You find an exception to this in the hands of people who are brilliant but
entirely unconventional. They may lack the fate-line.)
Your hands are not likely to be perfectly marked unless
you are either perfect or very simple. To be really badly
marked, the lines must be tangled or broken in several
places, and they must have an uncertain, wavering look.

To evaluate the exact combination of line type and
hand shape, see the table "How to Combine Hand Shapes
and Line Meanings."

GOT SOMETHING TO SAY?
— CARL SANDBURG

LARGE THUMB HELD CLOSE TO HAND — STRONG OPINIONS

THIS HAND HAS HIGH PADDING (SO HIGH THAT SHADED AREA WON'T PRINT) PLUS MANY DEEP LINES — PASSIONATE FEELINGS

HEART LINE

HEAD LINE

MANY CLEARLY MARKED INTUITION LINES — POWERFUL INTUITIVE IMAGINATION

Carl Sandburg

Many lines deeply marked, plus high mounts, show emotions so deep they must be expressed. This can be an advantage to a creative person.

Many twisted, islanded lines in this hand suggest the owner's hardest struggles are within herself.

HOW TO COMBINE HAND SHAPES AND
LINE MEANINGS

LINES	BROAD AND MEDIUM HAND	NARROW HAND
Few lines deep and well-marked	You are outgoing, purposeful, with clear, simple goals.	You are poised with clear personal goal
Lines few, deep and falteringly marked (especially with coarse skin)	You are energetic but not sure where you're going. When upset, like a bull in a china shop, or very depressed.	You are not sure of yourself — therefore, easily hurt—but may still have a clear over-all sense of direction.
Lines few, fine, and well-marked	Subtle perceptions and a clear goal.	You are subtle, sensitive and know how to get what you want.
Lines few, fine, and badly-marked	Slightly chained, islanded or feathery lines may show delicately tuned nerves. If the lines are *very* badly marked—delicate nerves and superficial emotions or hysteria.	If the lines are chained or feathery — delicate nerves and the need to be alone or quiet often. Very badly-marked lines —selfishness
Main lines deep and fairly well-marked, many other lines superficial	You are outgoing and purposeful enough to make your sensitivity to others an asset. With high mounts—very emotional. Example: Ernestine Schumann-Heink	You are intuitive, highly strung but can make this an asset (especially with a normal or large thumb) Example: Mary Martin
Main lines and spiderweb of fine lines, all equally superficial	You are impressionable and high strung, but if the hand is firm, energetic. If flabby, a dreamer.	You are so high strung that you need harmonious surroundings to keep on an even keel.
Many lines—all deeply marked	Deep feelings usually find an outlet. This is often the expressive hand of a writer or musician. Example: Maurice Ravel	Intense feelings. This is often the hand of the philosopher.
Many lines deeply and falteringly marked with many faults	Strong inner conflicts, possibly with the energy to manage anyway	Deep feelings but strong inhibitions. Tormented emotions.

CHAPTER VII

"GOOD" AND "BAD" HANDS

"It is easier to know water ten fathoms deep than a man one fathom tall."
— Old Korean proverb.

Judging by their letters to me, readers of my newspaper feature, *Helping Hands*, seemed to have two chief questions in mind: "Am I good or bad?" and "Am I lucky or unlucky?"

In general, the shape of your hand indicates your approach to life while your mounts show the kind of energy you have and how you use it.

Your lines reflect your own awareness of what you are and where you are headed. Therefore, your lines can change. The mannerisms of your hands, the way in which you hold them, their color and temperature provide clues to the state of your feelings.

Above all, you want to know: "What is there about my hand that shows chances for happiness and success?"

Happiness is most easily discovered by the person with a balanced hand in which no one mount is greatly out of proportion to the rest, the lines are clearly marked and medium in number, the fingers are straight and evenly set and the hand is neither remarkably flexible nor stiff.

If the vertical lines are also long and clearly marked, you can assume that the person is well balanced, sensitive and possessed of good sense of purpose. Such a hand is very rare, however. Most of us can get a great deal out of life with less balanced and clearly marked hands.

We often find genius in the very unbalanced hand. The owner of the unbalanced hand may be successful under the right circumstances.

The so-called "bad" hand shows us at a glance that this person has had a hard time getting along with himself. Almost all of us have at least one bad characteristic in our hands.

If you would imagine a hand with all the signs of a warped personality, you would find twisted fingers unevenly placed; scrambled and twisted lines with many breaks and islands; hollow mounts or one mount developed out of all proportion to the others; chalk white, alarmingly red or vividly yellow coloring; a hand tightly clenched or flabbily open like wilted lettuce; a very large or very small thumb out of proportion to the rest of the hand, especially the fingers.

Luckily, you probably won't be shaking hands with anybody like this, but you will come across hands with one or more of these faults. Any one of these qualities is the hallmark of a person who has trouble solving his problems, and two of them indicates that he is in even greater trouble.

For example, a small thumb is the sign of a person who lacks the will power to overcome natural faults. When the small thumb is combined with flabby or hollow hands, this person is not only unable to conquer his faults but feels that his faults have conquered him.

Old palmistry books, written before man knew as much as he does today about how to cure his mental and physical ills, were inclined to associate depressing predictions with problem hands. All of us have heard for example, that a short life-line is the sign of early death. As we shall see, this sign is not nearly as gloomy as tradition would have us think.

As you read hands, notice how they reflect the serious problems people have. But if your hand reflects your problems, it may also show those positive traits you need to solve them.

CHAPTER VIII

LIFE, LOVE AND WILL POWER

"Man is the only animal that blushes, or needs to."
—Mark Twain.

Don't bother pulling petals off a daisy to find out if your true love loves you—just look at her Mount of Venus. This mount shows instinctive warmth and vitality.

If your Mount of Venus is high and the line of life encircling it loops far out into the palm, you are most likely warm-hearted and vibrantly alive. This mount is associated with love—the instinctive, overflowing kind of love a person feels who has an excess of vitality.

The high mount also goes with a love for all the good things of life. The person with this mount is sensual as well as emotional. When we are overflowing with warmth, we sing, therefore it's not surprising that the high mount is associated with a love of melody.

When your Mount of Venus is a thin, low pad and the life-line runs close to the thumb, you are not sensual by nature and your love for your fellow beings is mental rather than physical. You are content to share their interests.

If the Mount of Venus is large and soft, it indicates an exaggerated love of pleasure. If it is large, soft and pink, it is a sign of cheerfulness and the desire to share cher-

PADDING HERE—
WARMTH

Helen Hayes
RIGHT HAND PRINT

LIFE LINE

*You are warm-hearted and vibrantly alive if your Mount of
Venus is high and wide.*

ished luxuries. If it is large and flabby and dead-white, you
are selfishly sensual.

If your mount is thick and hard and there are two
mounts of Mars that are also thick and full, your vitality
reveals another side entirely. You may be warm-hearted,
but you are extremely combative. No one should get into

If your Mount of Venus is thin and low, love for you is more mental than physical.

a fight with you unless they have as much push as you do— and that's a lot.

A grill of lines on the Mount of Venus shows a need for affection. On a high, full mount, a deeply marked grill is the sign of a passionate nature.

From time to time, the study of palmistry has been combined with the study of astrology, and a certain type of hand was supposed to show the influence of the planet Venus. This hand had (as you might expect) a large full Mount of Venus, but in addition it was generally small, plump, and dimpled. It was soft but not flabby and had short, smooth fingers and a short, flexible thumb.

You can see how such a hand would emphasize all of the spontaneous warmth and love of luxury associated with a full Mount of Venus. (It's interesting to note that this type of hand nearly fits the description of an endocrine type of the same general sort described in Charlotte Wolff's *The Hand in Psychological Diagnosis,* p. 22.)

THE LIFE-LINE

The boundary of the Mount of Venus nearest the palm is the life-line, which many people consider (quite mistakenly) an indicator of the exact length of one's life. At one time people thought that if this line were short in both hands, its ending indicated the natural time when you would die. Even in the early days of palmistry, however,

SHORT LIFE LINE SHOWS LACK OF VITALITY AND OF INSTINCTIVE FORCE IF FOUND IN BOTH HANDS WITHOUT LINE OF FATE

A SHORT LIFE LINE IS NOT NECESSARILY OMINOUS

STRONG FATE LINE BEGINNING LOW IN PALM REPLACES THE MISSING PART OF THE LIFE LINE people believed that with a strong will (shown by a large thumb) or great attention to health, you could outlive your natural span of years.

Today, life insurance tables show that most of us outlive what the nineteenth century considered our natural span of years. Many people reading this book have had their lives saved by modern medical techniques and drugs. And many of us, without realizing it, have extended our life span through improved public sanitation.

Still, the life-line shows a lot about ourselves. For example, the man with a short life-line would do better to live by his wits than his brawn. And a life-line that appears short may actually be lengthened by a strong fate-line on the lower part of the hand.

Palmists often read the timing of events on the life-line. But while some palmists date our childhood years from that part of the line that lies under the index finger, others begin down near the wrist. Both seem to obtain fairly good results—a sure sign that dating events along the life-line is really a matter of intuition rather than science. You'll read more about this dating system in a later chapter.

Regardless of which end of the life-line represents childhood, it's interesting to note that all systems of dating assign the age of thirty-five to the same approximate spot— the center of the line as it runs from the edge of the hand under the index finger all the way down to the wrist. Islands or breaks in the line are supposed to show periods of physical or nervous stress (the age depends, of course, on whether you're reading up or down the line).

The life-line tells us a good deal about our temperament and vitality. We don't need to follow a system of dating to learn that a line with many breaks or islands

HARRY GOLDEN

When the life-line sends a branch toward the index finger, it shows ambition.

belongs to a person who needs to take care of himself and get plenty of relaxation.

If your life-line curves far out into your hand, you are a person of action. Even if the Mount of Venus is fairly flat, a far curving life-line is the sign of a physically vigorous person. On the other hand, a life-line that curves closely around the thumb indicates you prefer mental rather than physical activity.

Under the index finger, the life-line may be attached and close to the head-line above it: this is a sign of great caution. Again, the two lines may be widely separated at the start—a sign of rash independence and impulsiveness—or the lines may be only slightly separated, which indicates a more moderate form of independence.

If your life- and head-lines touch at the point of origin, you have a balanced nature. If your lines are joined for as much as a third the length of your head-line, you are timid. This is particularly true in a conic hand. In a square hand, it is a sign of caution.

When the life-line ends out in the hand near the Mount of Luna, it indicates restlessness.

If your life-line displays a branch extending to the top of the Mount of Jupiter (the mount under the index finger), you will probably attain success through your abilities and determination.

If your life-line near the wrist curves around the Mount of Venus toward the outside of the hand, you probably have deep love of home—like the Texan who keeps a little urn of Texas soil on his mantelpiece when he's far from the Lone Star State.

On the other hand, if your life-line is almost a diagonal line across your hand that passes quite close to the Mount of the Moon, you are extremely restless and probably have a strong desire to travel.

You have worries if all lines that cross the life-line from the Mount of Venus continue to the middle of your hand. When you have a great number of these lines, you are someone who worries so much that you sap your strength and impede much of the progress you might make.

Traditionally, these worry lines are supposed to indicate specific worries depending upon the line or mount where they end. People with many of these lines need an important interest upon which to concentrate their mental energy.

Branches rising from the life-line are called "lines of personal effort." The person with such lines is making a strong bid to improve his life.

Lines on the Mount of Venus parallel to the life-line are called "lines of influence." Hindu palmists in particular emphasize these lines. Each is supposed to represent a person who exercises an influence on your life, and the influence is in proportion to the proximity of the line of influence to the life-line.

This system appears to work, though perhaps only because people with many lines on the Mount of Venus need affection and are influenced by many people around them.

Lines that cross the life-line from the Mount of Venus show worries.

A line running beside the life-line and inside of it on the Mount of Venus (which is almost as clearly marked as the life-line) is called the Line of Mars. It is not a line of influence, and in general it appears to show more power of resistance in a hand with a badly marked life-line and tremendous vitality in a hand with a stronger life-line. We'll learn more about this line in a later chapter.

CHAPTER IX

ALL THUMBS

*"The gentle Norman barons would seem to have been im-
pressed with the importance of (the thumb) when they
hung up their enemies thereby."*
                                    —Stanislas d'Arpentigny.

The thumb shows more about you at a glance than any
other part of the hand. While the Mount of Venus shows
whether you are warm and fiery or cool and collected, and
the life-line shows physical vitality and resistance, the
thumb shows whether you can deliberately make the best
of all your talents and abilities or whether your success
will depend on chance.

The average thumb reaches half way up the lowest section of the index finger.

A large thumb belongs to a person who works out a plan
and, as far as his other abilities allow, either sticks to the
plan or changes it after careful consideration—the way a
map-maker might change a map if he discovered a mistake
in it. A large thumb is said, therefore, to go with a strong
will.

The person with a small thumb is ruled by instinct and
emotion. On a short-term basis, such a person may seem
more willful than someone with a long thumb since he is

more influenced by the whim of the moment than by any long-range plan. He has less self-control than the long-thumbed person and a weaker will. This person depends on chance and the help of other people. With talent and intelligence, this person can be extremely successful, but he will succeed by fits and starts of inspiration rather than by any single-minded drive.

Small thumb belongs to the person ruled by emotion.

Women are inclined to have shorter thumbs than men, and most of the old jokes about women are aimed at the short-thumbed variety. For example, there's the old story about women in business: if you treat them like women, they get the better of you, and if you treat them like men, they cry.

The shape of the thumb and length of each section is important. Here's what it shows about you:

A long, broad tip section and short palm section are the

HEART, HEAD AND LIFE LINES START TOGETHER IN LEFT HAND—
NATURAL FEARLESSNESS

HEAD LINE AND LIFE LINE RUN PARTLY TOGETHER IN RIGHT HAND—
DEVELOPED CAUTION

(RIGHT HAND PRINT)

HEART LINE

HEAD LINE

HEAD LINE

LIFE LINE

INTUITION LINE (LEFT HAND PRINT)

LIFE LINE

TREMENDOUS, POWERFUL, WELL-SHAPED THUMBS ALWAYS BELONG TO REMARKABLE, DETERMINED PERSON.

Large thumb usually belongs to a person who goes by a plan and has strong will power. Sir Edmund Hillary's hands show will, plus caution and courage, that helped him conquer Mt. Everest.

signs of a steamroller will. If the tip section is slightly longer, look for some stubborness. If the tip section is much longer, you leap before you look and can't be reasoned with.

A *long palm section and short tip section* mean that you're better at giving advice than acting decisively. This might be called the "Hamlet" thumb since people who have it tend to go on thinking about what they ought to do until after they should have done it. They reach well-thought-out conclusions and their advice is likely to be good.

Two sections of the thumb of equal length with the palm section possibly slightly longer than the tip section means good equilibrium between knowing your own mind and doing something about it.

A *broad and stocky thumb of normal length* shows endurance, patience and stability.

A *waisted palm section* means tact (unless the tip section is overpoweringly larger).

A *long, slender thumb* shows a strong will and subtlety —the iron hand in the velvet glove.

A *marble-like tip on the thumb* is a sign of erratic will and fitful temper. This feature is also associated with fits of the blues.

A *double-jointed thumb* that bends back almost at right angles shows adaptability and usually extravagance. Sometimes the extravagance is emotional rather than financial.

A *double-jointed thumb that bends back slightly* shows adaptability. You will see a double-jointed thumb on the hands of many theater people.

A *thumb that's both short and double-jointed* is the sign of an impressionable person.

A *pointed thumb* means that you're quick and impulsive.

A *conic thumb* indicates less will than a square thumb,

but more than a pointed one. If it is very long, it is a sign of will and tact.

A *square thumb* indicates common sense.

A *spatulate thumb* is a sign of impatience.

A *flat, broad thumb* shaped like a canoe paddle shows a strong will backed by nervous energy rather than physical strength. Sculptors and potters often have a thumb like this with a little bump of flesh showing a concentration of nerve endings on the palm side of the tip section.

*   *   *

By combining what you know about the thumb and the Mount of Venus, here's how you might answer the question so often put to hand-readers, "Will I marry and live happily ever after?"

—High or medium Mount of Venus and normal or slightly large thumb—probably.

—High or medium Mount of Venus and huge thumb—marry somebody who wants a boss.

—High or medium Venus and small thumb—be careful or you will marry in haste and repent at leisure.

—Flat, grilled Venus and large thumb—you need affection and have the perseverance to find it.

—Flat, grilled Venus and small thumb—marry the person with a high Venus and large thumb. You need love and a boss too.

—Low Venus with life-line running close to the large thumb—you'll marry because of mutual interests.

—Low, small Venus and small thumb—you'll marry for security or will be perfectly happy unmarried.

*   *   *

The position of your thumb is also important. Several positions have already been mentioned, but check with your hand prints to see how you normally hold your hand.

*Thumbs held at right angles to the hands show an open mind;
in a bad hand, lack of self-discipline.*

A thumb held very wide, almost at right angles to the
hand, shows an extremely open mind. Hindu palmistry
says that the thumb opened at a 90° angle from the hand
is the sign of a balanced soul.

The normal angle between the thumb and hand is from
about 45° to 60°—a medium position. Self-reliant people
usually have this angle.

If you hold your thumb any closer to your hand, you
are a cautious person, usually set in his ways and sometimes secretive.

If your thumb is bent as though it were stooping to look
shorter, you are probably tense and lack self-confidence
to such an extent that you are sometimes anti-social and
hard to deal with. Like the turned-in thumb, this may
reflect a temporary state of mind.

A slightly turned-in thumb combined with the long, little finger that shows cleverness may belong to a person
who manages to compensate for any lack of confidence. A
successful business woman I know with a hand like this
does "dry runs" before every important appointment in
that part of her city that's not familiar to her. She makes
a trip during her lunch hour to the new address to be sure

*Held at a medium angle (45°-60°) to the hand, the thumb
suggests self-reliance.*

she knows how to get there and how long it will take.
Then she can arrive for the business appointment relaxed
and on time.

Sometimes you'll see a hand print in which a thumb of
normal length seems to be straining upward together with
the index finger. The owner of this hand is making a tremendous effort to carry out his plans. He is tense because

he senses that he is pushing himself beyond his strength.

The "best" thumb for any hand is the one that's in proportion to the rest of the hand.

A broad, firm, bulging hand with only an average thumb still shows plenty of drive.

STUBBORNNESS—
THUMB TIP LONGER
THAN LOWER
SECTION.

LARGE
THUMB—·
STRONG WILL

THUMB SET LOW
ON HAND — LOVE OF
INDEPENDENCE

A slender, sensitive-looking hand needs a slightly longer thumb—almost (but not quite) to the first knuckle of the index finger—if the person is to have the push and perseverance to turn his dreams into realities.

The extremely mobile thumb—one that offers no resistance when you bend it this way and that—shows inner flexibility and often extravagance.

The very stiff thumb, which can hardly be bent out of

its natural position, belongs to a dogmatic person. Don't waste your breath trying to make him change his mind.

Of course, a large thumb is not a talisman that insures perseverance. In a clumsy hand with tortuous-looking lines or almost no lines, this thumb shows a potentiality that for some reason you can't use.

CHUNKY, BALL-LIKE END OF THUMB SHOWS TEMPER WHEN AROUSED.

REASON.

WAISTED REASON PHALANX SHOWS TACT

LIFE LINE

The small thumb sometimes belongs to people who spend their lives helping others.

A person whose abilities must be consciously controlled —anyone whose work requires stick-to-itiveness—needs a thumb of normal or large size in order to succeed.

Those whose gifts are a welling-up from the subconscious may be successful by force of their talents without long thumbs—hence, the short thumb is sometimes found on the successful artist, wife, or missionary.

WIDE
SPACE
AT BASE·
BETWEEN
FINGERS—
MONEY RUNS
THROUGH
YOUR FINGERS

FATE

TIP OF
THUMB
BENDS BACK—
EXTRAVAGANCE

Back-bending thumb-tip goes with adaptability as well as extravagance. Latter is emphasized by other signs.

CHAPTER X

"PUSH"
AND THE BRAINS TO USE IT

"He who enjoys doing and enjoys what he has done is happy."
—Goethe.

The Mount of Active Mars (often called Lower Mars because it is below the head-line) is often treated as part of the Mount of Venus. It is located at the base of the thumb but above the Mount of Venus.

Both mounts together—Venus and Mars—indicate emotional warmth. But when the Mount of Mars is firm and bulges, this warmth takes the form of energy, push and combativeness. A true fighter will have bulges on both this combative Mount of Mars and the Mount of Passive Mars (on the other side of the hand).

The line of Mars, which starts on the Mount of Active Mars, looks like a double life-line. If the mount is high, this line indicates even greater physical resistance and a tendency to fight for what you want. Tradition has it that this line spells success in love for women and success in war for men. President Eisenhower has the line of Mars.

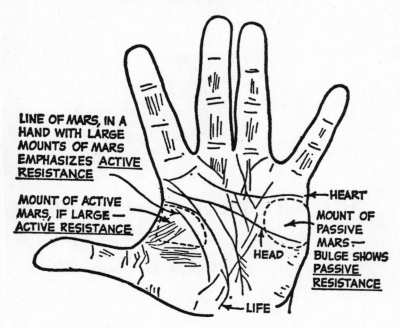

LINE OF MARS, IN A HAND WITH LARGE MOUNTS OF MARS EMPHASIZES <u>ACTIVE RESISTANCE</u>

MOUNT OF ACTIVE MARS, IF LARGE — <u>ACTIVE RESISTANCE</u>

←HEART

MOUNT OF PASSIVE MARS — BULGE SHOWS <u>PASSIVE RESISTANCE</u>

HEAD

LIFE

Active Mars shows constructive energy as well as active resistance.

THE HEAD-LINE

In a practical hand, the head-line will run across the hand, touching the life-line at the top boundary of the Mount of Active Mars. Then it will cross the plain of Mars and touch the lower part of the Mount of Passive Mars directly across the hand. One of the reasons why this line runs fairly straight is because the practical or useful hand is more flexible horizontally than vertically.

Basically there are two types of head-lines: the one that barely slopes and the other that slopes quite a bit. The former slopes only slightly and crosses from active to passive Mars. It is often found on a broad, practical hand, and even in a long, slender, sensitive hand it shows a streak of practicality. The go-getter has high Mounts of Mars with this line. If your Mounts of Mars are low and your thumbs large, you are less aggressive and more thoughtful but still a person of action.

The second type of head-line slopes, sometimes drastically. It may run almost all the way down to the wrist. This sort of line is likely to be found in a long, slender hand, partly because a sensitive hand is likely to be vertically flexible with many more up-and-down or sloping lines.

Even in a broad, practical hand this sort of head-line

ONE STRAIGHT HEAD LINE PLUS ONE BRANCHED HEAD LINE SHOW A PERSON TORN IN TWO DIRECTIONS

LEFT HAND PRINT

HEART LINE

HEAD LINE BRANCH TO MOUNT OF APOLLO SHOWS VERY STRONG LOVE OF BEAUTY

APOLLO

HEAD LINE STRAIGHT ACROSS HAND SHOWS PRACTICAL STREAK

HEAD LINE BRANCH TO MOUNT OF LUNA SHOWS HUGE INFLUENCE OF IMAGINATION

LUNA

LIFE LINE

The very imaginative head-line slopes sharply. A fork at the end of any head-line shows ability to see two sides of any situation.

reveals a strong note of sensitivity and imagination. This sloping line crosses the plain of Mars, but in extreme cases it will not touch either mount. In its most sloping form, it is often found in hands that lack any padding on the Mounts of Mars—indicative of the person who finds it difficult to push ahead or do anything useful with his ideas, however good they may be.

When you see this sloping line in a forceful hand with developed Mounts of Mars and a large thumb, you can assume that the person is likely to be both imaginative and productive. Instead of day-dreaming, he writes novels or poems. If he thinks up an invention, he'll try it out.

Aside from its general direction, the line may be either very straight or somewhat curved. A slight curve goes with a more flexible mind. A head-line straight as a ram-rod suggests a calculating person.

You may have heard that the length of this line indicates your intelligence. It would be nice if it were that simple. The head-line tells you many things about your thinking, but it won't reveal your I.Q. You must study your whole hand to find that answer. Then you can draw only a very general conclusion. If the shape and markings of your

STAR ON MOUNT OF JUPITER— PROBABLE <u>SUCCESS</u>

HEAD LINE

A branch of the head-line to Jupiter shows ambition. With a star at the end, it shows probable success.

hand have a look of style and vitality, you are doubtless quite intelligent. The head-line in such a hand is usually long. But in the hands of idiots it can be long.

What is the meaning of the different starting places for the head-line?

When it begins on the Mount of Jupiter and curves back near the life-line—ambition and a balance between independence and caution (a good sign for an actor or politician).

With a branch to Jupiter—ambition.

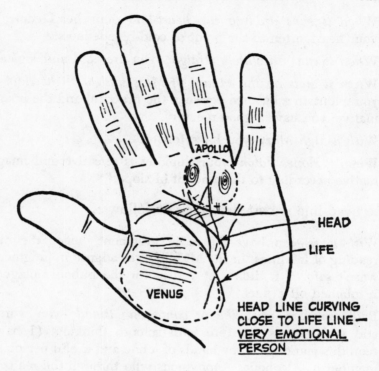

HEAD LINE CURVING CLOSE TO LIFE LINE— VERY EMOTIONAL PERSON

Slightly separated from the life-line—independence of thought, slight impulsiveness.

Widely separated from the life-line—impulsiveness to the point of rashness.

Curving across the life-line down into the Mount of Mars or with a strong branch curving down—perseverance in fighting your own shortcomings, sometimes a tendency to quarrel.

The signs connected with the progress of the head-line can be summarized as follows:

When it runs up into a mount or curves up toward a mount —that mount exercises an overwhelming influence on your mind.

When it runs up into the heart-line—your head controls your heart, often to the point of cold-bloodedness.

When it runs absolutely straight—you are cold and logical.

When it ends on the Mount of Mars with a slight slope—you maintain a balance between the practical and the imaginative; you have a good memory.

With a high Mars—you have fortitude.

When it slopes down—your thinking is sensitive and imaginative according to the amount of slope.

The head-line is best described as follows:

With gaps—you have lapses in judgment, hence the old reading of fatalities. In the Middle Ages a lapse in judgment wasn't safe. If it didn't let you in for the bubonic plague, it touched off a duel.

Badly marked, chainlike or containing islands—you worry and your nerves interfere with smooth thinking. (I have seen this marking on the hands of a fine and useful person, a member of Alcoholics Anonymous who through the realization of his own shortcomings and the desire to help others leads a satisfying life).

Wavering—you are pulled this way and that by desires and feelings. The quality of the mount under which the line bulges shows too much influence on your life; the quality of the mount under which the line dips shows a bad influence.

The length of your head-line is important:

The long line shows that you have a versatile mind. A long line is one that ends beyond the ring finger.

A *short line* ending under or almost under the long middle finger suggests a one-track mind. This sign has a more emphatic meaning in a long hand than a broad one.

DO YOU HAVE REMARKABLE INSIGHT?
—YOGI SACHIN MAJUMDAR

"MYSTIC CROSS"—
ADEPT IN
MYSTICAL
PHILOSOPHY

RING OF
SOLOMON—
NATURAL
ABILITY TO
UNDERSTAND
PEOPLE
INCLUDING
YOURSELF

LINE
OF SUN

HEAD
LINES

TWO
WELL-MARKED HEAD
LINES—REMARKABLE
POWER OF MIND

Sachin Majumdar

The double head-line is sometimes found in the hands of people who are both practical and adept in mystical philosophy. Cheiro had a double head-line.

And here is the interpretation of some unusual head-lines:

Double head-line—the old-fashioned reading of this was "luck in money matters." A later reading points up the qualities of versatility, command of language and the power

ARE YOU AN UNUSUAL PERSON?

JOINT HEAD AND HEART
LINE PLUS LARGE
THUMB-<u>POWER</u> <u>OF</u>
<u>CONCENTRATION</u>

←APOLLO

<u>EXPRESSIVENESS</u>

HEART AND
HEAD LINES
JOINED INTO
ONE —
<u>UNUSUAL</u> <u>PERSON</u>

LUNA

to analyze people. This line is generally found in the hands of people who lead two distinctly different lives or follow two fields of activity in which they reveal different sides of their nature or even opposite talents.

Head- and heart-line in one line—always the sign of an unusual person; if you have a large thumb, you have tremendous powers of concentration.

The space between head and heart lines is called the Quadrangle—

If the space between the head-line and the heart-line above it (called the quadrangle) is wide, it indicates broadmindedness; if your quadrangle is narrow, you are strict and set in your ideas. I don't mean that a man with a narrow quadrangle is conventional, but he has his own fixed ideas and sticks to them. I have seen a narrow quadrangle on the hands of an inflexible radical who prided himself on his "tolerant" mind.

CHAPTER XI

THE MAN WITH THE POWER

"Life consists not in holding good cards but in playing those you do hold well."
                                          —Josh Billings.

Below the index finger is the Mount of Jupiter, which is above the Mount of active Mars and divided from it by the life-line. Like all the mounts, this one is named to help you remember it—Jupiter was the ruler of the Roman gods.

This mount and the finger above it show how you wish to deal with other people. Do you want to govern them by running for political office, influence their minds or boss them around? Or maybe you just want to live and let live. Whatever the answer, it will show up on your Mount of Jupiter.

First, let's start with the extremes. A well padded or marked Mount of Jupiter and a long, strong index finger backed up by a large thumb and widely curving life-line are the marks of a born leader. How long is a long, strong index? You have to depend partly on your eye, but the normal length for the index extends to the middle of the tip section of your middle or longest finger (in comparing fingers, it is somewhat more accurate to measure from the back). A very long finger, called the "Forefinger of

Napoleon," will be longer than the ring finger. Fewer than ten persons in a hundred have a finger this long.

A short index with a flat, unmarked Mount of Jupiter shows a desire to take a back seat. Sometimes it indicates a lack of self-respect, especially if the finger is very short —for example, if it reaches the beginning of the tip section of the middle finger.

Either a long, strong, out-leaning finger or a high or much lined mount under it shows a desire to lead in some way. Usually these signs are accompanied by a normal thumb. If the thumb is small, you know immediately that the person has a problem: he desires to lead without the strength of purpose to carry through his plans. The general markings on your hand will show whether or not the problem is serious.

If you hold your hand tensely and your lines look tortured, it is indeed disturbing.

This combination of a long index and short thumb appeared in the beautifully marked hands of a teacher who intended to become a nun. She felt that what she had to offer could only be developed once she had the spiritual support of a group as well as her personal religion.

This brings us to another quality that goes with a well developed Mount of Jupiter—a strong feeling for religion, a sense that power should be spiritual as well as worldly. This is emphasized in hands with conic or pointed fingers.

If your Mount of Jupiter under your index finger is roundly padded or has several rising lines, a well marked star or a trident on it, you possess the creative power of leadership and a desire to influence other people.

A developed mount and a short index finger are sometimes found in a hand with a long ring finger, suggesting that this person wants to assert himself through self-expression rather than through any sort of ordinary leadership.

An undeveloped mount with a long, strong finger is the sign of an ambitious person who is extremely active but not inclined to originate any new ways of doing things. As a committee chairman, he would preside effectively but not make many suggestions.

Left from the link of palmistry with astrology is the description of the "Jupiterian Hand." The Mount of Jupiter may actually be found developed in many shapes of hands, but, as you will see, the hand shape called "Jupiterian"

MOUNT OF
JUPITER

When Jupiter is set high on the hand, it emphasizes ambition.

JUPITER

CROSS UNDER
FINGER OF JUPITER
—TRADITIONALLY
BELIEVED TO SHOW
HAPPY MARRIAGE

would be especially likely to belong to a quick-thinking, practical and ambitious man—the kind who might become a recognized leader.

The "Jupiterian Hand" is thick and massive with fairly long but thick, smooth, square-tipped fingers. The index finger alone is conic-tipped. The thumb ranges from normal to large with a large tip section. Both Mounts of Mars are fairly large, giving the palm a somewhat circular shape. The palm is pale red. Of course, it goes without saying that the mount and finger of Jupiter are large. An intellectual variation of the "Jupiterian Hand" might be paler with lower Mounts of Mars.

Because of its massiveness and thick fingers, this hand indicates a love of comfort and plenty, usually associated with a highly developed Mount of Jupiter.

While the size of the mount and finger of Jupiter indicates your degree of ambition and your leadership potential, the shape, position and divisions of your forefinger tell us more subtle things about the sphere in which you hope to be influential and the quality of your influence.

Old English books call the index the "showing finger." A long index means that you like to point things out to others. A straight index means that you see things in proper perspective and can point them out clearly to others. Your attitude toward life and the world around you is well balanced.

A very slight inward bend in both your index and little finger is normal. The crooked finger has a pronounced curve and shows a less balanced view of the world.

This may be confusing because a crooked index is often found on the hands of clever and able people. One reading interprets this bent finger as a sign of shrewdness in realizing ambitions. It is often the finger of the expert who has been defined as "a man far from home who knows more and more about less and less." The expert doesn't always have a well-rounded view of the world, because he may be so busy studying his own field that he may neglect to study anything else. He may still be an extremely useful and clever person. He is very shrewd in his own field.

In a clumsy hand with scrambled lines, the crooked index shows a decidedly unbalanced view of the world and hence misguided ambition. A man with such an index may find that his "success" consists of having almost enough money to pay the bills he wouldn't have if he weren't so "successful."

If the tip section of your index finger is the longest of the three inside sections, you want to be a leader in some abstract and idealistic way. You want to influence the ethics or ideals of those around you rather than influence their actions directly. This might be the hand of the religious reformer or the abstract intellectual.

If the middle section of your finger is the longest, you want to influence other men's actions directly. Your ambitions might be political.

If your palm section is by far the longest (it is often slightly longer than the other two), your ambitions are very down-to-earth. You want personal power and the symbol of it—money. You want to be boss. If the sections are balanced, the balance is reflected in your thinking.

SOLOMON'S RING

The Ring of Solomon, the line associated with the Mount of Jupiter, also shows that you have the power to understand and influence other people. This power seems to be both intuitive and intellectual and the line usually accompanies a high intelligence (lack of the "ring" certainly doesn't suggest a low intelligence).

In its strongest form, the "ring" goes all the way around the index finger and is marked on the back of the hand as well as the front. Sometimes it is a double or triple ring.

According to the old reading of this line, the subject had a talent for occult studies. It was also called a sign of divination.

The name "Ring of Solomon" is a reminder of the ancient days when hand-reading was related to magic. In the mythology of magic, Solomon was regarded as probably the greatest magician of all time, and he was said to have been the first to collect many of the spells and charms listed in the *grimoires* or grammars of magical procedure.

Stories say he had a ring of brass and iron joined together, engraved with a magical seal and set with the jewels of the angels of the four elements. By means of

ARE YOU PERSUASIVE?
— LISTER HILL

"RING" OF INTUITION IN UNDERSTANDING PEOPLE

WAISTED THUMB-TACT

BULGE OF IMAGINATION

HEART LINE

HEAD LINE

When these signs combine with the Ring of Solomon, as in Sen. Lister Hill's hand, persuasiveness is suggested.

this ring, he subdued spirits and made them do his bidding. It also gave him the power to understand the speech of birds and animals.

If you have the Ring of Solomon on your hand, you won't be able to understand the songs of the birds, but through intelligence and intuition you'll understand not only what people say, but much of what they leave unsaid.

CHAPTER XII

YOUR FATE AND WEIGHT

"As knowledge increases, wonder deepens."
—Charles Morgan.

Next to the Mount of Jupiter and under the long middle finger is the Mount of Saturn. Medium high or marked with one or two well formed lines and combined with a large middle finger (or a middle finger that draws the other fingers toward it), this mount shows a studious or philosophic turn of mind and a love for the solitude of nature. The Saturnian is also inclined to be a cautious person, and he is often a skeptic.

If this mount is high or covered with a number of disorderly lines, or if the finger above it is large and massive—out of all proportion to the other fingers—it indicates fits of depression. It also suggests someone who may be so preoccupied with bookish interests that he doesn't take the time to be orderly.

It must have been a Saturnian who said, "He who spends his time reading books has a disorderly attic." Abraham Lincoln, who has been called Saturnian, used to leave his law office in Illinois so messy that seeds sprouted in the dust.

You will often see that the mounts of Saturn and Jupiter are high, padded and linked together. Add a large thumb, and you have all the signs of the active philosopher, the man who wants to convince others of his philosophy or get ahead in the world through serious studies. If you find this combination of Saturn and Jupiter with a small or bent-in thumb, it is a likely sign of morbid pride.

If your middle finger is extremely short and pointed, you may be irresponsible. A normal finger is about half a tip section taller than the ring and index fingers. A slightly shorter finger may suggest someone who depends more on intuition than intellect. The short middle finger serves as a religious symbol, and is supposed to be one of the marks on the hands of Buddha.

Few of us ordinary mortals have such infallible intuition that we can do without a somewhat developed intellect to steer us. So with ordinary mortals, a short middle finger (almost the same length as the index and ring) suggests a possible lack of balance.

A developed Mount of Saturn, high or marked with lines, is (as you might imagine) emphasized in a long, rectangular and bony hand that often has knotty fingers underlining an inward trend of mind and a philosophic streak.

This "Saturnian hand" is usually found on people who love science and such earthy, basically lonely pursuits as farming or mining. Intellectuals with this type of hand love to study philosophy or psychology and prefer classical music or progressive jazz to more popular music.

The funniest humor has a core of serious truth. When we find life bleak and depressing, we need to keep joking to bear life at all. Therefore, it's not surprising that many humorists are Saturnians.

Saturn may be found in a broad hand, especially in

combination with the Mount of Jupiter or the Mount of Mars.

The middle finger shows how studious or down-to-earth qualities are used: if the tip section is the longest, an

FINGER OF SATURN

WHEN ALL FINGERS LEAN TOWARD SATURN IN LONG, BONY HAND — SERIOUS, SOBER NATURE

KNOTS AT BOTH FINGER JOINTS SHOW NEED TO PROVE FACTS — IN "SATURNIAN" HAND, SKEPTICISM

FINGER OF MERCURY WHEN LONG — CLEVERNESS, GOOD BALANCE FOR SOBER NATURE

HEAD AND LIFE LINES START JOINED — EMPHASIZES CAUTION NATURAL TO "SATURNIAN" HAND

HEAD LINE

LIFE LINE

RIGHT HAND PRINT

interest in philosophy is evident; if the middle section, we note an interest in such useful studies as science or agriculture. When the palm section is the longest of the three, it's a sign of concentration and staying power—and sometimes avarice.

THE LINE OF SATURN (FATE-LINE)

Under the serious finger of Saturn is the most controversial line in hand-reading. Everyone believes it means something very important, but *what* does it mean?

Desbarrolles called this line, in its lengthy, well-marked form, a sign of good fortune. The born ruler was said to have it—straight as an arrow from his wrist to the center

ARE YOU A WORRIER?

SATURN →

GRILL OF LINES
UNDER FINGER
OF SATURN —
DEPRESSED
MOODS

HEART LINE

MEDIUM
SMALL
THUMB —
LACK OF
STRONG WILL

WAVERING
HEAD LINE —
WORRY MAKES
YOU THINK
LESS CLEARLY

GRILL HERE —
YOU ARE EASILY
IRRITATED

HEAD LINE BRANCH
DROOPING TO GRILLED
LINES ON MOUNT
OF LUNA —
WORRYING NATURE

RIGHT HAND PRINT

Tangle of disorderly lines under Saturn shows discouraged moods. Other signs of a tendency to worry are often found in the same hand.

of his Mount of Saturn. Cheiro said much the same thing, but he admitted that he once found such a line in the hands of a tramp. Both writers computed time on the fate-line, beginning with childhood near the wrist and ending with old age near the fingers.

DO YOU KNOW WHERE YOU'RE GOING?
—ELEANOR ROOSEVELT

KNOTS OF MENTAL ORDER

HAND FULL OF TRIANGLES— WELL-DEVELOPED SKILLS

LONG, WELL-MARKED LINE FROM BASE OF HAND TO BASE OF MIDDLE FINGER— CLEAR SENSE OF PURPOSE

Eleanor Roosevelt

Well-marked fate-line from wrist to middle finger is usually seen with other signs of self-assurance.

Other writers have thought that the fate-line represents inherited outer circumstances or social adaptability, or that it showed the naturally productive moments in a man's life.

In my experience, a well-marked fate-line shows a clear sense of purpose. It is almost always more clearly marked on a conic, philosophic or psychic hand than on an elementary or square hand. Yet the square-hander is often successful because he is practical, hard-working and inclined to aim for the goals that are accepted as normal and proper by the people around him. This would be a problem only if he grew up among people with a warped sense of direction.

Since a clear, well-marked fate-line shows a strong sense of purpose, you see it on the hands of many people who are successful, both in material ways and as human beings. A refugee I know has been driven from her home twice, but has come through the experience alive and a fine person. She has a long, well-marked fate-line.

Whatever the explanation, the traditional meanings for the fate-line seem to work very well. Here they are:

No fate-line—you can only achieve success through hard work.

A badly marked line—you suffer many ups and downs.

WHERE YOUR FATE-LINE BEGINS

The starting place of your fate-line is also important:

Starts inside the life-line—you succeed with the help of relatives. The person with this line often feels he has received too much help and hasn't been allowed freedom to develop during his youth.

Starts from the center of the palm near the wrist—you'll succeed through personal effort.

Starts from the Mount of Moon—you'll succeed through the help of those outside the family or you depend on the whim of the public. When your fate-line starts here, it emphasizes the imaginative area of your hand. Thus you often see it on the hands of writers, actors and others who depend for their success on the help of those who are less temperamental than they.

The line begins well above the wrist—on a long hand, this indicates no definite purpose until later in life, perhaps

FATE LINE

Wavy fate-line shows many changes due to its owner's uncertain sense of direction.

during your middle years. On a broad hand it has less meaning.

THE END OF YOUR FATE-LINE

The place where your fate-line ends is very significant:

If it ends low in your hand, below your head-line, with no new fate-line or "sun-line" under your ring finger beginning

Fate-line that starts and stops, then starts again in another place means (by tradition) a change.

above it: traditional reading—the end of smooth sailing because of mental blundering; latest reading—if your hand is long, you may have bumpy going because you have no purpose or plan; if it's broad, you will work out your own fate.

If your fate-line ends and a new line begins—this indicates

MIDDLE FINGERS HAVE FLARED OR SPATULATE TIPS—LOVE OF ACTION AND ORIGINALITY

FINGER TIP PRINTS HAVE WHORL IN SKIN RIDGES—ORIGINAL AND INDIVIDUALISTIC

HEAD LINE STARTS SLIGHTLY SEPARATED FROM LIFE LINE—GO-AHEAD SPIRIT OF SELF-ASSURANCE

FINGERS SET IN ALMOST STRAIGHT LINE ACROSS PALM—SWASHBUCKLING SELF-ASSURANCE

HEAD

LIFE

THICK, STRONG THUMB—DETERMINATION

ABSOLUTELY SQUARE PALM—STRONG SENSE OF ORGANIZATION AND ORDER

The hand with virtually no fate-line may show other qualities that lead to success.

a change; if it ends high on a mount (traditional meaning), you will enjoy smooth sailing right through old age.

Ends on the Mount of Jupiter—your life is ruled by ambition; you will probably succeed.

OTHER DISTINCTIVE MARKS

A fate-line cut by many horizontal lines from the Mount of Venus—you'll have a bumpy ride through life because you are inclined to worry about this and that.

A wavy fate-line—your life will undergo constant changes; many small lines rising from your fate-line—you are hopeful and ambitious.

Many small downward lines—you are easily discouraged; when branches from your fate-line extend to a mount or the line rises high in your hand and then curves toward the mount—you will use your abilities as indicated by the mount, for example:

Jupiter, ambition;
Saturn, serious studies;
Apollo (under your ring finger),
          self-expression;
Mercury (under your little fin-
          ger), practical clever-
          ness.

CHAPTER XIII

STYLE AND PERSONALITY

"To the question 'what is art?' we answer: 'That whereby forms are transmuted into style.'"
—André Malraux.

When the Mount of Apollo (under the ring finger) is high, crowned with a star or marked with one or two straight clear lines, it promises a sense of style.

If you have a developed Mount of Apollo, then whatever you do—whether you sell cheese, recite Shakespeare, paint pictures or rob banks—you act in a stylish, dashing way. You are a spontaneous person. If you are smart, people describe you as brilliant. A not-so-smart person with this mount may be dashing or, at the very least (and worst), flashy.

The high Mount of Apollo signifies a great love of the beautiful and colorful, the ability to enjoy life and to convey that joy to others.

If your ring finger or finger of Apollo is longer than your index finger, you may be more interested in enjoying and sometimes creating the beauty around you than in dominating other people. When combined with a short thumb, the long ring finger indicates someone who finds

Star under the ring finger goes with a sense of style.

harmonious and beautiful surroundings as necessary as
food and drink.

If you have a long ring finger (especially one with a
high or starred Mount of Apollo beneath it) combined
with a long thumb, you like to use your brilliance crea-
tively—act, paint, write or do any job where success depends on dazzling the people with whom you deal.

A long ring finger, almost as long as the middle finger
and considerably longer than the index, usually goes with
artistic "temperament." Maria Callas has a long ring finger
like this.

Especially when it is joined with a short thumb, the
long ring finger hints at a tendency toward gambling—a
double-or-nothing turn of mind. With a long thumb, the
gambler has a better chance to win.

DO YOU HAVE HIDDEN TALENT?

APOLLO TIP WITH WHORL
FINGERPRINT—ORIGINALITY
IN EXPRESSION

NEAR APOLLO FINGER
IS SKIN RIDGE
WHORL OR
"SHELL"

APOLLO

APOLLO
LINE

APOLLO
LINE

HEAD LINE

LIFE LINE

LUNA

LUNA

LEFT
HAND
PRINT

RIGHT HAND PRINT

LONG APOLLO LINE SHOWS REAL FLAIR
IF IT'S LONGEST IN THE LEAST-USED
HAND — RESERVES OF TALENT YOU
HAVEN'T EVEN USED YET.

Producer-playwright George Abbott has creative talent marked in his hands by Apollo lines from the Mount of Luna and by "shell" markings on the Apollo mounts.

The importance of the mount and finger is emphasized in a hand whose whole form shows spontaneity and love of beauty and receptivity.

The hand is usually almost conic, but sometimes the fingertips are square. The Mount of Venus is inclined to be large, giving an oval shape to the palm. The fingers may have the knots of order nearest the palm but, beyond these, they are smooth. The thumb is usually turned out at the tip because most stylish, dashing people are adaptable and at least a little bit extravagant.

If the tip section of your ring finger is much longer than the other two sections, you love ideal beauty.

When your middle section is the longest, you have the ability to use your sense of style practically.

If your palm section is long and fleshy, you probably love luxury.

SHORT THUMB—
YOU MAKE OTHERS
FEEL IMPORTANT

SMALL HAND—THINKS BIG,
LIKES TO IGNORE DETAILS,
VOLATILE

LONG RING FINGER
PLUS SHORT THUMB
BELONGS TO
GAMBLER OR
WOMAN WHO
LIKES TO DEPEND
ON A MAN

NORMAL LENGTH
OF THUMB COMES UP
TO HERE

RING OF
SOLOMON
INTUITION
ABOUT
PEOPLE

MANY LINES
UNDER RING
FINGER—
VERSATILITY

HEART LINE

HEAD LINE

LINES ON LUNA
—RESTLESS
IMAGINATION

VENUS

LUNA

(RIGHT HAND PRINT)

Short thumb plus long ring-finger usually belongs to a gambler. In a feminine hand, this combination leads to the woman who likes to lean on a man.

The crooked ring finger suggests a kink in your ability to enjoy life. Sometimes it belongs to a person who gives up his own personal enjoyment for others.

When your ring and middle finger lean toward each other, it suggests a conflict between your sense of serious responsibility and desire for self-expression and the spontaneous enjoyment of life.

POSSIBLE TIPS ON THE RING FINGER

What kind of tip do you have on your ring finger?

Square—sense of form and line; are you an architect or a builder?

Conic—you are quickly inspired.

Pointed—your sudden inspirations strike like lightning.

Spatulate—you have a talent for expressing yourself dramatically, in pantomime, etc. Are you an actor, by any chance?

THE APOLLO OR SUN-LINE

Under the Apollo finger and mount, which show style, is one of the happiest lines you can have—the Apollo line or, as it was traditionally called, the luck-line. When

APOLLO

LINE OF APOLLO
OR SUN LINE
STARTING
ON MOUNT
OF MARS—
WILLINGNESS
TO FIGHT FOR
AMBITIONS.

MOUNT OF
MARS

clearly marked, this line is a symbol of self-realization. It seems to go with the mind's intuitive and creative power.

You find the Apollo line on the hands of writers who can always express exactly what they mean or business-men who always seize the right opportunity with such seeming ease that it looks like luck.

A long, well-marked Apollo line doesn't necessarily belong to someone rich or famous, but if his hand is well-balanced he has the intuitive power to achieve his deepest

Line of Apollo from the heart-line shows creative power if combined with a well-marked fate-line lower in the hand.

personal desires. In a distorted hand, it merely signifies a desire to show off.

The Apollo line is frequently unmarked on a broad hand. This person succeeds through steady, hard work rather than brilliant flashes of inspirations.

STARTING PLACES FOR THE APOLLO LINE

The wrist—some form of artistic talent.

The Mount of Moon—you show you are blessed with a creative imagination; actors who can "create" a part often have this line.

The Mount of Mars—you show a willingness to struggle for self-fulfillment.

The center of the hand—(traditional reading) you'll succeed after some tribulation.

The heart-line—this is the usual place for the line to start, and it means that you'll enjoy success after hard work.

ENDING OF THE APOLLO LINE

The Apollo line always ends near the base of your ring finger. If it curves toward the middle finger or sends a branch there, it shows the influence of wisdom. If it curves toward your little finger, you will use your talents in a practical way.

OTHER ASPECTS OF THE APOLLO LINE

More than three lines on your Mount of Apollo suggest a Jack-of-all-trades and master of none.

A well-marked star at the end of the line suggests creative ability and style—a winning combination. A trident at the end has the same meaning.

AN OLD TRADITION

If you have three lines on the mount, you will never lack money.

CHAPTER XIV

THAT EXTRA SOMETHING

"Take him up on top of the mountain, tie him to a tree, and he'll come back with ten dollars."
—North Carolina mountain saying.

The Mount of Mercury under the little finger endows a man with that "extra something"—the sure insight of the investor who beats the market; the flash of understanding that gives the scientist a new answer before he even realizes how he discovered it; the quick wit of the debater.

Like the Mount of Apollo, the Mount of Mercury signifies intuitive abilities; but they differ in the way you use them. The large or well-marked Mount of Mercury belongs to the man of the world. He is shrewd, and unless he has the Mount of Apollo too (a common combination), he would rather use his eloquence to win legal cases or an election than write poetry. Science appeals to him as a practical way in which to use his intuitive gifts. He can be a very successful businessman.

If you wanted one word for the Mount of Mercury, it would be "clever." If the mount juts out at the side of the hand, the owner of a sensitive hand would have the sort of quicksilver mind that would make him not only clever but unpredictable. This jutting-out in a practical hand underlines intuitive business sense.

As you might expect, the Mount of Mercury plays an important role in hands with fairly short, often smooth

ARE YOU A NATURAL DETECTIVE?
DR. SIGMUND SPAETH

FINGERS LONG WHEN MEASURED FROM THE BACK

CLEVER INVESTIGATOR HAS LONG LITTLE FINGER

INTUITION LINE

YOU LOOK INTO DETAILS

LARGE THUMB— STICK-TO-ITIVENESS

Sigmund Spaeth

Long little finger lends the support of cleverness to any other qualities shown in the hand.

fingers that emphasize quick thinking. The palm is often long and shaped like a top-heavy trapezoid.

It is the long little finger that makes the Mount of Mercury important, even when it is flat. The finger also tells us how you exercise your cleverness. The long little finger, even with a low or flat mount, belongs to an expressive person. He can find the right word or, more

CURVED LITTLE
FINGER—
SHREWDNESS

correctly, the right hundred words to express himself. If he is an actor, he can, as the expression goes, "act with his back."

The long little finger with a high mount indicates shrewdness, exceptional wit and tact. If the little finger is very long (if it extends as far as the nail of the ring finger) you should be on the alert—this person can deceive you.

Unless it is set very low on the hand, a long little finger is one that reaches the fingernail on the ring finger. Normally, your "Mercury" finger reaches the beginning line of the tip section of your ring finger. A short little finger would not extend that far.

A crooked finger with a high mount belongs to a person who can easily fool the people around him. Such a person may be a detective or intelligence agent or a crook. A slightly crooked finger emphasizes shrewdness without hinting at underhand practices.

A short finger with a high mount is in the hand of an impetuous and usually cheerful person. Together with a small, narrow Mount of Venus, it suggests someone who would be perfectly happy unmarried.

The low-set little finger is a sign of diffidence and shyness.

In a woman's hands you will often see a normal or even long little finger with a mount that juts out at the side of her hand. When she joins her fingers, her little finger and its mount are set so low that the finger *looks* short. The woman with such a little finger is both clever and shy. She's the sort who persuades her husband to see the mayor about a new public playground because she's shy about visiting him herself.

THE SECTIONS OF THE LITTLE FINGER

When your tip section is the longest, it means that you are eloquent or at least you love to talk.

When your middle section is the longest, you make practical use of your intuition and cleverness (are you a scientist?).

When your palm section is the longest, you are a shrewd customer and bear watching!

How is the tip of your little finger shaped?

If it's square, you love form.

If it's conic, you may be musical.

If it's pointed, you have a lightning wit.

If it's spatulate, you are probably inventive (are you a mechanic?).

AN OLD TRADITION

The horizontal lines on the side of the hand between the little finger and the heart-line below it indicate the number of times you will marry. If tiny vertical lines touch these horizontal lines, each means a child. The French call all the horizontal lines the "lines of sex appeal."

ANOTHER KIND OF LOVE

The heart-line begins at the outer edge of the hand below the Mount of Mercury. This line shows the ability to love, though not through an overflow of physical warmth, vitality and high spirits. That aspect of love is revealed on the Mount of Venus. Running, as the heart-line does, largely in the intuitive side of the hand, the heart-line shows the qualities of intuitive rapport and sympathy—the qualities of our emotions rather than the depth of our passions.

Normally the heart-line runs nearly as far below the ring finger as the length of the tip section of that finger. If it is much higher in the hand, it indicates that you lack subtlety and depth in your feelings. In other words, you are the sort of person who might sing, "I told you I loved you—now get out!"

If the heart-line is more or less straight, it suggests a more idealistic and mental type of love, like the couple who "looked adoringly at each other more than they kissed." If the heart-line has a definite curve, it suggests the opposite. These people need to express their love as concretely as possible.

HEART LINE SHORT—LACK OF STRONG EMOTIONS ABOUT FELLOW HUMANS

MARS

If this line is short, not running beyond the middle of the long middle finger, it suggests that love, for you, is not a matter of rapport and insight but either an overflowing of physical warmth, if the Mount of Venus is high, or a result purely of intellectual respect, if the head-line is long and well-marked.

At the other extreme, if your heart-line reaches all the way across your hand to the far side of the Mount of

Jupiter, you will feel the joys of great love but will also be at the mercy of your emotions.

If your heart-line ends under the center of your index finger, you are inclined to expect so much of the people

GIRDLE OF VENUS
SENSITIVITY

RING OF SATURN

UNUSUAL HEART
LINE ACROSS WHOLE
HAND, EDGE TO EDGE
— YOU ARE VERY
EMOTIONAL

GRILL

FATE

DOUBLE LIFE
LINE SHOWS
STRONG FEELINGS

LIFE LINES

RIGHT HAND PRINT

Other markings may emphasize the super-emotional nature of the person with a heart-line that embraces the whole hand. In a narrow hand, this suggests jealousy.

you love that you are frequently disappointed. When your friends fall off their pedestals, *you* are the one who gets hurt.

A heart-line that curves up between the index and middle fingers suggests a person who is realistic in his affection for other people and therefore usually happy in love.

When your heart-line ends in a number of forks, you are a warm-hearted and emotional person.

Heart-line that ends under the index finger belongs to a man who wants to idealize the people he loves.

When your heart-line joins the head- and life-lines, you are completely oblivious to danger. Desbarrolles describes people of your sort as the kind who walk along the edge of cliffs blindfolded. You incline toward extremes of intelligence—brilliance or feeble-mindedness.

Heart-line curving up between index and middle finger shows practical, realistic affections.

THE GIRDLE OF VENUS

Above the heart-line and more or less parallel to it is a line nearer the base of the fingers that sometimes circles the middle and ring fingers. This is the Girdle of Venus.

If you have this line, you are high-strung and emotionally responsive—qualities that can be good or bad, depending on how they are used. When this line is triple or quadruple, it means you have trouble controlling your emotions. Sometimes it indicates hysteria.

THREE MAIN LINES
JOINED SHOW
MAN WHO SITS
ON POWDER KEG
TO SMOKE

**GIRDLE OF
VENUS**

*Girdle of Venus, clearly marked in the hand of author Henry
Miller, is often found in the hands of writers and artists who
must feel things deeply in order to express them movingly.*

GIRDLE OF VENUS— SENSITIVITY

Double or triple Girdle of Venus belongs to a person who is too sensitive for his own comfort.

CHAPTER XV

STAYING POWER

"The art of living is more like that of wrestling than of dancing; the main thing is to stand firm and be ready for an unforeseen attack."

—Marcus Aurelius.

If your Mount of Mars, which is under the Mount of Mercury, is well padded in proportion to the rest of your hand, you have the power to bear up under difficulties, no matter how trying.

The quality of this mount is best illustrated by the ancient story of the poor couple who had such a beautiful and promising baby that they scraped together their pennies and went off to the soothsayer to find out what wonderful future lay in store for the child.

"When he's two," the soothsayer said, "he'll have measles; when he's eight, he'll have smallpox and lose his complexion; when he's fourteen, he'll scald himself and lose all his hair; and when he's eighteen, he'll marry the ugliest and poorest girl in the village."

"Won't anything wonderful happen to him?" the parents asked.

"Yes," said the soothsayer, "when he's twenty something very wonderful will happen. He'll get used to it."

When you can take your troubles calmly and bravely, you are a lucky person indeed.

If your Mount of passive Mars under Mercury is highly padded and the Mount of active Mars under Jupiter is also high, you are a person of action who gets what he wants by sheer energy, persistence and determination. You are a fighter.

If your hand brings out all the strongest qualities of the two Mounts of Mars, both passive and active, and suggests the indomitable fighter, it is firm and square-palmed with square-shaped fingers. The outside edge of your hand is

Both Mars high, many lines in the plain of Mars between them, plus other signs, add up to a violent temper.

ALL FINGERS AND THUMB
HELD CLOSE TOGETHER—
SHY CAREFUL NATURE

LOW-SET LITTLE
FINGER — SHYNESS

LOW, PASSIVE
MARS — IT'S
DIFFICULT FOR
YOU TO
ENDURE
HARDSHIPS

RIGHT HAND PRINT

Low mount of passive Mars is emphasized by other signs.

highly padded and forms a right angle at the base of the hand. Your fingers are big and probably stiff and straight. The Mounts of Mars and Venus are large. The lines in your hand are broad and red, and your palm is probably red. The Martian fighter is not always a boxer or soldier; he may be a crusading newspaperman.

The space between the two Mounts of Mars is called the Plain of Mars. If both mounts are high, the plain is full of disorderly lines and a number of lines are found on the passive mount, you'd better watch that temper of yours!

On the other hand, if your passive mount is high, firm and unlined, you are able to control your temper. And you can control it if you have a well-shaped thumb, preferably one that is slightly long.

CHAPTER XVI

IMAGINATION

"Exaltation is the going
Of an inland soul to sea."
—Emily Dickinson.

The Mount of Luna, located near your wrist on the side of your hand below the little finger, shows how imaginative you are and (to a certain extent) how you use your imagination.

Hand-readers list many qualities revealed by Luna, including daydreams, a love of the sea, a love of mystery, exaltation, a large vocabulary, contemplation, the creative spark of genius, lying, coldness and selfishness.

The imaginative person can create images and symbols within his own mind that seem almost as real as the objects he can touch and smell and taste and see. If he passes that "almost" point and his inner world becomes more real than the world around him, his imagination can make him cold and selfish. He may retreat into his own world of fancy and ignore other people. On the other hand, he may become so unable to see truth that he tells lies without even realizing it. Young children who are very imaginative often do this and are furious and hurt that their parents won't believe there really is a dragon waiting at the front door.

Fortunately, as we grow older, most of us can use our imaginations in a constructive way. Words are symbols for

LUNA

(RIGHT HAND PRINT)

In the long hand, imagination is usually shown by a long, kidney-shaped Mount of Luna marked by lines. By tradition, vertical lines show sea voyages.

things, and a large vocabulary depends on imagination, though not every imaginative person has a good vocabulary.

The day dreamer may dream about strawberry shortcake or the beautiful blonde who lives down the street, or he may compose novels or operas or paint pictures. A man who played the stock market had one of the largest Mounts of Luna I ever saw.

If your hand bulges noticeably in the Luna area or the mount is clearly marked by lines, you have a strong imagination. This is also true if the mount is red or one of the major lines of the hand crosses it. A skin whorl on the mount is the sign of an exuberant imagination.

If your Luna mount bulges near the wrist or most of its marks are down near the wrist, you have a kinesthetic imagination, one in which the images formed by your mind are likely to be in terms of physical feeling and movement. Very sensuous people and those who are attuned to such rhythms of nature as the tides and seasons have this kind of Luna.

If your Mount of Luna is most marked on the higher part of your hand that is nearer to Mars, your imagination is more sublimated.

The way you use your imagination is also shown by your other developed mounts and the general shape of your hand.

LONG, FLEXIBLE HAND

If you have a long, slender, supple hand, your receptive imagination is a great source of enjoyment. But for real fulfillment, you must constantly experience beauty in nature or art.

If your Luna is well-marked but does not bulge with high padding, you are probably an interpretive artist rather than a creator of new thought. You might be a fashion designer or a water-colorist. You probably have a knack for arranging flowers. In a hand such as yours, Luna is long and kidney-shaped and marked by lines.

If the mount is covered with a tangle of lines, the person with a receptive imagination finds it hard not to go over and over his worries in his mind's eye, as a squirrel goes around and around in a wheel. The mount marked by a few clear lines shows a happy use of the imagination.

In a hand with tangled lines, a branch of the head-line to Luna or strong markings on Luna show an overpowering imagination.

If Luna bulges noticeably, it is a sign of creative push. Many actors, for example, have long, slender hands with Luna and Venus bulging.

LONG, BONY HAND

If you have a long, bony hand with Luna highly developed, your strong imagination is still a source of escape and personal enjoyment. But a large thumb generally rides herd over it. Dreams and imaginings tend to be used as raw material for rationally decided projects. If the fingers have knots at both joints, the imagination finds its outlet in philosophy or science or some other field where system and order are more important than spontaneous inspiration. If Luna is flat but emphasized by lines, the owner of these knotty hands should avoid the inclination to express himself in a pedantic way, using long words even when it's clearer to use short words.

BROAD HAND

If you have a broad, firm, clearly marked hand, you are sure to put your imagination to practical use, especially if you have square fingers. You can cook imaginative and probably spicy dishes, paint pictures that sell or write clearly organized books. If you are in politics, you're working on new and better legislation.

If you have hands that are broad, fleshy and very soft with a well developed Luna, you are a daydreamer. But a large thumb indicates that you have the ability to turn dreams to practical use. Let's suppose that you have spatulate fingertips. This means that you are mentally active, though physically lazy.

If you have very small hands with a developed Luna, your imagination is strong, vivid, impulsive and usually original.

UNDERDEVELOPED LUNA

If your Luna is not curved out at the side of your hand or padded but is bony and flat, you may have so little imagination that it is hard for you to see the other fellow's point of view. Then you must guard against hurting others unintentionally through lack of insight.

However, you may be happier than the imaginative person because you will not feel that you are missing something out of life, and so you will have little desire for the unattainable.

If the Mount of Luna in the hand you use most has a lot of marks but the main lines are more clearly marked and the mount in your other hand is higher, you have had such painful experiences that you have retreated into the world of your imagination and neglected to develop your more active talents. If you take up some craft or art form as a hobby, you will begin to harmonize your activity and imagination.

LUNA INTENSIFIED

If you have short and smooth conic or pointed fingers, the Mount of Luna has much influence over your personality, as you might expect.

With a hand of this sort that is also soft, white and fleshy with a short thumb and fingertips so close as to overlap each other, the imagination is so strong as to be overwhelming. If you have a hand like this, you are a creature of whim and caprice. You must beware of becoming the victim of an overactive imagination.

These hands show imagination by their bulging Mounts of Luna. His is intensified by diagonal lines and shows active and restless imagination.

OTHER FACTS

A number of vertical or horizontal lines on the Mount of Luna indicate restlessness and a desire to travel. Traditionally, each is supposed to represent a voyage—vertical lines, a sea voyage; horizontal lines, a trip by land.

THE VIA LASCIVIA

A line across the Mount of Luna emphasizes sensitivity and restless imagination. If it crosses into the Mount of Venus, it shows a desire to escape. It is often found on the hands of the creative artist whose escape into his own imagination is translated into fiction or painting. It got its

DO YOU IMAGINE HORRORS?
CHARLES ADDAMS

LARGE THUMB — GOOD BALANCE FOR "VIA LASCIVIA," CAN MAKE WILD IMAGINATION AN ASSET

SATURN FINGER

HEPATICA

VERTICAL VIA LASCIVIA — LOVE OF EXCITEMENT

HORIZONTAL VIA LASCIVIA — CRAVING FOR ESCAPE

unfortunate name because it is also found on the hands of people who escape in less acceptable ways.

Another line parallel to the hepatica or health line is called the "Via Lascivia" by some authors. This line emphasizes nervous energy when well marked and usually goes with a love of excitement. Tortuously marked, it belongs to the over-excitable person who may easily become dissipated.

The Via Lascivia is best balanced by a large thumb. With such a thumb, in a well-marked hand, it emphasizes the artistic gift.

THE "MOONLIT" SIDE

Roughly speaking, the area of your hand from the thumb to the middle finger shows power for action and observation. The area between your middle and little fingers reveals the extent of your ability to feel, perceive and dream and sometimes sense things instinctively.

If your middle or Saturn finger leans at all, it slants toward the side of your hand that is most important in your life. In a practical hand, for example, when the middle finger leans toward your smallest digit, you have intuitive business acumen.

THE LINE OF INTUITION

The line that emphasizes the "moonlit" or intuitive side of the hand is called the line of intuition.

If you have a well-marked, curving line from Mercury to Luna, it suggests that your intuition is so strong that you probably possess some form of extra-sensory perception. A square-handed person with this line probably has strong hunches. If your hand is slightly long with conic or pointed fingers, you may even have prophetic dreams.

SMOOTH, CONIC-TIPPED
FINGERS — <u>MORE
INSPIRATION</u> THAN
LOGIC

RING OF
SOLOMON—
<u>INTUITION</u>

CURVED
LINE HERE
MEANS
<u>INTUITION</u>

*Curved intuition line under the little finger is seconded by
other signs of intuition.*

THE HEPATICA

A more or less straight line that slants up the side of the
hand from the life-line to Mercury or from Luna to Mercury is called the Hepatica or line of health. It is a sign of
good health whether it is clearly marked or non-existent.
When badly marked, it suggests sensitive nerves or **an**
improper diet.

Many talented performers like ballet star Edward Villella have a diagonal fate line beginning on the Mount of the Moon. Hence, the traditional reading: Success by pleasing the whim of the public. You'll find the same kind of fate line in the hands of Helen Hayes. (Original length of print 6-1/2 inches)

CHAPTER XVII

COMBINED MOUNTS

"The whole is more than the sum of the parts."

When certain mounts combine so that a section of the hand is emphasized, a special meaning is added.

We mentioned that the thumb side of the hand is related more to action, the little-finger side to perception. If the Mounts of Venus and Moon combine to emphasize the base of the hand, we have instinctive warmth and instinctive, earthy imagination. These usually combine to make for love of luxury, instinctive originality and spontaneity. It has been called the area of the instincts.

The two Mounts and Plain of Mars form another stripe across the hand. If it is the most developed part of your hand, you have a lot of practical "drive."

If your finger mounts are the most developed section of your hand, your mental energy is the key to your development. If your hand is broadest here, you have intellectual originality.

If your fingers are nearly as long as your palm, they emphasize the finger mounts even if these are not high or wide, particularly in a long hand. A hand shaped this way suggests the abstract thinker, especially if the fingertip

PERCEPTIVE SIDE

WHEN THE HIGHEST "MOUNTS" OR PADS OF
FLESH ARE ALL ON THE LITTLE FINGER
SIDE OF THE HAND—— YOU ARE GOVERNED
BY INTUITIVE "RADAR"

ACTIVE
SIDE

MANY BROKEN LINES IN HAND
SHOW INTUITION WILL ONLY WORK
IN CALM SURROUNDINGS, BUT NERVOUS
ENERGY TEMPS YOU TO HECTIC LIFE ——

*Most developed side of the hand shows whether you are more
active or perceptive. The lines show how best to follow your
natural bent.*

sections are long in comparison with the other sections.
If in addition you have smooth, conic or pointed fingers,
you may be such an idealist that you are constantly upset
by the cold, hard realities of life.

The highest mounts or those with the most markings do
not always form a large continuous area.

WHEN THE HIGHEST PADDING ON THE HAND
IS ACROSS THE BASE IT SHOWS YOU ARE
SENSUOUS, IMPULSIVE AND HAVE STRONG
BASIC INSTINCTS —

TURNED IN
THUMB —
LACK OF SELF
CONFIDENCE

MARS

MARS

Middle section of hand developed, or the two mounts and plain of Mars in a good hand, show practical push. Other signs—a bent-in thumb, for instance—may show that the ability to push ahead is limited by other character traits.

MOUNTS UNDER FINGERS COME TO PEAKS IN CENTER—— EMPHASIZE CLEVERNESS

BROAD—TOPPED PALM USUALLY HAS LARGE MOUNT OF MERCURY— QUICK UNDERSTANDING

HAND BROADEST ACROSS TOP OF PALM — CLEVER MIND

HEART LINE

HEAD LINE

TRAPEZOID OR SPATULATE PALM— WIDE AT TOP—PRACTICAL INVENTIVENESS

LIFE LINE

the top third of the palm is broadest, it emphasizes intellec- ual originality.

Here is a brief table of other mount combinations:

Most-Emphasized Mounts	Best Results	What to Beware of
Jupiter, Saturn	Wisdom in leadership or ambition in serious studies	Gloomy pride
Jupiter, Apollo	Style and ambition lead to development and use of talents	A desire to show off
Jupiter, Mercury	Ambition plus practical cleverness yield worldly success	Schemes to gratify personal pride, one-upmanship
Jupiter, Passive Mars	Ambition not easily discouraged	Inability to understand and sympathize with weaker souls
Jupiter, Luna	Enough ambition to use imagination creatively	Pride inflated by impossible dreams of glory
Jupiter, Venus	Outgoing, constructive ambition—humanitarian goals	Ostentatious generosity to inflate your pride
Jupiter, Active Mars	Aggressive ambition which lets nothing stand in its way	Tendency to pick fights
Saturn, Apollo	Talent used in a serious way	Gloom that inhibits self-expression
Saturn, Mercury	Serious understanding plus clever self-expression	Temptation to forget scruples because of skepticism about human race
Saturn, Luna	Studious and imaginative qualities of the "deep" thinker	Restlessness and black moods, strange ideas
Saturn, Venus	Kindness and dependability	Pessimism
Saturn, Active Mars	Love of outdoor life	Active grumbling and discouragement that makes action seem useless
Saturn, Passive Mars	Adherence to convictions	Gloom
Apollo, Mercury	Clever use of talent	Pretense and affectation

Most-Emphasized Mounts	Best Results	What to Beware of
Apollo, Passive Mars	Style and endurance — a winning combination	Ostentation
Apollo, Luna	Interpretive or creative talent	Squandered talent, lack of serious purpose, "temperament"
Apollo, Venus	Love of beauty and ability to create it. Music	Tendency not to plan ahead
Apollo, Active Mars	Ability to promote your own talents	Sense of self-importance and habit of sponging on others
Mercury, Passive Mars	Refusal to give up	Tendency to quibble
Mercury, Luna	Ingenuity — practical use of imagination	Fast talk—twisting the truth
Mercury, Venus	Cleverness, vivaciousness, warm-heartedness	Impetuosity
Mercury, Active Mars	Great business ability	Over-aggressiveness
Luna, Passive Mars	Ability to turn dreams into realities	Coldness
Luna, Venus	Energy and originality	Impulsiveness, restlessness and sensuality
Luna, Active Mars	Ability to do unusual out-of-the-ordinary things successfully	Struggle for impossible goals you have dreamed up
Venus, Passive Mars	Tolerance and sympathy, huge physical reserves of energy	Sympathy that is easily exploited by others
Venus, Active Mars	Loyalty and the determination to fight for ideals	Emotionalism
Active, Passive Mars	Great forcefulness	Too much aggressiveness

CHAPTER XVIII

ACCIDENTAL SIGNS

"Awareness of danger brings good fortune."
—I Ching.

How could there be any meaning to anything as coincidental-seeming as a star, a cross or a triangle in a certain part of the hand? The answer is that such signs aren't coincidental.

Groups of lines are found on those parts of the hand that indicate your most-developed qualities. If you use your hand surely and deftly, the groups of lines tend to be clearly marked in a balanced way, as in a well-formed star or triangle. In the hands of an awkward person, the lines have a scrambled and uncertain look.

In an uncertain hand, groups of lines tend to form a grill—an unfavorable sign. In hands covered with lines, single signs don't have much meaning unless they stand out clearly. The squares on your hand are protective signs that are supposed to shield you from possible disaster. For example, a square on the Mount of Jupiter suggests protection against the adverse effects of pride and the thirst for power.

In general, you find square markings on the hands of people who exercise a great deal of intuition in recognizing and escaping serious dangers. This is true even if these people are not intuitive in other ways.

Fig. 10.
The Star

Fig. 11.
The Square

Fig. 12.
The Spot

Fig. 13.
The Circle

Fig. 14.
The Island

Fig. 15.
The Triangle

Fig. 16.
The Cross

Fig. 17.
The Grille

Signs found in the Hand.

*An old picture showing common hand-markings (including
a circle, traditionally believed to show dangerous brilliance).*

CROSSES

By and large, it seems best to read crosses quite simply as well-marked or badly marked lines on the mount where you find them—depending, of course, on whether they are clear or falteringly marked.

A cross roughly in the middle of the palm, between the lines of head and heart, is called the Mystic Cross. It may be formed by the fate-line and a horizontal line connecting the head-line and heart-line, or it may be quite separate. It denotes some form of mysticism—anything from religious mysticism to just plain superstition, depending on how well marked and well formed the rest of the hand may be.

Here are some *traditional* meanings of various crosses, just for fun:

Cross	*Meaning*
On Mount of Jupiter:	Happy marriage.
On Mount of Saturn:	Melancholy mysticism.
On Mount of Apollo:	Obstacles to artistic success.
On Mount of Mercury:	Dishonest nature; kleptomania.
On Mount of Mars:	Enemies.
On Mount of the Moon:	Exaggeration, self-deception.
At end of life-line:	Happy old age.
On Mount of Venus:	A single, tragic love.
On lowest section of index finger:	Lewdness.
On lowest section of ring finger:	Chastity.

STARS

Here is what stars mean when they appear on various mounts:

Star	Meaning
On Jupiter.	Great ambition, usually leading to proportionate success.
On Saturn:	Fatalistic view of life, probably gloomy moods. Scholarly success.
On Apollo:	Dash and sense of style, often leading to fame or wealth.
On Mercury:	Talent for science or commerce, or eloquence.
On Luna:	Soaring imagination, hence (traditional reading) fame won through imagination.

And, just for fun, here are some of the *traditional* meanings:

Star	Meaning
On lines circling wrist:	Inheritance.
On Passive Mars:	Honor through fortitude.
On Luna:	Shipwreck.
In center of quadrangle (in a man's hand)	Ruin by a woman; losses recouped.
On tip of Saturn finger:	Danger.
On tip of other fingers:	Good luck in anything you touch.
On tip of thumb:	Success through strong will.
At base of thumb:	Troubles caused by women, or fall from a ladder.
On Mount of Venus:	Success in love affairs.
At end of life-line:	Wealth in old age.

GRILLS

A grill or network of criss-crossed lines on a mount shows so much nervous energy that it is almost bound to be destructive. The more tangled the lines are, and the more they wriggle like swimming snakes, the more the grill suggests self-destructive tendencies.

If a hand is covered with a network of fine lines, don't consider there is a grill on every mount. Take another look at the tables of general line meanings in Chapter VI. To have its strongest connotations, a grill must stand out clearly in the hand.

A firm hand and a large thumb may help you control the unfortunate leanings shown by a grill: so strange and complicated is human nature that, under some circumstances, our very faults can be useful.

For example, a grill on the Mount of Saturn indicates fits of depression. You often see this grill in the hands of a humorist or comedian whose sense of humor has been developed to offset his tendency to feel depressed. In private, however, he will still have blue moods.

A grill on the mount of Apollo shows a desire to show off. In a hand with many twisted lines and a small thumb, this would amount to vanity. On the other hand, you will often see this grill on the hands of successful actors and actresses. Because such people have talent, their way of showing off is pleasing to us and profitable to them.

A grill on the Mount of Venus is very common and shows a need for affection.

GOT A DRAMATIC FLAIR?
"SCHULTZY"

"SPATULATE" TIP ON RING FINGER — DRAMATIC FLAIR IN SELF-EXPRESSION

"GRILL" UNDER RING FINGER — YOU NEED THE SPOTLIGHT TO BE HAPPY

GIRDLE OF VENUS — IN DRAMATIC HAND, ABILITY TO "EMOTE" WHEN NECESSARY

HEART LINE

HEAD LINE

LIFE LINE

RIGHT HAND PRINT

Many actors and actresses who feel at home in the public eye have a grill under the ring finger.

Here are some other grill meanings:

Grill	Meaning
On Mount of Jupiter:	Destructive pride.
On Mount of Mercury:	Instability, sometimes dishonesty.
On Mount of Passive Mars:	Irritability.
On Mount of Luna:	Overactive imagination; constant worry.
In quadrangle (center of palm):	Overawareness of difficulties.

TRIANGLES

If you use your hands deftly, the lines are likely to form triangles, small and large. Therefore, traditionally, most triangles in the hand show some form of skill or good luck. It is an excellent sign if the main lines of the hand make a large, clear triangle.

Here are the meanings of smaller triangles:

Triangle	Meaning
On Mount of Jupiter:	Skillful leadership, tact.
On Mount of Saturn:	Talent in serious studies.
On Mount of Apollo:	Inspired craftsmanship.
On Mount of Mercury:	Shrewd diplomacy; wit; money sense.
On Mount of Luna:	Wise use of imagination.
On Mount of Mars:	Probably calm in crisis.

And here, for fun, are the *traditional* meanings:

Triangle	Meaning
On Mount of Venus:	Calculating in matters of love.
At end of life-line:	A wagging tongue.
On lines around wrist:	A rich marriage.
At end of head-line:	Power of divination.
On Mount of Saturn:	Skill in black magic.

Notice how many triangles are formed by the lines in the skillful hands of artist Norman Rockwell.
(Original length of print 7-1/8 inches)

CHAPTER XIX

AT YOUR FINGERTIPS

"Better thou wert never born than on a Friday pare thy horn."
—Old jingle.

"Drops of water" is the traditional name for the tiny bumps of flesh on the inside of some fingertips. They are mainly composed of nerve-endings and emphasize sensitivity. People with a subtle and refined sense of touch have such bumps.

DO YOU LIKE TO CRITICIZE?

WIDE SHORT
NAILS BELONG
TO <u>CRITIC</u>

KNOTS AT
FINGER
JOINTS—
<u>ANALYTICAL</u>

HIGH
BULGE HERE
BELONGS TO
<u>FIGHTER</u>

FINGERNAILS

Here are some more clues to character right at your fingertips:

Short nails that are slightly broader than they are long—you crave activity.

Very short nails—you are irritable (or are you a critic?).

Long nails—you are shy with an even temper.

Vertically ridged nails—you suffer from nervous irritability, sometimes because of a run-down condition.

Strong horizontal ridge, especially in the thumb-nail—this often results from a nervous or physical shock in the past—one that has taken place within the last six months, since that is how long it takes the nail to renew itself.

Hard nails—a sign of vigor.

OLD TRADITION

White spots on the nails are a sign of good luck.

These fingernails show (l. to r.) *shyness, frankness, activity, criticism.*

CHAPTER XX

FINGERPRINTS AND SUCH

"Fingerprint figures that whirl around in a circle are the 'whirl-pool type' and those running in a water-course are the 'stream type.' . . . Figures and combinations of fingerprints actually tell the fortune of a person's entire life."
—Yusuke Miyamoto, 1963.

The ancient Chinese believed that thumb-print patterns composed of closed circles showed a more focused and powerful mind than prints made up of arches and loops. A Japanese fortune-telling system equates the circle or near-circle fingerprint with the *yang,* or active, male, creative principle, and all other prints with the *yin,* or passive, female principle. Hindu hand-readers believe that a circle pattern on palm or sole is a sign of talent. The science of dermatoglyphics also involves the study of these circular and related spiral prints, or whorls, and the facts scientists have discovered provoke interesting questions.

Why, for example, do men tend to have more whorls on their fingers than women? Why do North American Indians, Chinese, Japanese, Jews and Arabs, for example, tend to have more whorls on their fingers than Dutchmen, Norwegians, Britons or African bushmen? (Readers who want to know more about dermatoglyphics may want to

HIS

LARGE THUMB AND WHORL FINGER PRINTS — <u>YOU CAN'T BE PUSHED AROUND</u>

SIMPLE ARCH FINGERPRINTS— "SALT OF THE EARTH" SIMPLICITY

WHORL FINGER-PRINTS — DYED-IN-THE WOOL <u>INDIVIDUALIST</u>

SMALL THUMB AND ARCH FINGERPRINTS — YOU <u>DON'T WANT TO BE BOSS</u>

HERS

RIGHT HAND PRINTS

read *Finger Prints, Palms and Soles,* by Cummins and Midlo.)

Some readers may want to stop at this point and learn a little extra about papillary ridge markings, which have been in the news in the last few years because of medical use of skin ridge patterns.

Intriguingly, modern scientists who study human hand and foot patterns as part of dermatoglyphics have given special attention to one of the marks mentioned in age-old Buddhist scriptures:

"The Exalted One addresses the monks. . . . There are thirty-two special marks of the superman . . . wherewith endowed, two careers lie open to him and none other: that of a monarch, turner of the wheel . . . that of a Buddha supreme."

These marks include long fingers and toes, "soft and tender" hands and feet, physical proportions with the "symmetry of the banyan-tree," hands and feet "like a net" and skin "the color of gold" and so "delicately smooth that no dust cleaves to his body."

And the mark that is relevant to dermatoglyphics is this:"Moreover, beneath on the soles of his feet, wheels appear thousand-spoked, with tire and hub, in every way complete and well divided. That this is so counts to him as one of the marks of the superman."

You may have "wheels" in your hands. The tiny papillary skin-ridge designs have been classified into types and named. One of these skin-ridge patterns, either in the form of a spiral or concentric circles is called a whorl, and this formation seems, in its most perfect concentric circular form, to be the wheel called one of the thirty-two marks of the superman. It is still widely used in oriental fortune-telling.

*If, like Senator Wayne Morse's hand, yours has whorl finger-
prints on all fingertips, it shows forceful character even if the
tip section of the thumb (the will section) is short. You will
think for yourself and not care whether other people agree.*

One modern system of reading from fingerprint whorls is oversimplified until it is like a child's counting-out rhyme. This Indian method says that one lone circle fingerprint out of ten prints means you are clever; two, good looking; three, you love luxury; four, you will be very poor; five, you are well-educated; six, clever even among scholars; seven, a recluse; eight, dirt-poor; nine, a king; ten, you will work for the government.

A more common type of whorl than the perfect circle is the spiral, and spiral fingerprints have their reading too: one, you will be a Raja; two, a wealthy man; three, a yogi; four, a poor man; five, a rich man; six, a yogi; seven, a very poor man; eight, a rich man; nine, a yogi; ten, a poor man.

Indian ideas spread to China with Buddhist missionaries after 217 B.C., and possibly this is the origin of another fingerprint fortune-telling system, still in use, keyed to an ancient Chinese philosophy and fortune-telling book, the *I Ching*. This fingerprint-reading system seems more serious and a little closer to modern ideas. This is the system that calls either the circle or the spiral fingerprint *yang* or creative masculine principle. All other fingerprints are then *yin* or yielding, receptive, feminine. Masculine and feminine are not used here to tell merely what is to be expected on the fingerprints of a man or a woman, for in fact a woman is occasionally seen who has all *yang* or "masculine" fingerprints, a man with all *yin* or "feminine" fingerprints. In the *I Ching* and related Chinese philosophies, the masculine and feminine are used to suggest the two polar forces of the universe that are needed to complete each other. You read a man's left hand or a woman's right hand. The no-whorl hand is the completely yielding, receptive hand. Says the oriental reading: men and women with no-whorl hands "grow old in peace and comfort just as a huge tree with increasing annual rings."

At the opposite extreme, the all-whorl hand has concentric circles or a spiral in every fingerprint. The oriental reading calls the owner like a "lone tree in the middle of a plain"—proud, self-respecting, outspoken and self-made. Even the more common hand with whorl prints on all fingers except the thumb has a strong reading: "He must push and progress with intensity . . . (and) is predestined to live his life with thrill and strength."

The oriental system reads thirty-two possible fingerprint combinations. I have not studied and used this system so thoroughly that I can say whether I think it all works. The all-whorl hand has, however, in my experience always belonged to a strong individualist, whether it be a leader or an anarchist, and the no-whorl hand usually belongs to a more flexible person. But the intriguing fact is that not only Buddhist scriptures but oriental fortune-telling still in use finds the whorl-marking means something out of the ordinary. And so do scientists.

It was a whorl near the heel of his own hand, a marking he noticed was more common on the paws of monkeys than the palms of his friends and acquaintances, that piqued the curiosity of Francis Haythorn Wilder, a biologist, in the late 1800s. He studied the paw-prints of monkeys galore and took the palm and foot prints of groups of European descent, Maya Indians, Chinese and Negroes, studied duplicate twins and other groups to see what sort of prints were typical of each.

And Wilder wasn't the only scientist studying hand-markings. As interest grew, identification experts, anthropologists, geneticists, zoologists and anatomists all contributed to the growing store of statistical knowledge about hand and foot markings.

Now, if you find a whorl on your right ring finger, you

1 Composite 2 Tented Arch

SQUARED FINGER TIPS
SHOW YOU'RE SOMEWHAT
PRACTICAL — GOOD
BALANCE FOR
FLEXIBLE HAND

LOOP PRINTS
ON ALL
FINGERS —
FLEXIBLE
MIND

FINGERS
BEND
BACK 90°

VERY FLEXIBLE
HAND CAN JUMP
FROM ONE THING
TO ANOTHER LIKE
BOUNCING BALL.

HEART LINE

LIFE LINE

WAVERING
HEAD LINE —
CHANGEABLE

BACK-BENDING THUMB —
ADAPTABLE, VERSATILE

(LEFT HAND PRINT)

*The flexible mind, shown by loop fingerprints, can be under-
lined by other markings. This hand shows a mind flexible to
a fault.*

can know that, statistically, this is one of the most usual places for a whorl to be. (Thumbs and ring-fingers are more whorled than other fingers, the right hand more whorled than the left.) If there is a whorl on your little finger, however, this is rarer. Little fingers are most often tipped with loops.

If there are no whorls or few whorls on your fingers, you can know that this is slightly more usual if you are a woman. Women have fewer whorls and more arches among their fingerprints than men. Intriguingly, this dovetails with the Chinese idea that whorls are *yang*, which is firm and masculine, and all other prints are *yin*, which is female as well as yielding.

One out of every five persons has no whorls on his fingerprints at all. Many others have only a few of these "whirlpool" prints. In fingerprints and toe-prints, many whorls are the exception. A hand with few whorls is quite usual.

It is much rarer to find a whorl in the tiny skin ridges of the palm of your hand, or on the sole of your foot, than to find a whorl in one of your fingerprints. And, to scientists, the rarity of these whorls makes them seem significant. Because whorls are much rarer on human palms and soles than on the elevated pads of monkey's paws, and because whorls are scarcer on the more advanced great apes than on the more primitive smaller monkeys, dermatoglyphic authorities Cummins and Midlo believe they are a mark not of the superman of Buddhist scriptures, but of the primitive.

If you have whorls on your palms and soles, this could leave you—and also Mr. Wilder, who helped start it all—in an uncomfortable position.

Psychiatrist Dr. Charlotte Wolff came to the conclusion

CAN YOU THINK FAST?
JACK PAAR

LONG, POINTED LITTLE FINGER —QUICK ON THE UPTAKE

LONG SUPPLE HAND—QUICK SUBTLE WIT

WHORL OF LIGHTNING WIT

HAND BROADEST ACROSS BASE— IMPULSIVE

Jack Paar

A whorl on the Mount of Mercury shows wit, which is what you'd expect to find on Jack Paar's hand.

that whorls on palms belonged to people with a primitive, atavistic streak in their personalities. Certain families, she believed, tended to produce brilliant off-beat members and subnormal members—not much in the "normal" range in between. Members of these families tended to have whorl on their palms, particularly on the heel of the hand.

Of course, the theories that scientists use to make their findings fit into a meaningful picture can change with new discoveries. But it's interesting that what these scientists gleaned from years of painstaking research is not entirely different from the Buddhist scriptures. The scriptures never said that whorls alone marked a superman, but that they must be one of thirty two marks. And these included long fingers, soft, fine, well-colored skin and beautifully shaped hands and body—and the numerous fine lines typical of sensitive hands.

If whorls indicate the out-of-the-ordinary for better or worse, wouldn't whorled hands and feet with other signs of balance, sensitivity and good health belong to a brilliant original? In my limited experience of the rare hands that approach these standards, the owners have been talented and unique.

Modern British hand-readers who have been interested in character-reading from fingerprints have also come to the conclusion that whorls show strong individuality and originality. The man who has these prints on all his fingers thinks for himself. If you see whorls on certain fingers only, you know their influence is confined to the abilities indicated by these fingers. You'll often find whorls on mounts in the palm, and these signs indicate an intensive and original use of the quality signified by the mount.

The simplest form of fingerprint is called the "simple

arch" and is composed of bent lines like a sergeant's stripes. This arch always reveals a quality of simplicity, often an old-fashioned salt-of-the-earth simplicity. You may find this quality in people of high intelligence. However, people who have these prints on all fingers do not like to work under pressure.

Modern palmists give meanings to all other types of prints, but I have not found they are as important in interpreting a hand as the two extreme types mentioned above. The others are the loop, which indicates a flexible mind; the tented arch, sign of an idealistic, sometimes artistic mind, and the composite, which symbolizes the ability to see both sides of a question.

CHAPTER XXI

THE PAST

"... We must respect the past, remembering that once it was all that was humanly possible."
                                                        —Santayana.

Why can you read the past in your hands? The oldest theory is that our hands show our horoscopes. Even today, some Indian hand-readers can determine the planets' positions at the time of your birth by studying your hands. V. A. K. Ayer believes that these unusual hand-readers are other-worldly men who cannot entirely explain their methods.

Another theory maintains that our hands reflect whatever we know subconsciously. This is possible if parts of your hand are represented in separate areas of the brain (see Wood Jones' *Principles of Anatomy as Seen in the Hand*) and if detailed memories of the past are stored in specific parts of the brain. Experiments in the stimulation of parts of the brain by electrical impulses tend to support the theory.

In the May 15, 1958, issue of *The Reporter*, Maya Pines said: "Dr. Wilder Penfield, director of the Montreal Neurological Institute, developed a theory that the brain is permanently altered by everything we do. According to him, for each experience we have ever had, there is a corresponding record, like a strip of film ready to be activated by electrical stimulation. Each spot seems to contain only one experience, and always the same one—a moment in one's childhood, a song, a conversation, a dream."

The theory that seems most provable and compatible with other theories might be defined this way: since our hands show what we are, they make it obvious what sort of past we have had. If your hands are full of tortured lines, you have had a lot of troubles.

You can learn more details about your past by comparing your hands. If a line or mount is well marked in the hand you use most frequently and badly marked in the other, you have definitely made progress in mastering your life and realizing your desires and ambitions.

Since the most-used hand is connected with the center of the brain where learned skills are recorded—even such basic ones as talking (see *The Master Hand* by Abram Blau, American Orthopsychiatric Association, 1946)—if the least-used hand is marked much more clearly than the other, your education and training was destructive to the kind of person you were naturally suited to be. Perhaps you had a natural talent for vaudeville but were raised in Boston.

A more clearly defined left hand reveals a right-handed person's possibilities for development; a right hand with clearer markings shows the helpful effect of early training or attempts at self-improvement (maybe you had a temper, but you've learned to control it).

Suppose your least-used hand is flexible, but your most-used hand is stiff. You have become less flexible in your thinking. (The right hand is usually slightly stiffer.)

Suppose your fate-line is badly marked in your active

LEADING INDEX FINGER — AMBITION

THUMB STRAINING UPWARD — YOU TRY EXTRA HARD TO CARRY OUT ALL YOUR PLANS

LINE OF PERSONAL EFFORT

SUN LINE FROM MARS — SUCCESS THROUGH EFFORT

HEART LINE

HEAD LINE STRAIGHT IN RIGHT HAND, DIPPING IN LEFT — DEVELOPED PRACTICALITY

LUNA

Difference between left hand and right hand show the way you have changed.

hand but well marked in the passive. You have a poor sense of purpose due to improper training or destructive experiences, but you are capable of developing a clearer aim in life (probably your instinctive sense of direction only comes to the fore in emergencies).

Suppose the sun-line is well marked in your most-used hand and badly marked in the other. You have developed a sense of style and perhaps talent as well.

It's fascinating to read your own past because, at the same time, you are taking stock of yourself. If you don't like the direction in which you've been traveling, this is the first step toward changing that direction.

And it's also fun to observe how others are doing and where they are headed.

CHAPTER XXII

READING THE FUTURE

"Of course, it is only by long experience and constant practice that the exact dates, even in the past, can be correctly read, and the most experienced palmist is always liable to make mistakes."
—Mrs. A. Robinson, *The Graven Palm.*

Can you predict the future with absolute accuracy by reading hands? Fortunately, no, though you *can* tell what a man's future is *likely* to be. Even Cheiro, who was somewhat of a fatalist, felt men could alter the future revealed by their hands.

Suppose you undertake to tell the details of a life, past and future, from a hand—not just the general direction, but more exact events.

For example: "Five years ago there was a big change to satisfy ambition. In the 35th year there will be another change because of the conniving of an enemy—but in the long run it will turn out for the best. There will be a brilliant success in the arts before the age of 45" . . . and so forth.

You will find that, in most cases, the subject reports that his past fits your reading. Then, later, the subject usually

RARE
HEART
AND HEAD
LINES
COMBINED

LIFE
LINE

FATE
LINE

In the Middle Ages the head-line and heart-line combined was read as a sign of an evil life and an evil death. As a matter of fact, the owner of this hand was murdered, but the combined line is by no means a "sign" of murder. Original print tracing: 8¼ inches long. (Original length of print 8-1/8 inches) will report he has been surprised by how exactly the future happened as you said it would.

Clairvoyance may possibly explain some future readings, but it can't possibly explain the fact that certain lines tend to accompany certain events over and over.

The occultist believes that your hand reflects your past and future because it reveals the influence of the stars that largely, but not entirely, determine your actions.

But there are other explanations, for at least some parts of future-reading, that don't necessarily rule out the occultist's view but are independent of it. Modern findings and old readings seem to be connected though not the same.

Traditional palmists read each broken line as a sign of a particular trouble or unhappiness: A broken heart-line means a terrible shock to the emotions or a heart attack; a broken head-line equals damage to the head or at least a breakdown temporarily impairing the intelligence; a broken fate-line means a change—though this last is not necessarily for the worst.

Dr. Wolff kept records of the hand-markings of neurotics, "normal" people, patients in mental hospitals, a number of talented writers, poets, dancers and the like—in other words, both the sick and the healthy, in body and mind. She found that the lines tended to be broken more often in the nervous hands of those who were highly strung or under a physical or mental strain.

Palmists call a long, well-marked fate line a sign of a successful life. Dr. Wolff found that the line tended to be fragmentary or missing in the hands of social misfits or people with little sense of social conscience.

Palmists of the Middle Ages called the line formed by the heart and the head lines joined into one a sign that a man would lead an evil life and come to a bad end.

Age, as marked on the life-line and fate-line, as shown in an old palmistry book.

Recently, one of the birth defect clues found by Dr. Achs and Dr. Harper was a heart and head line combined into one line, called the simian line by the scientists. Life must indeed have been "evil" and often short for people with physical defects in the days when there was virtually no treatment for, for example, a malformed heart.

But the simian line is not always a sign of birth defects. It is also sometimes found on people who are apparently entirely normal. The old reading worked—but not exactly, and not always.

My own hunch is that much of future reading from the hands is based on germs of truth—sometimes over-simplified, sometimes exaggerated and sometimes mixed with the most poetic fables. It works well enough to be fascinating but not well enough to be worth the nightmares caused by irresponsible predictions of unavoidable death and catastrophy. Over-simplified traditional readings can sometimes be quite wrong. And remember—hands change; lines fade and appear as the owners' stamina or sense of inner harmony changes.

Yet there is always a fascination in these old readings— and here they are, hopefully to be used with discretion and common sense.

First of all, divide the lines in your hand into ages. An illustration shows how you can indicate various ages on the fate- and life-lines. Make a print or outline of your hand and mark the lines accordingly.

Now trace the course of your life-line from infancy to old age, indicating the traditional meaning of each irregularity:

A star at the very beginning of the line (see A, page 210) is a sign of good fortune in life.

An island on the life-line (B) indicates a period of physical strain.

A break in the life-line (C) means that an illness or shock took place at the time indicated.

A square on the line (D) is a protective sign that

guards you against some threat to your life; if the square is red, you are being protected from fire.

A "worry" line (a line from the Mount of Venus that crosses the life-line) indicates by the lines it cuts what your trouble is all about. You actually began to fret at the point where this line cuts your life-line.

A "worry" line that cuts your heart-line (E) means that you are disturbed by love.

A "worry" line that cuts your head-line (F) indicates that your disturbance can lead to foolish acts.

A "worry" line that cuts your fate-line (G) means that you're worried about money.

A "worry" line that crosses the sun-line (H) concerns your reputation.

A well-marked sister life-line behind the regular line protects you against the troubles marked on the life-line.

Downward branches on any line are traditionally a sign of weakness. The point on the life-line where downward branches begin thus indicates the age when your body begins to weaken. Downward branches on both sides of the life-line mean bad health and many losses. Upward branches are good omens. Branches from the life-line that reach the head-line without cutting it mean riches and honors. A large number of upward branches on the life-line means satisfied ambition and excellent health.

Upward branches are not always read in a cheerful way, however. When they are cut by horizontal or diagonal lines from the Mount of Venus, read them as "law suits." An upward branch cut by a line from Venus to—but not cutting—the Line of Sun means a lawsuit won. But if the upward branch is cut by a line that also cuts the Sun line, it tells of a lawsuit lost. An upward branch cut by a line from Venus to Mercury means divorce.

For every short bar crossing the life line, there will be a

*Tradition says downward branches are marked on the life-line
at the age when vitality begins to lessen.*
(Original length of print 8-1/8 inches)

minor illness. For every dot on the line, there will be a minor accident at the age indicated by the position on the line.

Each minor line inside the life-line and parallel to it stands for someone who influences you. The time when he is a force in your life is read by the dates on the part of the life-line each parallels. The importance of the influence is in proportion to the closeness of the influence line to the life-line.

By tradition, a double life-line, in which the inside line begins near the forty-year mark and runs parallel to the life-line like a separate railroad track (I) predicts success followed by exile. Henri Rem says Napoleon III had a line like this.

If your life-line is short, reread Chapter VIII before you get alarmed.

A mole on the life-line announces riches.

The prediction of the future by moles was once known as "moleosophy." A mole on the right hand was supposed to indicate success in business; a mole on the left hand revealed an artistic disposition.

THE FATE-LINE

The fate-line may be lacking in the hand of a go-getter who determines his own fate.

To trace the years on your fate-line, begin at the wrist and work up. (Turn to the illustration on page 209.) Mark the meaning of the line's irregularities on a hand-print.

The most important events of your life *traditionally* happen at a time when your fate-line is most deeply and clearly marked.

A cross on this line is indicative of a change (see J, page 210).

Deep lines that cut the fate-line (G) signify obstacles

*"Dukkerin" or Gypsy fortune-tell-
ing signs, placed on houses.*

Go on. Nothing here. They don't
believe in fortune telling.

This woman has just had a pro-
posal of marriage.

Wife here is unfaithful!

People here have quarrelled over
an inheritance.

Husband here is unfaithful!

Man here is a widower.

Here died an old woman recently.

Very kind people, don't impose on
them.

When you tell her fortune, say she
will have children, because she
wants them.

Woman is a widow.

This woman can have no child.

220

that you must overcome.

Breaks in your fate-line (K) indicate changes in your life. If the ends of your fate-line overlap, it means you have switched your course without trouble.

Lines that rise from your fate-line (L) indicate successful projects. A fate-line with many well-marked rising lines forms what hand-readers in India call the "Line of Tree" and is considered a wonderful sign. Gladstone had one.

In the hands of a gambler, a star on the fate-line (M) foretells the date of his losses.

Small lines parallel to the fate-line (N) are signs of good luck and help in meeting challenges on the dates where they are marked. If one of these supporting lines joins the fate-line, marriage is likely. You can confirm this by checking the horizontal line or lines on the edge of your hand just below the little finger (O)—they are the signs of a deep love or marriage.

An island on the fate-line (P) indicates a period of difficulty. French hand-readers say the trouble is the result of a love affair, but others say money is the cause. But your own particular weakness, as shown by the rest of your hand, is likely to be the cause.

If a long-marked fate-line runs high onto the Mount of Saturn, you can expect remarkable good luck throughout your life.

If a well-marked fate-line runs to the Mount of Apollo, your triumph will be artistic.

If a fine fate-line runs to the Mount of Mercury, you will be wonderfully successful in business.

If a beautiful fate-line curves toward the Mount of Jupiter, your worldy ambitions will be fulfilled—perhaps because you will marry well.

But if the line is deep red and runs across the Mount of Saturn and well into the lowest section of the Saturn finger, you will die in a shameful way or go to prison.

The fate-line beginning inside the Mount of Venus tells that your family has ruled your career.

The clear line running from the Mount of Luna to the Mount of Saturn means that your success will be due to the help of someone of the opposite sex.

The fate line ending abruptly at the head-line means that your success in life will be spoiled by poor judgment.

But if it end suddenly at the heart-line, disappointment in love ruins your luck.

One thing you can predict with absolute certainty: if a person has a fate-line with many different markings, his life may be full of ups and downs, but it will never be monotonous.

The dates marked on the sun-line (R) are more or less parallel to those indicated on the fate-line. An island on this line indicates a time in your life when you can't trust to luck or talent but must get what you want by hard work and careful planning.

THE HEAD-LINE

When the head-line twists up and ends on the Mount of Saturn: a fatal head wound.

When the line is very short: early death or loss of mental abilities.

Broken under the Mount of Sun: danger to the eyesight.

Broken under the Mount of Saturn: a head wound, recovery if the ends of the line overlap.

(I have never seen any of these traditional head-line readings come true. But I have seen a very short head-line

HOLDING-ON-TO-MONEY
HAND IS LONG,
WITH KNOTS
AT FINGER
JOINTS AND
AN EXTRA-LONG,
LARGE LITTLE
FINGER

AVERAGE LITTLE
FINGER REACHES
BEGINNING OF TIP
SECTION
OF RING
FINGER

HEART
LINE

HEAD LINE

LIFE LINE

FATE LINE

*The fate-line to the base of the little finger (Mount of Mercury)
traditionally means you will be brilliantly successful in business. If so the rest of the hand will second the motion.*
(Original length of print 7-1/2 inches)

BROAD TIP ON RING FINGER (ABOUT AS BROAD AS BASE)— GOOD <u>EYE</u> <u>FOR</u> <u>LINE</u>

LIFE LINE MAKES <u>WIDE</u> <u>CIRCLE</u> AROUND THUMB BASE —ENERGETIC <u>CHEERFUL</u>

HEART LINE

APOLLO "LINE OF TREE" ✸

MARS LINE

HEAD LINE

The "line of tree" or upward branches on fate-line or Apollo line traditionally means brilliant success; on Apollo, artistic talent too. Notice how the rest of the hand follows suit.
(Original length of print 8 inches)

in the hands of a boy suffering from a serious mental break-down. When he had received treatment and appeared much better, the line lengthened.)

THE HEART-LINE

If the line is chained where it crosses the fate-line, love troubles hurt your career.

The heart-line long and much-branched at the end bodes many minor love affairs. Count the branches—each is a love affair.

Lines drooping from the heart-line under the Mount of Apollo tells of troubles caused by friends.

The heart-line joined to the life-line under the Mount of Saturn means terrible misfortune caused by violent passion.

When many small bars cut the heart-line, repeated disappointments in love are shown.

A break in the heart-line is interpreted differently under each mount. Under Saturn, it says a tragic end to a love affair; under Apollo, a love affair ended by your own inconstancy; under Mercury, a love affair ruined and ended because of greed. If the heart-line overlaps at the point of the breaks, the trouble may be patched up.

All the heart-line breaks are also read as health warnings.

Like the life-line and fate-line, the head-line and heart-line can be dated and used to pinpoint the time of an event. The simplest system is Henri Rem's. He drops a line from the center of each finger.

Here's how he dates the head-line: ten years is marked directly below the index finger; twenty-five years is indicated below the middle finger; fifty below the ring finger

EACH FINGER TIP LONG IN PROPORTION TO OTHER FINGER SECTIONS — INTUITIVE

HIGH PADDING UNDER RING FINGER—QUICK RESPONSE TO BEAUTY

APOLLO LINE

HEART LINE

HEAD LINE

WIDE AND HIGHLY PADDED MOUNT HERE — EMOTIONAL RESPONSE

Many branches on the heart-line are read "many love affairs,"
one love for each branch.
      (Original length of print 7-3/4 inches)

and seventy-five below the little finger. Mental strains and difficulties, shown by islands, bieaks, cross-lines and pits in the line, are dated according to this system.

He dates the heart-line from the opposite direction—ten years is marked below the little finger; twenty-five below the ring finger, fifty below the middle finger and seventy-five below the index. Heartaches and heartbreaks, shown by islands, breaks and cross-lines, are dated this way.

Nearly every great hand-reader has worked out his own system of reading dates from the lines, but while there is some agreement about dates on the fate- and life-lines, there are so many conflicting systems for the other lines that it seems obvious the fate- and life-lines give more consistent results in dating events.

There is a good, practical reason why dating events on the fate-line in an upward direction gives remarkably accurate results:

When we are young, imagination and animal spirits are usually enough to make us happy and successful. Therefore, if the lines are well-marked in the lowest third of the palm where these qualities are represented, we are likely to do well in early life.

In middle life, we have the greatest need of physical energy and staying power—the qualities represented in the middle section of the palm. When the lines are most clearly marked here, our best years will be between thirty and forty-five.

In our autumn years, it is the quality of our minds that makes the difference. Even if we have not had the push in middle life to be financially successful, we may have acquired a wisdom and philosophy to enjoy our later years. Since our intellectual drives are related to the top third of the palm, well-marked lines here show our chances of success in later life.

And the hand will suggest how to deal with its own special temptations and pitfalls, too. For example, the owner of the pale, hollow hand needs to do everything possible to build himself up, mentally and physically. He needs to be sure of proper diet, medical checkups, healthful exercise and enough pleasant companionship.

The owners of the pell-mell-ambitious and luxury-loving hands can perhaps realize they are spending the coin of life too fast and in self-destructive ways that can leave them bankrupt later. Good qualities, too, are in most hands —perhaps an ability to work hard and pride in a job well done, in an ambitious man; or great generosity in the luxury-lover; or the ability to understand other people's problems in the hollow hand.

Self-knowledge of good qualities as well as bad provides the way to compensate for weaknesses and avoid temptations that future-readings call signs of coming disasters. So, while parts of future-reading are merely points of interest about an interesting old folk-art, other parts may be truly useful.

In regard to periods of "luck" and in other ways, only the character reading that goes with a future reading and explains it makes a hand reading ring true.

For example, a long series of breaks in the fate-line cut by many worry lines suggests a period filled with difficulties. The faults shown in the hands will tell why. Is it because the owner of the pale, hollow hand gives up too easily? Or because the owner of the hand with a high, grilled Jupiter mount is blindly ambitious? Or because the owner of the very soft hand with smooth, fat fingers and a huge Mount of Venus is too extravagant and cares only for luxurious today, forgetting to look out for the future? Probably it is.

CHAPTER XXIII

SUMMING UP

"We say again, and we cannot repeat too often, that a single mark in the hand is not enough to form your opinion . . ."

—Adolphe Desbarrolles.

Beginners at hand-reading are sometimes confused when they find that the same general quality shows in different ways in different hands and that the same quality may be marked in several ways in one hand.

Actually the key qualities to a person's character are always repeated in his hand in a number of ways.

Let's take originality as an example. There are many kinds of originality, and a truly original person can find several varieties marked in his hand. The number of marks and their nature tell us *how* original he is and *in what way*.

If he has whorl fingerprints on most of his fingers, we know he is a person who has to think things out in his own way, a natural-born individualist. If what he does is original, that is just a result of his natural way of thinking.

If he has spatulate fingertips, he is restless, likes to stay busy and is by nature an explorer. He likes to explore places or ideas just because they are new. If he has a

SATURN →

ONE LINE STRAIGHT ACROSS WHOLE HAND — REPLACES HEAD AND HEART LINES — BELONGS TO TRUE ADVENTURER OF THE MIND

FINGERS LEAN TOWARD "SATURN FINGER" — SCIENTIFIC INTERESTS

FATE LINE SLANTS TOWARD INDEX FINGER — PRIDE IN WORK LIKELY TO LEAD TO UNUSUAL ACHIEVEMENT

HEAD AND HEART LINES

FLATTENED THUMB LOOKS POINTED FROM SIDE VIEW — NERVOUS ENERGY KEEPS YOU BUSY

FATE LINE

LIFE LINE

Henry A. Wallace

The inventive person like pioneer geneticist and ex-vice-president Henry A. Wallace, will have more than one sign of originality in his hand. (Original length of print 8 inches)

spatulate palm too, exploring is his passion; the tried-and-true bore him.

If he holds his thumb and fingers wide apart, we know that he is uninhibited.

If at the same time he has a large and much-lined Mount of Luna, he is extremely imaginative and dreams up exaggerated and unusual ideas.

And on top of all this, if he has an unusual and wild-looking pattern of lines in his hand, you're dealing with an eccentric—a person so out of the ordinary that you are sure he is a genius or a crank or possibly both.

Money-sense also shows in hands in different ways. A long little finger suggests the cleverness to get money, especially if the mount under the finger is high.

If your head-line curves up under the little finger, you are influenced by the desire for money. If the line is fairly straight across the hand, you are practical.

If your fingers are plump enough near the palm so that no light shows through them when you hold them together, you like luxuries and keep yourself supplied with them by holding on to your earnings.

If you have knots on the lower joints of your fingers, you are pragmatic and appreciate money for what it can do for you.

If you have a star or long line under the finger of Apollo, you have style and dash to enable you to make money, though the chances are that you'll spend it freely.

If your little finger is crooked as well as long, you're shrewd. If it's very crooked, watch out! You may be tempted to pull a fast deal.

If your palm and fingertips are square, you are probably basically practical. Along with other signs of practicality in financial affairs, the squareness means that you'll succeed in business.

FEW LINES — YOU <u>DON'T</u> FRET OR STEW

LONG RING FINGER — YOU <u>LIKE</u> TO TAKE <u>CHANCES</u>

HEAD LINE

HEART LINE

LINE OF MARS — CALM ASSURANCE IN FACING REAL DANGER

MARS

LUNA

BOTH MARS AND LUNA AREAS FIRM AND HIGHLY PADDED — <u>GREAT DARING</u>

LIFE LINE

Galla Shawn

Any important quality in a hand will be marked in several ways, as daring is repeated in the hand of circus performer, Galla Shawn. (Original length of print 6-3/4 inches)

DO YOU SHOCK PEOPLE?
SALVADOR DALI

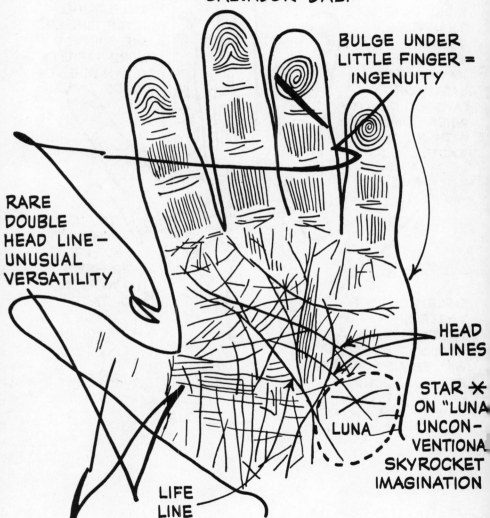

BULGE UNDER
LITTLE FINGER =
INGENUITY

RARE
DOUBLE
HEAD LINE —
UNUSUAL
VERSATILITY

HEAD
LINES

STAR ✳
ON "LUNA
UNCON-
VENTIONA
SKYROCKET
IMAGINATION

LUNA

LIFE
LINE

Artist, Salvador Dali's hand makes it obvious in several ways why his art has been a violent shock to some of his contemporaries. (Original length of print 8 inches)

INDEX LONGER THAN RING FINGER— YOU ENJOY HAVING THE LAST WORD (A GOOD QUALITY WHEN COMBINED WITH WIT AND TACT)

LONG, STRAIGHT OUTLEANING LITTLE FINGER LIKE POINTED SWORD—ABILITY TO WIN DUEL OF WORDS

HEART LINE

TRIANGLES UNDER INDEX AND LITTLE FINGERS— WIT AND TACT

HEAD LINE

DISCRIMINATING TASTE SHOWN BY PADDING HERE— SHOWS COMEBACK WILL BE APPROPRIATE FOR OCCASION

LIFE LINE

Quick wit is shown in a number of ways in the hand of Hermione Gingold. (Original length of print 7-1/2 inches)

DESTRUCTIVE GAMBLER'S HAND ISN'T LIKE MR. HUROK'S, BUT MORE LIKE THIS

RING ALMOST AS LONG AS MIDDLE FINGER— YOU ENJOY TAKING CHANCES (FOR BETTER OR WORSE DEPENDING ON REST OF HAND)

LONG, LARGE LITTLE FINGER WITH HIGH PADDING ALL THE WAY DOWN SIDE OF HAND UNDER IT — INTUITION TO TAKE CHANCES AND WIN

LARGE AREA OF PADDING AT THUMB BASE AND HIGH PADDING BELOW RING FINGER USUALLY BELONG TO GENEROUS PERSON WHO WON'T GAMBLE SELFISHLY

If an extra-long ring finger suggests that, like impresario S. Hurok, you enjoy taking chances, the rest of your hand will show exactly what kind of "gambler" you are.
(Original length of print 7-3/4 inches)

The person with a large forefinger or a developed Mount of Jupiter is a natural leader who realizes the power of money. These signs are usually indicative of a love for the good life that money can bring.

As you see, you can find endless combinations that describe a man's attitude toward money.

Desbarrolles describes the avaricious hand in this way: the thumb and fingers incline toward each other; the fingers are very square or pointed, stiff, long, thin, dry and knotty; the skin on the back of the hand is hard, dry and wrinkled; the fingers are held together so that no light shows through; the head-line is very straight and forms a bar across the whole hand; the Mount of Venus is flat and feeble; the Mount of Mercury is well developed and grilled, and a large line begins at the short, branched and tortuous heart-line and extends to the little finger.

Warmheartedness also reveals itself in many ways: A high Mount of Venus shows physical vitality and warmth, a long, deep heart-line adds affectionate rapport, and a high Mount of Jupiter further adds a desire to help weaker persons.

A low Mount of passive Mars added to a high Mount of Jupiter in a woman's hand usually signifies shyness and a desire to help others. The woman knows from experience what suffering is. This is especially true if the inside of the fingertips have the sensitivity pads or "drops of water." And a pink hand shows warmheartedness through an overflow of good health.

How about determination? You usually find this quality in a firm hand. (If the person has a long thumb, he may be determined even though he has a soft hand.)

An impulsively wilful person may have a short thumb. This is also true of someone who works well as part of a

DO PEOPLE LISTEN TO YOU?
THIS WEEK — HAL HOLBROOK & MARK TWAIN

OUT-STANDING
INDEX FINGER—
YOU SPEAK WITH
AUTHORITY

LARGE OUT-STANDING
LITTLE FINGER PLUS
OUT-STANDING
INDEX =
ORATOR

MARK TWAIN

PRONOUNCED KNOTS HERE SHOW GOOD SENSE OF TIMING

HEAD LINE

LIFE LINE

Here are several marks of a talent for public speaking, seen in the hands of humorist and lecturer Mark Twain, and actor Hal Holbrook, who is famous for impersonating Mark Twain.
(Original length of print 8-1/4 inches)

group, though it does not apply to the consistently determined person who plans ahead.

The fate-line or sun-line from the Mount of Mars contributes the necessary will power to struggle for what you want.

The two high, firm Mounts of Mars add energetic willingness to fight against odds. The mount and finger of Jupiter lend the additional incentive of ambition. And whorl fingerprints in a determined hand add a bonus of individualism, the inability to be a part of the herd.

As you read hands, you will learn how to search for the way qualities are repeated and combined to show clearly the most important abilities and motives in each hand.